PENGUIN BOOKS

THE PARTITION

'An excellent exposition of how the border came into
existence . . . based on deep research and particularly good
on the personalities involved and the unusual political climate
in the aftermath of the First World War'
Marianne Elliott, *The Times Literary Supplement*

'A layered and mostly fair assessment of the dynamics, deal, prejudices
and delusions that created the Border in Ireland . . . This is a timely
and important book, not just because of the centenary of the creation
of Northern Ireland but because so much of its content remains relevant
to understanding contemporary preoccupations and controversies'
Diarmaid Ferriter, *Irish Times*

'Charles Townshend has routinely displayed both scholarship
and objectivity. In *The Partition*, he shows how the necessity
arose to divide Ireland into unequal parts, down roughly
Protestant and Roman Catholic lines'
Simon Heffer, *Daily Telegraph*

ABOUT THE AUTHOR

Charles Townshend is the author of the highly praised *Easter 1916: The
Irish Rebellion* and *The Republic: The Fight for Irish Independence,
1918–1923*. *The Partition* forms the third part of his trilogy on how
Ireland became independent. His other books include *When God Made
Hell: The British Invasion of Mesopotamia and the Making of Iraq,
1914–21*.

CHARLES TOWNSHEND

The Partition
Ireland Divided, 1885–1925

PENGUIN BOOKS

PENGUIN BOOKS

UK | USA | Canada | Ireland | Australia
India | New Zealand | South Africa

Penguin Books is part of the Penguin Random House group of companies
whose addresses can be found at global.penguinrandomhouse.com

First published by Allen Lane 2021
Published in Penguin Books 2022
001

Typeset by Jouve (UK), Milton Keynes
Printed and bound in Great Britain by Clays Ltd, Elcograf S.p.A.

The authorized representative in the EEA is Penguin Random House Ireland,
Morrison Chambers, 32 Nassau Street, Dublin D02 YH68

A CIP catalogue record for this book is available from the British Library

ISBN: 978-0-141-98573-2

www.greenpenguin.co.uk

To my grandchildren

Contents

List of Illustrations

Chapter 1: 'Our Dan'. In August 1864, loyalists paraded and burned an effigy of the Irish nationalist leader Daniel O'Connell (whose statue had just been unveiled in Dublin), sparking twelve days of street fighting in Belfast. (*Historical Images Archive/Alamy Stock Photo*)

Chapter 2: The great ships built in Belfast yards – like the White Star liner *Olympic,* then the world's biggest – were potent symbols of the city's global commercial position, which Unionists argued would be imperilled by Dublin rule. (*Bettman/Getty Images*)

Chapter 3: 'King Carson'. With suitably set jaw, the Ulster Unionist leader Sir Edward Carson inspects a detachment of the loyalist Ulster Volunteer Force at the height of the Ulster Crisis in early 1914. (*Central Press/Getty Images*)

Chapter 4: Opposition to compulsory military service in the British army after 1916 united Irish nationalists – the Irish Party leader John Dillon here sharing the platform with Sinn Féin at an anti-conscription rally in Roscommon – but aggravated the division between them and Ulster loyalists. (*George Rinhart/Getty Images*)

Chapter 5: David Lloyd George, prime minister from 1916 to 1922, here leaving Downing Street with Lord Birkenhead and Winston Churchill, directed the adoption of partition to end the stalemate over Irish home rule. (*Fremantle/Alamy Stock Photo*)

Chapter 6: Loyalist shipyard workers' attacks on Catholic dockers in July 1920 led to repeated clashes in the streets of central Belfast, with some 10,000 Catholics driven from their homes. (*Hulton Archive/ Getty Images*)

Chapter 7: The apotheosis of Ulster Unionism – the State opening of the Northern Parliament by King George V in Belfast City Hall on 13 June 1921. (*Mirrorpix/Getty Images*)

Chapter 8: A blood-spattered and bullet-riddled remnant of the train on which four members of the Ulster Special Constabulary were killed in a gun battle with the IRA at Clones station in February 1922. (*Topical Press Agency/Hulton Archive/Stringer*)

Chapter 9: The Boundary Commission goes forth – Justice Richard Feetham with his fellow commissioners Joseph R. Fisher (on his right, with Francis Bourdillon, Secretary to the Commission) and Eoin McNeill (on his left, with Fisher's private secretary) at Armagh in December 1924. (*Courtesy of the National Library of Ireland*)

Epilogue: The frontier. The British army – the Lincolnshire regiment here on the Northern Ireland border in late 1922 – would shortly leave; it would return with more up-to-date fortifications fifty years later. (*Bettman/Getty Images*)

List of Maps

Ireland in 1885

N

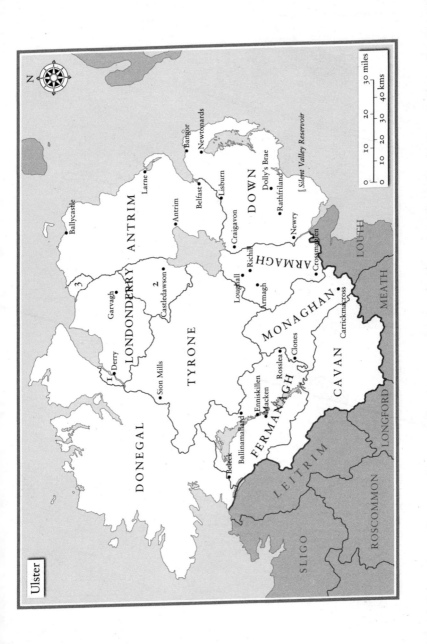

Ulster

N

DONEGAL

LONDONDERRY

Derry
Garvagh
Castledawson
Sion Mills

3
2

ANTRIM

Ballycastle
Larne
Antrim
Belfast
Lisburn
Bangor
Newtonards

TYRONE

DOWN

Dolly's Brae
Rathfriland
Rathfriland
Craigavon
Newry
Silent Valley Reservoir

Loughgall
Richhill
ARMAGH
Armagh
Crossmaglen

LOUTH

MEATH

Ballinamallard
Enniskillen
Macken
Belleek

FERMANAGH

Rosslea
Clones

MONAGHAN

Carrickmacross

CAVAN

LEITRIM

LONGFORD

SLIGO

ROSCOMMON

0   10   20   30 miles
0   10   20   30   40 kms

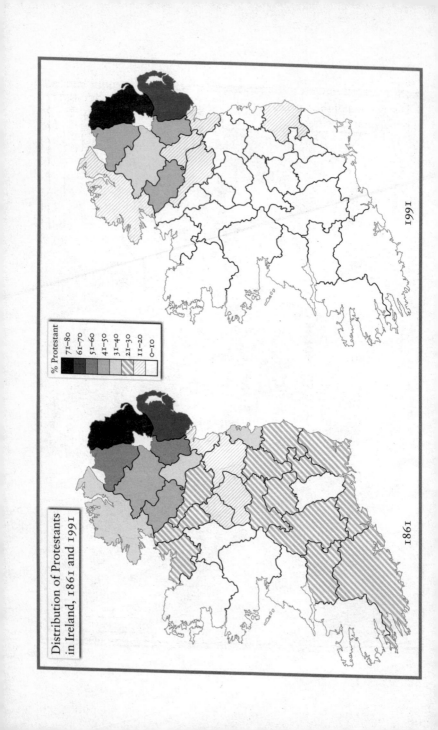

Distribution of Protestants
in Ireland, 1861 and 1991

% Protestant

71–80
61–70
51–60
41–50
31–40
21–30
11–20
0–10

1991

1861

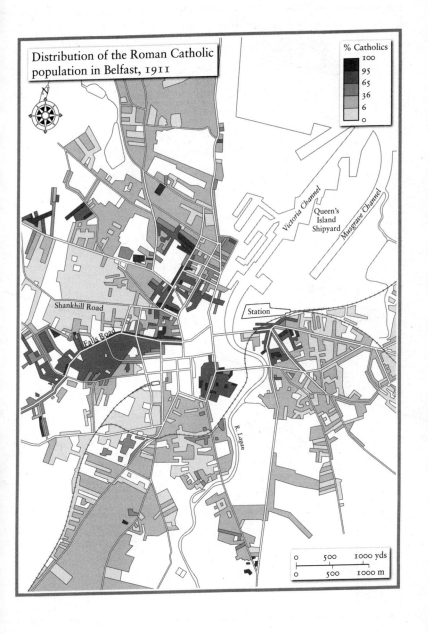

Distribution of the Roman Catholic population in Belfast, 1911

% Catholics
100
95
65
36
6
0

Victoria Channel

Queen's Island Shipyard

Musgrave Channel

Shankhill Road

Station

Falls Road

R. Lagan

0   500   1000 yds
0   500   1000 m

The 1925 Boundary Commission

N

DONEGAL

•Derry

LONDOND

•Omagh

TYRONE

FERMANAGH

•Enniskillen

LEITRIM

MONAGH

CAVAN

Coleraine

R Y

A N T R I M

Ballymena

Belfast

D O W N

A R M A G H

Newry

Crossmaglen

0   5   10 miles

0   5   10   15 kms

List of Abbreviations

The following abbreviations are used in the text and the notes

AOH	Ancient Order of Hibernians
BP	Belfast Protestant Association
BLSUU	British League for the Support of Ulster and the Union
BMH	Bureau of Military History
BNL	*Belfast News-Letter*
CCBS	Centre for Cross-Border Studies
GIA	Government of Ireland Act
GOC	General Officer Commanding
HC Deb	Parliamentary debates, House of Commons
ILPU	Irish Loyal and Patriotic Union
INA	Irish National Archives, Dublin
IRA	Irish Republican Army
IUA	Irish Unionist Alliance
NA	National Archives, London
NEBB	North-Eastern Boundary Bureau
NLI	National Library of Ireland, Dublin
PA	Parliamentary Archive, House of Lords
PR	proportional representation
PRONI	Public Record Office of Northern Ireland
RIC	Royal Irish Constabulary
ROIA	Restoration of Order in Ireland Act
RUC	Royal Ulster Constabulary
SC	Special Constabulary
UCDA	University College Dublin Archive

UIL	United Irish League
USC	Ulster Special Constabulary
UUC	Ulster Unionist Council

Prologue

Two days before Christmas 1920, the Government of Ireland Bill – or fourth Home Rule Bill – became law. It set forth two devolved governments in Ireland, southern and northern. Southern Ireland remained in the realm of political imagination, but Northern Ireland was firmly established when its parliament met in June 1921. The three previous Irish home rule bills had precipitated what may have been the most serious political and constitutional crisis in modern British history. The first two, introduced by the Liberal leader William Ewart Gladstone in 1886 and 1893, had split one of the two great governing parties; the third bill, introduced by his successor Herbert Henry Asquith in 1912, had brought the kingdom to the brink of civil war. Hundreds of thousands of men in Ireland had enlisted in citizen militias opposing or supporting home rule, and at Westminster the leader of the Conservative and Unionist Party had pronounced Asquith's Liberal government 'a revolutionary committee which has seized on despotic power by fraud'. Political negotiations were deadlocked, and the British army in Ireland was in turmoil. The 'Ulster crisis' was overwhelmed by events on an even vaster scale in Europe in August 1914, but it was never resolved.

The partition – the drawing of a political border within Ireland – happened because the Irish home rule project, the British government's acceptance of the Irish nationalist claim that Ireland should not be ruled from London, was resisted by those who refused to accept that claim. The roots of the home rule crisis lie in the original connection between the two main 'British Isles' – as the English call them – cemented by Henry II's expedition to secure the submission of Strongbow (Richard de Clare), the Norman adventurer who had

seized control of eastern Ireland in 1171. The connection tightened
and relaxed over long periods of time, but two key moments shaped
the issue which wracked the country in the nineteenth century. Oliver
Cromwell's campaign in 1649–50 determined the essentially military
nature of English control of Ireland, and fixed in Irish minds its
essentially Protestant character. The passage of the 1801 Act of Union
ended Ireland's colonial status along with the limited autonomy of
the Irish parliament, launching an attempt to turn the 'British isles'
into a single political community. Defence or destruction of that
union would then form the hinge of what became known as the 'Irish
Question'.

Whether or not British statesmen intended the union to end the
'Protestant Ascendancy' and integrate Catholics in a single United
Kingdom body politic, the daunting scale of any such project was
already established. As a historian of County Monaghan (on the
Ulster border) put it, by the end of the eighteenth century 'if a person
was a Catholic, it invariably meant that he was of old Gaelic stock,
that his ancestors were a defeated race, that he was never to be fully
trusted' – in the minds of the 'planter stock', who in turn were seen
as foreigners, persecutors, privileged persons, enemies. The political
meaning of this cocktail of racial perceptions was unambiguous: the
intention of the Catholic was 'some day . . . to become master in his
house again'.[1] This 'zero-sum' analysis – in the language of game
theory – the belief that a gain for one community must be an equivalent loss to the other, would militate against compromise in all
future political negotiations. Political consensus, the animating idea
of the English constitution, was hobbled in Ireland. The result was
forty years of political crisis.

To speak of such a protracted crisis may seem to abuse an overused
word. Can a crisis last so long? In clinical terms, crisis is by definition
transient, 'the point in the progress of a disease which is decisive of
recovery or death', as the dictionary says. Extended to the social or
political sphere, its meaning is not so precise. 'A turning point in the
progress of anything . . . or a state of affairs in which a decisive
change for better or worse is imminent.' Measuring such serious matters is necessarily more subjective, but in the nature of things 'normal'
political crises reach some resolution in a matter of days rather than

weeks. The head-on confrontation over Irish home rule did not follow normal patterns, and could not be resolved by normal political
adjustments. At stake was the self-definition of the United Kingdom.

This composite polity had been put together after the violent
upheavals of the seventeenth century in what can look like a deliberately pragmatic manner, avoiding issues of definition. The debates
on the fundamentals of politics conducted in the church by Putney
Bridge in 1647 would remain unique. (Moreover, that uncharacteristic moment of English self-analysis did not happen in parliament, but
the army.) But another moment of national destiny arrived in 1885,
when Gladstone's acceptance of home rule – it has often been called
a 'conversion' – broke up the conventional parameters of parliamentary politics, producing an extended sense of crisis, widely and
repeatedly experienced, over four decades, from 1885 to 1925. At its
core, beyond the immediate alarms and excursions, lay a systemic
crisis, a fear that the breakdown of consensus rendered all the struc-
tures and assumptions of the British political world ineffective.

The intensity of the hostility generated by the home rule project
can be difficult to grasp today.[2] Neither of the first two home rule
bills offered more than limited devolution of power to an Irish administration, but the fierce and increasingly well-organized opposition
which brought Gladstone's bills down raised fundamental questions
about the home rule project, the survival of the United Kingdom, and
the limits of democratic consensus. Was devolution desirable – was it
even possible? Did it defy the laws of politics to propose a status part
way to independence? What rights did Irish people who refused to
accept home rule have to resist it?

The third Home Rule Bill aimed, just as had the first two, to preserve the union by allowing Ireland limited self-government, and
hardly went beyond them in the powers it offered to the devolved
administration. But it precipitated the greatest intensification of the
recurrent crisis, focusing and magnifying all these issues. Unionists
were no readier than they had been in 1893 to accept that home rule
would maintain the union: it was, they held (and many believed),
simply a new name for the ancestral Catholic longing to secure independence and ultimately dispossess the Protestants. Home rule would
be 'Rome rule' – illiberal and incompetent, if not actively malignant.

The argument convulsed parliament and spread beyond it into popular mobilization. Hundreds of thousands signed pledges to resist home rule. Quasi-military militias with six-figure membership lists were formed to put pressure on the government either to abandon it – or push it through. They raised the spectre of civil war, with political questions that the liberal consensus was unable to answer. Could the threat of armed resistance to the law ever be justified?

As the crisis intensified, Unionists concentrated in north-eastern Ireland faced a new issue. If home rule could not be stopped altogether, could they be excluded from the devolved Irish substate? The idea of 'exclusion' was rejected in 1912 but never went away afterwards. So was another idea, a kind of federal arrangement, maybe modelled on the Dominion system of Canada and South Africa, which might contain the conflicting democratic rights of nationalists and Unionists. In 1914 Unionists in Ulster prepared to act unilaterally, and the government's monopoly of force seemed to be disintegrating. How real was the threat of meltdown? This issue has always been a matter of dispute, but in the event the threat was submerged by the indisputably greater threat posed by Germany in August 1914. Only when a fourth home rule plan was set out after the war, amidst an armed Irish republican bid to establish a separate state, did it become certain that the hangover of that debate would be a formal division of Ireland.

The 1920 Government of Ireland Act, dividing Ireland by devolving powers to southern and northern parliaments, forms the focal point of this book. Its passage was long drawn out, though in parliament it was far less stormy than its predecessors. The storms were outside, as British rule across most of Ireland – Ulster excepted – was paralysed by the IRA's guerrilla campaign to establish an Irish Republic. In Ulster, the pre-war preparations for unilateral action were revived with the (often reluctant) cooperation of the British government. In an atmosphere of civil war, too readily evoking seventeenth-century memories, a 'state under siege' was put together. The 1920 Act established its frontier, the line of partition, but it remained open to question for years. Few people apart from Ulster Unionists saw it as either sensible or just. The Anglo-Irish Treaty in December 1921, which morphed 'Southern Ireland' into the Irish Free State, with Dominion status, entailed immediate adjustment of the border in line with 'the wishes of the inhabitants', but the civil war within the Free State delayed this until 1924. The eventual Boundary Commission did not report until December 1925, so border revision remained a hope or fear in the air for five years after the 1920 Act.

The Irish border has always been contentious, both its course and indeed its very existence. A recent study of Ireland's long century within the United Kingdom concludes that partition was not inevitable, but it was logical.[3] So was partition just a mistake, a failure of statesmanship, or an unavoidable necessity? Or was it, perhaps, as Irish nationalists have always believed, a deliberate device to preserve British power? The question whether it should, or could, be reversed has driven political action and paramilitary violence on both sides, nationalist and Unionist, but as its centenary approached the border seemed to be more settled than ever before. The decision of the United Kingdom in 2016 to leave the European Union unexpectedly brought the status of the frontier back to the centre of the political vortex; at its centennial moment an understanding of the forces which brought it into existence is more than ever necessary.

I

The Union

'What can we say for a set of Irishmen, that fell out with each other in a state of ebriety, for private animosity, and when the law has sobered some of them, then to fall a quarreling about their respective creeds?'[1]

John Byrne, Armagh 1787

THREE BATTLES

By a crossroads near Loughgall in County Armagh, on 21 September 1795, a group of Protestants with firearms on the hilltop beat off an assault by 'swarms of Defenders', killing perhaps thirty. It was a one-sided fight, a 'turkey shoot'; the fact that the assault was pressed in such an unfavourable situation testified to the desperate determination of the Catholic assailants, members of a semi-secret semi-vigilante society. Colonel William Blacker, who wrote an account of the conflict a generation later, lamented, 'Happy had it been for the Protestant name if the Protestants had contented themselves with the defeat of their enemies at the Diamond and the formation of a protective society. Unhappily it was not so, a spirit of vengeance and retaliation had sunk too deeply in many of their minds to be thus easily satisfied . . . A determination was expressed of driving from this quarter of the country the entire of its Roman Catholic population.' ('Many were "quiet in the land" and had taken no share in such proceedings, but revenge, like love, is blind.')[2] The 'protective society' became known as the Orange Order; Blacker had in fact been one of its senior officers.

The 'battle of the Diamond', superficially a scruffy local set-to,

achieved a kind of immortality for this reason. It signalled and symbolized an unwavering repressive streak which ensured that whereas
anti-Catholicism in Britain gradually faded, ceasing to be the defining
attribute of Britishness, in Ireland it retained a living function in the
construction of collective identity. British anti-Catholicism sometimes
burst into public discourse, as it would famously do in 1850 when the
Liberal leader Lord John Russell denounced the re-establishment of
the Catholic hierarchy in Britain as 'insolent and insidious' Papal
interference, but it no longer routinely erupted into public violence.
Outbursts of sectarian conflict in Ireland became more noticeable as
they declined in Britain.

In July 1813, when England was gearing up for the final showdown
with Napoleonic France, another fight was going on in Garvagh,
County Londonderry. Several hundred Catholic 'Ribbonmen' attacked
the King's Arms, where the Orange lodge met; Protestants flocked to
the tavern bringing enough yeomanry muskets to disperse the attackers (who had only bludgeons). This 'battle of Garvagh' was kept from
obscurity by an Orange ballad and took its place in a ritual succession
of Orange triumphs.[3] The Catholic losers also memorialized these
battles in song and story.

In July 1829, at Mackan in Fermanagh, when Orange marchers
attacked youths who had jeered at them, Catholics replied by gathering with pitchforks and billhooks and attacking the Orangemen.
Three were killed, and four Catholics sentenced to death for the murders. Three of these were transported, and the fourth executed. They
became the subjects of folk legend, ballads of 'the battle of Mackan
Hill', still repeated in the late twentieth century. One of the longest
chapters in the anthropologist Henry Glassie's remarkable study of
the border village of Ballymenone charts the recurrence of this tale.
Mackan Hill, he judged, 'coils with the live force of "serfs" in rebellion against "bigotry" '; it 'becomes the tale of Catholic frustration . . .
just vengeance is meted out on men who do no real harm, who are
not the cause but only the medium . . . men who are available . . .
neighbours'.[4] For the anthropologist, this was a strategy of using the
past to frame the present.

By the time the Orange Order was taking form, and the 'Defenders' were reacting against it, the sense of a frontier was already etched

into what has been called the 'shatterbelt' – a zone on the fringe of Ulster 'where both religious groups had significant demographic strength', and a wider zone where they 'felt vulnerable to attack or colonization'. The reciprocal dynamic has been likened to Newton's third law of motion: every Orange action 'created equal and opposite support for the Defenders'.[5]

INVADING ULSTER

Less than a year before the Mackan fight, when Daniel O'Connell's Catholic emancipation campaign was reaching its climax, his lieutenant Jack Lawless, vexed by the dramatic shortfall in Ulster contributions to the 'Catholic rent' (the penny subscription to the Catholic Association) – just £204 out of £2,899 – launched an 'invasion of Ulster' – the first use of a fateful label. Leaving Carrickmacross on the Monaghan frontier on 17 September 1828, he planned to hold a series of mass meetings, declaring he would have 50,000 followers by the time he reached Ballybay six days later. Ballybay, a Presbyterian town, was an inhospitable place for Catholic agitators, and 8,000 Orangemen reportedly mustered there – 'in general armed with muskets; but failing these, swords, bayonets, pitch-forks, scythes, &c.' – to stop Lawless, many of them having made their wills before they set out. Lawless was headed off by a force of police and troops, but even so there was a clash near Rockcorry in which two of his followers died. In Lawless's next proclaimed objective, Armagh, where once again armed Protestants assembled on 30 September, local Catholics persuaded Lawless to stay away.[6]

The invasion was a fiasco and has largely been forgotten; but its motivation remains important. The Catholic Association leaders assumed that Protestant resistance to emancipation was weak, manipulated by elites rather than spontaneous eruptions, and could be called out and overawed. This assumption would recur repeatedly over the next century. And while the Ballybay standoff passed without major violence, it might have triggered a truly destructive conflict, a civil war in which the 'massacre of the Catholics of the North' might have been followed by a mass invasion of Catholics from the south.[7] O'Connell's campaign in the 1820s cemented an informal process of politicization which had taken shape over the previous generation. At many social levels, Catholics picked up the tools of the day-to-day trade of democracy – 'organising the signing of petitions, electing delegates, drawing up agendas, conducting debates' – and many once unpolitical social occasions 'took on a highly charged political character'. It has been argued that even before O'Connell launched his movement, this wide skein of communal activities represented 'the emergence of the Irish Catholic nation'.[8] The consequences of this could hardly have been more epochal.

UNIONISM?

After Catholics were eventually conceded the vote in 1829, O'Connell began campaigning to repeal the 1801 Act of Union, requiring Irish candidates in the 1832 election to take the 'repeal pledge'. It was resistance to this Irish nationalist mobilization against the union which would, ultimately, lead to partition. The centre of that resistance was in Ulster, and the resistance movement was labelled unionism. That much is plain enough; but what the union was, not so. Unionism did not exist before the creation of the United Kingdom in 1801, and at that point, beyond the rudimentary motive of national security, there was no Unionist programme or ideal underpinning the union. Those who forced the union through the Irish parliament did not know what it was for, nor how it should be made to work. 'Incorporation', the idea of full integration, was advocated by some, but without ever becoming a definite policy. Even for William Pitt (the Younger), the prime minister, who had spoken long before of 'making England and Ireland one country *in effect*', the creation of a United Kingdom identity as such was not a significant objective.[9] He did of course see Catholic emancipation as a crucial step which could not be taken without union, but it was merely a preliminary one. And this policy had negative origins; ministers were criticized – in terms that would echo throughout the union's life – for never thinking of Ireland 'except when she became troublesome'.

In the absence of any coherent governmental impulse towards

'incorporation', Britain's Irish policy drifted; the two countries remained separate in almost every respect after 1801. The Irish administration would be seen time and again – as it was by the future Lord Melbourne when he served as chief secretary – as 'anomalous and unsatisfactory'; yet it was left that way. Twenty years into the union, one advocate of integration, who maintained that it had been 'expected . . . that Ireland should become the same as a county of England', fumed that since Ireland was being governed 'as our slave colonies were' – by a viceroy and colonial establishment – 'Jamaica might be called, with as much propriety, a part of the United Kingdom as Ireland'. This was an exaggeration, certainly: Ireland sent a hundred MPs to Westminster. But they did little to establish Ireland's status of 'equality of laws' (one of Pitt's favoured ideas). Westminster did not ignore Ireland exactly, indeed it passed many special Irish laws, but that very fact displayed the absence of 'blending' (another such idea). For London, Ireland remained a foreign land (if not, as the future Duke of Wellington bluntly described it, 'an enemy country'). The cheerful confession of ignorance of Irish matters would be a standard line for British statesmen over the next hundred years. Against it, Irish MPs battled in vain, even though, as the Anglo-Irish playwright and Whig politician Richard Brinsley Sheridan said, the union made such protestations 'as ridiculous as to say they knew nothing about Middlesex or Yorkshire'.[10]

The London and Dublin administrations remained separate through inertia rather than deliberate choice, except perhaps for the theory, sometimes embraced, that only 'the man on the spot' could deal with the peculiarity and ungovernability of the Irish. The racial perception of Irish 'mendacity, corruption and violence' may have been toned down over the years, but a sense of fundamental difference would still be an underlying presence at Westminster when partition was debated in 1920. (Lord Hugh Cecil, for instance, clinically identified 'the kind of exaggeration which so often makes Irish speeches quite ineffective to an English audience'.)[11] Time and again British policy was reduced to the hope that once the country was 'reduced to obedience', as one lord chancellor put it, it might ultimately converge towards English values and behaviour.[12] This hardly qualified as a constructive or coherent programme of unionism, and it is hard to deny that the union was a major example of what has been called 'state-building failure'.[13]

Small wonder it was unpopular in Ireland – or rather, as Wellington put it, detested. If the positive meaning of the union was ill-defined, its negative effects were definite. As one pioneering student of devolution remarked, 'After 1801, the will to Irish unity disappeared'.[14] Although nationalists would always summon up the history of the democratic movement (embodied in the Volunteers) as proof of Irish unity, the 'generous enthusiasm which had for one flickering moment illuminated the Irish political scene' was lost, and lost for good. The psycho-political and social significance of the union changed with the uneven economic development of Ireland in the nineteenth century; Belfast and the north more generally came to see it as the framework of prosperity.

Even Catholic emancipation, the union's only positive achievement, was so long delayed that its constructive character was lost. The union was premised on Catholic consent, offered in the belief that it would be a prelude to emancipation; the failure to deliver it lost perhaps the last chance of legitimizing the British state by enrolling the Catholic elite.[15] Catholics were pushed into a political posture in which the only solution was reduction or removal of 'British rule'. And the ineffective performance of the state in reconciling Catholics left the field open to a very different project, the 'Protestant Crusade' to complete the union by converting Catholics to Protestantism. In the 1820s, O'Connell's mobilization for emancipation coincided with the so-called 'Second Reformation', a proselytizing campaign which not only failed to achieve mass conversion, but seriously exacerbated sectarian animosity.[16] Catholic resistance could take violent forms, and the fear of proselytism became etched deep in the attitude of the Church.

In one crucial sphere the union did attempt a constructive Irish policy, one which was ahead of Britain's own. In 1831 the Irish national system of education was launched to establish primary schools throughout the country. School building grants, teachers' salaries, and approved textbooks were centrally directed by an unpaid commission. Within two years over 100,000 children were enrolled in 789 schools; by mid-century there were half a million in 4,547 schools, and by the time a British national system was set up in 1870 there were nearly a million in 6,800 schools. All were non-denominational – in theory. In practice, despite the original aim of having schools run jointly by Protestant and Catholic clergy or laymen, by mid-century fewer than 4 per cent were under joint management; three-quarters were run by clergy of a single denomination. By 1870 the system was effectively denominational – 'almost as denominational as we could desire', as the Catholic hierarchy noted at the end of the century. The main result of the national system, as one leading historian has put it, 'was to bring about a dramatic increase in the educational resources of the Irish Catholic Church'.[17]

This unintended outcome was in large part the product of denominational geography; in overwhelmingly Catholic or Protestant areas, if the government had insisted on mixed schools, it would have ended up with no schools. In areas where the population was mixed, the failure of state policy was more serious. In the north-east, the education issue was a long-running battleground, with the Catholic Church unyielding in its determination to secure control – not least because so much Protestant support for 'non-sectarianism' was couched in terms of hostility to Catholicism.[18] In consequence, as a leading historian of Irish education puts it, 'now not only were the schools effectively segregated institutions, but the Protestants and Catholics assumed directly polar ideological positions concerning schooling'.[19]

PRESBYTERIANS INTO ULSTERMEN

The north-east of Ireland would become politically distinct for one key reason: its concentrated Presbyterian population, a very distinct community – fissiparous yet dynamic – with its centre in the growing city of Belfast.[20] Not all Protestants were Presbyterians – indeed until the Church of Ireland was disestablished in 1869, 'Protestant' meant 'Anglican'; Presbyterians were 'dissenters'. In this lay their special quality. The potency of a sense of victimhood in driving and sustaining resistance – sometimes violent – has come to be widely recognized. It existed long before the recent rise of 'victim culture'. For Irish

Presbyterians the sense arrived early on, shortly after the great triumph over Catholicism of 1690. The 1704 Test Act effectively expelled them from local government, and a series of disabilities gave 'frequent fortification' to their 'sense of persecuted purity'.[21]

James Craig, who would become prime minister in the first Northern Ireland government in 1921, belonged to the first generation of Presbyterians who would be unambiguously labelled 'Protestants'. In his biography, *Craigavon: Ulsterman* – a book 'so angry even Lady Craigavon and the Stormont Cabinet were upset'[22] – the playwright St John Ervine announced that his project was not to write a formal biography but to explain why the once anti-establishment Presbyterians had become conservatives; 'why was the Henry Joy McCracken of my childhood a Unionist when his renowned kinsman a century earlier was hanged as a rebel in Belfast?'[23] Ervine doubted 'if there are many Presbyterians in Ulster who cannot claim at least one rebel in their family history', and that reflects a view still widely held. The prominence of radical Protestants in the revolutionary movement was striking at the time and even more so in hindsight. But as an eminent historian of Ulster Presbyterians has cautioned, 'those who mourn the extinction of the pre-lapsarian Presbyterianism – enlightened in religion and republican in politics – which supposedly prevailed' before the emergence of the firebrand populist preacher Henry Cooke in the 1820s, 'would do well to recall its fragile and conditional nature'.[24] Presbyterians were at the forefront of the United Irish rebellion in 1798, but in the United Irish mobilization 'the basic categories of ethnic and denominational identity', and the seventeenth-century colonial settlement patterns, determined the geography of Ulster republicanism. The 'Scotch' (as Presbyterians were widely known) had been involved in sectarian violence for years and their Catholic antagonists never dropped their guard.[25] And 'the speed with which the Presbyterian radicals shifted their ground' after the failure of the 1798 rebellion 'tells its own story'.[26]

An account of 'the evolution of the Ulsterman', written at the height of the early twentieth-century Ulster crisis, argued that the identity was already formed by the time of the union. The 1608 Ulster plantation scheme, R. H. Murray said, had 'planted a new race in the northern province', which, unlike most such migrant groups, 'never coalesced with the inhabitants'. They remained 'as distinct as if an ocean rolled between them'.[27] The 'character of the Ulsterman' was shaped in the 'severe school of adversity'. This 'new being', the Ulsterman, it has been suggested, took shape during the crisis over the second Home Rule Bill in 1892; and then a literature developed giving him a special 'character', 'heritage', and 'destiny'.[28] There was ample material to hand already: forty years earlier, in 1852, a series of articles in the newly founded *Ulster Journal of Archaeology*, examining 'the origin and characteristics of the population in the counties of Down and Antrim', found them to be Anglo-Saxons with 'the inherited virtues of thrift, capacity for hard work, and respect for law and order'.[29]

The consistency of the characteristics attributed to 'Ulstermen', or northerners more generally, over several generations, has certainly been quite striking. Recently Marianne Elliott boiled them down to 'a peculiar accent, a blunt manner, a philistine outlook on life, an intransigent frame of mind'.[30] The graceless accent has even been explained as a deliberate rebuke to the graceful southern 'brogue'. Others have lengthened the list, or reduced it to, say, 'grit' (versus southern 'grace'). As the human geographer Marcus Heslinga noted, in quoting a raft of such menus 'for what they are worth', quite apart from the fact that regional characteristics are inherently 'rather intangible', appreciations of them are highly subjective. But both regional and denominational differences have been repeatedly registered. So, for instance, northerners are more provident whereas southerners lean more on Providence; the southerner works to live while the northerner lives to work; and so on. Northern Catholics are northerners – Eoin MacNeill said 'hardly less grave, sedate, unresponsive, taciturn, laconic, keen on a bargain, tenacious of his own . . . than the typical Ulster Presbyterian' – and, however hospitable, have a hard core not found in the south.[31] For James Winder Good (an acute critic of unionism) the Ulster 'temper' had become so distinct that 'the Ulsterman of all creeds contrasts more sharply with the natives of the other provinces than the Black Country does with the Home Counties'.[32] Jack White would later point to the 'mixture of contempt and defensiveness' that marked the Ulster provincial character.[33]

Applied to Protestant northerners, though, the label 'Ulstermen' took on a special character as an identity with distinct political meaning. Crucially in the nineteenth century the previous sharp division within Protestantism, between Episcopalians and dissenters, steadily dissolved. The Presbyterian ethos stayed central; they have been called a 'covenanted people' whose special relationship with God gave them a legalistic turn of mind and a precise sense of place.[34] The special religiosity of Ulster Presbyterians, the 'almost ostentatious plainness' of their church interiors, extending to a fear even of musical ornamentation, marked a simple culture which did not encourage the reading or writing of imaginative literature.[35] The moralistic intensity of Dr Henry Cooke, whose activism over three decades did more than most to push Presbyterians into the conservative, unionist camp, fused theology and politics to show the equation of Protestantism with liberty. 'Without civil liberty a man is nothing – without religious liberty, a Christian is nothing,' he insisted in 1850. He did not neglect to point up the contrast between free Protestantism and 'enchained Rome'.[36] This would become a ceaseless undertone in the long struggle over home rule.

For Protestants, Ulster came to stand not only for a homeland but for a way of life, a sense of identity which might – and sometimes would – be seen as akin to nationality. Heslinga indeed concluded that the 'Ulster' identity, which he labelled 'Ulsterism', is 'essentially a form of nationalism' – because it had too many political implications to be considered 'mere regionalism'.[37] The political implications are beyond doubt, but implications are not the same as intentions. The term 'nationalism' does not resolve the theoretical problem here, not least because nationalism is a notoriously imprecise concept, which has been taken to rest on various and sometimes inconsistent foundations. But it involves conscious intent – what Ernest Renan called 'the daily plebiscite'. What mattered was a sense of separateness, assiduously maintained. Because in much of Ulster, as a historian acutely attuned to the relationship put it, thanks to the 'haphazard nature of the conquest and settlement', Catholics and Protestants were not gathered in 'solid blocs . . . but interspersed amongst each other in tiny islands, the necessity to keep one's distance and preserve one's identity was paramount from the beginning'.[38]

The corollary of this was that 'insecurity became a permanent part of their psychology'.

The economic uniqueness of Ulster in the nineteenth century (with the so-called 'Ulster custom' governing landlord–tenant relations, the growth of the linen industry, and the emergence of Belfast as a manufacturing city) confirmed rather than created Protestant identity. Linen – 'the Protestant's potato' – allowed the rural population to grow to 'fantastic densities'. Forced social change produced unrest, with Protestant violence generally directed at landlords rather than Catholics. Only the bitter sectarian conflict in north Armagh primarily targeted Catholics, but violence against landlord power did so indirectly, because Catholics were assumed to be willing to pay 'any rent' for tenantries. Whatever strategic logic they adopted, the loyalist 'bands' were ostentatiously Protestant. The Hearts of Steel boasted of being loyal Protestants, 'not one RC is ever suffered to appear among us'. The objective was to impel landlords to return to the old ways, which meant privileging Protestant tenants.

Belfast's urban culture was the product of a rural society which migrated there on the back of the city's astonishing growth, from 13,000 in 1782, to 50,000 in 1830, 122,000 in 1861, reaching 350,000 by 1901. The speed of in-migration from the countryside (common in early industrial cities) sucked in rural patterns of behaviour directly, unchanged. The religious complexion of its citizenry altered significantly: almost entirely Presbyterian in the eighteenth century, it became one-third Catholic in the 1830s. By 1861, Presbyterians made up hardly one-third of its citizens. For a long decade after the Orange Order was suppressed in the 1830s, Protestants could not visibly dominate the city. But the repeal movement concentrated minds. When O'Connell was due to speak in Belfast in 1841 – 'when you *invade* Ulster', as Henry Cooke, Moderator of the Presbyterian Synod, put it – he was challenged to a public debate by Cooke, and refused the challenge. Plans for a great repeal procession were dropped amidst fears of serious violence. A triumphant Cooke – for whom repeal was 'just a discreet word for Romish ascendancy and Protestant extermination – invoked the 'genii of Protestantism and Liberty', together with the 'genius of Industry', to explain Belfast's miraculous growth and prosperity. 'And all this we owe to the Union.'

'Look at Belfast,' he challenged, 'and be a Repealer if you can.'[39] The visit demonstrated that 'virtually all sections of Protestant political opinion and clerical leadership', as well as a very large part of the mass Protestant population, could be 'mobilized to defend the Union'.[40]

The special self-image of Belfast as a hub of enterprise and progress would become ever more sharply defined. The north-east was not spared the impact of the great famine which prostrated Ireland over four years from the winter of 1845–6, especially during the most bitter winter of 1846–7. In the spring of 1847, Belfast was struck by a typhus epidemic which spread throughout Ulster. In 1848 there was a second wave of fever. Even so, a ten-year project to cut a new channel to open Belfast harbour to heavy ships was pressed ahead, and the channel was opened with a spectacular maritime ceremony on 10 July 1849. For the *Belfast News-Letter* it formed one of the 'brightest pages in the history of the progress of Belfast towards the enviable rank she is hastening to attain among the commercial *entrepots* of the British Empire'.[41] The contrast with the haphazard programme of public works commissioned under the government's famine relief policy – roads *'that will never be finished'* as one local official sadly remarked, *'useless* or *injurious Works'* in the splenetic view of one ratepayer – could not have been sharper.[42]

WRATH AND DEFIANCE

The all-male, all-Protestant Orange Order has, for much of the last two centuries, been the most assertive bearer of Protestant identity. It was an odd mix of secrecy and triumphalist public display. Its origins in opposition to Catholic secret societies imprinted a suspicion of subversive conspiracy, suspicion nourished by the Europe-wide wave of secret-society activity in the late eighteenth and early nineteenth century – a real phenomenon which was hugely exaggerated in the minds of the authorities.[43]

The first attempt at a full history of the Order, R. M. Sibbett's *Orangeism in Ireland and throughout the Empire* in 1914, described the answer of an Orangeman who – asked how long his Order had existed – said it could be traced back to the garden of Eden, as 'a thoroughly accurate statement'. This because 'all the essentials of a perfect nature and an exalted religion were to be found in the primal day of our race'. The journalist James Winder Good, writing just after the Great War, would interestingly invoke the Islamic concept of *jihad* to characterize Orange anti-Catholicism. He cited the public sermonizer Dr Thomas Drew's warning that 'under the downward progress of British legislation, God will be made angry', and his insistence that Protestant unity and 'testimony' were required 'to deprecate God's indignation'.[44]

As Winder Good noted, it was 'simple enough to describe the surface appearance of Orangeism, but by no means so easy to analyse the qualities which give the faith its hold over the minds of its adherents' – and 'make it so formidable a political force'. As he said, few such powerful communal ideas had found quite so few 'reputable defenders'.[45] This shortage of sympathetic analysis has persisted; for every attempt at understanding there have been many brusque invocations of mere bigotry (often invoked as self-explanatory). The Orangemen's aim was formally respectable: to help maintain 'law and order'. But their 'order' – a fruitful ambiguity in their organizational title – was a particular social order – Protestant ascendancy. This followed the logic of the view (firmly voiced by Henry Cooke) that only Protestants were truly law-abiding. By the time Good was writing, ascendancy was played down, and the call to put 'the rascally Papishes under my feet' heard less loudly. He anticipated much subsequent analysis in his acid comment that, 'As usual in Ulster religious fanaticism was so directed as to subserve economic ends'.[46]

A more sophisticated approach has suggested that as the modernization process disrupted the old landlord–tenant relation, which had privileged Protestants, land became more marketable, and Protestants needed a way of maintaining their position. The Volunteer movement of the 1780s provided the mechanism, enlisting 'riotous assemblies' like Hearts of Oak and Hearts of Steel and turning them into 'decent tranquil meetings' where 'a connection with their superiors begets affection'.[47] After the union, Protestant energy was directed away from the 'ideal of 98' to Orangeism, which by the 1830s incorporated over half the adult male Protestant population. Its function was not so much to conduct an economic struggle against Catholics as to cushion the impact of social change by sustaining a sense of unity between the lower orders and their betters. Although Orangeism might initially have been a response to a particular crisis – like earlier 'public bands' – unlike them it survived, and indeed strengthened over succeeding generations because it fulfilled this social need.

Orangeism's British dimension has often been overlooked – its leading historian called the British lodges 'merely a series of miscellaneous clubs . . . hostile to the catholics' and viewed with suspicion by all governments.[48] But it would contribute to stoking the febrile political atmosphere of the anti-home rule reaction. The numbers directly involved did not approach the level of those in Ulster, though in Liverpool some 20,000 Orangemen marched on 12 July 1859. After the dramatic growth of the Order in mid-century Liverpool, it spread across the industrial heartland as Irish immigration accelerated.[49] The Order has generally been given at most a marginal place in late-Victorian British society, but it had real popular appeal, and certainly played a part in raising awareness of 'Ulster'. This could of course be negative. While the liberal press might reluctantly concede that the Order reflected 'a grand epoch in our national history' – 'when Protestant religion gained its first ascendancy over the Romish Church' – more often liberals were alienated by its activities. ('Some people of seventeenth-century ideas are still in the flesh.')[50] Above all, the July Twelfth celebrations could be as divisive in Britain as in Ireland.

Even so, Orangeism's function as a pan-Protestant movement was not negligible. In Ulster, its role as an umbrella organization for Protestants of all denominations has made it so important that its role may often be exaggerated. A careful scholar has argued that the institution of the Order 'was not the cause of sectarian strife but a reflection of it'.[51] The Order did not always take the lead in direct action, but rather nursed the worldview that powered action. It and Fenianism may both be seen above all as mental attitudes, one of domination, the other of defiance. The assertion of dominance through the garish triumphalism of processions, 'walking' with ear-shattering drumbeats, erecting big castellated arches at key points on the communal divide, decorated with ropes of coloured paper and festoons of orange lilies or sweet william, all counterbalanced the secrecy of the lodge organization with its masonic initiation rites and quasi-occult grades of power.

Its appeal as a vehicle of frontier culture was quite real. Winder Good evoked the way the early July Orange preparations brought 'a gleam of brightness into dull lives'; the arches were 'thickest in the streets that abut on Nationalist territory', 'there the Orange lilies are most lavishly spread, the inscriptions are more provocative ... the din of fifes and drums all night long makes sleep impossible, and youthful braves, like knights before their investiture, keep watch and ward beside bonfires in expectation of a raid'. His phrase for this frontier zone, 'debatable land', was a telling one.[52]

The great Orange fiesta was 12 July, the anniversary of William of Orange's victory over James II at Aughrim, but the most psychologically telling memory, with enduring effect on political behaviour, was the Siege of Derry. The anniversary of the lifting of the siege had been celebrated since its centenary year, 1790. Macaulay's vivid retelling of the story in his runaway bestseller, the multi-volume *History of England* (published between 1848 and 1855), projected it from the local sphere into mainstream awareness. It 'gave Ulster Protestants a central place in the myth of the unfolding British constitution', as Ian McBride puts it – and is still quoted by Unionists to demonstrate Ulster's centrality to 'the struggle for civil and religious liberty, for representative institutions, and ultimately for democracy itself'.[53]

But the climax of the celebration, the burning of a looming effigy of the city's governor, 'the traitor Lundy', has etched a parallel fear of betrayal into the loyalist outlook. On its first appearance, in 1788, the effigy was 'represented in a very humorous style' by 'some of the lower class of citizens'.[54] Subsequently, the humorous element became perhaps less noticeable, the neurotic element in the fear of 'Lundyism' more so. The tension between Macaulay's negative view of the Protestant ascendancy's 'hateful laws' and his respect for Protestant resolution in times of peril has been remarked, and he saw the Derry celebrations likewise, as two-sided: while a people must take pride in the achievements of their ancestors, this 'pious gratitude' had 'too often been mingled with words of wrath and defiance'.[55]

VIGILANTES, VANGUARDS

The Order evolved in an age of rioting, by no means all of it sect-arian. Practically every contested election in Ulster, like many across the rest of the kingdom, was embellished by hired mobs intent on intimidating voters, and violent clashes often followed. Economic protests frequently took riotous form. 'Faction fights', the semi-ritual clashes of gangs – 'parties' – with no recognizable political or rel-igious affiliation, pre-dated the formation of sectarian groups, some of which indeed started out as factions. (The first Peep O'Day Boys, and some early Defenders, seem to have been recruited from both religious denominations.) Still, Henry Cooke insisted in 1825 that 'the names of Orangemen and Ribbonmen which have become notorious' were 'merely the coming out of the leaven that had infected the lump before'. And by mid-century, working-class Catholics and Protestants acquired an ideological legitimacy for their sectarian prejudices, and conflict 'became more clearly a political one'.[56] Sect-arianism shaped nearly all Belfast riots.

Orangeism's effectiveness and legitimacy were variable. The Order was initially too weak to establish lodges in Belfast and was rather loosely organized by contrast with its image. Catholic emancipation, while it brought the average Catholic little immediate material bene-fit, 'did wonders for him psychologically'.[57] One significant result was that Orange parades were now challenged at every level. The Mackan fight of July 1829, the year after emancipation, was an early token of this. The government formally suppressed the Order in the late 1820s, and a Party Processions Act in 1832 ushered in twenty years or more of relative quiet. Indeed the Order dissolved itself after a parliamen-tary inquiry suggested that it threatened to subvert discipline in the army. But the Act was never consistently enforced, and it lapsed in 1845. Orangemen resumed marching, matched once again by Ribbon-men, the successors of the Defenders.

The logic of these patterns of counter-vigilantism, 'feuds and conflicts with a life of their own', has been pithily explained: only 'universally accepted law and order systems' can break the cycle of fear which for much of history and in most of the world has led to 'potentially endless spirals of revenge and chaos'. No such system existed in Ulster. In the 1830s one of the union's most capable administrators, Thomas Drummond, Under Secretary at Dublin Castle, went far to establish a regular legal regime which could supersede the sectarian vendetta system – a framework 'in which people of influence had to understand that tranquility depended on accommodation with the Catholic clerical and middle-class leadership'.[58] Such accommodation remained fragile, and whenever it lapsed, the Orange Order resumed its function as upholder of the deterrence system. Vigilantes could be seen as vanguards, accepted, at least tacitly, by their community.

The endemic threat of vanguard rivalry was magnified by the advent of railways in the mid-1840s. In their first railway 'excursion', a big Orange parade assembled in Belfast on 12 July 1846 to take the train to join a meeting in Lisburn; returning later, they paraded along Bridge Street before being attacked with stones and brickbats by a Catholic crowd as they tried to enter Donegall Street. (The *Belfast News-Letter* lamented that 'the harmony of the day' had been marred by 'the intolerant spirit of Romanism'.) Railway stations henceforth became new sites of conflict, as crowds of supporters and opponents gathered to meet parades when they returned from other towns. (Criticizing the authorities for their inaction, the *News-Letter* pointed out that the 'Repealers and Ribbonmen' had made their intentions clear – 'they paraded the streets with green boughs, headed by a fife and drum, collected in several places in great numbers and manifested every symptom of intended opposition'.[59] July 1848 brought an unusually big procession in Belfast, to refute the ill-advised claim by the recently formed Protestant Repeal Association that most Orangemen had embraced repeal.

The famine hardly mitigated the intensity of the rivalry. Rathfriland in County Down was hit by severe destitution in 1847–8, yet it witnessed one of the most emblematic rural battles of the century on 12 July 1849. An Orange march from Rathfriland to Tollymore Park followed a route where there had been serious clashes the previous year, one carefully chosen to provoke the Ribbonmen. As the military commander sent to police the march with a troop of light dragoons and an infantry company – a formidable force – drily observed, it was such a long detour (via the Catholic village of Magheramayo) that the

Orangemen were 'epicures to choose it'. Some 1,400 Protestants with banners and bands, 'armed to the teeth', marched out without incident, but on their return ran into hundreds of Ribbonmen armed with pitchforks, pikes, and muskets, at the Dolly's Brae pass. While 'the Ribbon party were constantly "blazing away" with their arms', Major Wilkinson noted, 'no breach of the peace occurred'.[60] In this 'regular field day' an unknown number of Catholics – estimates vary from six to eighty – were killed; a parliamentary inquiry condemned the magistrates for permitting the march amidst a population consisting of 'two contending bodies, whose prejudices and feelings are inflamed against each other from old recollections and religious differences'.[61] Next year, the Party Processions Act was revived.

Before this, though, the government, faced with the threatened Young Ireland insurrection in 1848, briefly enlisted Orangemen in their yeomanry guise to defend the state. This history of partial suppression buttressed Catholic suspicions that the Orange movement was officially inspired, though for most of the nineteenth century it was viewed with distaste not only by officialdom but also by many middle-class Protestants (for whom it manifested the disruptive threat of the 'dangerous classes'). Class tension within the Order was contained; the radical tendency amongst working-class loyalists – 'Protestant populism' or 'radical bigotry' as one writer has memorably labelled it – often surfaced, but never undermined the common political posture.[62] As the Catholic population surge in Belfast faded, Orangeism revived. After serious riots in the early 1850s, marked by the increasing use of firearms, the 'Orange party', in the view of one newspaper, were 'inspired with confidence in themselves ... ably organized, skillfully disciplined'.[63] The Irish Lord Chancellor thought Orangeism had remained 'extensively organised' in spite of its supposed suppression, having changed its 'system and rules' to protect it from legal prosecution. In the mid-1850s it kept up 'through large districts of the north a spirit of bitter and factious hostility', provoking 'violent hostility and aggression'.[64]

The railways which enabled larger Orange assemblies also made possible the great rally of Ulster popular Protestantism in 1859, the year when 'the Protestant province went on a gigantic evangelical spree'. The rally in the Belfast Botanical Gardens was the climax of a

mass revival movement which saw even the Church of Ireland holding open-air evangelical meetings. Dramatic manifestations of
conversion cascaded across the province, with women prominent
amongst the 'smitten'; a big feature of the 'awakening' was 'its almost
electric spread among female workers'.[65] Women would cry out in
anguish as they recognized their sinfulness, even go into extended
trances with visions of heaven. This was in essence a spiritual,
unpolitical – even as some have thought a quasi-sexual – movement,
but it had a definite, negative effect on community relations. It was
unmistakably Protestant, and the strenuous efforts of Catholic
organizations to prevent conversion sharpened tensions in working-
class areas. The two new churches – Presbyterian and Church of
Ireland – built in Sandy Row in the wake of the revival both had committed Orangemen as ministers.[66] The number of Orange lodges in
Belfast surged from forty-two in 1856 to 147 twenty years later.

The fact that a number of Catholics embraced Protestantism during the revival signalled a wider impact on communal relations. The
number was probably quite small, but, as one authority suggests,
more were probably converted 'by this experience than by every effort
at overt proselytization before or since'.[67] It was more than enough to
trigger the Catholic Church's ever-present anxiety; its reaction in
turn fuelled Protestant hostility. One Episcopalian paper which initially took a dim view of the revival concluded that since 'Romish
priests' pronounced it a device of the devil, that was 'a strong argument in its favour'. What the political scientist Frank Wright called
'accommodative relationships' were put under direct pressure in some
places, and the Presbyterian 'heartlands . . . became more vulnerable
to sectarian rivalries'.[68]

PROCESSIONS AND RIOTS

The basic shape of Belfast fighting was fixed early on – the first significant riot, organized on sectarian lines, was in July 1813 – and
never much altered later. The culture of riot in Belfast has been widely
studied, of course, and possibly given too much attention. But it is
hard to argue that the escalation of rioting in the nineteenth century

did not have a major political significance. After 1851 there were dozens of minor riots, and four whose violence and duration exceeded any of those that happened before. This escalation reflected growing collective cohesion: in Belfast as elsewhere the severity of riots increased as the wider community increasingly supported them. Even when the Party Processions Act was in force, there were frequently violent clashes around 12 July – in eighteen of the thirty-five years before 1886. Violence threatened, whether the Orangemen marched to special church services or merely beat their drums and fired shots in the air.

The Act was in force in 1857, the year of one of the fiercest riots. Orangemen in Sandy Row marched without sashes to hear a special sermon by Dr Drew in Christ Church, putting their sashes on when they arrived. While Drew delivered a ferocious address, evoking a global battle between Catholicism and the Protestantism of the British Empire and the United States, a Catholic crowd gathered around the police cordon guarding the church. From then on, as the commission of inquiry suggested, it was just a matter of time before 'the two parties' had the opportunity 'to bring their conflict to a bloody issue'. Both sides prepared stocks of bricks and paving stones, and loopholed walls, so that by 14 July the Sandy Row and Pound districts 'presented the appearance of actual battle being waged between two hostile forces prepared for a deadly encounter'.[69] The ensuing clashes lasted almost a week. The worst effects were due not so much to gunfire, which often seemed mainly symbolic, but the house-wrecking and workplace intimidation which manifested the intensity of sectarian hostility.[70] After a brief lull, confrontation began again in August, when Drew launched a series of open-air sermons on the steps of the custom house, and went on through September.

This lengthening became a feature of the most intense disturbances which followed, the first in August 1864, when the political battle lines were more unambiguously drawn. Twelve days of street battles with stones and firearms, with attacks on churches, schools, and a female penitentiary, began with the burning of an effigy of O'Connell, and an attempt to bury the remains in a Catholic cemetery. Funerals of dead rioters provoked further retaliation. When a big group of Catholic 'navvies' arrived in town and wrecked a national school in

Brown Street the fighting escalated, with most of west Belfast suffering serious damage. The riot commissioners concluded that 'the elements of contention were never more rife amongst the population than at present', but found an additional cause for alarm in the 'perfectly astounding' participation of evidently respectable people – notably in the select neighbourhood of Donegall Place.[71] Equally alarming for the future, there were several clashes between Protestant crowds and the police. The belief that the authorities were shipping in Catholic police reinforcements became widespread and opened a potential rift between loyalism and the state authorities. The twin themes of cross-class Protestant mobilization and alienation from the state were ominous.

The warning of a Belfast constabulary officer in August 1864 that, but for the big deployment of troops and police, 'scenes of violence would have been witnessed . . . without a parallel in the annals of any civilized community', hyperbolic as it was, perhaps began to be realized in 1872, after the repeal of the Party Processions Act. This confession of legislative failure was significant, both in itself and in the way it came about. The law had never sat comfortably with the principle of freedom of expression, and even less so did the 1860 Party Emblems Act which banned displays of 'any banner, flag or symbol' (including the Union flag itself), and any 'playing of music', if judged a threat to public order. The effective ruler of Ireland, Under Secretary Thomas Larcom, noted in 1864 that 'in the North' marching and drumming had not generally been directly interfered with – the police merely took down the names of offenders and prosecuted them later. This had little effect, but Larcom optimistically suggested that Orange parades were 'in truth sinking into little more than something between Guy Fawkes and a Carnival'. The former prime minister Sir Robert Peel, irked by the erection of the 'ugly' O'Connell statue in Dublin, had professed that he could not understand 'why people have not as much right to burn O'Connell in effigy in one place, as to glorify his memory in another'.[72]

The Party Processions Act was repealed after four years of parliamentary sniping by William Johnston 'of Ballykilbeg', a minor County Down landlord whose persistent defiance of the Act had led to his imprisonment in 1868 and, shortly afterwards, his election to parliament for south Belfast. The organization which backed his candidacy, the Belfast Protestant Working Men's Association, was a portent for the future – a cross-class 'pan-Protestant' movement.[73] Its working-class membership notwithstanding, it put Protestant solidarity above class issues. Johnston's mass procession against the Party Processions Act at Bangor, County Down, on 12 July 1867, assembled over 25,000 demonstrators. By 'revitalising the cross-class Protestant alliance on which Orangeism was predicated', it has been suggested, Johnston's campaign provided the essential foundation for the formation of an Ulster Unionist political movement in the following decade.[74] Johnston's invocation of Ulster was very precise: 'we in Ulster,' he announced in 1864, 'shall never endure tyranny in the name of the law'.[75]

In proposing repeal in 1872, Chief Secretary Lord Hartington had admitted the 'injurious effect' of an act, 'constantly violated and never enforced', being maintained 'with a semblance of partiality'. This injurious effect was rather abstract, perhaps, compared with the immediate effect of the repeal. The 12 July 1872 Orange parade passed off without violence, but the newly founded Home Rule Association then organized its own inaugural demonstration, conspicuously featuring a supposed representation of Ulster in the form of 'a boy dressed in green mantle trimmed with white and gold and mounted on a white horse with green trappings'.[76] This was attacked as it set out from the city centre and again, more violently, at the brickfields – a frontier between the Falls Road and Shankill districts, where a month-long spate of house-wrecking followed. By the end of it some 840 families had been driven out, and their formerly mixed streets 'had become almost entirely Catholic or Protestant'.[77] After 1872, loyalists offered a violent challenge to every Catholic or nationalist procession in Belfast. As the home rule movement grew, a kind of guerrilla street-politics was already prepared to oppose it.

HOME RULE

Nationalities habitually define themselves in opposition to an Other; national identities can remain latent and diffuse until they face what is felt as an existential threat. The nature of Ulster identity would have remained an ethnographic curiosity, but for the development of the Irish nationalist movement in the nineteenth century. 'As nationalist aspirations became more sharply defined, so also did an Ulster sense of difference.'[78] For Irish nationalists, the defining 'other' was England, and the precondition of national freedom was, as Wolfe Tone put it, to 'break the connection'. After Tone's death in 1798, the changed political form of that connection meant that the Act of Union became the primary target: it would have to be done away with, either by outright repeal or by drastic remodelling. Daniel O'Connell's repeal campaign brought forth what may be seen as the first partition proposal. Macaulay, a decade before he began his epic *History*, argued in parliament that O'Connell could not 'find a reason for having a parliament at Dublin which will not be just as good for having another parliament at Londonderry'.[79]

When the repeal campaign failed in the 1840s, the alternatives were either to wrest freedom from Britain by force or somehow adjust it to fit within the union. The failure of 'physical force men' – first Young Ireland and then the Fenians (Irish Republican Brotherhood, IRB) to liberate Ireland in 1848 and 1867 opened a space for the second approach. Home rule, an attempt to square the circle of union and freedom, began as a unionist alternative to O'Connell's repeal, which the founder of the Home Rule Association, Isaac Butt, thought was too negative, lacking any progressive dimension. Butt, a Donegal Protestant lawyer who became a nationalist hero for defending the Fenian rebels of 1867, thought repeal would merely pitch Ireland back into the clearly unsatisfactory political system of the eighteenth century. He also saw the union itself as having potential virtues, enlarging Ireland's role in the world. His home rule was basically a federalist idea (and he chose not to resolve some of the vital issues, like the taxation powers of the Irish parliament, which would dog home rule throughout its career). It sparked neither strong enthusiasm nor violent objection. Butt's own character was partly responsible: he lacked the 'exasperation' which his successor, Charles Stewart Parnell, had in spades.[80] Under Parnell, home rule would generate both mass enthusiasm and organized resistance.

As president of the Amnesty Association, pressing for the release of

Fenian prisoners, Butt had publicly identified with the IRB; the far more militant and anti-English Parnell may have joined it. So even though home rule would never offer Ireland more than autonomy within the union, it could well seem viscerally connected to separatists who demanded an independent republic. Both Butt and Parnell insisted on the unity of Ireland; both were Protestants. Butt saw home rule as the only political structure which could reconcile nationalism and unionism; Parnell seems to have simply ignored the potential problem of unionist resistance. The trajectory of home rule, though, painfully drawn out over half a century, could only aggravate that problem.

This modest devolutionary scheme would rapidly provoke a hostility – in Britain as well as Ireland – which can now appear disproportionate. It proposed transferring domestic administrative powers to an Irish government, while Ireland would remain part of the United Kingdom, sending MPs to the Westminster parliament, with very limited fiscal independence, and without any role in foreign policy or defence. Whether, if home rule had been enacted speedily, it might have resolved the 'Irish Question' – avoiding partition – is a central question in Irish history. Any answer must hinge on whether the resistance movement which instantly emerged in Ulster became more formidable as time passed, to the point at which it presented a real threat of civil war; there were, and still are, those who hold that the manifestations of loyalist militancy were a sham, a bluff which should have been called. This issue lies at the heart of the story that follows.

Home rule would be stymied for reasons which touch the core of the British political system's governing capacity. It was well said, a few years after the partition, that 'the failure of England [sic] to provide a solution to the Irish question was not a failure for which this or that statesman could be held responsible, but it was a failure in the political conception of a nation', as it were 'a regrettable *lacuna* in English political thought'. 'A people which prides itself on a genius for political compromise displayed a legal pedantry which precluded compromise on the most significant problem in politics of the last century. A question which demanded . . . a great effort of creative imagination was approached with caution and enduring pessimism.'[81]

2

The Remote North

On 16 October 1883, moments before T. M. Healy, the recently elected Irish nationalist MP for Monaghan, was due to address a National League rally at Roslea, on the county line between Monaghan and Fermanagh, a large column, some two thousand strong – described by one of its leaders, Lord Rossmore, as 'a most respectable, determined-looking body of men' – advanced towards the meeting site from Clones. Rossmore had 'the whole country placarded calling on all loyalists to assemble' there; his notices carried slogans like 'Down with Parnell and rebellion', and 'Emergency and Boycott men to the front'. When the local Resident Magistrate (one of the few Catholic RMs – Rossmore thought him 'quite insufferable'), with a force of over 500 troops and police, called on him 'in a very impertinent manner' to take a detour, Rossmore simply told him 'my men have made up their minds to go straight on'. When threatened with arrest, he warned 'on you and you alone will rest the blame of having transformed this orderly body of men into a leaderless mob'. He was allowed to pass.

In his own account, Rossmore – himself a justice of the peace – pointed out that although 'there was only a hedge and a ditch between the two bodies of demonstrators', only verbal insults passed between them. 'Not a blow was struck, not a shot fired, or a missile thrown.'[1] He depicted, as has been remarked, 'a finely judged exercise in social control for the greater good'.[2] But if this was a peaceful confrontation, the terms of Rossmore's address to his followers, pledging 'to resist in every way in our power any attempt to place Ireland under a government of murderous butchers and socialistic rebels' – 'that scum on the hill beyond' – suggested that the peace was fragile.[3] Indeed, when Rossmore was dismissed from the magistracy for 'deliberately endangering the public peace', the loyalist reaction was fierce. Military intervention was needed to control a pro-Rossmore 'counter-demonstration' at Dromore in County Tyrone, and a loyalist linen worker was fatally wounded in the melee when the Orange marchers tried to attack the nationalist meeting.

The Roslea face-off was a leading example of the counter-demonstration tactic adopted by the Orangemen, aimed at forcing the authorities to ban both meetings. Loyalist action could be pre-emptive too, as when the Londonderry Apprentice Boys occupied the city hall to prevent a nationalist meeting due to be addressed by the Lord Mayor of Dublin, who was fired on from the hall. Two people were wounded. The 'volatile political atmosphere' reflected rapidly increasing political polarization in the early 1880s. The first home rule candidate to be put up in Ulster was heavily defeated in the 1881 Tyrone by-election, a personal humiliation for Parnell. The 1882 Phoenix Park assassinations, when the Chief Secretary for Ireland and the Under Secretary had been killed with butchers' knives – hence Rossmore's identification of Irish nationalism with butchery – 'produced an appalling effect' in Ulster.[4] It seemed a chilling warning of the intentions of underground republican terrorist groups. The Land League, a tenant-right movement (which a number of Orangemen had taken part in), was succeeded by the openly political National League – immediately identified by loyalists as a front for physical-force republicanism. Orange lodges which had supported the Land League were punished by expulsion from the Order.

Healy, formerly MP for Wexford, had agreed to stand in Monaghan 'to raise the banner in the remote North'.[5] (The phrase speaks volumes about the perspective from Dublin.) His victory on 30 June 1883 – an electrifying moment – heralded what he pugnaciously labelled the nationalist 'invasion of Ulster', a racking-up of confrontation encouraged by Parnell himself. (Although neither he nor Parnell mentioned home rule in their election speeches, his Conservative opponent insisted that the nationalists were 'coming forward to establish an Irish Republic'.)[6] And franchise reform – which would give the Irish nationalists a bare majority of the Ulster seats at the next general election – was imminent. The announcement of the Roslea meeting summoned the 'men of Fermanagh and Monaghan' to prove they would 'never rest contented until the land of Ireland is the property of the whole people of Ireland, to be administered by government existing for and by the will of the Irish nation'.[7]

Before he was removed from the magistracy, it had been made clear to Rossmore that if he were to declare he had not appreciated the risk that his action could lead to violence, he would not be dismissed. He refused. Objections to his dismissal were not confined to the streets of Monaghan. The Viceroy, Earl Spencer, had to threaten resignation to prevent the House of Lords condemning it. Five years later – shortly after calling Gladstone 'a mad dog that ought to be destroyed' – he was restored by the (now Conservative) government.[8] But it was, he grumbled, 'done in a very hole and corner fashion'. The government eventually banned counter-demonstrations, but the ban was not easy to enforce.

'HOME RULE IS COMING . . . BUY A REVOLVER'

The difficulty of grasping, at this distance in time, the divisive impact of Gladstone's Irish Home Rule proposal, a very limited measure of devolution explicitly designed to preserve the union, has often been noted. Its shock effect stemmed in part from the suddenness of the prime minister's conversion: 'the strangest conduct of public men and great political parties in the recent constitutional history of England' was, as the editor of the leading Liberal paper in Belfast wrote, 'painful to dwell upon'. And it was 'all the more painful . . . because the great statesman who gave the signal for such an astounding change of front was the leader of the great historical Liberal party which boasted of having fixed principles'.[9] The editor of the *Northern Whig*, Thomas Macknight, agonizing at length over the effect of the shift, even compared it with 'the feeling of consternation' in Paris on 'that memorable Sunday in the August of 1870', when the first news of German military successes reached the capital. Indeed this was worse: 'the Unionists of Ulster' had not been beaten by a foreign enemy: they found themselves 'in a moment . . . handed over to a hostile Nationalist majority . . . by whom their very loyalty would be regarded as treason'.[10]

This was an educated perception, but for ordinary people the challenge was still more fundamental: the threat of dispossession. Protestant farmers and workers believed that 'their right to continue living in Ireland was literally at stake'. Late in 1885 rumours swept through the north that in remote Catholic chapels 'raffles', auctions or lotteries were already taking place to ensure an orderly transfer of land possessed by Protestants. (Such rumours would be exactly repeated in evidence to the 1925 Boundary Commission.)[11] Zero-sum politics was visceral: the story of a Catholic used-furniture trader telling a Protestant customer 'our turn is coming now, and, by God, we'll learn you what we can do', may have been apocryphal but was instinctively believed.[12]

But the roster of objections to Irish Home Rule was more extensive yet. In 1886 an armload of them was gathered up by one of the most eminent of all English jurists, Albert Venn Dicey, Vinerian Professor of English Law at Oxford, whose *Introduction to the Study of the Law of the Constitution* became the most authoritative codification of the notoriously unwritten British constitution. Interestingly, Gladstone read it, with strong approval, in late 1885 when he was finally preparing to commit himself to Irish Home Rule, and he cited its central message – 'the absolute supremacy of parliament' – in introducing the Government of Ireland Bill in 1886.[13] He was less persuaded by Dicey's 1886 polemic *England's Case against Home Rule*, which set forth 'the immense evils of a policy which no Englishman can regard as other than most injurious to the whole United Kingdom'. Home rule might be primarily a scheme for the government of Ireland, but it was also 'a plan for revolutionizing the constitution of the whole United Kingdom' – and one that, Dicey held, would be more dangerous to Britain than would outright Irish independence.[14]

Dicey's argument depended on dismantling the basis of the Irish nationalist case. He argued that if the demand for home rule rested on the complaint that Ireland was misgoverned under the union, the rational solution was not to transfer power but to reform the union. If, however, it rested on 'the outraged feeling of nationality' – a desire for national freedom – then home rule would not suffice: it could only be 'a half-way house to Separation'. A true nationalist could not be a home-ruler: 'home rule will not turn the people of Ireland into a nation'. Dicey was well aware that making the union work – first by enforcing 'obedience to the law of the land' – would be a heroic undertaking, involving 'gigantic inconvenience, not to say tremendous perils'. The union's defects were deep rooted; Irish history was 'a record of incessant failure on the part of the Government and incessant misery on the part of the people'. The failure of English statesmanship had produced 'the greatest evil which misgovernment can cause. It has created hostility to the law in the minds of the people.' But 'to complain about the nature of things is childish . . . we must all of us look facts in the face'. Understanding 'the circumstances of the times, the very nature of things', required the recognition of English power: the union was 'essential to the authority of England [sic] and to the maintenance of the Empire'.[15]

Dicey's full-on rejection of home rule left him no space for consideration of special treatment for Ulster. But, invoking England's civilizing mission, he made no bones about its basis: the uneven development of Ireland, and hence Irish discontent, was a product of religion. It had been a 'grievous misfortune' that 'the people of England were ripe for Protestantism at a time when the people of Ireland had hardly risen to the level of Roman Catholicism'. While he charitably exonerated the 'people of Ireland' of any fault in this – 'inevitable ignorance is not the same thing as wickedness' – the implication that the other people in Ireland, the Protestants, merited special consideration was inescapable.

Dicey's fierce polemic was a warning that the issue was going to be serious, even though his arguments bounced off Gladstone's Liberals. James Bryce – who in predicting that home rule would soon come had added the advice to 'buy a revolver' – was the only leading Liberal to sound a warning about Ulster. A home ruler through 'despair', because he could see no viable alternative, Bryce's report to Gladstone on the state of Ireland in December 1885, making clear that 'things could not go on much longer the way they were', had helped to shape Gladstone's rethink. Now, as the home rule bill was being prepared in the spring of 1886, he warned the Cabinet that Ulster opposition to home rule was genuine, and much wider than crude Orangeism. Ulster Presbyterians were not fanatics; they really believed that if they were placed under a Dublin parliament there

32

would be civil war.[16] But Bryce's uncertainty about how to modify the bill to cope with this meant that his warning was smothered by the argument that no 'section' should 'refuse to take, *pari passu* with the rest of their fellow countrymen, their share in the government of their common country'. Conferring 'any separate autonomy upon Ulster as a whole, or that small part of Ulster which may be called distinctly non-Catholic', would be 'impossible' without 'great peril to the experiment of a national parliament'.[17]

This argument was put not by a nationalist but a Liberal Catholic lawyer, Sir Charles Russell, like Bryce a recent and reluctant convert to home rule. But its logical basis, the inherent unity of Ireland, was a keystone of nationalist thought, which Gladstone instinctively accepted: he could not 'allow . . . that a Protestant minority in Ulster' ('or elsewhere', he oddly added) 'is to rule the question at large for Ireland'.[18] And just as the loyalist stereotype of 'the Fenian' was by now firmly fixed, nationalists were driven by their need to believe that all inhabitants of Ireland were members of the Irish nation to construct a profile of 'Ulster' Unionists that would attribute resistance to the national movement to the bigotry of a small violent minority, exploited and controlled by Orange leaders (who could turn violence on and off at will), under the influence or even the direct control of British Tories. Thus talk of armed resistance was bluff, and warnings of civil war wild exaggeration. This crucial argument would reappear at every critical juncture over the next twenty-five years. As a new Ulster Unionist party was emerging, the nationalist John Dillon breezily dismissed its leader's 'habit of talking about civil war' because he cracked so many jokes that he seemed not to care 'a half-crown whether Home Rule is granted or not'.[19] Was this justifiable scepticism, or fatal misjudgement?

There were, certainly, Tories who took an instrumental view of loyalism – as a vital barrier to home rule rather than something admirable in itself. Two in particular had a noticeable effect on the level of communal tension in the north in the 1880s. Stafford Northcote's visit in 1883 at the height of the 'invasion' created something of a stir, but nothing to compare with the high-voltage performance of Lord Randolph Churchill in February 1886, when he urged his audience in the Ulster Hall (with its seating removed to make more room)

to organize and prepare for the catastrophe of home rule. His peroration would echo for a generation: 'I do not hesitate to say and to tell
you, and tell you most truly, that in that dark hour there will not be
wanting to you those of position and influence in England who are
willing to cast in their lot with you – whatever it may be.'

An eminent constitutional writer has argued that, had the first
Home Rule Bill contained provisions to safeguard Ulster Protestant
interests, the case for its adoption would have been immeasurably
strengthened. Unionism had not yet acquired that 'feverish antagon-
ism to Irish proposals emanating from a Liberal government' that
would soon follow – very soon, indeed; the 'chances of establishing a
Home Rule parliament for all Ireland had passed by the close of the
year'. The Conservative Party has rarely been decisively influenced by
pronouncements from the extreme right: the one exception (at least
before the issue of leaving the EU) being the party's attitude to Ulster,
which was determined by the opinions of the extreme Unionists.[20]
This Tory alignment was to be fateful in British politics, though it
was not the cause of the still more fateful crystallization of Protestant
and Catholic electoral blocs in north-eastern Ireland.

Up until this point, it was possible to see northern Irish politics as
normal; political behaviour in mid-Victorian Ulster largely followed
the mainland pattern. But in the 1880s its shape was dramatically
recast. During the agricultural depression of the late 1870s a strong
alliance of Presbyterian and Catholic tenant farmers had been formed,
under the aegis of the Liberal Party, to take on their Anglican landlords, but while this alliance could function in the agrarian sphere, it
was overwhelmed by the political clashes of the 1880s. The 1884
franchise reform transformed the electoral geography of Ulster: now
a much-increased Catholic electorate could contest seats without the
need for Presbyterian allies. The ever more explicit Catholicism of the
nationalist movement reached a peak in 1885, with open involvement
of the clergy and endorsement of Catholic educational policy.[21] The
elections of 1885 and 1886, which have been labelled 'a milestone in
Irish history', dealt the final blow to any expectation that voting
behaviour might follow economic interest rather than religious affiliation. Many Ulster Catholics benefited from the union, but almost
all supported home rule. (Some would have maintained that there

was no contradiction in this.) The Protestant vote, which had been divided along British party lines, with distinct differences between Presbyterians and Anglicans, now became solidly Unionist.[22] The intensity of Unionist anxiety invested the result – the 'psychologically important majority of one in Ulster' – with tremendous symbolic force.

A 'GREAT CRISIS'

Dicey's Unionist call to arms flagged up the word that would be repeatedly invoked as the home rule conflict intensified: this was a 'great crisis in the fortunes of our country'.[23] Its first manifestation was an epochal split in the Liberal Party, for the last fifty years the United Kingdom's natural governing party. In a painful psychological drama, where personality and policy fused, it became evident that home rule was a uniquely divisive issue. The veteran radical John Bright called it 'a measure so offensive to the whole sentiment of the province of Ulster so far as its loyal and Protestant people are concerned'. 'I cannot agree,' he said on 18 May, 'to exclude them from the protection of the Imperial Parliament.' (He would go even further the following year, arguing that 'Ulster may be deemed a nationality differing from the rest of Ireland at least as much as Wales differs from England.')[24]

Following Bright's line, his anointed Radical successor Joseph Chamberlain judged Gladstone's emerging idea of home rule 'truly absurd' ('unless we are all in a dream'). He was not against some devolution of power, and he favoured an alternative project: federalism. But the 'central board' scheme he proposed for Ireland in 1885 made no special provision for Ulster, and nor did his first plan of UK federalism: 'four bodies resembling the States Governments in the United States'.[25] As the crisis intensified, Chamberlain added another body, and his resignation – which clove his party in two – was in part over his insistence that Ulster should receive not merely special provision within home rule, but a separate parliament. This was truly a key moment: it has been said recently that the exclusion of Ulster 'crossed [Chamberlain's] mind', but it clearly did more than this.[26]

When he set out his final terms for a reconciliation with Gladstone over home rule, he made a 'separate assembly for Ulster' a vital requirement.[27] The following year he went on to propose county plebiscites to determine the separate area.[28]

The first response to this in Ulster itself was muted, though Lord Ernest Hamilton, the newly elected MP for North Tyrone, embraced it enthusiastically, saying that Ulster's boundary must be set 'to enable it to afford a refuge for all the Protestants of Ireland'. He even spoke of an 'Independent Ulster', a 'splendid refuge for the expropriated land-lords, the businessmen and manufacturers of the South, who would flock within its borders with their capital and industry'.[29] But on 12 April in the Commons, Hamilton's leader Edward Saunderson explic-itly rejected Chamberlain's idea 'that Ulster should be excluded ... or treated in a different way from the rest of Ireland' (Gladstone shook his head at this). He declared 'on the part of Ulster' that they would 'stand or fall with every loyal man in Ireland'. Thomas Macknight, a profes-sional Ulster observer, found this sentiment 'not general', and 'certainly not sympathized with by the Liberal Unionists and the commercial classes in Belfast and the north' – who were evidently looking out for themselves. While he insisted there was 'no desire for a separate Ulster, or part of Ulster', he believed that 'they would prefer absolute sep-aration from Great Britain' to any Irish parliament in which they would 'always be hopelessly outnumbered'.[30]

The moment when British political parties ceased to contest Irish seats was decisive. The Irish Unionist Party was established on 25 January 1886, out of the Irish Loyal and Patriotic Union (ILPU) cre-ated the previous year. From then on it replaced the British Conservative Party in Ireland, and the end of Liberalism as a party effectively came when Liberals joined Unionists in a mass anti-home rule meeting in the Ulster Hall on 13 April. The once-Liberal Macknight lamented that the 'implied compact' with those who 'crossed the sea on what was believed to be a great colonizing and civilizing mission' had now been broken; abandoning them to 'those who regarded them as intruders, and as enemies'. Prosperous, educated Presbyterians began to return to the Orange order – which they had usually held in contempt – resuming leadership in the 'public band' tradition, which had 'for several generations been kept alive mainly by their social inferiors'.[31] Like Macknight and Thomas Sinclair, a leading Presbyterian Liberal who had been an enthusiastic Gladstonian – and also a vehement opponent of Catholic demands for state-funded denominational education – many saw Gladstone's conversion to home rule as a betrayal and surrender.[32] Sinclair would take the initiative in organizing the spectacular Belfast anti-home rule convention six years later. The Ulster Liberal Unionist Association was established on 4 June, four days before Gladstone's Home Rule Bill was defeated. In the general election of July 1886, Gladstonian Liberals – who took fourteen seats in 1880, and nine in 1885 – were reduced to three. Nationalists reached the dizzying total of eighty-six – 'the 86 of '86'. The Irish Unionist Party took nineteen seats, just two of them held by southern Unionists.

A gradual, almost imperceptible, separation between Ulster and all-Ireland unionism began; an Ulster Unionist Party emerged, and by 1893 the ILPU (renamed the Irish Unionist Alliance in 1891) was generally accepted as representing only the Unionists of the three southern provinces.[33] The eventual fate of the home rule project – the first measure fell after Chamberlain's resignation in 1886, the second fell in the House of Lords in 1892; the third and fourth would both be enacted, in 1914 and 1920; but none was implemented – rendered the complex financial and administrative details of the scheme, which occupied so many days of parliamentary time, sadly irrelevant to the future shape of politics. But Chamberlain's proposal of an Ulster parliament laid down a marker which would prove indelible.

'THE LOWEST HALF OF THE POPULATION'

Whether or not Unionists could have been persuaded to accept home rule with special treatment for Ulster in 1886, it would have been impossible to persuade nationalists. Nationalist analysis of Ulster unionism combined contradictory elements; either unionism was illusory, or it was real but held to by a small minority. Ulster Protestants in 1782 were routinely invoked to show that their community was essentially nationalist; but if asked for proof that Ulster was actually nationalist, nationalists invariably identified nationalism with the Catholic community and argued that it equalled or outnumbered the Protestant and Unionist community.[34] Thus John Redmond, Parnell's future successor, informed the House of Commons on 13 May 1886 that the province was 48 per cent Catholic, and if Belfast was omitted, Catholics were '55 per cent of the whole population'. His colleague Justin McCarthy held that statistics showed that Ulster was 'a Nationalist province of Ireland'. Thomas Sexton presented a different argument, that if there were to be two Irish parliaments, 'you would have not one but two oppressed minorities' (risking the dangerous implication that it would be better to have just one, i.e. the Protestants), to bolster the conclusion that there was 'no safe standing ground except to treat . . . the demand of Ireland as a demand of the people of Ireland'. Leading English Liberals picked up the line taken by Charles Russell, that the loyalist case was morally dubious – identified with Protestant bigotry. For them, the fear of Catholic rule was bogus, a mask for Orangemen's wish to dominate and discriminate against Catholics.

The ILPU endeavoured to confront directly the belief of 'those politicians in England who think that they are bound to entertain Mr Parnell's demands, because he makes them in the name of the "Irish people"'. Numbers were not everything, they insisted. Parnell's constituency was 'the lowest half of the population' – small tenant farmers who wanted the land they tilled 'without the usual preliminary operation of paying for it'; 'labourers who covet the land occupied by the farmers'; but 'chiefly the disaffected masses who have been taught for the past forty years by the seditious newspapers that find their way into every Irish peasant's house, to hate everything English'.[35] This analysis, crude as it might have been, reflected an underlying, and often explicit, loyalist trope – the danger of giving power to those without a stake in the country.

Fear of the 'have nots' – not of course unique to Ireland – had a special edge where the history of dispossession in Ulster was concerned. A 'remarkable feature of the northern response' to home rule was the 'widespread assumption on the part of Protestant farmers and workers that their own right to continue living in Ireland was at stake'.[36] 'Home Rulers' to the young Leslie Montgomery, who would grow up to be the writer Lynn Doyle, were 'a dark, subtle and dangerous race, outwardly genial ... but inwardly meditating fearful things'; any moment they might 'rise, murder my uncle, possess themselves of his farm, and drive out my aunt and myself to perish on the mountains' (for them, Slieve Gullion in County Down). In his aunt's stories, 'it was on the mountains we always died'.[37]

The uniqueness of the 1886 electoral result – Parnell's triumph in 'commanding for a time all parties' was short-lived, and 'the peculiar moment was soon to pass away' – might have offered the ILPU's interpretation some support.[38] But the Liberals never seriously questioned his party's mandate to speak for all Ireland – the last prime minister in a Liberal government, Henry Asquith, would maintain this until both his party and the Irish Party were swept away in 1918. In Ireland, though, a subtle distinction between northern and southern nationalist attitudes began to appear. After the triumph of the 1886 election, it has been suggested, home rule seemed so inevitable that many southern Catholics began to forget the contest system in which their fathers had been involved, and so found it increasingly hard to grasp why Protestants refused to regard home rule as a gain for all Irishmen rather than a defeat, humiliation and unparalleled disaster for their side. Northern Catholics did not develop this perception; for them, politics still remained a zero-sum game.[39]

In the desperate final phase of his life, Parnell – as well as invoking the shadowy 'hillside men' – seemed to adjust his former indifference to Ulster unionism, declaring in Belfast in May 1891 that until 'the religious prejudices of the minority' were conciliated, Ireland could 'never enjoy perfect freedom'. It could never be united and independent 'as long as there is an important minority who consider rightly or wrongly that the concession of freedom to Ireland means harm to them'. But though his successor, John Redmond, held to this conciliatory line of seeking to win the hearts and minds of the unionists, mainstream nationalists dismissed it as 'the pathetic attempt of an adulterer to curry favour with the Orange lodges'.[40] And conciliation called for a long-term perspective; when he became leader of the reunited Irish Party at the turn of the century, Redmond eventually returned to the idea of using the power of the British state to neutralize or override Ulster opposition.

WOULD ULSTER FIGHT?

The reverberant phrase 'Ulster will fight and Ulster will be right' raises several questions. The least important, and easiest answered, is whether Randolph Churchill actually said it (not in his famous Ulster Hall speech, but in a letter written after the event). The bigger question, whether Unionists really meant to fight if necessary, has proved more difficult to answer. A kind of militarism – drilling, quasi-military organization, the collection of weapons – set in much earlier than the official Ulster Unionist story would suggest. Ronald McNeill's influential *Ulster's Stand for Union* indicated that drilling began 'almost by accident', when at the great rally at Craigavon in September 1911 it appeared that one contingent had learned to drill, unleashing a 'spirit of emulation' in the rest.[41]

But it seems that if emulation needed exemplars, they were to be found earlier. Even before Healy's invasion, the future Ulster party leader Edward Saunderson had urged Orangemen in border areas to begin military drilling.[42] Sometime in 1886 – probably for much of the year – a group of about fifty men met in the Demesne and Temperance Hall in Richhill, County Armagh. The Royal Irish Constabulary (RIC) identified twenty-nine, over half of them agricultural labourers, with a couple of servants, drivers, and shoemakers, one carpenter and just three farmers and one merchant. They were led by a solicitor and a 'gentleman'.[43] An attempt to prosecute these leaders failed, with significant consequences for the future. At Armagh petty sessions in June the right to breach the Statute of Liveries for the purpose of defending the 'constitution' was established. Extravagant celebrations followed, with the Richhill band parading amongst several hundred gleeful burghers, cheering the leaders and 'groaning' at Gladstone and Parnell. A meeting at the Temperance Hall was told that they had the right to drill because 'they had a right to be in this country and they meant to be in it', whoever might think 'they ought to be out'.[44] Their struggle was set in an apocalyptic frame: the exercises of this section of the 'Grand Orange Army', as a Belfast paper reported, were 'preparations for the civil war to be waged against the Queen's forces in resisting Home Rule'.[45]

Not much changed in the years between the first and second Home Rule bills; in 1892 another shoemaker appeared as leader of a drilling group at Ballinamallard, one of five recorded incidents (though there were probably others). The police counted some 200 men in all, and reported comfortingly that none of them had carried real firearms. Nor did the 'volunteers' assembled by Gerard Irvine, a twenty-five-year-old major in the Fermanagh Militia (and a recently appointed JP), who told the police 'frankly that he had enrolled about 140 volunteers for the purpose of defending the Union'.[46] But since at least one of the next generation's drilling groups – in Lisburn – asked its recruits whether they knew where the rifles issued between 1886 and 1892 now were, there seems to have been a belief in their existence.

The biggest anti-home rule meeting yet, the Ulster Convention in Belfast on 17 June 1892, when almost 12,000 delegates from across the province processed through the city to a rally in the Botanical Gardens, strongly indicated that the Unionist organizers' ideas were evolving dramatically. First and foremost, this was an Ulster manifestation, and a 'superbly orchestrated' one.[47] The press, reaching for terminology to describe its animating spirit, fixed on the word *Bund* – a reminder of how central German romanticism and nationalism were to nineteenth-century thinking. The keynote was activism. Declaring 'we are children of the revolution of 1688', the leading Liberal Unionist, Thomas Sinclair, insisted that if any parliament was ever set up in Dublin 'we shall simply ignore its existence'; its laws would be 'waste paper', its police would find the barracks occupied by 'our own constabulary', its judges would 'sit in empty court-houses'. This forceful evocation of civil resistance did not go so far as to say that they would go beyond simply paralysing the Irish executive, and set up their own government, but did not fall far short of it. And while it had been left to the maverick Churchill to demonstrate mainland Tory solidarity with such resistance in 1886, now the party leader Lord Salisbury and his nephew Arthur Balfour ('Bloody Balfour' to nationalists since his term as Chief Secretary) both stood tall.

'WHAT ULSTER MEANS'

When Balfour was finally persuaded to visit Belfast in April 1893 (standing in for his indisposed uncle) he was treated to a large-scale 'march-past' by more than 100,000 in Donegall Place, where a copy of the Home Rule Bill was ceremonially burned 'and stamped upon amid great cheering'. As he stood on the platform for four hours, the square was crammed with 'one vast sea of heads . . . something which all who witnessed it declared they had never seen paralleled'. In the Ulster Hall later he promised that 'if the British people can only have it brought home to their minds what Ulster is, and what Ulster means, not all the forces arrayed against you can prevail'.[48] He made clear that resistance might well not be passive: 'what is justifiable against a tyrannical king might . . . under certain circumstances be justifiable against a tyrannical majority'.[49]

Salisbury's eventual visit to Belfast – when the crowds, as Macknight defensively noted, were smaller than those for Balfour (which had of course been intended for Salisbury), because such a demonstration 'could scarcely be repeated in the course of a few weeks' – was notable in part because of the route he took. Like many Belfast Unionists, who now preferred to avoid going through Dublin on their way to Britain, he crossed from Stranraer to Larne. He went on to Derry, where – maybe for the first time – Union flags put out to greet him were taken down by the police as 'party emblems'.[50] This proved unsurprisingly contentious. The marquess reinforced the emerging identity of Ulster by writing in *The Times* of what he called Ulster's 'moral nature'.[51]

Moreover, at this point the most eminent soldier of the late Victorian era, Field-Marshal Wolseley, weighed in with a grim warning: 'If ever our troops are brought into collision with the loyalists of Ulster, and blood is shed, it will shake the whole foundations on which our army rests.' He predicted that officers would resign to 'join Ulster'; no army could stand 'such a strain upon it'. For good measure he added that Ulstermen's resistance 'to the uttermost' would not be treason: they would not merely be justified on the ground of self-preservation, but would be 'in reality fighting for the cause of the

Empire'.[52] Such sentiments would re-echo much amplified twenty years later.

Whether leaders developed formal strategies to organize resistance or not, their potential followers were always ready to mobilize on their own. This spontaneity has been disputed. A key element in nationalist views of the mechanics of loyalism was that, as Healy said, 'an Orange rioter never moves without orders'. Orangemen, unlike the 'nationalist mobster', were 'a disciplined unit', and when 'things get out of hand' their leaders control them by 'touching the "soft pedal"'. This image of mechanical control certainly reflected the Orange order's own self-image, but it was surely overdone. The dynamics of conflict were seemingly ubiquitous. In June 1886, for instance, a Catholic mob attacked Protestants in Sligo who, they believed, had tried to murder the Bishop of Elphin by 'dangerously unhinging the gates of his residence'. This rather indirect sabotage, it turned out, had actually been carried out by a nationalist leader who then organized the posse.[53]

The seriousness of quasi-military behaviour could be played down or dismissed as posturing. But in 1886 there was a more immediately alarming outbreak of communal violence in Belfast, not only more lethal but with a political edge more threatening than earlier riots. Some one hundred Protestant shipworkers, 'Island men', left Harland & Wolff's yard at their dinner hour on 4 June, 'armed with sticks and various missiles', to attack Catholic dockworkers at the Alexandra Dock: those who failed to escape were beaten or thrown into the water and pelted with rivets. Another thousand or so assailants followed, according to the police, who arrived too late to prevent the assault, but did try to prevent attacks on the Island men as they went home after work. Next day the Island men were attacked as they marched to work through Catholic districts, and over the following week there were repeated attacks on houses of both communities. By this point in the city's evolution, 'the extremity to which party and religious feeling has grown' (in the words of the commission of inquiry) was 'shown strikingly by the fact that people of the artisan and labouring class, disregarding ordinary considerations of convenience, dwell to a large extent in separate quarters . . . the boundaries of which are sharply defined'.

This was as far as the riot commissioners went in pointing to structural causes: though the riots were exceptionally destructive – with thirty-two killed and almost 400 injured – even by the standards of nineteenth-century Belfast, their recommendations were limited to 'tinkering with the police'. The riots had quickly become a determined attack by the Protestant mobs on the police as well as the Catholics; at one point the magistrates had urged that the police be withdrawn from the Shankill Road. The commissioners worriedly noted the belief amongst Protestants that the government had been packing Belfast with Catholic constabulary, and reported, 'we are not aware of any other period at which the animosity of a vast number of the Protestant community of Belfast, many ... from a respectable walk of life, was so fiercely directed against the Constabulary'.[54] Even so, they turned down the Belfast Corporation's repeated demands to remove the 'semi-military' Royal Irish Constabulary from the city.

The commissioners mistook the significance of this unprecedented hostility, but it is hard to mistake in retrospect. The instinct to nose out treachery, the 'Lundy syndrome', would gather force, as when Unionist organization was accelerated again by the 'Devolution crisis' in 1904. The eagerness to scent betrayal went as far as indicting Balfour, whose standing with the 'orange working man' (according to the future gunrunner Fred Crawford) sank to the point that they 'think worse of him than they did of Gladstone'.[55]

In the last year of the nineteenth century, the national trauma of the Boer War brought an interrogation of British identity. With the Irish Party still divided after the Parnell split, no nationalist leader was in a position to take the line that John Redmond would take in 1914, of supporting the British war effort. With the prospect of home rule remote, such an attitude could have broken the nationalist movement apart. The centenary of the 1798 rising had accelerated the growth of a reborn radical separatist tendency, while local government reform enlarged the ground of electoral contention. In 1899 the victorious nationalist candidate in the county council election in Strangford, County Down, delivered a street speech in front of the house of a prominent Unionist organizer: 'these people ... have no right of inheritance in this country no more than the meanest beggars who crawl the streets of Strangford. This is our land and we will have none here but those professing the ancient religion of the country.'[56]

So nationalists were almost all instinctively pro-Boer (no more worried by Afrikaner oppression of blacks than Arthur Griffith, a prominent pro-Boer and advocate of dual monarchy on the Austro-Hungarian model, was worried by Magyar oppression of minorities in Hungary). Separatists like Maud Gonne campaigned against recruitment to the British army and held Boer victory meetings. Dublin Corporation resolutions against the war were opposed by very few councillors, and while John Dillon privately disliked the Irish Party's fraternal embrace of President Kruger, he accepted that to 'create a united party' the best available means was 'a fighting policy on the Transvaal Question'.[57] Some separatists went the whole distance, like the Irish brigade formed by Gonne's future husband, and future 1916 rebel, John McBride, which fought with the besiegers of Ladysmith. Since most British people saw 'pro-Boer' as synonym for treason, and jingoism was so rampant that British critics of the war were in danger of violence, this was unfortunate. It 'invigorated the imperial aspect of Ulster Unionism'.[58] James Craig, a captain in the militia battalion of the Royal Irish Rifles, naturally served in South Africa. (A commemorative postcard showed him as 'he who volunteered for England in her deadly Boer War'.)[59]

TWO NATIONS:
THE PRICE OF SOUL-SEARCHING

The year before Gladstone's conversion to home rule, Edward Saunderson published his provocatively titled *Two Irelands*. The division he expounded was political – 'loyalty versus treason' – and this trope would re-echo throughout the conflict over home rule: why should loyal subjects be placed under the rule of the disloyal? It was augmented by a more cultural, or indeed ethnic, sense of difference. Nationalists often spoke of 'home rule for Ireland', but of course a land (however sacred) cannot govern itself, even in theory – only a people can. Ireland as such was not a nation, however often the phrase might be repeated – but who constituted the Irish nation?

45

For the founders of German nationalism like Johann Gottlieb Fichte, and most of the nationalists of Europe who followed them, it was an article of faith that 'where a separate language is found, there a separate nation exists'. Irish nationalists did not all adhere to this creed: Daniel O'Connell, a native Irish speaker but a true child of the Enlightenment, saw diversity of language as 'a curse' ('first imposed on mankind at the building of Babel'), and in 1833 acknowledged the 'superior utility of the English tongue as the medium of modern communication'.[60] Thomas Davis, on the other hand, though not a native speaker, firmly embraced the German romantic idea of organic national unity – a language which 'grows up with a people, is conformed to their organs . . . mingled inseparable with their history and their soil' was uniquely fitted to expressing their thoughts. This was to have profound consequences for how the Irish nation was envisaged.

At the turn of the century, mainstream nationalist theory, as represented in the party of Parnell, was still set in the form it had taken when nationalism itself first emerged – the 'United Irish' insistence that 'the common name of Irishman' must ultimately transcend all divisions. 'Irish' people were all the inhabitants of the island of Ireland, a natural as well as rational political unit. The title of the organization which brought the party, fractured after Parnell's fall, back together in 1900, the United Irish League (UIL), suggested that this inclusive nationalism still prevailed, but the reality was rather different. One historian has placed among 'the greatest imperialistic coups of the nineteenth century' the capture by Ireland's Catholic politicians of 'the term "Irish" for themselves and their co-religionists'.[61] The essential question then became whether Irish nationalism could be 'more than simply the expression of the grievances of the Irish Catholic democracy'.[62] It has been strongly argued that the last chance of maintaining a civic nationalist framework for home rule was lost in the early years of the twentieth century, when the efforts of the UIL founder William O'Brien to build an inclusive movement were defeated by the 'narrow, traditionalist' element led by John Dillon.[63] Internal conflict, notably the 'radical agrarian' urge to repossess the land occupied by large-scale farmers, provided the energy needed to maintain the national struggle. The resolution of such conflict threatened to undermine the demand for self-government.

But while the home rule party became 'in effect a confessional or ethnic' movement, it had no interest in making this identity explicit.[64] Outside the realm of formal politics, a more radical concept of Irish identity was taking shape, aiming not merely to end British rule but to eliminate British cultural influence. In the 1890s the Irish-Ireland movement centred on the effort to 'de-Anglicize' Ireland, revive the Gaelic language, re-create a Gaelic literature, and replace English sports and pastimes by authentic Gaelic games and dances – 'racy of the soil'. Leading spirits of the movement spoke of Anglicization as 'cultural murder'; P. H. Pearse denounced the national school system, which had accelerated the disappearance of Gaelic speaking, as the 'murder machine'. The underlying belief, pungently expressed by the fierce polemicist D. P. Moran, was that 'the foundation of Ireland is the Gael, and the Gael must be the element that absorbs'. Implicit in this was a redefinition of the national unit. Moran explained that though 'we can conceive, and have full tolerance for a Pagan or Non-Catholic Irishman' (a truly provocative yoking of adjectives), 'he must have respect for the potent facts that are bound up with Irish nationality'.[65]

The language movement, and the impulse to 'de-Anglicization', was not explicitly political. Indeed the founder of the Gaelic League, Douglas Hyde, a Protestant and a Unionist, protested that wanting 'the Irish race to develop along Irish lines, even at the risk of encouraging national aspirations', was 'no political matter'. Hyde was a believer in bilingualism and did not 'for a moment advocate making Irish the language of the country at large', and certainly not the 'National Parliament'.[66] But whether consciously or not, the movement was politicized. Early in the new century, Gaelicists began to talk of 'the Irish language' rather than Gaelic, automatically (and deliberately) rendering those who did not speak it less Irish, and those who did not even acknowledge its status as non-Irish. This created, it has been said, 'a world of polar opposites', with the English language and people the antithesis of the Irish.[67] Moreover, some argued that the language was a product (or producer) of biological difference. 'Racial unity of speech' was determined, according to a philosopher of the language movement, by the fact that, 'under pressure of similar inward experiences', the 'organs of speech will utter similar articulate sounds'.[68]

And just as German nationalists had denounced the French language ('the slime of the Seine'), Irish-language enthusiasts denounced English, 'overrun with the weeds of triteness and vulgarity'; English was 'the language of infidelity'. In 1901, Mary Butler called for 'a war to the death between Irish ideals and British sordid soullessness'. Eoin MacNeill identified the Irish language as essentially religious, and though the Gaelic League refused to entertain any special link with Catholicism, this message (Protestant involvement in the language movement notwithstanding) 'gradually came to dominate'.[69] 'Given the ways in which it attempted to utilize the Irish past', the Gaelic revival was 'bound to have a powerful, albeit unspoken, Catholic complexion'.

Even Griffith, a notably practical nationalist (with Ulster Protestant ancestry), would spell out – at the height of the Ulster crisis – that 'when we say we love Ireland we do not mean by Ireland the peasants in the fields, the workers in the factories, the teachers in the schools, the professors in the colleges ... we mean the soul into which we were born and which was born into us'.[70] The opposition of 'civic' and 'cultural' nationalism could not be more starkly expressed, and surely negated his condemnation of the crusading Gaelicist D. P. Moran for 'seeking to arouse the antipathy of the Irishman of fifty generations against the Irishman of five'. Griffith gave equally pungent expression to the immutable nationalist assumption that the island of Ireland was a natural political unit, indeed a divinely created one: 'when God made this country He fixed its frontiers beyond the power of man to alter while the sea rises and falls'.[71]

Oddly, in Ulster the only significant impetus to cultural self-expression before partition came as a by-product of the Irish revival. When a move to found a branch of the Irish Literary Theatre in Belfast was 'somewhat coldly received' by Dublin – indicatively, perhaps – a separate body, the Ulster Literary Theatre, was founded in 1904. Most of those who wrote for it (including St John Ervine) became less interested than its republican founder Bulmer Hobson in propagating nationalist ideas than in giving voice to what they called the 'Ulster genius', which they took, F. S. L. Lyons suggests, to be 'satiric'.[72] After a while a distinctive art form, the 'kitchen comedy', rustic drama reflecting 'something inherent in the character of the province, the down-to-earth temperament of the Ulsterman', evolved. Commercially the Ulster Theatre was never more than marginally viable, but it was symptomatic of the awkward fit between Dublin and Belfast.

The logical implication of the Irish-Ireland movement was partition – the exclusion of those who did not identify as Irish. Few Irish nationalists (then or even later) could accept this logic, however. One of these few was Arthur Clery, a Catholic believer in what he called 'the sect of the Gael'. A lawyer-journalist who wrote for Moran's *Leader* and the *New Irish Review*, Clery argued that partition was the only way of dealing with Protestants without 'abandoning your principles'. He reacted against William O'Brien's attempt to move nationalists into agreement – 'unity by consent' – arguing that 'the attitude of Ireland [sic] towards the Ulsterman is not a little like that of the English towards ourselves'. Both endeavoured 'to gloss over the existence of the horrid thing'. In reality, he held, 'the chances of our absorbing Ulster under Home Rule' were about the same as those of 'England absorbing us if we do not get it'. It could only be done, if at all, by methods which 'just men will prefer not to see'.

Clery shared Moran's dislike of Protestants, or at least Ulster ones – 'turbulent and bigoted aliens'; he borrowed a notorious Boer nationalist word to label them 'Outlanders'. But he insisted it was 'mere futility' to deny that their opposition to home rule was sincere. In fact, he recognized that all the methods they had used to propagate their ideas – exactly the same methods as the nationalists' – 'have all borne witness to their national faith'. If they were indeed 'distinct in nationality', Clery concluded, they should have their 'national independence'. The fundamental point was to prove that 'Irish freedom causes bondage to no man'.[73]

Even nationalists who did not share the Catholic aversion to Saxon materialism and immorality had difficulty including all the north in their vision of Ireland. Stephen Gwynn, a Protestant home ruler who became MP for Carlow in 1900, had just written a travel book about Donegal and Antrim in the *Highways and Byways* series. His aim was to show that Ulster was at least as Irish as the rest of the country, and since he clearly could not do this at the political level, he took the physical landscape as the subliminal key to national consciousness.

So even at Larne, he said, with all its Scottish Covenanting memories, 'you will still be conscious of the Celtic fringe'. Belfast, though, was different, a city whose prosperity was built on the destruction of native industry and whose politics were despicable. The articles written by William Bulfin in Griffith's *United Irishman* hammered the point home: Belfast was 'not an Irish city'.

Unionists were at first not much readier to take the 'two nations' concept beyond Saunderson's essentially political analysis, but their frame of thinking about the issue was now changing. In the mid-1890s, Thomas Macknight concluded his sprawling survey of twenty-five years in Ulster, *Ulster As It Is*, with the assertion that 'there are two antagonistic populations, two different nations in Irish soil'.[74] Arthur Balfour spelled out that the 'two nations' in Ireland evidenced 'two sets of aspirations, two sets of ideals, two sets of historic memories'.[75] This terse catalogue of the elements of nationality would reappear in formulations proposed when home rule returned to the centre of political debate after 1910. Linked with it – though Balfour himself resisted the linkage – was the idea of Ulster as a Unionist polity. Journalists led the way for politicians in this. In October 1910 the editor of the *Observer* (and Joseph Chamberlain's biographer), J. L. Garvin, set forth a plan for a 'distinct Belfast assembly' for what he called 'the great Northern conclave'. His tone was reluctant; to guard against 'permanent vivisection', Irish unity could be maintained by an all-Ireland 'upper house' or national council. The sharpness of the break implicit in Garvin's proposal was disguised by making 'the whole arrangement provisional': after a 'probationary interval' Ulster could decide whether to stay separate or 'throw in its lot completely with the Common Irish system'. This could be done 'by referendum'.[76]

St Loe Strachey, editor of the *Spectator*, took a slightly different line, proposing that in the first instance Irish counties should be allowed to opt out of home rule individually, and stay part of the United Kingdom. Otherwise there should be two home rule systems. (He thought a referendum too risky, but noted that fortunately the Liberals hated the referendum 'with such deadly dread that they will never consent to its use in any shape or form'.)[77] 'There are two nations in Ireland & therefore two national units,' Strachey instructed Bonar Law, leader of the Conservative Party, in November 1911, suggesting this could be a 'weapon'. (He called it a 'fighting argument', which might produce 'confusion and difficulty', forcing the government into maintaining that there was 'something sacred in the area in which they choose to apply self-government'.) Separation of Ulster would be a 'thoroughly bad arrangement', he admitted, but better than forcing Ulster under a Dublin parliament, and certainly 'better than civil war'. The real hope, Strachey said with classic British high-mindedness, was that the demand might in itself 'prove to the people of England and Scotland the folly of the whole thing and so smash the HR bill'.[78]

He may have taken this line partly to increase his proposal's appeal to the Tory leadership. (He would still be arguing in late 1913 that 'the cry of Ireland one and indivisible is enough to ruin any scheme of exclusion'.)[79] Strachey may possibly have believed in the intrinsic merits of partition from the start.[80] In this, if so, he was some way ahead of his time. The future 'king of Ulster' Edward Carson would take years to accept the idea of Ulster separation as anything more than a weapon, and he was too mindful of the sensitivity of 'Unionists outside Ulster' to see any merit in the county option idea, which he dismissed in 1911 as 'unworkable if not ridiculous'.[81] Still, this was the way that partition would, at last, formally enter the high-political home rule debate.

3

The Crisis

Home rule was off the agenda for a long decade after Gladstone's second bill was vetoed by the House of Lords. Returning to power in 1906 after a landslide victory, the Liberal Party had mixed feelings about its Gladstonian home rule heritage. The younger generation of radicals saw Irish home rule as probably an electoral liability, certainly as no asset – it had barely figured in the 1905 election manifesto – and as an impediment to the progressive 'new Liberal' programme they wanted to press ahead with. At best it was inevitable: a recognition that the union had failed 'the test of nationality' and proved not to be 'justified' because the demand for autonomy remained 'clear and persistent'.[1] Some on the right of the party, so-called Liberal imperialists ('limps'), actively disliked it. It was 'a cause with the glamour gone from it, a dead thing'.[2] The Irish Council Bill of 1906, the most the surviving Gladstonians could manage, fell well short of home rule – indeed hardly went beyond Chamberlain's central board scheme. The party seemed to be settling into a pattern of 'step by step' incremental Irish reform rather than big constitutional change.

Ironically it was one of the most prominent younger radicals, David Lloyd George, who as Chancellor of the Exchequer indirectly recharged the home rule project. The rejection of his 1909 'people's budget' by the House of Lords – breaking the unwritten convention that the upper house did not interfere with money matters – triggered a constitutional crisis which ended, after two narrow Liberal general election victories in 1910, in legislation to abolish the Lords' veto power. The 1911 Parliament Act made possible not only death duties, but also Irish home rule. As the Act passed, the prime minister H. H. Asquith announced that a third home rule bill would be brought forward. Enraged Tories denounced this as the result of a 'corrupt bargain' to keep the Liberals in power with Irish support – the budget was disliked by the influential Irish liquor trade, and home rule was the price of pushing it through. There was probably no deal as such, and the Liberals had in any case, thanks to Labour support, a comfortable majority. 'A general understanding' that home rule would follow, it has been reasonably suggested, was 'surely the natural result of the long history of Liberal commitment' to it.[3]

This was the Liberal line; but of course the Irish Party did hold the balance of power at Westminster in the sense of having the power to put the government out, and then perhaps make government impossible. This was the high-risk strategy which Parnell had adopted, and his successor John Redmond certainly threatened the same. His threat to vote against the budget – highly credible because its liquor tax provisions were disliked by his constituency – caused a Cabinet crisis. Liberal imperialists like the Foreign Secretary, Edward Grey, who resented Redmond's influence, wanted to 'tell the Irish to go and be damned'. With the fall of the government in prospect, however, those ministers – not least the prime minister himself – who preferred to stay in office ensured that policy shifted sufficiently to keep Redmond onside.

The commitment may have been more than merely tactical, but it was evidently a cerebral more than a visceral one. Asquith gave some insiders the impression of 'disliking the Irish' (and Redmond in turn, Margot Asquith thought, 'hates Henry'), while Lloyd George, personally unreligious to the point of anticlericalism, had 'a good deal of the Protestant in him' in a cultural sense. (Later, as prime minister, he gave one of his close advisers the strong impression that 'below the surface of his mind there was this deep primitive "No Pope here" of Ulster.') He certainly argued that Wales had a better claim to national independence than Ireland, not only because its language gave it a deeper identity, but because it 'had no Ulster'.[4] One pithy assessment of his qualities did not mince words in judging him 'profoundly anti-Catholic'.[5] Winston Churchill, who may have been offered the Irish Chief Secretaryship in 1910, but preferred the Home Office, was a guarded convert to home rule; in his role as an international historian he had written that 'the Catholic Church has ruined every country in wh[ich] it has been supreme'.[6]

The fact that the Tories knew of the dissent in Asquith's Cabinet, and indeed that Asquith was probably one of the least enthusiastic home rulers in a party which was mostly fearful that the policy was electoral suicide, cemented their conviction that a dishonest deal had been done. This was what destroyed the clubby political atmosphere of Westminster and brought forth extremes of political language not heard there since the seventeenth century. When Edward VII died in May 1910 (in between the two general elections), Asquith made an attempt to reconstitute the club – and so escape his dependence on the Irish vote – by organizing an inter-party conference to help the inexperienced King George V navigate the crisis he had suddenly inherited. This constitutional conference lowered the political temperature for a while – it met from mid-June to mid-November, with a very long summer recess – but when it eventually broke down, the atmosphere became still more toxic. The key Unionist demand had been that if the Lords' veto was removed, there should be special provision for fundamental constitutional changes: if the two houses disagreed, 'the nation should be consulted'. Irish home rule was a pre-eminent instance of such fundamental change.

Of course, Conservatives exploited (some no doubt cynically) the political leverage of public dislike of home rule. Some of the enthusiasm they had felt in 1893 had been eroded by prolonged contact with the 'foul Ulster Tories', but they had a respectable constitutional point in the call for a national vote, and maybe also the argument that an unprecedented reconstruction like this must be approved by an 'English majority'. With no formal provision for such major change (of the kind which would call for a two-thirds majority in many written constitutions), it was reasonable to challenge the government's assumption that the United Kingdom might be redefined by a single parliamentary vote. It was not only Conservatives who believed that if the Liberals had declared a commitment to home rule they would have lost the general election. As it was, as the rising Tory star F. E. Smith fumed, 'the only argument these scoundrels ever use to show that Home Rule was before the country' in 1905 'is that *we* said so'.

'ROME HAD JUSTIFIED
THE OUTRAGE'

The revived home rule project confronted Unionism in its most vigorous form yet. Suspicions of betrayal, already acute, became sharper still after the 'devolution crisis' in 1904. A limited devolution plan developed under the Conservative Chief Secretary George Wyndham was furiously denounced, even though its originator intended it to head off the demand for home rule. The furore brought Walter Long, a Tory squire seemingly wedded to his job at the Local Government Board, into the centre of the home rule dispute. He was persuaded or flattered by Balfour into taking on the Irish Chief Secretaryship, and set himself to convince Irish Unionists that they could depend on Britain. With the mantra 'patience and firmness' he succeeded, though in the process Long inevitably tilted the policy balance from 'conciliation' towards 'coercion'. So at least thought conciliators like Wyndham and Balfour's private secretary Jack Sandars, who judged 'Walter . . . honest & simple as the day, but he is a tool in the hands of' a 'malevolent cabal' who found it easy to work on his 'vanity and his hopes'. This was not the last time he would be dubbed an easily deceived dupe.[7]

Long emerged from his brief spell in Dublin Castle as an expert on Ireland (a status rather too easy to achieve in British politics), and after losing his Bristol seat in the 1905 landslide, he stood and was elected for South County Dublin in January 1906. He was picked as leader of the Irish Unionist Alliance after Edward Saunderson's death in October. Later that year Long was chosen as Saunderson's successor to lead the Ulster Party in parliament, and early in 1907 he became Vice-President and virtual head of the Ulster Unionist Council (UUC) – a curious journey for a Wiltshire squire. But grumbling later that year that 'Ireland and Irishmen are not grateful recipients of one's endeavours', Long gradually migrated back to British politics, leaving his Dublin constituency for the Strand in the 1910 election. His place as Ulster leader was taken by a man of a very different stamp, the lawyer Edward Carson.

A celebrity barrister, famously pugnacious, who had been briefly appointed Chief Secretary by Balfour in 1904, the Dubliner Carson was scarcely more of an 'Ulsterman' than Long. He had long since built an English legal and political career. Like Long – both of them martyrs to ill-health – he might have secured the Conservative Party leadership when Balfour resigned it, but they both stood aside (as did Austen Chamberlain) in favour of Andrew Bonar Law. He did not look a likely leader of the Ulster Unionists; not only was he a Dubliner representing a Dublin constituency, but he had become more an English than an Irish political figure, and had played very little part in Irish politics. James Craig, a Belfast Presbyterian, the youngest son of a millionaire whiskey-maker, and a very effective MP since 1906, looked much more likely. Carson's own motives for risking his 'career and reputation' by taking on the UUP leadership at the age of fifty-eight have remained unclear.[8] But he possessed serious charisma, and was rapidly embraced as a symbol of Ulster defiance. Craig, less obviously charismatic, but highly capable and more embedded in the loyalist world, became the perfect lieutenant.

The historian F. S. L. Lyons saw the years 1903–7 as a 'watershed' for Irish nationalism, and an Ulster watershed lagged only a little behind. Ulster leaders would suggest that the upsurge of militancy after 1911 was a justified response to the 'corrupt bargain' and unconstitutional Liberal action, but the ground had been well prepared. The 'devolution crisis' of 1904 electrified Unionists and triggered a new level of Ulster organization. The Ulster Unionist Council, with the very successful Ulster Clubs movement it fostered, began to construct the mechanics of a popular mobilization. This first popular coordinating body for northern loyalism signalled a 'decisive rejection of the British political forum'.[9] Just as importantly, the Clubs, more 'respectable' than the Orange Order, aided the reinvention of Orangeism after 1905, a renaissance helped by its reabsorption of the breakaway Independent Orange Order; it was rebuilt as a cross-class movement with its relaunch in 1911.[10] The idea of distancing Ulster unionism from southern unionism began to gain traction; according to the (not wholly reliable) Fred Crawford, his resolution to confine preparations for resistance to Ulster, passed by the Ulster Unionist Council standing committee, was decisive. Southern Unionists were dismayed, he said, but 'when we asked them for an alternative they could suggest no alternative'.[11]

The spectre of 'Rome Rule' got a popular boost in the early years of the century with a spate of books by Michael McCarthy, a renegade Catholic polemicist, whose Cork family business had failed after a conflict with the Land League. Now forgotten, or smothered by nationalist outrage, McCarthy's self-promoting productions sold in multiple editions and influenced people as varied as the Independent Orange leader Lindsay Crawford and the writer James Joyce. His 1902 book *Priests and People in Ireland* used a striking photomontage of a colossal church tower looming over a small Irish village to herald his analysis of clerical power.[12] It went through four editions in twelve months.[13] In *Rome and Ireland* (1904), a series of lectures delivered to suitably enthusiastic Protestant audiences, McCarthy expatiated on the disastrous effect of Catholic control of education. The southern Irishman had 'surrendered from his infancy the right to think freely'; 'every difference of opinion from the theocracy is hushed up, or crushed to death'. He suggested that Ireland was 'a microcosm of the continents of Europe and America' in the 'contrasts in character between North and South'. His audience was surely happy to be told that the 'virility' of northerners stood out against the 'effeminacy' of the southerners, and McCarthy mercilessly flayed the victim culture of his fellow nationals, forever blaming their failures on ill-fortune: 'that expression "only for" is never out of our mouths'.[14]

Protestant antipathy to the Roman Church as a hostile and aggressive global power was (if possible) racked up further by the 'intolerant mood' fostered by the reign of 'the most reactionary of modern popes', Pius X, and particularly his 1907 decree *Ne temere*, which required that the children of mixed marriages be raised as Catholics, and effectively made what had been implicit Catholic disapproval of such marriages explicit.[15] There was little public reaction at first, but shortly after it came into effect at Easter 1908 a Catholic father, told by a priest that his Presbyterian marriage was invalid, left his wife and took their children with him when she refused to raise them as Catholics. She petitioned the Viceroy to recover them. The 'McCann case' electrified the Protestant community, provoking protest meetings in Dublin, Edinburgh, and London as well as Belfast. The Anglican Bishop of Down suggested that the decree had 'been enforced in Ireland in a manner which must seem impossible to Englishmen' (used to the 'mild and cultivated form' of English Catholicism). It defied the civil law, but the Irish executive was 'afraid to do its duty because Rome had spoken and justified the outrage'.[16] There had, the bishop said, never been a time 'when there was in the minds of Irish Protestants so deep a dread of Roman aggression and so firm a conviction that the object ... is the complete subjection of the country to Roman domination'.

For the Reverend Samuel Trenter, Moderator of the Presbyterian General Assembly, the 'religious difficulty' of home rule sprang from 'the essential and fundamental genius of Romanism', whose 'whole ideal of life differs from the Protestant ideal'.[17] The Unionist MP Ronald McNeill pointed out that no Irish nationalist MP had 'protested against the cruelties' of the decree. Indeed, the opposite; the northern nationalist leader Joe Devlin saw the spat as a 'wretched domestic quarrel' and thought Mrs McCann had deliberately made trouble. The new Chief Secretary, Augustine Birrell, noting that her petition had been drafted by her Presbyterian minister, agreed that she could have taken a less public legal action. But the trouble was infectious: Devlin's Belfast constituency was placarded with the slogan 'Will you vote for Devlin and have your Protestant children kidnapped by the priest?'[18]

Almost as striking as Protestant outrage was Catholic incomprehension of it. A similar pattern of reactions followed the papal rescript (*Motu proprio*) of 9 October 1911, *Quantavis diligentia*, forbidding any Catholic to bring any ecclesiastic before a civil court without his bishop's permission. This appeared – to Protestants at least – to take the clergy beyond the law, and was argued by extension to apply to any Catholic MP who voted for a law which would be 'held to invade the liberty or rights of the Church of Rome'. Clearly, the Ulster Unionist Thomas Sinclair said, Catholic members of a Dublin parliament would be 'under the absolute control of their hierarchy'. Not only would the legislative independence of a Dublin parliament be 'destroyed', but the same would happen to the legal profession, so 'confidence in the just administration of the law, which is at the root of civil well-being, would be fatally destroyed'.[19] A *Daily Chronicle* correspondent called on the Irish Party to issue an official disavowal of 'this monstrous claim on the part of the Papacy' or risk losing

Liberal support for home rule. The Catholic response, led by Archbishop Walsh, was to tell Protestants that the matter had nothing to do with them as it concerned Catholics only.[20]

The *Ne temere* decree was more significant for its political resonance than for any chilling effect it may have had on the likelihood of mixed marriage; which was showing little sign of increasing. Even in Dublin, where the residential segregation so evident in Belfast did not exist, the low level of mixed marriage provided 'impressive testimony to the separateness of the social worlds' fostered by the different denominations. And at the same time Protestant fantasies of Roman imperialism were matched by Catholic fears of proselytism, which drove the creation of many Catholic social organizations at the turn of the century. Insofar as proselytism persisted, it was 'less important for the number of converts/perverts it produced' than for the way the belief in the gravity of the threat stimulated 'the formation of a network of strictly denominational institutions enclosing the Catholic community'. Before the First World War, Dublin's largest private charitable agency engaged in poor relief, for instance, the Society of St Vincent de Paul, was gripped by 'a constant and almost obsessive concern with the activities of Protestant missionaries'.[21]

'THE PROTESTANT PROVINCE OF ULSTER'

In the nationalist view, Ulster's move towards a separate path was, if not initiated by, certainly dependent on Britain. Any sign of spontaneity can be elided in even sophisticated modern nationalist accounts.[22] Yet it is hard to ignore the manifestations of what Canon John Hannay (the novelist George A. Birmingham), a quizzical observer – and a Gaelic Leaguer – called 'that north Irish democracy which is probably less imaginative and less reasonable but more virile than any other in the world'.[23] The gradual separation of Ulster from 'southern' Unionists, well advanced by 1910, would prove crucial, and it rested on the simple fact that Ulster's claim could be vindicated outside Westminster.

The Ulster Unionist Council's 'more gritty and more populist' political faith, articulated through the revived Ulster Clubs – 164 of them by the end of 1911, 232 by February next year, and 316 six months later – was always likely to produce a quasi-military manifestation. By November 1910, schemes for Orange arming and drilling were being prepared, and on 22 November a secret UUC committee established to negotiate with arms dealers authorized Frederick H. Crawford to secure quotations for 20,000 rifles and a million rounds of ammunition.[24] Just before Christmas another Orange leader, Colonel Robert Wallace, reported that numerous Orange lodges would shortly begin to learn basic military drill – 'learning to form fours and re-form two deep, and simple matters like that'. The UUC had made its first major allocation of cash to buy guns by March 1911; and James Craig had by then gone beyond any idea of mere bluff, assuring Crawford of his commitment to secret and sustained importation of arms. In April 1911 he wrote that if a 'steady supply' of arms was not begun, 'we will be caught like rats in a trap'.[25] (For his part, Carson told Craig in late July 'I am not for a mere game of bluff' – talk of resistance was no use 'unless men are prepared to make great sacrifices which they clearly understand'.)[26]

By 1911, both the idea of Ulster separation and the mechanisms for staking out its claim on the ground were in place. Unionist political strategy at the national level still aimed to use this threat to block home rule in its entirety, but the genie was escaping from the bottle. The stormy passage of the Parliament Act fuelled an increasingly torrid political atmosphere, culminating on 23 July in Asquith being silenced with shouts of 'Traitor!' – the first time a prime minister had ever been refused a hearing in the Commons. When the Act finally passed on 10 August and the Lords' veto was truncated to two years, the parliamentary defences against home rule were breached. The impulses towards direct action immediately went public with two big Unionist rallies in September 1911. At the second, on the day of the first reading of the Home Rule Bill in parliament, Orange lodges and Unionist clubs combined to muster the 50,000 who met for the 23 September rally at Craigavon. They 'walked' past Carson as the biggest-ever Union flag was broken out. Carson's charismatic presence was amplified by the setting – on a platform above the lawns and meadows sloping down to Belfast lough – and his oratorical intensity. 'The immense multitude', as his colleague Ronald McNeill recorded, 'felt instinctively the grip of his power.' 'I now enter into a compact with you, and every one of you,' Carson declared, 'and with the help of God . . . we will defeat the most nefarious conspiracy that has ever been hatched against a free people.' It was not enough simply to reject home rule: direct action had to be taken. They must make preparations to 'carry on for ourselves the government of those districts of which we have control. We must be prepared, the morning Home Rule passes, ourselves to become responsible for the government of the Protestant Province of Ulster.'[27] Four hundred delegates assembled for the UUC meeting four days later appointed a committee to draw up the constitution of a provisional Ulster government. The Craigavon rally, often seen as the beginning of the militarization, was the culmination of an extended process. Ulster Unionism, as its leading historian puts it, had developed since 1905 'from an essentially parliamentary movement into an army of resistance'.[28]

It helped change the thinking of the Tory grandee Lord Milner, a lukewarm federalist who had resigned himself as early as April 1910 to the fact that 'we are in for Home Rule in some form', but thought that as long as it was federal ('like Quebec to the rest of Canada', rather than like Canada to the United Kingdom), 'not much harm would be done'. At that point he had assumed that 'the Irish' would not want Canada-like independence. Now he began to envisage the Tories giving 'ultimate support' to a 'reasonable revolt of Ulster'. Ulster's present rebellious course was 'intolerable' but if it stepped back and insisted simply on not being 'disinherited', keeping its UK citizenship 'with the security which it alone can give them against oppression', he thought 'we ought to back them'.[29]

When A. V. Dicey, the high priest of the constitution, reissued his 1893 tract *A Leap in the Dark* in 1911, the looming national crisis he had diagnosed earlier was full-blown. He now asserted that the government, through the Parliament Act, had obtained 'strictly unlimited and dictatorial power' by intrigue. It had 'treated with scorn the idea of an appeal to the people'. Although he took comfort in the fact that 'political devices, however crafty, break down whenever they are opposed to the nature of things' – i.e. the English 'supremacy and predominance which is the real bond of union' – he still insisted that serious damage would be inflicted by home rule, even in the apparently more innocuous form of 'home rule all round' federalism.[30] But despite his own heated language, Dicey was alarmed by the rapidly escalating rhetoric of confrontation, horrified when the prime minister was shouted down, and uneasy about signs of organized resistance. When Winston Churchill went to speak in Belfast early in 1912, Dicey judged the 'deplorable stupidity' of the loyalists who tried to stop him even worse than the 'unutterable' moral guilt of the minister himself – who aimed at 'exciting the loyalists of Belfast to violence'. Why, he asked Bonar Law, 'can't they perceive they are rushing into a trap set them by Winston Churchill?'[31]

Dicey was an inveterate opponent of 'home rule all round', which he had first condemned years before Gladstone's conversion to Irish home rule. But federalism had one of its periodic 'moments' in 1911. In February, Asquith, who was certainly not an enthusiast for federation, perhaps typically set up a Cabinet committee to discuss it; a hefty one, though, chaired by the Lord Chancellor, Lord Loreburn, with Lloyd George, Churchill, Haldane, Grey, and Herbert Samuel as well as Birrell. Most of them – Birrell was a notable exception – leaned towards federalism to a degree that some found alarming.[32] Loreburn himself not only opined that 'home rule all round' was 'the right principle', but later that year told C. P. Scott of the *Manchester Guardian* that a start should be made with Ireland as the beginning of a United Kingdom scheme.

The *Spectator*'s editor, St Loe Strachey, suggested to Bonar Law on 17 November that 'if we use the Ulster arguments properly we can almost certainly defeat the HR Bill'; but believed that it would still 'take some time to get the ordinary English and Scottish public to understand the Ulster case'. Exclusion, for him, would be a vital 'safety valve' to stop home rule bringing civil war. They needed to argue that the 'county option' was really practicable (however undesirable), and show that 'any Irish county might quite well become a county of England' [sic]; the police, for instance, could easily be divided, Strachey held – why not put the North East Ulster police under Commissioners on the Metropolitan police model?[33] Addressing practical issues like this showed that the implications of 'partition' were beginning to be thought through. Carson himself, though, thought it could not be done. 'Stracey's [sic] suggestion is impracticable,' he told Bonar Law: it would be 'unworkable if not ridiculous' for a county to 'remain outside'. And whatever he thought about British opinion, Carson knew that southern Irish Unionist opinion was not ready for partition. It might 'be necessary at some stage to raise the question by an amendment', but to 'agitate' it at this point would alienate support in Ireland outside Ulster. Southern unionism, with its narrow social base – at least outside Dublin – might lack the democratic power of Ulster, and might have lost much of the leverage provided by its strength in the House of Lords, but it remained well organized and vocal.[34] Leading southern Unionists like Lord Midleton and Lord Lansdowne, leader of the opposition in the Lords, were significant figures at the heart of the political establishment. Southern unionists, absolutely opposed to home rule and still more to partition, were capable of heading off any Conservative leaning towards a compromise solution.

EXCLUSION

As it would in the next great British constitutional crisis – the 2016 referendum on leaving the European Union – parliament was now playing catch-up as popular action set the agenda. By the time the bill was launched in the Commons on 11 April 1912, the crisis was already well advanced. The bill itself – in retrospect at least – looks too moderate to provoke such intense hostility. There is a kind of 'imagination gap', one historian suggests, making it hard to 'figure out why people were so upset by the 1912 bill'.[35] The more so, perhaps, as it went little further than the second Gladstonian home rule plan. The Irish assemblies (called Legislative Council and Legislative Assembly in 1892) were renamed the Senate and House of Commons, and the Irish representation at Westminster was almost halved (down from eighty to forty-two). The Crown representative, the Lord Lieutenant, was retained, and actually given an additional power – 'reservation' of the royal assent to Irish legislation, potentially postponing enactment indefinitely.[36] Otherwise the same battery of legislative powers were 'reserved' to Westminster, some permanently (the Crown, war and peace, foreign policy, defence, and overseas trade), some for varying periods (old age pensions for one year, the police for six). The Irish administration could levy taxes, but not customs duties. This was not anything like full self-government, and it was ostentatiously designed to maintain the union. To allay Unionist fears it added to the earlier bill's prohibition of religious discrimination a specific ban – clearly in response to the uproar over *Ne temere* – on making the validity of marriage dependent on any religious belief or ceremony.

The bill was loudly silent about any special position for Ulster. Whether Asquith 'missed a magnificent opportunity' by failing to incorporate such a provision has been a vexed question. It is clear that the bill would still have faced opposition on both sides, but equally clear that a settlement would have been easier to impose and sustain in April 1912 than at any later point.[37] As it was, when Carson's notion of an amendment appeared, proposed by an otherwise undistinguished Liberal backbencher, Thomas Agar-Robartes, MP for St Austell, it was resisted by the government. A polo-playing Devon yeomanry officer, and heir to a viscountcy, Agar-Robartes was a firm Roseberyite Liberal imperialist with a dislike of Irish home rule. (He was not the only south-western nonconformist Liberal to take this line.)[38] When the bill went into committee, on 11 April, Agar-Robartes put down an amendment calling for the four north-eastern counties – Antrim, Armagh, Down, and Londonderry – to be excluded from the jurisdiction of the home rule parliament. His argument was blunt: 'I think everyone will admit that Ireland consists of two nations different in sentiment, character, history and religion.' It was 'absolutely impossible to fuse these incongruous elements together'.[39] This chemical metaphor showed that the amendment was not a technical device to secure the passage of home rule; Agar-Robartes was disputing the fundamental assumption which Gladstone had taken from the Irish nationalists. His list of the component elements of nationality was more workmanlike than Balfour's 'aspirations, ideals, memories', but equally devastating to the nationalist party's claim to represent the Irish nation.

His amendment invited not only a dramatic adjustment of the moral logic of home rule, but also a major adjustment of Unionist thinking. Nearly all the Unionists who spoke on it tacitly accepted the inevitability of home rule for the rest of Ireland. Exclusion offered the only way of saving something from the wreck. Agar-Robartes was wrong in one crucial respect, though: not everyone would 'admit' the incongruity of the two 'elements'. Home rulers rejected it with fierce passion: Redmond fumed, 'the idea of two nations in Ireland is to us revolting and hateful'. While Liberal and Unionist contributors to the debate preferred to speak of 'exclusion' rather than 'partition', with its negative historical associations and air of finality, Redmond was less squeamish. 'The idea of our agreeing to the partition of our nation is unthinkable.' The idea of cutting the Protestants off from 'the national traditions and aspirations of the Irish race sounds to many of us something like sacrilege'. Nationalists expected 'to see the Irish nation in the near future made up of every race and every creed and every class'.[40] (Though the implication that there were at least two 'races' in Ireland could not be missed.) Redmond also dropped in – rhetorically no doubt – another highly charged word, when he pledged that 'the setting up of permanent dividing lines between one creed and another and one race and another' would be resisted 'most violently as far as is within our power'.[41]

The amendment also angered many Unionists. The *Irish Times* instantly detected 'a trap designed to secure an admission that the Northern Unionists were willing to abandon the Unionists in the rest of Ireland to their fate'.[42] Balfour, pioneer of the 'two nations' concept, vehemently opposed partition. And even those who voted for exclusion said they did so purely to bring down the whole measure. Thus while Carson accepted it, he insisted that this acceptance was strictly a wrecking manoeuvre: they did not accept it 'as a compromise' on the fundamental home rule issue. 'There is no compromise possible'; if Ulster succeeded, 'Home Rule is dead' – for the whole of Ireland.[43] They were as convinced as Redmond that partition was unthinkable. Lord Hugh Cecil took the opportunity of declaring that 'Ulster would be perfectly right in resisting'.

Leading for the government, Chief Secretary Augustine Birrell took a perilous line, dismissing the danger of Ulster resistance and calling for proof that Ulster 'desires to cut herself off from the rest of Ireland' – 'it would take a very great deal of evidence'.[44] This was mildly ironic, as Asquith's promise to George V to make 'careful and confidential inquiry as to the real extent and character of Ulster resistance' seems to have been stymied by Birrell himself.[45] The Chief Secretary had oscillated for months between smug dismissal of it and alarm about the possibility of 'civil war' (a term he was the first to use since the onset of the crisis). In August 1911 he admitted to Winston Churchill that although Ulster's 'rodomontade' had been ridiculed in the past because it had 'cried "wolf" so often and so absurdly', the situation had changed: 'her yells are genuine'. There was 'great ferment and perturbation of spirit', fed by a mix of hatred of Catholicism (among the poor) and, among the 'better to do', the belief that home rule would make Ireland 'a miserable, one-horsed, poverty-stricken, priest-ridden, corrupt oligarchy'. He even floated at this point the idea of a county-by-county referendum, which he thought would leave only Antrim and Down standing out against home rule. 'It might then be suggested,' he proposed, 'that for the transitional period, say 5 years', they might stay out; then 'there should be a fresh referendum to settle their fate'.[46]

If Churchill was still unconvinced, he got a strong steer when he decided – without telling Birrell or any of his colleagues – to deliver a pro-home rule speech in Belfast in January 1912. His meeting had to be moved from the Ulster Hall (where his father had delivered his legendary anti-home rule speech) to Celtic Park in west Belfast, because of boiling Unionist fury. Churchill junior was denounced as going to 'dance on his father's coffin'. The Ulster Unionist Council formally resolved to prevent the meeting: senior Unionists saw this as a 'great opportunity of proving that [Ulster] is capable of doing what it says it will', and one was reported as predicting 'there may be bloodshed – I think there will'.[47] In the event there was not, but Churchill (who took his wife, Clementine, with him) did encounter open hostility even in their smart hotel; he was branded as 'disloyal', arousing, as Ronald McNeill fumed, 'the same bitterness of anger and contempt which soldiers feel for a deserter in the face of the enemy'. Their car was mobbed by shipyard workers when they left: it might have been overturned 'if the police had not driven off the people immediately'.[48]

Agar-Robartes's action in putting down his amendment may have been annoying to the government, but it reflected the fact that there had been a noticeable volume of Liberal chatter about exclusion and referenda while the Home Rule Bill was being finally prepared. Not that Ulster itself was directly discussed: a bigger concern for the Liberal Party at large was the possibility of 'Dominion status' (on the model of Australia and Canada), the subject of a full-scale study by the Clerk of the House of Commons, Erskine Childers.[49] The very first time the Cabinet addressed the Ulster issue – Gladstone himself had sidestepped it – was on 6 February. The previous day, Lloyd George told some dinner companions that (partly because there was not enough support for home rule in Britain) 'it could not be imposed upon Ulster by force'; 'if possible the Protestant counties [sic] should be exempted'.[50] He and Churchill submitted a proposal for exclusion on the basis of 'county option' for every county in Ireland. Since minutes of Cabinet meetings were not taken (the only account being the prime minister's reports to the monarch), we do not know its details, or indeed whether it was intended to be written into the draft bill or kept in reserve as a possible amendment. Asquith, whose unofficial motto was 'wait and see', told the king he had persuaded his colleagues to do just that – see whether 'fresh evidence of facts, or the pressure of British opinion' would 'render expedient' certain changes: if it became clear that 'some special treatment must be provided for the Ulster counties', the government might amend the bill, or even decide not to use the Parliament Act to 'press it on'.[51]

Loreburn now shifted his position, becoming the most recalcitrant opponent in Cabinet – 'most violent' in his opposition according to Lloyd George; 'Loreburn repulsed us in the most blood-thirsty manner,' Churchill noted.[52] Most noticeable, though, was the indifference of most of their colleagues – above all Asquith and Birrell, who appear to have offered no view of the issue. Birrell, like many Chief Secretaries, often blamed ministers for their lack of interest in Ireland, but at this point he had only himself to blame. In the debate on the amendment, Asquith took a line which would often be heard over the next decade: by detaching from Ireland 'that body of the Protestant minority which is best able to protect itself', the amendment would 'leave without any kind of redress or protection' Protestants in the south and west – including those in the other Ulster counties. (The suggestion that they might need protection may have been unwise.) Churchill was absent, and Lloyd George said nothing, but – significantly – abstained in the vote, as did nineteen other Liberals. Although the government defeated the amendment, it was with a reduced majority of sixty-nine.

Whether or not Agar-Robartes had been laying 'a trap' (as F. E. Smith, like the *Irish Times*, called it), his amendment was a crucial moment in the crystallization of partition. Ronald McNeill called it a 'landmark in the history of the movement', when Ulster's leaders 'for the first time publicly accepted the idea of separate treatment as a possible alternative to the integral maintenance of the Union'.[53] Next year, when the bill went into its second circuit, Carson himself would put down an amendment calling for the exclusion of all nine Ulster counties. A wrecking amendment again, but it also further bolstered the perception of Ulster as an entity.[54]

ULSTERIA

Meanwhile, the 'very great deal of evidence' of Ulster's wishes which Birrell had rashly demanded was ominously stacking up. The early summer of 1912 saw another burst of rioting and shipyard expulsions, triggered by a clash at Castledawson, where a group of 'Hibs' – the Ancient Order of Hibernians (AOH) – tried to seize a Union flag carried by one of the children in a Sunday school procession. Protestant outrage boiled over, and a Catholic Vigilance Committee protested against the failure of the authorities to 'chastise' the attackers. The AOH itself, widely seen as Joe Devlin's private army, was (like the Ribbon Society before it) in some ways a mirror image of the Orange Order; both were ostensibly 'friendly societies', both were political enforcers for their communities. The *Irish Times* naturally labelled the Hibernians 'at least as brutal and aggressive as the worst Orangemen',[55] but they were also disowned by much of their own community too. (For the Catholic Archbishop of Armagh, Cardinal Logue, the AOH was also 'an organized system of blackguardism' and 'a cruel tyranny'.)

Orange mobs were a familiar kind of evidence, but the mighty rally held in the Agricultural Society showgrounds at Balmoral on the

Easter Tuesday holiday was very different. It featured opening prayers delivered by the Primate of All Ireland and the Moderator of the Presbyterian Church, and the singing of Psalm 90 ('Teach us to number our days'), long an Orange favourite, by men who arrived from all across Ulster in seventy trains; over 100,000 marched past in military order 'against the backdrop of the blue Antrim hills'.[56] After this event Rudyard Kipling (who had built a drill hall at his Sussex home to train the locals during the Boer war) wrote his fuming poem 'Ulster 1912', with its electrifyingly ultra-Orangeist language, cataloguing Catholic qualities – 'murder done by night, treason taught by day, folly sloth and spite' – and warning of 'the war prepared on every peaceful home' ('terror, threats and dread in market, heath and field'). Above all, 'the hells declared for such as serve not Rome'. This kind of anti-Catholicism had not been heard in England for generations. Invoking a quasi-fascist mantra, 'one law, one land, one throne', Kipling committed 'the North' to violence: 'if England drive us forth, we shall not fall alone'. It may be that, as Benedict Kiely would later write, 'we are left to wonder at the ingenuousness of the minds that could have taken it seriously'.[57] But wonderment – shared not just by Irish nationalists, but English Liberals and probably most Conservatives – was beside the point.

This amounted to a sort of anthem of 'Ulsteria' – a state of mind identified (usually mockingly) by journalists as the crisis intensified. Thomas Kettle's unconvincing attempt to dismiss Ulster loyalism in his book *The Open Secret of Ireland* diagnosed it as 'largely a problem of hysteria'. Explaining the Ulster question to an American audience in 1913, Sydney Brooks presented the business people of Belfast ('the Chicago of Ireland') as 'rough-tongued, hard-headed, not particularly ingratiating or cultivated', but 'with a clearness of vision, a remorseless energy and fixity of purpose in pursuing their ends, and a general ruggedness of character that command instant respect'. Belfast was 'the headquarters of Ulsteria', he said, but these qualities 'run with astonishing consistency through all the Ulster Protestants of whatever class or occupation'. As a community they were 'as dour, stubborn, self-willed and self-reliant a body as one is ever likely to come across – taciturn of speech, fixed in all their ideas, obstinately faithful to the men who are capable of winning their reluctant trust'. Crucially, they were 'absolutely differentiated from the ordinary Catholic Irishman of the south and west'. And worryingly, 'the rougher elements among them are as turbulent a mob as you will find in all Europe', while 'mingling with all these traits is an intense strain of emotionalism'.[58]

An Orangeman, Brooks suggested, looked on the idea of being governed by a Catholic-farmer parliament much as a 'white planter in Texas' would regard handing over the state administration 'to the negroes'. 'It is not merely an insult; it seems to him positively unnatural', a personal degradation, a lowering to the level of 'an alien and abject civilization'. As ignorant of the rest of Ireland as the average American of Mexico, 'a little world of hallucination that is all his own', Brooks warned that 'the brutal fact that lies behind Ulsteria' – Ulstermen's readiness to eliminate Catholics – was 'concealed from the British public as much as possible'. Carson himself, he said, had no trace of the odium theologicum, but the 'unedifying and indisputable fact' was that it 'furnishes most of the motive power for the anti-home rule agitation'.

Brooks dissented from the kind of idealistic optimism hawked by nationalists like Kettle – 'people are wrong who think that Ulster is bluffing' – but he hedged his bets on whether its resistance could succeed. He did not 'rate them, with their insurance policies in their pockets, as the stuff out of which successful rebellions are made'. He thought that the idea of pitting them against the British army had been abandoned in favour of establishing a provisional government. Rebellion would be bad for business.[59]

Undoubtedly though, 'Ulsteria' now became a potent political force, focusing not only the collective energy of northern Unionism, but also the commitment of the British Conservative leadership. Balfour, however dedicated to the union, had never been able to muster much enthusiasm for Ulster as such; his successor Andrew Bonar Law was very different. Balfour backed away from the partitionist implications of his pioneering 'two nations' argument, and now played down ethnic division – arguing in 1912 that the ethnic mix in the British Isles was so thorough that 'there is no race frontier'. Bonar Law played it up. For him, though he might rehearse the well-known battery of arguments against home rule, 'the strongest objection' to it lay in the fact that Ireland was not a nation. Nationality was 'the only intelligible ground on which home rule can now be defended', yet Ireland was 'two nations separated from each other by lines of cleavage which cut far deeper than those which separate Great Britain from Ireland'. This was no longer unionism, but Ulsterism – it was 'the Unionists of Ulster' who gave this argument its decisive weight.[60]

A Canadian-born Presbyterian, Bonar Law shared some of the cultural characteristics identified by Brooks. Combined with intense outrage at the 'corrupt bargain', they led him to the most unambiguous declaration of solidarity, in language reminiscent of the English Civil War. At the biggest Unionist rally to take place outside Ulster, in the grounds of Blenheim Palace on 29 July 1912, he labelled the government 'a Revolutionary Committee which has seized upon despotic power by fraud', which could not be opposed by the methods of an 'ordinary constitutional struggle' – there were 'things stronger than parliamentary majorities'. In a phrase which would resonate long afterwards, he declared, 'I can imagine no length of resistance to which Ulster can go in which I should not be prepared to support them'. The overwhelming majority of the British people, he believed, would do the same.

The emergence of Ulster as an autonomous political force reached its climax on 'Ulster Day' (28 September), when nearly a quarter of a million men signed 'Ulster's Solemn League and Covenant', whose words – though altered from those of the seventeenth-century Scottish original, which might not have played so well in England – conveyed its spirit quite authentically. Signatories pledged themselves 'to stand by one another in defending our cherished position of equal citizenship in the United Kingdom, and using all means which may be found necessary to defeat the present conspiracy to set up a Home Rule Parliament in Ireland'. Even more women (barred from committing themselves to 'using all means' – which were taken to include fighting) signed a parallel version. The theatricality of the event was magnified in Belfast, where the Covenant was signed on a round table draped in a Union flag under the dome of the magnificent new city hall, a striking symbol of Britishness.[61] Some would think this a 'strange and even improper' use of a public building, Ronald McNeill noted, but the citizenry saw it as exactly fitting its purpose.[62]

A DEMOCRATIC ARMY

The 'drilling craze' launched by the Craigavon rally produced ad hoc local groups wherever magistrates were ready to certify that they were drilling – banned in 1819 by the Unlawful Drilling Act unless by 'lawful authority' – to make them 'more efficient citizens for the purpose of maintaining their liberties'. Few magistrates in Ulster were unwilling to do this. Meeting in Orange halls or schoolhouses, the majority of the groups, though by no means all, were in north-east Ulster.[63] Not until this had been going on for over a year did the UUC take steps to pull them together, by forming the Ulster Volunteer Force, whose name evoked eighteenth-century precedents while trumpeting the newly emerged entity of 'Ulster'. Membership was open to men aged between seventeen and sixty-five who had signed the Covenant. Most existing groups went into the UVF, including the Young Citizen Volunteers of Ireland, established in Belfast a few months earlier to 'develop the spirit of responsible citizenship' and 'cultivate ... a manly physique, with habits of self-control, self-respect and chivalry'. It had previously described itself as 'non-sectarian and non-political', possibly to aid its (unsuccessful) application for official recognition and funding.[64] Some of its members evidently took that description seriously, and resisted being 'taken over' until early 1914, but the group's financial straits left it little alternative. Other groups adhered more readily, like the Enniskillen Horse, formed by the editor of the *Impartial Reporter*, William Copeland Trimble, and consisting mainly of farmers (according to the police, who reported that 'prominent people' disapproved of it altogether).[65] Within six months the UVF had a full command structure and a general staff, with a retired Indian army general as commander-in-chief.

The force's nature remains somewhat elusive. It has been called a 'private army' or a 'stage army', while less hostile observers have preferred labels like 'citizen' or 'democratic army' (the term used by the *Times* military correspondent), or even 'armed democracy'.[66] The great majority of its recruits do seem to have been volunteers; the owners of some industrial villages (such as Sion Mills in Tyrone) appear to have more or less conscripted their employees, but whether they would have joined in any case is impossible to say. Landlords sometimes followed their tenants into the force.[67] Socially, it was fairly representative, though class balance varied across units; rural battalions seem to have resembled the quasi-feudal levies in the Volunteers of nineteenth-century England, while in Belfast the majority of young businessmen joined the Young Citizen Volunteers, leaving many urban battalions socially unbalanced. However composed, it was an element within the British state unknown since the fifteenth century, and certainly supposed to have been impossible since Henry VII's Statute of Liveries.

Militarily, its capacity and intentions are also hard to pin down exactly. What would it actually do? Whatever Sydney Brooks thought, setting up a provisional government would certainly involve violence at some point. Ulster Volunteer leaders had a preference for 'open' fighting – as would many of their Irish Volunteer equivalents – though the UVF's territorial structure seemed to militate against concentration. (Charles Repington, the *Times* military correspondent, thought that even so it could be concentrated much faster than the British army could be mobilized.) The Boers had made guerrilla fighting politically as well as professionally obnoxious. Wilfrid Spender, the UVF's most capable staff officer, prepared a plan – called 'The Coup' – to strike 'a sudden, complete and paralysing blow', in which railway and telegraph lines would be cut, arms depots seized, and roads into Ulster blocked.[68] He may have hoped that the British government would back off in the face of this, but it was a risky strategy if the object was to avoid bloodshed.

Spender himself vividly illustrated the impact of Ulsteria. As the youngest staff officer in the British army, and secretary to the Home Defence committee of the Committee of Imperial Defence, he had seemed marked for high achievement. Then what a military inquiry called his 'too active conscience' impelled him into the home rule dispute, of which he knew nothing until he discovered (he later wrote) that on mobilization two of the army's six divisions would be detailed for Ireland, reducing the force that could be sent to France by a third.[69] He signed the Ulster Covenant, organized a national petition against home rule, and tried to resign his commission and stand for parliament. Embroiled in a dispute with the War Office over resigning his commission – for which royal authority was needed – he sought legal advice from Edward Carson, who cannily arranged for him to join the staff of the UVF – infuriating the Chief of the Imperial General Staff, Sir John French, who then urged the Secretary of State for War that he should be cashiered *'pour décourager les autres'*. He failed; although French and Seely were close friends, the minister was not ready to take such action.[70] But Spender was born again as an Ulster stalwart.

The government had no interest in seeing the UVF as disputing its monopoly of armed force, and therefore as a direct political challenge which would have to be dealt with. It preferred to leave it be. The question why the government did not clamp down on this spectacular breach of the ancient Statute of Liveries remains a big one, and hard to answer. Was it bias, or mere vacillation? Reluctance to wake sleeping dogs, in the hope that a political settlement would render them irrelevant, would certainly have been the prime minister's instinctive course. This quietism survived the accumulation of evidence that the UVF was acquiring weapons; arms importation – legal since the lapse of the Peace Preservation Act – occurred, though unobtrusively, and overall stocks could only be guessed at. (They seem to have been smaller than the force liked to imply.)

Late in 1913, the rank and file grumbled about the arms issue – tired of drilling with wooden dummy rifles, and annoyed that news of the fresh ban on arms importation had not been passed on in time for 'a large extra number of arms to have been imported'. The UVF staff met with Ulster Unionist political leaders to ask 'what early developments' they should be prepared to meet. The issues were carefully set out: what should be done if the government tried to seize UVF weapons, what if action were taken against leaders, what if the Belfast population were to 'show grave signs of getting restive'? What, indeed, if the government began to draft large numbers of troops or police into Ulster? To this the leaders replied that they must hear of it beforehand, and action would only then be considered. They were hardly more forthcoming on the question of arms importation, saying that no steps should be taken to continue it, but conceding that plans should be prepared for future importation 'on a large scale'. To the demand that they guarantee to give the military leaders at least a month's notice before such plans should be put into effect, they seem to have given no reply.[71]

Would the UVF fight? Nationalists persisted in seeing it as yet another manifestation of Ulster bluff. Sydney Brooks saw 'the indemnity fund to guarantee all "rebels" against personal loss' as a symptom of its military limitations, though he rejected the notion that Ulster was bluffing. The fund (which Arthur Griffith unwisely mocked) was not a normal feature of military service, certainly, but surely a sensible provision for a volunteer militia, and could equally be seen as evidence of serious intent. The real question probably was, fight who? George Birmingham's wryly prophetic novel of militia-building and gun-running, *The Red Hand of Ulster*, written months before the UVF emerged, climaxed with a serious street battle between the rebels and the British army. (After that, of course, the British government gave way.) No UVF people could admit to any intention to do this, but that was the ultimate logic of their posture. It was also the reason for the creation of a Special Service Force, enrolling 3,000 men from the Belfast battalions, which was pushed ahead early in 1914.

Lord Dunleath, a leading figure in the County Down UVF, laid out for Carson's benefit a strikingly candid analysis of the force's attitude. He pointed out that 'we are a democratic force', without regular army discipline: so 'orders even from general Richardson would not necessarily be carried out', if such orders embodied a policy which 'failed to commend itself to the men and to their officers'. He himself did not believe 'that our men are prepared to go into action against any part of His Majest'y [sic] forces, and we should not consider ourselves justified in calling upon them to do so.' So though 'many of us are undoubtedly willing, if necessary, to risk our lives', he recommended a policy of passive resistance, if Ulster was not excluded from home rule. Only when a home rule government tried to collect taxes would they fight: 'our men would like nothing better than to go out against the Nationalists'.[72] In the event, the more urgent question would become whether the British army would fight them.

'ULSTER SHALL BE FREE'

Not long after 'Ulster Day', another parliamentary amendment proposing exclusion was put down, this time by the Scottish home ruler and federalist D. V. Pirie, and this time excluding a full nine-county

Ulster unit. It went the same way as the county option proposal, but clearly showed that exclusion was likely to be more not less substantive. It took two years of tinkering with ideas of special treatment for Ulster within all-Ireland home rule – evolving from an Ulster committee with veto power to 'home rule within home rule', a subordinate administration – to convince Asquith that no such arrangement would neutralize Unionist resistance. All this time, pressure for exclusion remained persistent, and it came, tellingly, from practically the only senior ministers to give any serious or sustained thought to the Ulster issue, Lloyd George and Churchill. Churchill now decided, as he told the chancellor, that 'action about Ulster must be settled' immediately: 'we ought to give any Irish county the option of remaining at Westminster for a period of 5 or 10 years', or 'some variant of this'.[73] A month later, on 12 September, in a major speech in his Dundee constituency he gave unusually detailed attention to the idea of establishing 'a workable federal system' which might involve 'perhaps as many as ten or twelve' self-governing regions such as Yorkshire, the Midlands, and London.

Politics became ever more ill-tempered in autumn 1912 – indeed blood was actually shed in the House of Commons when Asquith refused to resign after the government lost a snap vote on the home rule financial provisions. Amidst 'considerable disorder' as the House adjourned, Ronald McNeill, irked by Churchill's taunts, flung a leather-bound copy of the Standing Orders at his head, drawing blood, and the two had to be restrained from hand-to-hand combat by their supporters. The Government of Ireland Bill passed its first circuit early the next year, and was vetoed by the Lords on 30 January; it was passed and vetoed a second time in mid-July. With parliament in deadlock, the struggle moved out into the public sphere. Unionists demanded a general election, and put heavy pressure on King George V to dissolve parliament. The king resisted; Carson lamented that the new monarch's idea of 'constitutionalism' translated into 'doing everything his P.M. tells him'. ('What a good King,' he sarcastically added.)[74] Dicey advised 'the constant holding of meetings' in favour of dissolution, though he and Selborne also proposed a referendum as a possible substitute; even Bonar Law himself thought a referendum acceptable.[75] They were convinced that the public would support them, and so probably was Asquith. He stoutly resisted dissolution; the king was dismayed by the royal prerogative power being publicly examined, notably in *The Times*.

In late March a 'British League for the Support of Ulster and the Union' – the word order was significant – was launched by Lord Willoughby de Broke, one of the 'Ditchers' who had defied the threatened mass creation of peers in 1911, forcing the final vote in the Lords on the Parliament Act. A public letter signed by 100 peers and 120 MPs announced that 'Ulster will be the field on which the privileges of the whole nation will be lost or won'. Some 10,000 people signed up over the following months, committing themselves to direct action to prevent home rule being imposed on Ulster. This was a potentially alarming symptom of Ulster militancy spreading into the mainland. In June the government was questioned in parliament over a shipment of rifles seized in Belfast which was allegedly linked with the League. The radical MP Josiah Wedgwood called on the government to 'indict for conspiracy those responsible for the formation of the society', but the government held that there was not enough evidence to take action.[76] There was, though, no doubt about the British League's readiness to use violent means; as Willoughby de Broke told Bonar Law on 11 September, 'in the absence of the old Constitution, the only thing left is physical force'.[77]

On 24 September the UUC formally constituted itself as the Ulster Provisional Government – a tag which had been in common parlance for some two years – with a Central Authority seventy-six strong, a Military Council, and four administrative committees as proto-ministries. Carson conducted a two-week tour of Ulster, inspecting 22,000 UVF men in six counties, culminating in a parade of 4,300 Volunteers at Armagh. In November, Bonar Law, Carson, and Austen Chamberlain appeared at a rally in the Birmingham Hippodrome, where they were regaled with an anthem as passionate as Kipling's – with lines like 'Steadfast rank and glittering steel/Strong to guard a nation's weal ... Ulster shall be free, [chorus] Ulster for the right/ Ulster know your might/Raise your hand and guard your land/With Ulster for the right.'[78]

'THESE GRAVE MATTERS'

How serious was the situation? Dicey was certainly now thinking about outright war in September 1913 – 'Civil war will bring untold evils to every part of the United Kingdom'. There were English Unionists who appeared to imagine that 'the mere sight of war in Ireland' would arouse such indignation against the government that it would fall. He saw this as a dangerous delusion. Just as worrying was the growing movement to subvert the discipline of the army and encourage officers to resign. Barely veiled incitements to mutiny were profoundly menacing to democracy, and would rebound on any conspiracy; 'English opinion will not tolerate any attempt of the Army to determine the policy of the nation.'[79] In any case, he doubted whether officers could legally resign their commissions without the Crown's permission.

When the publicist F. S. Oliver wrote a pamphlet pushing federalism as a solution to the crisis, he called it *The Alternatives to Civil War*. Evidently it suited him to stress the depth of the political cleavage, to increase the attraction of his proposed third way, but for him the reality of the danger was clear enough. Each side questioned the determination of the other to face the consequences of its declarations, but that was natural. While 'we may be pretty certain' that for every 'fire-eater who likes the idea of going out with his rifle' there were 'at least one hundred Ulster Volunteers who hate the thing most heartily', that was no cause for comfort. It was, he argued, the very fact that, though hating it, they were determined in certain circumstances to 'undertake it' that demonstrated the strength of their resistance. He was almost certainly right to say that 'the Ulster grievance is the only point of the Irish question which the ordinary elector in Britain knows or cares anything about'.[80]

Others were also ruminating on the issue at this point; St Loe Strachey wrote a series of *Spectator* articles on civil war (a perilous subject, he said, 'ringed round with all that is most hateful and ill-omened to the good citizen'). He pointed out that under the 'English constitution' military duty did not divest the soldier of the obligations of the citizen. Common law had established 'a kind of spiritual dualism'; obedience to orders could not justify taking life if the circumstances did not warrant it, and such latitude as the military had was given to them as 'civilians who happen to have arms in their hands', not as soldiers.[81] 'A man's defence of his acts is made neither better nor worse by his being under military discipline.' So refusal to obey orders could be not mutiny but good citizenship. And besides, as Strachey contemptuously asked, 'Does anyone really suppose that the present Government ... would have the pluck to hand over to a firing party the first half dozen officers who sent in their papers and, when told they were not accepted, disobeyed orders and absented themselves from duty?'

The government line remained against exclusion through this, though it was hardly discussed between early 1912 and late 1913 when some ministers complained about the lack of information about Ulster 'goings-on'. Birrell belatedly produced a report on *The Movement in Ulster* on 21 October, quickly followed by two more, making all too clear that the situation had drifted potentially beyond governmental control.[82] Birrell's authority was compromised, and Lloyd George again took the initiative with a scheme for the 'temporary exclusion of Ulster', with 'automatic inclusion at the end of the term'. The chancellor thought this should be from three to five years. The logic was 'to knock all moral props from under Carson's rebellion', either making it 'impossible for Ulster to take up arms' or 'if they did, put us in a strong position with the British public when we came to suppress it'.[83]

At last there was distinct movement towards acceptance of exclusion, led by Asquith and Lord Crewe, Lord Privy Seal, with only lightweight ministers holding out for the 1912 bill unaltered. The most sustained objection to partition came from Herbert Samuel, who had done more work on that bill than any other minister, and whose elaborate financial provisions for home rule were already too complicated for most of his colleagues to grasp. He believed that no 'workable financial scheme can be evolved, based upon a fiscal separation between Ulster and the rest of Ireland'. He denounced exclusion not only for 'the injury it would do to the principle of nationality', but also 'the difficulty it presents in providing for the proper government of that [excluded] district'. It was a 'counsel of despair'.[84] But after his own proposal of 'home rule within home rule' – an 'Ulster House' without a financial veto – was rejected by the Cabinet, he did not dig his heels in.

At this crucial juncture, leading nationalists also backpedalled: John Dillon had to accept that 'if . . . we were faced with a real firm proposal of allowing the HR Bill to go thro' with an option for the four counties, our position would be an extremely difficult one'.[85] Here, 'extremely difficult' was political language for 'untenable'. Conflict lines were hardening: Canon Hannay was driven out of the increasingly politicized Gaelic League. Strachey thought 'all the signs of the times point to the fact that Asquith is going to give us exclusion'. He urged 'Ulster people' not to 'rush their fence': if what Salisbury might have called the 'Celtic fringes of Ulster' were left out, 'you would gain immensely in strength because you would be a concentrated Protestant Teutonic community'.[86]

Shortly before Christmas, Asquith set up a cosy get-together of fellow barristers, 'old professional friends' as he put it to the king, meeting secretly with Carson to discuss his ideas on home rule within home rule. His 'few rough suggestions' revolved around a concept of 'statutory Ulster' with powers of veto in an Irish parliament. Ulster would apparently be left undefined, or perhaps self-identifying. Carson undertook to put the idea to Bonar Law, before declaring that since it kept Ulster within the Irish parliament it was 'useless'. Asquith met Carson again early in the new year, twice, trying to sell the idea of 'veiled exclusion' as against 'naked exclusion'; now Ulster would remain outside the jurisdiction of the Dublin parliament, and (as Carson understood it) 'would continue as at present to send members to the Imp[erial] Parl[iament]'. This was in fact exclusion rather than home rule within home rule – indeed it appeared to be just what Carson had been calling for – but he still turned it down.[87]

Asquith now told Redmond that he needed to do something, not just to deprive Ulster resistance 'of all moral force' but more urgently to stop the king using his prerogative power to 'dismiss his Minister', effectively dissolving parliament. The king was inclined to believe 'the reality of the civil war threat', and felt he had to turn to the country to resolve the crisis. Whether or not the Liberals would win the ensuing election (and this was clearly doubtful at best), the parliamentary sequence of the Home Rule Bill would be broken, and 'the last two years would have been wasted'.[88]

There was a certain air of inevitability to the Cabinet's eventual decision that Lloyd George should dust off and re-present his 1912 exclusion proposal. Asquith's effort to soften Redmond up went on until (fearing, as Lloyd George saw, that 'it would be an unpleasant task') he deputed his chancellor to have a 'preliminary conversation' with the Irish triumvirate on 27 February. They still insisted that the threat of civil war was exaggerated, but eventually conceded that 'as the price of peace' they were 'ready to give our acquiescence to the . . . standing out of for three years by option of the counties of Ulster'. Redmond demanded that whatever scheme was now put forward by the government 'would be their last word' – there would be no further concessions. Lloyd George assented: he, like others, assumed that 'Ulster' could not reject his scheme and retain its 'moral force'. But within a few days, Asquith told Redmond that he had just realized that the exclusion period must be no less than six years, to ensure that there must be a general election before it expired.[89]

Finally in March 1914, as the bill came up for its third parliamentary circuit, Asquith formally offered exclusion for six years – which would ensure a general election before the issue was finally resolved. 'County option' would include Belfast and Derry as separate plebiscitary units. Redmond now found, to his surprise, that northern nationalists – notably the senior clergy – were not as hostile to this proposition as he assumed. (At least they would 'submit', even if 'not with the best grace', as Devlin reported to him.)[90] Carson on the other hand rejected the proposal with one of his most lethal blows, as a 'sentence of death with a stay of execution'. Few people now imagined that (whatever the outcome of an election) exclusion could be ended without Ulster's consent, but Carson wanted permanence written in. He went further, accusing Asquith of 'making no genuine effort to achieve a settlement', but merely 'trifling' to get 'platform material' for Churchill and others to use 'for party advantage'. So much for old professional friendship.

Churchill predictably ramped up the confrontation, declaring at Bradford on 14 March that the Ulster Provisional Government was 'engaged in a treasonable conspiracy' with a 'sinister and revolutionary purpose'. There were 'worse things than bloodshed even on an extended scale' – defiance of the law foremost among them. If the civil and parliamentary systems 'under which we have dwelt so long, and our fathers before us, are to be brought to the rude challenge of force', 'let us go forward together and put these grave matters to the proof'. George Dangerfield judged this 'by all odds, the best Liberal speech of a decade'.[91] If things had been left to Churchill, they might have been put to the proof by direct confrontation. But things proved more ambiguous. He had received warnings about rumblings in the army the previous year, but seems to have been confident that as long as a fair offer was made to Ulster, nothing would come of this. Still, even to be contemplating the question whether the government could rely on the army was an alarming sign. It was well known that retired senior officers were involved in the training and command of the UVF, and most serving officers will have been aware of Garnet Wolseley's opinion, which was echoed – even amplified – by his successor as the *beau idéal* of Victorian soldiery – and Kipling's favourite general – the last Commander-in-Chief, Lord Roberts. Roberts would play a key role in the potentially catastrophic military intervention known as the 'Curragh mutiny' (indeed Asquith regarded him as its instigator). He had already gone a long way in 1913, encouraging the Tory leadership's idea of using the Lords to vote down the annual Army Act – an unprecedented and almost unthinkable step, with dangerously unpredictable consequences. Roberts has been charitably credited with 'doing his best to prevent a split in the army', convinced it could only be held together if it was not used in Ulster, but there was no doubt which side he was on. He thought the government was making 'a dastardly attempt to bring on Civil War'. He warned Sir John French, in a phone call at the height of the crisis, that he would 'cover himself with infamy' if he associated himself with 'this band of (certain epithets were used which I could hardly catch)'.[92]

Whether or not Carson's party-political allegation was intentionally provocative, Churchill was certainly provoked. He told the Cabinet ('united in determination to meet force by force', C. P. Scott heard) he would send a battle squadron to Lamlash, to support the movement of strong forces from the central military depot at the Curragh to secure northern arms depots. This, clearly an attempt to forestall possible UVF raids, became in Unionist rhetoric 'the plot against Ulster', designed to provoke direct confrontation which would turn public opinion against the loyalists. The army's officers could hardly object to securing arms depots, or even to 'overawing' the UVF, but the plot was in another category.

Was this really a deliberate attempt to provoke resistance that could be crushed by force? Or just culpably tardy action to vindicate the law? No doubt the government delayed taking action, either on drilling or on importation of guns, long after its professional advisers made absolutely clear that the UVF represented a serious threat. As early as May 1912 the army's law officers warned that former military officers who were drilling the UVF were almost certainly engaged in 'seditious resistance to constituted authority' rather than some glorified boy-scout activity. There was a spate of reported arms shipments, and one or two were sent back; some were shown to be mistaken, but the Royal Irish Constabulary (RIC) cautioned 'it would be unsafe to treat the rumours of armed resistance as mere bluff'.[93] Not until November 1912 were the police instructed to 'keep a careful watch upon the sale of revolvers and rifles in Belfast, and report the results'. When Trimble's Enniskillen Horse paraded with sixteen carbines and 143 lances early in 1913, the Irish Attorney General pronounced 'these demonstrations of armed forces ... highly criminal' – 'in fact acts of treason'. Despite this he cautioned against police action, beyond taking the names of the participants. When the police were told that Trimble was storing arms in Enniskillen, they reported that they could not get any information about arms deliveries, and thought them 'unlikely'.[94] After alarming information was received about a consignment of Winchester rifles in the Imperial Hotel, there was a sigh of relief when they turned out to be 'cheap single-barrel shotguns of American make'.

Scotland Yard reported multiple deliveries of revolvers and cartridges in late 1912; one Shankill pawnbroker was 'importing arms and ammunition direct from Belgium on a very large scale'. Hardware merchants and cycle dealers were also involved.[95] The tempo of arms importation quickened late in 1913, with several deliveries of Martini-Enfield rifles to the Belfast pawnbrokers Adjey and Murphy. When they were sent two cases containing no fewer than 740 sword bayonets from the Midland Gun Company in Birmingham (which labelled the shipment 'hardware') on 1 November, it was noted that 'the Customs were aware of the consignment, inspected the cases, but took no action'. An identical shipment followed five days later.

Finally the Attorney General, Sir John Simon, concluded that possession of documentary authorization from two Justices of the Peace could not shield a 'seditious conspiracy' from prosecution under the Unlawful Drilling Act – 'indeed the Justices of the Peace who gave such authority would be accessories to the crime'.[96] Even so, no prosecutions were ever launched. And, as we have seen, Sir John French urged exemplary action against army officers who were drifting over to the UVF, and contemplating even more dramatic action.[97] The eventual ban on arms importation in December 1913, though it led to several UVF shipments being cancelled (with 'serious monetary loss', the would-be gunrunners complained), was not enforced. It was most famously breached when Fred Crawford organized the running of 20,000 rifles into the port of Larne on the night of 24 April.

The police were certainly given no orders to intervene, and it was tacitly understood they would not (an understanding that applied throughout Ireland, but was ignored by the Dublin police when the Irish Volunteers landed rifles at Howth in July). For John Regan, a Catholic RIC officer in Lisnaskea, Fermanagh, the arming of the UVF – for good or ill – 'had nothing to do with me as a police officer'.[98] Interestingly, when C. P. Scott met John Dillon just after the gunrunning, and suggested that 'we had perhaps made a mistake in not checking [the] volunteer movement sooner', Dillon 'strongly deprecated any action even now which might lead to actual conflict'.[99] The military significance of the Larne gunrunning may be debated, but though it perhaps did no more than confirm that a direct military confrontation with the UVF was now unthinkable, it was another demonstration that collective organization was being taken to a different level.

'A REALLY EFFECTIVE RESISTANCE'

The scale of British popular mobilization against home rule has been seriously underplayed in most historical accounts. Willoughby de

Broke's militant BLSUU group never became a mass movement, but that was hardly surprising. A far bigger movement emerged in March 1914, when Lord Milner (who had made no contribution to the home rule debate since his ambivalent ruminations on federalism in 1910) launched the 'British Covenant'. Milner, still looking for a way of realizing his vision of national greatness without entering the grubby world of 'politics', was an iconic figure to a generation who shared that vision. Late in 1913, Lord Roberts, who had 'let the King know that a British regiment could not be called upon to fire on citizen soldiers who are fighting under the Union Jack', suggested he take a 'more prominent part in politics'. Milner decided that the issue of the coercion of Ulster was – as he told Carson on 9 December – a 'business [which] goes far deeper than ordinary party struggles'. If 'what would be technically a rebellion in Ulster' were to fail, it would be a disaster, but 'it must fail unless we can *paralyse the arm* which might be raised to strike you'.

Once convinced of this, Milner was prepared to go to extraordinary lengths to achieve that paralysis. He aimed at action 'falling short of violence or actual rebellion' – 'or at least not beginning with it' – which would both divert the government's attention from Ulster and actually prevent the movement of troops (with 'sufficient men in the railways, at the ports, in the service of army contractors, who had pledged themselves to strike rather than facilitate the movement of troops to operate in Ulster'). He needed to ensure that 'the stalwarts' had 'some sort of rudimentary organization, not leave everything to the last moment'. The organization itself hinged on a British version of the Ulster Covenant, the brainchild of Leo Amery. Its exact purpose was debatable – for some it was intended to avoid precipitate action, though Milner himself wanted 'to furnish a really effective resistance' and ultimately 'an organized and immediately successful national uprising'.[100] It was deliberately less extreme than the BLSUU – which Amery thought was limited by its focus on 'a contingency which the British public refuses as yet to contemplate', that was 'fighting with a rifle in Ulster'.[101] But there was much wider support for the idea of preventing a violent showdown. The British Covenant insisted that passing home rule 'without submitting it to the judgment of the Nation is contrary to the spirit of our Constitution', and its signatories declared themselves 'justified in taking or supporting any action which may be effective' to prevent the home rule act being enforced, 'and more particularly to prevent the armed forces of the Crown being used to deprive the people of Ulster of their rights as citizens of the United Kingdom'. The public letter that launched the Covenant on 3 March was signed by Milner, Roberts, Dicey, and the composer Sir Edward Elgar, as well as Kipling and the President of Magdalen College, Oxford.

Barely a fortnight later, the long-brewing army crisis finally broke. The ineptitude of the authorities played a bigger part than the mutinous intrigues of Tory officers. After Churchill issued his Bradford challenge, the Irish commander-in-chief, General Paget, was ordered to report his plans to deal with 'an organized warlike movement of Ulster Volunteers'. He argued that any demonstrative action risked provoking confrontation; the Belfast commander, General Gleichen, was acutely conscious of the army's awkward position. On 18 March, Paget was summoned to London, and ordered to carry out a series of military moves, including sending significant reinforcements to the north, on 21 March. Gleichen was to be replaced by General Nevil Macready, who had won political kudos for his careful use of troops in the Welsh miners' strike, and would go to Belfast with a dormant commission as military governor. Officers who preferred not to take part would not be permitted to resign, though those who lived in Ulster would be allowed to 'disappear'. Given these frankly odd instructions, Paget decided to sound out his officers, and those of the Cavalry Brigade responded by declaring they would resign their commissions rather than 'march on Ulster'. The doubts expressed by Dicey and Strachey were partly confirmed. The government made clear – one of the few clear points in a murky and confused episode – that officers would not be permitted to do this: they would have to refuse a direct order, and then be 'cashiered'.

It never came to this: the crisis was defused by a wholly unconstitutional undertaking by the government not to use the army to crush opposition to home rule, but this hardly disguised the scale of the setback. If not technically mutiny, the political intent of its leading spirit Johnny Gough is beyond question. It certainly rocked the government; this was the culmination of 'Ulsteria'. L. T. Hobhouse, the intellectual leader of New Liberalism, glumly ruminated on the significance of the 'surrender', which he anticipated from the moment he read 'Asquith's sonorous declaration about vindicating the law'. ('He always talks like that when he means to do nothing.') Hobhouse now thought it would be 'better far to lose Home Rule than accept a compromise based on the dictation of Carson with the backing of the army and society'. He had been in favour of a county option, but not 'under coercion'. As it was, 'we have given in after a fashion which must have permanent and most serious reaction on political methods'.[102] He probably did not know that Major-General Macready, sent to Belfast with a dormant commission as military governor if martial law had to be declared, was briefed by the prime minister not to interfere if special companies of UVF were sent, fully armed, to the border area, nor intervene if fighting broke out between loyalists and nationalists. But these 'heroic instructions' would no doubt have deepened his gloom.[103]

'When in our lifetime,' Milner mused, 'have thousands upon thousands of sober steady-going citizens deliberately contemplated resistance to an Act of Parliament, because they sincerely believed it was devoid of all moral sanction?' A month after the Covenant was launched in the press on 3 March, yet another League (of British Covenanters) was formed, and at its rally in Hyde Park on 4 April nearly half a million people assembled to hear speeches by Milner, Long, and Carson. Over the next few weeks nearly two million people signed the Covenant, a process enthusiastically documented by *The Times* newspaper. Just what they were committing themselves to remained vague – and none of them, it seems, signed in blood – but this was a formidable political demonstration by any standard. Demonstrations in many other places followed – Eastbourne, Leeds, and Newcastle as well as Glasgow and Liverpool. The Covenant's own journal ominously celebrated the excitement of 'the long processions, the waving of countless flags, the thunder of the old covenanting hymn, the vast array of faces fixed on the orators, the stern enthusiasm of the packed assemblies'.[104] The 'feverish paroxysm' of the crowds at these rallies has indeed been likened to Italian and German far-right assemblies in the fascist epoch.[105]

The Tory leadership may well have been less enthused by the

Covenant than their followers, but certainly 'it would have been difficult to avoid the British Covenant in the spring of 1914'. It may well now seem, as has recently been suggested, 'astonishing that open drilling should have been taking place in Britain for the first time since the Chartists were forging pikes and swords'.[106] Prone though he was to alarmism, Walter Long did not much exaggerate when he wrote to Herbert Samuel in July, 'this is no ordinary crisis ... it is something more terrible than that, namely, is there to be a civil war or not?'[107] The government could hardly doubt that the home rule issue was politically explosive in England itself.

Ulsteria would never recur with the same intensity, but from here on there was no possibility of implementing Irish home rule without the exclusion of some part of Ulster. Which part, and on what basis, remained to be negotiated. Birrell consulted several people about possible dividing lines; the results were not encouraging. His own Under Secretary, Sir James Dougherty, after stalling for some time, concluded that 'whatever plan may be adopted', the exclusion concept 'bristles with difficulties'. 'At the moment I confess I do not see how they are to be surmounted.'[108] Sir Henry Robinson of the Irish Local Government Board was more sanguine, drawing up maps showing how rural districts rather than counties might provide a way forward. (Dougherty simply dismissed the use of local government units.) But he warned Birrell unambiguously that 'you will find that the Ulstermen's minimum will be six entire counties, and no option'.[109] When Bonar Law and Carson met with the former chief whip Lord Murray (acting as Asquith's go-between) at the beginning of July, they discussed a quite precise area – four counties 'with the exception of part of south Armagh and a strip of south Down'. The area also included 'a strip of Donegal', and discussion 'showed that [the government] were willing to put within the excluded area a strip of Monaghan and possibly of Cavan'.[110] What turned out to be the last negotiation, at Buckingham Palace between 21 and 24 July 1914, showed that all the options were still on the table. The county option (excluding four counties) was as far as Redmond could go, while Carson stuck to a clean cut for the whole of Ulster. Bonar Law, more prophetically, had come to see six counties as the workable unit. Asquith proposed a more complicated arrangement, excluding south

Tyrone and north Fermanagh but including south Armagh in the home rule state. But though this was far more intelligent as a line of division, it was rejected by both sides. The impasse was complete, and there was no sign that any way forward could be found.

The day after the conference broke up, the Irish Volunteers ran a cargo of rifles into Dublin. British troops, having failed to seize the weapons, were stoned by an angry crowd as they returned to barracks; they opened fire, killing four Dubliners. 'In this little spatter of blood and bullets' on the Liffey quays, George Dangerfield wrote, 'an end was written to the Civil War.'[111] Asquith told the king he would present the Amending Bill on 28 July in its original form, 'but with the omission of automatic inclusion after a term of years, and the substitution of a fresh power of option'.[112] General Macready was sent back to Belfast, fearing that his soldiers' blood would be 'shed in a useless encounter with fanatical enthusiasts'. While he was on his way, the German army was moving to its assembly areas on the frontier with Belgium; on 4 August, Churchill's fear that 'we shall have a bloody peace' was laid to rest.[113]

4

The War

On the face of things, the home rule project and the Unionist resistance to it went into hibernation when the European war broke out. The government insisted on enacting the third Home Rule Bill, the first Government of Ireland Act, in September 1914, but Asquith specified that it would be suspended until the cessation of hostilities – and repeated 'not later than the end of the present war'. That proved, in the event, to be an unexpectedly imprecise concept. The final – fourth – Home Rule Bill would not be laid before Parliament until April 1920, nearly eighteen months after the Armistice. By that point, though, the whole nature of the issue had changed, and partition – hazily and hesitantly implied in 1914 – had become fixed, both in principle and in form. It is perhaps misleading to suggest, as did a leading political analyst, that the Irish question was 'on ice for the duration' – 'there were no great debates, no dramatic moves'. The question was in fact transformed.[1]

Getting the 1914 Act on the statute book was contentious in itself; the opposition saw it as an abuse of the party truce agreed informally by the party leaders on the outbreak of the war – which was supposed to exclude controversial measures. On the somewhat lawyerly argument that (having passed through all its parliamentary stages) the bill was no longer 'actively' contentious, Asquith opted to ignore the sharp protests from the opposition. Even the well-behaved Austen Chamberlain fumed to Winston Churchill that he was 'trading on the patriotism of his opponents, to carry a most controversial Bill in its most controversial form'. Although Churchill insisted reassuringly (and surely accurately) that the government was achieving nothing more than the 'sentimental satisfaction of having an inoperative bill on the Statute Book', the atmosphere once again became poisonous.[2]

While the Unionists stormed out of the chamber, the Liberals and Irish nationalists abandoned the conventions of political decorum and exulted noisily.

Great debates and dramatic moves may have been missing, but during the war the political landscape shifted significantly. After ten months, amidst mounting criticism of his energy as a war leader, Asquith brought the Conservatives into the Cabinet; alongside Bonar Law and Balfour, they included Walter Long and Edward Carson. The implementation of home rule would henceforth be in the hands of a coalition whose Conservative element steadily increased. John Redmond, offered a place in the Cabinet – several times – found it politically inexpedient to accept. By the end of the war his party, which for a generation had embodied nationalist opinion, no longer did so. Its capacity to hold the British government to deliver the commitment to home rule without partition, already faltering at the beginning of the war, was annihilated.

The turning point was the rebellion launched by the anti-Redmondite fragment of the Irish Volunteers at Easter 1916. The first eighteen months of war had seen the position of the home rulers become more difficult. Redmond's politically risky commitment to support the war effort in 1914 was not answered by any positive gestures from the British authorities. Asquith no doubt saw enacting home rule as enough, and in turning down a Cabinet post Redmond lost the power to push through his cherished project of turning Irish National Volunteer recruits to British regiments into an 'Irish army' by keeping their own formations, officers, and visual distinctions. This was doggedly opposed by the military command with what Lloyd George would later brand as 'stupidities beyond belief' that 'almost look like malignancy'; too late, sadly, to do anything about it.[3] The War Office's early concession of pastoral provisions for Catholic troops was as far as it would go. 'Everything, almost, that we asked for was refused, and everything, almost, that we protested against was done,' Redmond told parliament in October 1916, by which time his warning that military policy would turn Irish public enthusiasm into 'affront, disheartenment and hurt' had been amply borne out.[4]

Meanwhile, the 'Ulstermen' enlisted ostentatiously, carrying their identity firmly with them. The UVF ancestry of the 36th (Ulster)

Division was clear, even if UVF recruitment into it fell short of expectations.[5] It wore the Red Hand of Ulster as its divisional badge, just like the UVF (albeit without the UVF's accompanying motto, 'For God and Ulster'). The name Ulster had never figured in the army list before. In Newtownards, on the night of 23 April 1915, 350 soldiers of the Royal Inniskilling Fusiliers and Royal Irish Rifles sallied out of their depot to the town hall. Headed by a band, they marched through the streets with banners celebrating the anniversary of the 'Ulster Gun-Running', singing and 'using party expressions'. To still any alarm in London, the police noted reassuringly that this was 'merely an isolated outburst', adding that on Easter Sunday eighty Irish National Volunteers had been suffered to assemble in Lisburn and march unmolested to take the train to Dublin to take part in a national review. Before the war such a parade would 'have provoked a riot'.[6]

A year after the National Volunteer review in Phoenix Park, when some 20,000 Volunteers paraded, the force had effectively died. Redmond committed the Volunteers to the war in September 1914, but in doing so he split the movement; those who stuck with him, renamed the National Volunteers, were then the overwhelming majority, but the minority proved to be far more coherent, dedicated, and determined in their aims. The republican group which quietly took control of the minority organization was not just opposed to Britain's war effort, it believed that the war offered a unique opportunity to launch its own war for independence. On Easter Monday 1916 the breakaway Irish Volunteers staged a rising in the centre of Dublin and a few provincial areas. The 1916 rebellion was a military failure, but it presented Redmond's party with a potentially lethal political threat. Since the outbreak of war Redmondites had energetically denounced 'Sinn Féin' as a lunatic fringe, but the sharpness of their hostility if anything gave greater substance to what was until then an outlook rather than an organization. At organizational level, Redmond could plausibly call it a 'little group . . . circulating anti-recruiting handbills and publishing little wretched rags'. There had been no successful Sinn Féin challenges to the Irish Party in by-elections. The initial public reaction to the rebellion, at least in Dublin, was unsympathetic. But the rebellion effectively humiliated the Irish administration, and the heavy-handed military repression that followed rapidly drained the majority support which John Dillon claimed was 'the fruit of our life work'; now, as he angrily told the government, it was 'washing out our whole life work in a sea of blood'. For Unionists, Dillon's desperate protest was no more than 'flamboyant rhetoric'. His 'blurting out his sympathy with England's enemies', Ronald McNeill wrote, 'justified the whole basis of Ulster's unchanging attitude towards Nationalism'.[7]

Asquith bestirred himself to make an extended trip to Ireland in mid-May – unprecedented for a prime minister in office. Casting about for a successor to Augustine Birrell, who had resigned as Chief Secretary amidst the collapse of civil government in Dublin, and resisting Tory pressure to appoint Walter Long, he took on the job himself for the time being. Although one of the senior officials he talked to in Dublin cattily suggested that 'the wearied PM' had not got beyond 'perfunctory' conversation about casual topics, he reached some awkward conclusions. The Irish administration had been tested to destruction. Shortly after he returned on 19 May, he told his Cabinet colleagues that the suppression of the rebellion had 'aroused a good deal of uneasiness and sympathy' among many who had 'lent no countenance to the outbreak'. Did this outbalance the fact that on his walkabout in Dublin he had been 'received, not only without disrespect, but with remarkable warmth'?[8] Asquith naturally hoped so, which sustained his hope that the old home rule policy would still work, but in Belfast he was brought up sharply against its limits.

The Lord Mayor, Sir Crawford McCullagh – 'a level-headed and public-spirited man', Asquith thought – had already told him that he could not accept the proposal 'that all Arms in Ireland should be forthwith delivered up to the Crown'. Attempting to enforce it would be likely to lead to disturbance, 'as it would be looked upon by the population that they were being punished for the offence of the Sinn Feiners'.[9] When he met Asquith, McCullagh delivered a blast of pure loyalist angst. 'We,' he said, had already sent 'the best of our manhood to the front'; if more joined up, 'we shall be left defenceless against a possible, even probable, Nationalist invasion of our province'. 'Our wives, our children, our homes, our industry. Our religion will be at the mercy of our hereditary foes.'[10] Most Unionists saw the rebellion not just as proof of their long-held conviction that Catholics were disloyal, but also as an opportunity to crush the nationalist threat for a generation. As one Belfast man put it, 'it is good business its having come to a head & I hope we shall deal thoroughly with these pests'. But others, notably the Irish Attorney General, insisted to Asquith that 'the only way to escape was by prompt settlement of the whole problem'.

'SETTLE IRELAND': LLOYD GEORGE'S PROJECT

In August 1914, Asquith had (privately) expressed his relief that, at least, the Irish imbroglio had been pushed aside. That temporary relief was now rudely ended. Not much relishing a return to the stalled pre-war negotiations, and still 'in despair for a Chief Secretary' to replace Birrell, Asquith enlisted Lloyd George to make 'a bold effort on fresh lines' to find a viable home rule measure. Having decided that the Irish Viceroyalty was a cumbersome throwback, sitting awkwardly alongside the Chief Secretaryship, he also proposed to merge the two posts, offering the Minister of Munitions a full-scale job as Minister for Ireland.

This he refused; and why he took up, even 'for a short time', as Asquith suggested, the *unique* opportunity' of finding a 'permanent solution' – given how consuming the work at Munitions was – is not easy to say. It seems unlikely that he was seduced by Margot Asquith's suggestion that 'if you want to please Henry and me and do a *big thing* settle Ireland'? (She mischievously added that 'anyone with wit and a sense of humour must enjoy Ireland, trying as the Irish are'.)[11] Lloyd George never gave the impression of being amused by or truly interested in Irish issues, but his interventions in the pre-war Ulster crisis showed his natural inclination to find technical solutions to structural problems. They also clearly mapped a path towards a solution which would not find support amongst all his Cabinet colleagues. He was given an imprecise brief – at 'the unanimous request' of the Cabinet – which he interpreted as a free hand. The Unionists seem to have assumed, in line with a speech by Asquith at Ladybank on 14

June, that there would be no final settlement until the end of the war – when, the prime minister said, 'relations' both between Britain and Ireland 'and between the UK and our Dominions will of necessity be brought under close and connected review'. Asquith had also told the Cabinet in May that the Home Rule Act could not come into operation until the end of the war. But he also invoked the need for a 'prompt settlement' of the immediate Irish crisis.

Lloyd George unsurprisingly took this as a call to rapid action, and a mandate to offer home rule immediately if he could get the consent of both sides in Ireland. As early as 19 May, even before the Cabinet asked him to begin, he told T. P. O'Connor, 'if I am allowed to make some arrangement about Ulster I can promise to get you Home Rule for all the rest of Ireland'.[12] On 10 June he warned Dillon that 'unless the settlement goes through quickly, nothing can be accomplished until the war is over'. In light of the situation in Ireland it was already clear that Redmond would and could negotiate only on the basis of immediate home rule, but the pace and scope of the discussions Lloyd George launched dismayed hardline Unionists like Lord Lansdowne and Walter Long, who also protested that the negotiations had been supposed to be confidential. They were, in the sense that no record of them was made, but they became uncomfortably public when the leaders eventually set out to secure the consent of their followers.

Up to that point, Lloyd George's negotiating technique seemed to be working. Frances Stevenson, his secretary, deftly outlined it: 'he would take one party into one room and tell them one thing, and the other into another room and tell them another'. This was meant not to mislead, exactly, but to 'influence their minds and bring them together'. The question was how different the 'one' and 'other' thing were. Whether Lloyd George was entirely honest in these Irish negotiations has been disputed ever since. He may have exceeded the Cabinet's (somewhat opaque) instructions in offering immediate home rule, and it is easy enough to see why, but he went beyond this in suggesting to Carson that his colleagues had called for a settlement before the end of the war, and also suggesting that they saw American opinion as a crucial factor in the issue.

In May 1916, Lloyd George offered Carson and James Craig the exclusion *en bloc* of six Ulster counties. This was a major shift from the kind of exclusion terms discussed before the war. It was a clear improvement, from a Unionist viewpoint, on the offer of a county-by-county plebiscite, but Carson knew it would be a hard sell because most unionists still clung to the idea of excluding the whole nine-county province of Ulster. The truly vital concession Lloyd George now made was that exclusion should become permanent. The need for this concession spoke volumes about loyalist fears and suspicions. Many had noted by this stage that in practice temporary exclusion would almost inevitably become permanent – it would be virtually impossible to reverse a temporary exclusion, to force excluded counties back under an Irish government – but loyalists were not impressed by such pragmatic arguments. Permanence had to be spelled out in principle, in writing. This Lloyd George did in a note he gave Carson on 29 May – 'We must make it clear that at the end of the provisional period Ulster does not, whether she wills it or not, merge with the rest of Ireland.' The meaning of this was not, in fact, absolutely clear (indeed it has been called 'ambiguous'), but it did the trick.[13]

Carson presented the idea of six-county exclusion to the Standing Committee of the UUC on 3 June. The atmosphere was chilly: 'they received me as coldly as any audience has ever received a man who has a proposition to put before them'. In the end, only the fact that the Home Rule Act was already on the statute book – its repeal was 'not practical politics' – and the argument that 'in this crisis in the Empire's history, it is our duty to make sacrifices', swayed them. The abandonment of their co-religionists outside Ulster had at least been envisaged for some time, but the prospect of 'losing' three counties of the covenanted province (Cavan, Donegal, and Monaghan) still dismayed many. The belief that they were betraying the 1912 Coven-ant damaged their cherished sense of consistency. When the UUC met on 6 June, Carson had to intensify the 'practical politics' argu-ment, and add a dose of military psychology. 'I tell you honestly, I was as keen on the rifles and volunteers as ever a man was', but he called on his audience to imagine the British soldiers who had 'fought the battle of the Empire with our men at the front'. If Ulster went on resisting home rule for the whole of Ireland, 'They will come and ask you, "What are you fighting for?" . . . They will say. "You were offered six counties clean and free and you would not have it. You would rather go on and rather fight . . ." 'It is not possible,' he thundered, 'I tell you it is not possible.'[14]

Loyalists found several reasons for following their leader. One reluctant UUC convert, Hugh de Fellenberg Montgomery, was 'convinced that [Carson and Craig] were convinced that the Cabinet was unanimously resolved to do this and that American and Colonial complications were of a sufficiently serious nature to account for (though not to excuse or to justify) such a very unfortunate decision'. He accepted that 'if we did not take this offer we should never get as good a one again', and argued that 'we should be in a better position to hold our own and help our friends with only six counties returning 16 unionists and 9 Nationalists' – better placed also 'to help Unionists in any part of Ireland than if we formed a portion of a permanent minority in a Dublin Parliament'.[15] Fred Crawford later wrote a pamphlet justifying his decision to vote for a six-county unit, arguing that it was not a breach of the Covenant because a loyal Ulster would strengthen the Empire. He called up a vivid simile – including the other three counties would be like overloading a lifeboat. 'If they get into the boat they will go down just as surely as if they had stayed on the wreck, and they will have drowned the lifeboat load of passengers who would otherwise have had their lives saved.'[16]

Southern Unionists were all too aware that they were being left to 'go down'. Although the divergence between Ulster Unionists and the rest had been growing over time, this was the first point at which Ulster accepted a scheme which would formally divide them. As Henry Robinson would tell Walter Long, the southern Unionists had 'had a bad shock over the way Bonar Law, Carson etc have chucked them'.[17] The shock would prove fatal to the Lloyd George plan. As early as 23 May they met to denounce the reopening of the home rule issue 'in disregard of the party truce', and 'deprecate any permanent change being made . . . without the prior consent of the electors of Great Britain and Ireland'.[18] In response Lloyd George quickly brandished the war situation – urging the leading southern Unionist Lord Midleton that not only was the situation in Ireland itself 'very threatening', but since the Easter rebellion Irish-American opinion had turned pro-German, which might prevent the election of any pro-Allied president, and eventually terminate the supply of American munitions. This was laying it on rather thick, and Midleton was resolutely unimpressed, also disputing Lloyd George's insistence that the proposal would remain provisional until the end of the war. 'A parliament once given could not be taken away.'[19] (This argument would reappear often over the next few years.) In June, Lloyd George reported to Dillon that 'the Southern Unionists are working hard and skilfully against settlement ... bringing unwonted pressure to bear on the Unionist members of the Cabinet; ... sending paragraphs to all the London newspapers of the most gruesome character as to disloyal demonstrations in Ireland'.[20]

Enlisting Herbert Samuel to deal once again with the complex fiscal issues, Lloyd George pressed on with preparing legislation to bring home rule into effect immediately, with the six counties excluded and placed under the administration of a Secretary of State – an arrangement that could be extended (by Order in Council) if no other agreement was reached within a year of the war's end. A permanent Irish settlement would be discussed after the war by an Imperial conference, where the Dominions would join in recasting the government of the Empire. 'Possibly something of this sort might do', hazarded the parliamentary draftsman, A. T. Thring.[21] Or possibly not, as soon became clear. Technically, the exclusion offered to Ulster was provisional, and this was the definite impression that the nationalist leaders took from their meeting with Lloyd George in May. All he seems to have said to them, though, was that if the nationalists accepted the arrangement he and the prime minister would not agree to 'any further concessions being thrust upon us'.

Redmond set out to gauge the likely response to the proposal amongst northern nationalists. In early June he met the Belfast party leader, Joe Devlin, and Jeremiah McVee, the MP for South Down, who painted an unpromising picture. Three northern Catholic bishops had come out against it even before it appeared in the press (on 12 June, reporting the Ulster debates), and perhaps even more seriously the *Irish Independent* – owned by William Martin Murphy and a long-standing opponent of Redmond's party – had launched a ferocious anti-partition campaign. Its intensity can be judged by the number of its hostile editorials – thirty-eight out of fifty-two issues in June and July, including unbroken runs of thirteen in June and sixteen in July, featuring international echoes – 'No Irish Alsace' – as well as verbal plays on 'mutilation' and 'perdition'.[22] In light of this, Devlin's first effort to sell the settlement in his Belfast constituency on 17 June was a striking success. But to carry a bigger meeting of over 500 nationalist delegates from all six counties on 23 June not only required Devlin's unique political skill in opposition to the clergy, but also drew deeply on Redmond's dwindling reserve of political capital. His announcement that he would resign if the proposal was voted down (which had left the Catholic bishops unmoved) proved enough to carry it. The size of the majority – 475 to 265 – briefly encouraged the party to think there was a way through. A party meeting at the Mansion House in Dublin expressed extravagant praise for the 'magnificent spirit of patriotic self-sacrifice' displayed by the northern nationalists.[23]

The partition issue was still one which most nationalists found impossible to deal with rationally. Their reluctance to confront it would long persist. When, in 1972, he raised the question of how the 1916 leaders thought 'an unpartitioned Ireland could be won', Conor Cruise O'Brien noted that 'our school histories do not seriously discuss the ideas and policies of the men of 1916 in relation to the Protestants of Ulster'. Indeed he thought there had been 'no previous discussion of this problem, at any level'. As a preliminary contribution, he presented an extended analysis of James Connolly's writings, which 'like almost all Irish nationalist writing' was 'touched by a curious flicker or stammer when this question comes into view'. He traced Connolly's erratic use of the phrase 'the people of Ireland' to both include and exclude 'non-Catholics', and dwelt on Connolly's 'astonishing and ominous' elision of nineteenth-century Belfast from his *Labour in Irish History*. It was hard, he suggested, not to conclude that 'the Protestant workers of Belfast, *as they actually were and with the feelings and loyalties they actually had*, were not consistently felt by Connolly to be part of Irish History'.[24] They had excluded themselves from the Irish nation, yet they remained part of it, and would ultimately have to accept that.

As the 1916 negotiations unfolded, there was in fact a hint of public debate, with a handful of nationalists trying to weigh the inevitability, and maybe even the desirability, of partition. One remarkable contribution, by Fr Michael O'Flanagan (who would the next year become Vice-President of Sinn Féin) in the *Freeman's Journal* on 20 June, presented a theoretic exploration of the concept of nationality, insisting that 'in the last analysis the test of nationality is the wish of the people'. (As in Ernest Renan's famous formula, the nation was a 'daily plebiscite'.) O'Flanagan accepted that the Unionists of Ulster had 'never transferred their love and allegiance to Ireland'; they might be Irelanders in a geographical sense, 'but they are not Irish in the national sense'. Endorsing the argument that nationalists instinctively rejected, he pointed out that 'we claim the right to decide what is to be our nation', but 'refuse them the same right'.[25]

Alongside O'Flanagan's reluctant realism, Edmund Vesey Knox, a former Irish Party MP (who had sat for both Cavan and Londonderry), offered a more positive take: because nationality was about 'community of thought' rather than territory, division would actually be a good thing, allowing the Catholic, Irish Ireland to flourish as a homogeneous people and – he observed – avoiding the kind of mistake Germany had made in seizing Alsace and Lorraine. Such wide perspectives, though, were unusual, and generally repudiated in favour of the instinctual identification of the nation with the island. As a contributor to the *Irish Independent* protested, 'Ireland is a compact, perfect nation, bounded on all sides by the broad Atlantic . . . We hold it in trust for our children and our children's children until the end of time.' Partition was therefore not just undesirable but impossible: 'we cannot give away that which we have not to give'.[26]

THE PROJECT STYMIED

Five days before the Mansion House meeting, the coalition Unionists had finally discovered that Lloyd George's plan would bring home rule into effect immediately, not at the end of the war. A Cabinet crisis erupted, threatening the survival of the coalition government. Hugh Montgomery wryly opined to his son that Bonar Law, Walter Long, and other British Unionist leaders had been 'Asquixiated', and Carson had kept his head better. But while Bonar Law was indeed curiously complacent, Long was one of those – alongside Lords Selborne and Lansdowne, and Hugh Cecil – who never accepted the Lloyd George scheme. Long told Lloyd George on 29 May, before he knew any of its details, that he should be careful not to give the southern Unionists any impression that he was negotiating with 'the Ulster people' and the nationalists 'behind their backs'. When Long got to see a rough draft of the scheme next day, he instantly announced that 'no Unionists, Irish or English, would accept either the immediate setting up of a Parliament in Ireland, which was contrary to what I understood to be the intention of the Government', or 'the suggestion that the exclusion of Ulster was to be subject to revision at the end of the war'.[27] He hot-footed it to Lansdowne, who in turn immediately visited Lloyd George to tell him he 'could not accept' the scheme. After both men attended a Cabinet committee meeting with Asquith, Lloyd George, and Lord Crewe on 1 June, Lansdowne sent Asquith an extended critique of the proposals.

Lansdowne denounced not only the plan's failure to protect 'the loyal minority outside the excluded area', but also the (he claimed) 'much discredited' idea of exclusion itself. The only viable possibilities for him were 'home rule within home rule' or some kind of general scheme of devolution for the whole of the United Kingdom. But such a concept of UK federalism, which Long favoured, was obviously 'a gigantic enterprise which no sane politician' would envisage in the midst of a war. He protested that if 'Castle government' disappeared and an Irish parliament with its own executive was established, 'the triumph of lawlessness and disloyalty would be complete'. Still, he was at least prepared to go along with Asquith's idea of abolishing the lord lieutenancy so the Chief Secretary could govern directly with an Irish council.

So far, Long's opposition to the scheme had been more muted, but early in June he realized that he was being accused of being more than 'Asquixiated', but (notably by H. A. Gwynne, editor of the *Morning Post*) of abandoning the Unionists and indeed the union itself. Seriously jolted, he set about defeating the project. On 11 June he lectured Lloyd George on the dangerous state of Ireland – 'very different from what I believed it to be . . . not the moment to embark on any political experiment' – and complaining that 'the Unionist

Party in Ireland are being driven by the prime Minister and the Minister of Munitions into accepting a situation which they know to be morally wrong and wrong politically'. He could not, he concluded, 'assent to any agreement including the adoption of Home Rule'. Lloyd George chose to take this as a personal betrayal, complaining rather shrilly that 'it would have been fairer to a colleague who was undertaking a risky & a thankless task had you expressed [these] views at the time I was chosen to negotiate. When I consulted you some days ago it was not too late to avert irretrievable committal.' But now things had gone so far 'they cannot be put right except by my resignation'.[28] (His letter of resignation remained a draft, however, as Long may well have expected.) Long, 'really amazed at your letter' as he said, pointed out that he could not have objected when Lloyd George took up the task, since at that point 'no mention was made of any scheme'. As soon as he had got wind of the argument put to the Ulster leaders that the Cabinet had authorized Lloyd George to say that 'national emergency and especially the fear of complications with America rendered necessary an *immediate* grant of home rule', he had objected to it.

Long quickly fired off a barrage of memos to the Unionists in the Cabinet, charging Lloyd George with having 'misunderstood his position from beginning to end', and committing the Cabinet to 'wholesale and drastic changes' which the facts did not justify.[29] Lord Selborne weighed in on 16 June, telling Asquith that not only had he not agreed to the Lloyd George scheme, he had never even heard it discussed – and unless it was publicly repudiated he would resign. The Unionist ministers met next day at Lord Curzon's house to consider Long's memoranda, and Curzon then went with Cecil to confront Asquith. They found that the prime minister had failed to grasp the scope of Lloyd George's proposals, but would not repudiate them. The issue came to a head at two Cabinet meetings in late June, showing how far the Ulster Unionists, who had accepted the Lloyd George scheme, had become divided from those who opposed any grant of home rule during the war, and still rejected partition in principle. The latter were teetering on the brink of resignation. Austen Chamberlain, who had accepted Carson's line, lamented Asquith's 'failure to consult the Cabinet', and told Balfour that if Cecil,

Lansdowne, Long, and Selborne resigned, 'I don't think I can stop in'. Asquith was reduced to the desperate defensive line that 'at this critical juncture in the war, a series of resignations' – probably causing the government to collapse – would be 'not only a national calamity but a national crime'.[30]

Long, a four-square Tory for whom political imagination was potentially suspect, was deeply disturbed. For him, to sacrifice the union in order to win the war was absurd: the two objectives were equally vital. Home rule was 'sheer madness', but it was (as he wrote to the Irish Attorney General, James Campbell, on 29 June) 'very hard work fighting Carson and all his Ulster colleagues'. 'Fancy James Craig,' he added incredulously, 'spending ¾ hour here trying to persuade me, with tears in his eyes, to vote for Home Rule!' He was 'utterly puzzled by the line adopted' by Bonar Law, Balfour, and Carson, wondering if there could be 'some reasons operating with them which I know nothing about'. He now trusted 'nobody a bit outside this office'.[31] Carson reciprocated: Lloyd George told Asquith he was 'very angry with Long who has actually been telling his Ulster people to throw Carson over'. Carson's wife was contemptuous of the Cabinet – 'all playing a low game except LG' – and especially Long (who 'says he is an honest gentleman', she sardonically noted in her diary on 19 June). He 'would be better hoeing turnips than in the Cabinet'.[32]

If any Unionist leader had been 'Asquixiated' it seemed to be Balfour, no less, who now decided that home rule with partition was the best available outcome. His argument was 'if we must have Home Rule, let us at least exclude from its operation as much of Unionist Ireland as is possible'. Before the war, exclusion had looked likely to apply to four counties; under Lloyd George's scheme six Ulster counties would secure their permanent place in the United Kingdom 'by consent and without bloodshed', so averting what he coolly described as 'the hazard of civil war'. He challenged any of his Unionist colleagues to say that 'if their fate be deferred till peace is declared, terms equally good could be obtained without a dangerous struggle.' He also dismissed the danger which nearly all Unionists claimed would be posed by an autonomous Ireland: 'personally, I do not think there is the least chance of the Irish representatives deliberately making themselves willing instruments in the hands of our enemies'.[33]

As Foreign Secretary, Balfour was particularly concerned about the American attitude, but (as Hugh Montgomery noted) the Cabinet fretted about it throughout the war. In 1916 it seemed to be especially worrying: at the moment Lloyd George was conducting his discussions, American opinion was fuming against the execution of the rebel leaders in Dublin. Irish-Americans were outraged, the British ambassador in Washington chillingly reporting that they had 'blood in their eyes when they look our way'. Even former President Theodore Roosevelt, no Anglophobe, remarked that he wished 'your people had not shot the leaders of the Irish rebels after they surrendered'.[34] At the end of June, Roger Casement was sentenced to death in London (the only 1916 leader to be charged with high treason, the prosecution being led by Carson's friend F. E. Smith), triggering an intense American public campaign for a reprieve. Lloyd George took US opinion very seriously, warning that the Irish-American vote might 'break our blockade and force an ignominious peace on us, unless something is done'.

How serious this bogy really was might be debated: Lansdowne agreed with Long that they were being 'bluffed by the American peril'. It was roundly dismissed, in the sharpest ministerial critique of the Lloyd George negotiations, by Robert Cecil, the blockade minister – Ulster had been pushed into them by an exaggerated alarm about 'serious American and Colonial complications'.[35] Like Lord Midleton, Cecil maintained that Ireland must be kept under martial law while the war lasted, with home rule granted in principle only (as of course it already had been). Still, most of his colleagues were acutely sensitive to American opinion, and remained so even after the United States entered the war in April 1917. (Indeed, President Woodrow Wilson would immediately instruct the US ambassador to let Lloyd George know that the only barrier to 'absolutely cordial' Anglo-American relations was 'the failure to find a satisfactory method of self-government for Ireland'.)[36]

As the Cabinet crisis intensified, Lloyd George must have feared he was being hung out to dry. When Asquith urged the nationalist leaders to come to London immediately, Redmond hesitated, suspecting it would be 'as well not to be there' since the government was likely to call on him for more 'concessions'. He had an encouraging report from Devlin and O'Connor after meetings with Lloyd George, Bonar Law, and Craig, but on 29 June Lansdowne announced in the Lords that the Cabinet could not be bound by the proposals unless they could satisfy parliament that they were necessary to 'prevent a recurrence' of disorder – something they could not demonstrate. Dillon, who had 'all along suspected treachery', fumed that he had never expected 'anything so cynically treacherous'.[37] To keep Lansdowne on board, Asquith and Lloyd George came up with a guarantee that while the war lasted, there would be 'special safeguards for the maintenance of Imperial control of all Naval and Military conditions in Ireland'. The prime minister convened another Cabinet committee to consider the necessary modifications of the Home Rule Act that would be needed, and the Unionists agreed to stay on until it reported – Long only 'at Lansdowne's urgent request in order to help him'.[38] Lansdowne had now clearly decided not to resign, and began to work steadily on Long, urging him to help in the effort to secure 'the kind of safeguards for which Bob Cecil and I are fighting at this moment'. Someone leaked to *The Times* the story that Long was taking a harder line on the proposal than the other Unionists in the Cabinet, and an extraordinary delegation of sixty-four Unionist MPs and six peers called on Long at the Local Government Board on 4 July to press him not to go.

Finally, at a Cabinet meeting the next day, Long conceded. Reluctantly (his position, he complained, was a cruel one) he recognized that 'a considerable section of the Unionist party' would follow him if he resigned, and this might seriously weaken the government at a critical time in the war. A relieved Asquith praised the 'patriotism and public spirit' he and Lansdowne had shown, and went on to make the settlement proposals public in a Commons statement on 10 July. He stressed that they were provisional, until a permanent agreement was reached after the war. But while reiterating that [Irish] 'union can never be brought about without the free will and assent of the excluded area', he made clear that he still believed it should be the ultimate goal. When Carson called on him to confirm that 'the six counties will definitely be struck out of the Act of 1914', and asked whether 'at any time afterwards they could be included by a bill?', Asquith said 'they could not be included without a bill'.[39] It would therefore remain technically, if not politically, possible to pass a home rule act for a united Ireland.

This time it was Lansdowne who jibbed at the implication that the exclusion of Ulster might not be permanent. He instantly went back on the offensive, spelling out in the Lords on 11 July (in a debate on the Royal Commission report on the 1916 rebellion) that the maintenance of order in Ireland was the priority, and insisting that the structural alterations to the 1914 Home Rule Act in the bill resulting from the Lloyd George negotiations would be 'permanent and enduring' – this meant that partition would be irreversible. Lansdowne went further, trampling gratuitously on Irish nationalist sensitivity by spelling out that the Defence of the Realm Act would remain in force, indeed its emergency powers would be strengthened if necessary, and that an Irish parliament – 'whenever it is called into existence' – would never be able to interfere with it. General Maxwell, the military commander in Ireland (wrongly believed by many to be military governor), would be given whatever support he required, and jury trial would be superseded by special Resident Magistrates' courts in unsettled areas.

Once again Lansdowne was effectively holding Asquith to ransom, challenging him either to accept his interpretation of government policy or to sack him from the Cabinet. Redmond was outraged, denouncing this 'gross insult to Ireland' and 'gross breach of faith' – breaking the terms of the new proposal and amounting to 'a declaration of war on the Irish people'. If Lansdowne was speaking for the government, it would mean 'an end to all hope of settlement'. Redmond's own position was perilous; the hostile *Irish Independent* celebrated the 'bursting of the "temporary" bubble' as a humiliation for the Irish Party.[40] He made one more effort to get Asquith to adhere to the agreed terms, above all the 'temporary and provisional character of ALL the sections of the bill', but on 19 July the Cabinet confirmed Lansdowne and Long's interpretation – the exclusion of the six counties would be permanent.

It may have been influenced by a well-timed meeting of the parliamentary Imperial Unionist Association (ninety-eight MPs and seventy-six peers) a couple of days before, which warned that establishing a home rule parliament during the war would be 'a serious danger to the peace of Ireland and the Imperial interest'. Although Redmond went to a meeting with Asquith and Herbert Samuel three days later, nothing changed: Samuel had been sharply reminded by Carson on 21 July that 'to leave a suggestion in the Bill that the question of inclusion was to come up for consideration when the war is over is quite impossible'.[41] Redmond was simply presented with the draft bill, which he duly told them would 'meet with the vehement opposition at all its stages of the Irish Party'. The sequel was inevitable: Asquith noted that the bill would not be taken forward. 'There can of course be no question of introducing a bill to which you and your friends are not prepared to assent.'[42]

The date of 22 July 1916 has been labelled the moment that 'really finished the constitutional party and overthrew Redmond's power'.[43] The last chance, almost certainly, to rescue the home rule idea and head off the upsurge of separatist republicanism was lost. Why was what the *Manchester Guardian* branded 'a little aristocratic clique' able to torpedo the Lloyd George scheme? 'An appalling failure of judgement and nerve' on Asquith's part, it has been suggested – by Lloyd George's biographer, for whom Lloyd George also came up short when his repeated threats of resignation were revealed as bluff. Even the loyal Frances Stevenson at first thought he would have 'done himself less harm by leaving the Government . . . I don't think he has quite played the game'.[44]

Timing was also important. While the Cabinet was fencing over home rule, the Somme offensive was beginning: the stupendous bombardment opened on 24 June, and the assault was scheduled for the 29th. In fact it was launched on 1 July, giving an extra edge to Asquith's plea for government stability. This profoundly wrong-headed operation, with its grievous human cost and apparent futility, also presented a searching test of faith in the British army and those directing it. Ulster, by chance, was at the centre of this, and the losses suffered by the 36th Division on the first day of the battle – the anniversary of the 1690 battle of the Boyne – emphatically symbolized the reality of Ulster loyalty (a quality which had sometimes been – and would still more often in future be – impugned). Despite the ineffectiveness of the artillery bombardment the division had a dramatic success, reaching the fourth German trench line at Thiepval, but was left exposed when units alongside it failed. Its casualties were huge – over 5,000 on the first two days – and the 12 July celebrations were replaced by a day of public mourning.

James Craig's elder brother Charles, the MP for South Antrim, was, incidentally, taken prisoner at Thiepval. Also in the battle was Wilfrid Spender, now a General Staff Officer in the 36th Division, who won a Military Cross there. The Somme was soon to be celebrated, in part, as a decisive rebuke to those who had implied that the construct of the 'Ulsterman' was imaginary.[45] The Devonian Spender wrote on 2 July, 'I am not an Ulsterman but yesterday . . . as I followed their amazing attack, I felt that I would rather be an Ulsterman than anything else in the world'.[46] (The division won 'undying fame', he later judged, because it 'was largely composed of men who had the true Crusading spirit'.) The 'Ulster division' immediately assumed a key place in the projection of those men's ethnic identity; its striking war memorial at Thiepval would be built in an assertively Scottish 'baronial revival' style.

THE GREY EMINENCE OF
WALTER LONG

The stalling of the Lloyd George project marked the end of negotiations between the government and the Irish parties. Also the end, for four years, of Lloyd George's close involvement with Irish policy: when Redmond met him early in 1917 he could see that 'though he had [Ireland] on his mind he had not given it any serious attention'. On the brink of the June 1916 Cabinet crisis, Lloyd George had gloomily told Dillon that should his settlement fail, 'I shudder at what may happen meanwhile in Ireland'. If the country could not be governed with the assent of the Irish people, 'there is no doubt it will have to be governed by force. But nobody knows better than you,' he added, 'what coercion would mean under these conditions.' British people were getting 'accustomed to scenes of blood. Their own sons are falling by the hundred thousand, and the nation is harder and more ruthless than it has ever been.'[47] This was no doubt intended to rack up the pressure on the nationalists to accept partition, but it was a chilling insight. Oddly, though, when his project failed and he abandoned any direct involvement in Ireland for the duration, Lloyd George handed responsibility for it to an arch-coercionist. After he became prime minister in December 1916, leading a refounded co-alition with a markedly more Conservative cast, he increasingly brought Walter Long into the centre of Irish policymaking.

It was clear that unless Long was on board he could be an awkward opponent, but his influence also stemmed from the fact (so typical of British politics) that he was almost alone amongst ministers in having a deep and abiding interest in Ireland.[48] His view might have been blinkered, but it was assertively held. The archetypal 'backwoodsman', his very consistent echt-Toryism ensured him a substantial following in the Conservative Party (which he always called the Unionist Party), and might well have propelled him to its leadership in succession to Balfour if his ambition had been better focused. A grim encounter he had with Bonar Law just after Lansdowne's 11 July speech showed the difference between them: Long witheringly dismissed his leader as 'in Carson's pocket as regards Ireland & in Lloyd George's as regards all other affairs of Government'. Worse yet, he had 'entirely lost his nerve. As the boys say, "he is in a blue funk".' Bonar Law 'moaned' that the government would break up, '& what is to happen then?' Long icily asked him if he was 'prepared to make a stand for anything'.[49]

When the question of the Irish Chief Secretaryship came up once again, Long seemed an obvious candidate, but he had enough polit-ical awareness to back off. Perhaps, if 'it were made clear that it was my duty, and that I should be given a free hand and be backed by the whole Cabinet', he thought he might consider it, but he knew the reality 'would be very different'. Eventually the uninviting respons-ibility was taken up at the end of July by another straight up-and-down Unionist, Henry Duke. ('We must have a Unionist' as Chief Sec-retary, Asquith explained to Redmond.) This was balanced by a sort of 'greening' of the Irish Administration, with three Catholics – two of them Irish – appointed as Under Secretary, Inspector General of the Royal Irish Constabulary, and General Officer Commanding the army. (Maxwell's unofficially assumed title of commander-in-chief lapsed with him when he was transferred in November.) Crucially, although the Viceroy was re-appointed, he was not in the Cabinet; the Chief Secretary was now the sole minister responsible for Irish policy.

Long stayed in London – moving from the Local Government Board to the Colonial Office when Lloyd George became prime minister – but he was not prepared to cede control of Irish policy to the steady, colourless Chief Secretary. Long first thought Duke 'nearly, though not quite, as good as anybody there is' for the job, but soon had to lecture him on his role – he had not been sent to Ireland to achieve a settlement. Later in 1916 he was insisting that Duke was 'wrong both in his general view of the situation and in his conclusions'. Duke's idea that 'the present feeling of soreness against England' sprang from a belief that the home rule negotiations had broken down because of the 'bad faith of the English Government', Long dismissed as 'pure nonsense'. When the Irish prisoners began to be released at Christmas he protested, 'I don't understand Duke's policy, the release of some of the worst Sinn Feiners is deplorable', and if anything had worsened the problem of recruitment.[50] Worst of all was Duke's sanguine notion that partition need not happen. In December he seemingly laid out before Redmond the idea of a statutory commission of five Irishmen who might bring the Home Rule Act into operation as soon as possible for 'all Ireland'.

Duke started out from the standard position of knowing almost nothing about Ireland, and never managed to assert his status as the Cabinet's expert on it. By 1918 he had to face not just the withering contempt of Long's friends in the Irish administration, Robinson and Campbell – who told Bonar Law that Duke had 'lost his nerve if he ever had any' – but also the disappointment of Liberal ministers. When Duke jumped ship during the spring 1918 conscription crisis, his Cabinet colleague H. A. L. Fisher crushingly noted that he had given the Cabinet 'no steady counsel' as Chief Secretary.[51] Steadiness was what Long had, or seemed to have, in spades. In fact, his frequent memoranda, usually presenting 'absolutely reliable' reports from his Irish contacts, often mirrored their alarmism, but they were underpinned by a simple psychological analysis, repeatedly reiterated. The Irish were docile if firmly governed, but they were 'bad people to run away from'. Long blandly assured Lloyd George in February 1917 that he was 'not of opinion that the whole cause of Ireland's trouble is her [sic] connection with England.' It was, rather, 'due to her inability ever to be content with anything'.[52]

Long's inexorable movement towards becoming the lynchpin of the coalition's Irish policy was signposted early in 1917 when he was semi-formally appointed as the Cabinet's main contact with the Irish administration. He began to argue that the Irish be given responsibility for negotiating a settlement – telling the Cabinet in May that 'Ireland will never accept a scheme devised on this side'. He was also, and perhaps more surprisingly, drawn to the programme of UK federalism which was currently being promoted by F. S. Oliver, Leo Amery and others – clever men on the fringes of power. Its charm for Long was precisely that it offered a framework for incorporating Irish home rule into a series of devolutionary divisions of the whole United Kingdom. It had other virtues: the current 'congestion' of the British parliament under a much too complex legislative burden would be simplified by devolution. But enlarging the constitutional framework, possibly bringing in Long's South African experience, was paramount. He had made an extended trip to South Africa in 1909, met Jan Smuts and Sir Leander Starr Jameson (who had gone on from his disastrous raid to become prime minister of Cape Colony), and discussed the constitutional convention which had debated various federal and unitary systems for the four colonies. This convention was clearly in Long's mind in 1917.

At the same time, Lloyd George commissioned Professor W. G. S. Adams, a leading member of his private secretariat (the 'garden suburb' housed in the back yard of 10 Downing Street), as special adviser on Irish affairs. In March, Adams – who had once worked in the Irish Department of Agriculture and Technical Instruction, and now held the Gladstone chair of politics at Oxford – pointed up what the Cabinet was still reluctant to grasp: Sinn Féin doctrine was becoming more pervasive, while the Irish Party's influence was in obvious decline. At the same time, Ulster had become even more detached since the rebellion. Adams perceived that Sinn Féin was more an atmosphere than a formal party, though his suggestion that 'there are no recognised leaders' – reasonable enough at the time – was potentially misleading. With the argument that any settlement 'depends on the Irish themselves', he suggested convening an all-party convention.[53]

Long, who had done as much as anyone to accelerate the collapse of the Irish Party, still thought it could survive if Sinn Féin was repressed, and for him the absence of significant figures in the Sinn Féin organization was encouraging. Lloyd George now floated the idea of self-government for south-western Ireland only, and in mid-April a three-man Cabinet committee was set up to draft a bill as a basis for discussion between the Irish 'parties'. Long was not a member (it was chaired by Curzon, with Duke and Addison), but handed out erratic advice, urging the prime minister in April that it was 'far better to postpone and again rather than have failure', yet soon telling him 'it is the moment for a bold policy'. In May, Lloyd George offered Redmond the choice between the Curzon committee's bill and a national convention, and as Long predicted ('partition they won't have') Redmond opted for the latter.

CONVENTIONAL WISDOM

The Irish Convention which met from July 1917 until April the following year has received fairly short shrift at the hands of historians, who have seen it as a classic talking shop, a 'gigantic irrelevance', intended to kick the can down the road – 'to divert the energies of the Irish parties and to clothe Lloyd George's nakedness before the USA'.[54] The remark of the editor of *The Times*, that 'every day it sits is a day gained', seemed to bear this out, as did the Attorney General F. E. Smith addressing that vital American audience early in 1918: 'Let them keep on talking.'[55] By that point the Convention had been talking for six months. Actually the logic of the Convention was irrefutable: given that the British government was not prepared (then or later) to impose an arrangement by force, only a settlement agreed by all significant Irish political groups had any chance of working. And, as its chairman Sir Horace Plunkett defensively pointed out, while technically the Convention's task was to draft an Irish constitution, 'it would be more correct to say that we had to find a way out of the most complex and anomalous political situation to be found in history' – or even, he added for good measure, in fiction.[56] In reality, sadly, its seemingly interminable discussions – not made any less convoluted by Plunkett's idiosyncratic chairmanship – seemed to produce nothing.

The Convention's eventual report – signed up to by fewer than half its members – was already nugatory because two key groups either sidelined or boycotted the Convention. The Ulster Unionists sent a well-organized delegation, with simply a watching brief – they took no real interest in the various forms of home rule picked over for month after month. The only scheme of government they presented, Plunkett said, 'was confined to the exclusion of their entire Province'. Since 'the time had gone when any other section of the Irish people would accept the partition of their country even as a temporary expedient', and the Ulster Unionists rejected all nationalist 'concessions', there was no common ground. In a bid to persuade the Ulster group chairman Hugh Thom Barrie to 'lift his province to the high level of this opportunity', Lloyd George was not above pulling out the American bogy even as late as January 1918. The Irish were 'now paralysing the war activities of AMERICA'; if the southern Unionists were to agree with the nationalists and Ulster refused, 'everyone would say that we were sacrificing the interests of the war to that of a small political section'. If America 'goes wrong, we are lost. I wish Ulster would fully realise what that means.'[57] They did not.

Given that the United States had been a belligerent for the best part of a year, the prime minister's alarm signal cut no more ice than it had done while America was still neutral. Hugh Montgomery curtly dismissed it as 'absolute bunkum', asking, 'would handing over the administration of a great part of this country to the friends of the enemy' (or at least 'persons either in sympathy with friends of the enemy or in dread of the friends of the enemy') help to win the war?[58] Demotion to 'a small political section' also registered with Unionists, a former editor of the *Northern Whig* writing acidly that 'noble-hearted Ulster' was now told by the same people who recently urged it to resist to the last ditch 'that it takes but a narrow and selfish view of the question'. The argument that 'Ulster must now embrace home rule because the empire is in danger' was simply 'quaint'.[59] As for the southern Unionists, Adam Duffin – after a 'very interesting pow-wow with the southern unionist lot' in late November – concluded witheringly that they were 'a cowardly crew and stupid to boot'. They 'want to capitulate and make terms with the enemy [sic] lest a worse thing befall them'.[60]

The absence of Sinn Féin, which refused to take part, seemed, at the start, rather convenient. It was still seen by most mainstream nationalists as hopelessly idealistic and was still in the early stages of political organization; it had so far won only a couple of by-elections. Its conditions for taking part – that the Convention be elected on universal suffrage (male and female) and be able to recommend full independence rather than home rule – looked typically unrealistic. But its victory in Longford in May, organized by Michael Collins, in the face of an energetic Irish Party campaign, was a heavy blow to the 'constitutional movement', and served notice that home rule's viability was ebbing away with worrying speed.

It was not surprising, in these circumstances, that the issue of exclusion did not take up much of the Convention's time. Both nationalists and southern Unionists were stridently hostile to partition, so all debate focused on ingenious variations on the single Irish parliament model. As Lloyd George helpfully confirmed to Plunkett in February 1918, 'the Convention has given much thought to the method of overcoming objection on the part of Unionists, North and South', to a single legislature for Ireland, involving schemes giving additional Unionist representation by nomination or election, and one envisaging a single Irish parliament with two locations: it would sit in Dublin and Belfast either in alternate sessions or in alternate years.[61] The prime minister declared this encouraging, and noted that the South African Convention had made progress by placing the legislature, administration, and supreme court in three different places. Under this proposal, Ulster members of the Irish House of Commons would form an 'Ulster Committee' with power to veto legislation, as well as an administrative role in manufacturing and labour, liquor supply, and education.[62] This device had, by now, been repeatedly rejected by Ulster.

There may have been a faint chance of agreement. Lord Curzon told Redmond on the last day of 1917 that if the Convention accepted a scheme proposed by southern Unionists (for home rule with customs powers reserved) with 'substantial agreement' – meaning that the only opposition was from Ulster – the prime minister was committed to doing 'all he could' to implement it. This was not nothing, and the fear of a Redmond–Midleton arrangement seems to have been enough to impel Carson to resign from the Cabinet early in 1918, to regain his freedom of action.[63]

'WHY TOUCH H.R. NOW?'

The British perspective was sharply displayed in the Cabinet's most extensive (and perhaps only serious) discussion of Ireland in late October 1917. It certainly put Ireland in its place: viewing the situation as a whole, 'in relation to the vast problems with which the Government was confronted', the Irish question 'was so small a matter that it might be undesirable to pay too much attention to it' – particularly if it would 'involve the country in serious difficulties'.[64] The biggest issue here was, once again, the likely effect in the United States of 'a drastic policy'. So how much attention would be too much? The Curzon committee's tinkering with home rule – including, as Lloyd George had mentioned, a peripatetic legislature – was about the limit. No steps seem to have been taken to find out if this idea held any attraction in Ireland.

Coincidentally, this meeting took place just a few days before the first national convention (Ard-fheis) of Sinn Féin on 26 October, when the organization took the final shape in which it would go on to challenge British rule in Ireland. Next day, the national convention of the Irish Volunteers did the same for the parallel republican military movement. 'Serious difficulties' would follow directly from this formidable separatist mobilization, and the world war would be the catalyst. When that war would come to an end could only be guessed at, but at this point, with the American war effort gearing up, there was general confidence about how it would end. This changed alarmingly when the Bolshevik revolution took Russia out of the war, freeing the troops which allowed Germany to launch the most dramatic military operation on the Western front since 1914. The German spring 1918 offensive, threatening a disaster by now assumed to be impossible, turned the persistent but usually low-key issue of Irish recruitment from a nuisance into a full-scale crisis, triggering the most decisive moment in recent Irish politics.

The attack which opened on 21 March broke through the British line with a speed unseen since trench warfare had set in. After a week the Cabinet decided to impose conscription in Ireland, but quickly had to face the question whether it could be implemented. The Viceroy – who had taken more interest in the recruiting issue than any other – now protested that imposing conscription before the Convention reported would 'cause an explosion in Ireland'. Ministers like Milner and Balfour turned the issue over and over, worrying that if conscription was resisted the attempt to enforce it might actually reduce the number of troops available ('the naked truth' being 'that Ireland is a sheer weakness', as Balfour bleakly said), but also well aware that to admit this and do nothing would be unacceptable to 'England'. On 9 April the government announced a Military Service Bill, to operate as soon as the Convention delivered its report (expected that month). The response to this measure – which did not exempt priests from service – was an unprecedented nationalist resistance movement, spearheaded by Sinn Féin together with the Catholic bishops, also impelling the Irish Party MPs to withdraw from Westminster and return to Ireland.

Maurice Hankey, the powerful Cabinet Secretary, tried on 10 April to 'persuade the PM to take a more conciliatory line with Ireland', but found him 'quite implacable'. His assistant, Tom Jones, found him 'depressed' by this. Two days later the Cabinet was considering whether it was 'worth while keeping the priests in the Bill because of the opposition it would arouse'. France had begun to conscript priests, but as Lloyd George mischievously remarked, 'the French are an infidel nation'. Hankey even enlisted Sir Mark Sykes, famed for his wide knowledge of the Near East (he had founded the Arab Bureau in Cairo and negotiated the Sykes–Picot agreement dividing Arabia between Britain and France), but less so for his knowledge of Ireland. Sykes plunged in with characteristic brio, proclaiming that conscription could not be imposed by force, whatever the army might think. 'Military people always believe in the effects of terrorism,' he rather startlingly asserted; but if the war had shown anything it was that 'terrorism fails in the long run'. The post-war world would be 'a period of great unrest', he predicted, and if Britain found itself holding Ireland only 'by brute force at the period when brute force is being broken up we shall be as people in an inflammable dwelling situated near a bonfire on a windy day'. So how could the government go about 'getting men' – its primary objective? Sykes recognized that the nationalists had 'lost influence' but – like most British observers – thought that Sinn Féin were 'normally a minority [and] only form a majority through special circumstances'. If the circumstances were changed, and especially 'if enthusiasm for the war could be aroused', Sinn Féin would become a negligible force.

Aside from floating the idea of himself serving as Chief Secretary, and offering to act as 'mediator' if Carson and Devlin could be persuaded to meet to discuss the situation, Sykes's prescription – setting up a committee of 'Nationalists and Ulstermen to prepare a proper Home Rule bill' – was hardly original. His suggestion of withdrawing the Military Service Act, setting up a 'Provisional Government to take over the government of Ireland' immediately, and relying on it to introduce and operate conscription, was more striking. So was his idea of allowing Irishmen 'who profess to love freedom but to hate England' ('like the Sinn Feiners') to enlist in the US Army.[65] Sykes's idiosyncratic analysis, somewhat loosely moored in Irish reality, may have brought some light relief to overwrought Cabinet ministers, but Hankey's enthusiastic endorsement of it mainly indicated how short of reliable guidance they were.

In fact, by the time Sykes reported, control of Irish policy had been recast once again: the former commander-in-chief, Field Marshal Lord French, was appointed as Viceroy, while the broken Duke was replaced by a Liberal, Edward Shortt – Asquith's rule notwithstanding. French believed that he was 'a quasi-military' governor, and though he was wrong, many others took the same view.[66] The Viceroy's primacy in Irish policy was restored as he was made a member of the Cabinet, and Long's equal eminence was confirmed when he was formally made responsible to the Cabinet for Irish administration. He had a direct telephone line from his office to Dublin Castle to keep 'in constant and close touch with all that is going on in Ireland'.[67]

Long also took over the ungrateful task of preparing yet another home rule measure. He chaired a hefty new Cabinet committee, based on Curzon's three-man group, and bringing in Jan Smuts as well as the Home Secretary, George Cave, the Labour leader G. N. Barnes, and H. A. L. Fisher. Long was aware that he was now in a distinctly odd position. 'Why touch H.R. now?' he plaintively asked Bonar Law on 26 April – since without 'appeasing Nationalists' it was 'enraging Ulster'.[68] The answer was surprising. Although the committee was supplied with another draft home rule bill, prepared by Professor Adams – more or less a replica of the draft considered by Curzon's committee – it took a new turn. Long opened the first meeting by saying that the House of Commons was unlikely to approve a bill 'which did not fit into a federal system'. Cave agreed that federalism 'was one way of avoiding controversy', and Austen Chamberlain had already insisted – as a condition of joining the Cabinet – that any Irish measure should be 'consistent with federalism'.

Long's embrace of the federal idea suggested that it might at last, after many years of shadowy presence in constitutional discussions, become a real possibility. F. S. Oliver had revived the federalist campaign early in the year, and 'roped in' Long together with Selborne and Chamberlain. Carson was already an enthusiast. But efforts to enlist Lloyd George had failed – 'he does not apply himself to any Federal plan of any kind', preferring 'a patched up truce however unsymmetrical'. Oliver was well aware of Long's limitations too: 'he never knows what he wants, but he is always intriguing to get it'. Still, his backing was clearly crucial, and Long now saw the unique virtue of the federal idea in solving 'the very serious difficulties with which we are confronted'. As he told Lloyd George on 18 April, it should be acceptable to British opinion and placate Ulster; crucially, it might now be 'possible to devise a title for the Bill which would get rid of the words "Home Rule for Ireland"'. This was no mere semantic matter. He reminded the prime minister of the power of the slogan 'No Home Rule' in mobilizing Ulster resistance: it had become 'a sort of sacred creed'.[69]

By the time the Irish committee held its fifth and final meeting on 10 June, many of its members had become dispirited (Curzon saw no line of advance, Cave thought they were ploughing the sands), and

Long – tasked with preparing yet another draft bill – had decided that the state of Ireland prohibited any constitutional change. Walter Long and Edward Shortt would not always see eye to eye but they agreed that 'the dual policy of the Government' could not carry on. 'Owing to the marching and drilling which is becoming the invariable practice of the younger men' in much of Ireland, and illegal acts like 'raiding houses for arms, assaults upon individuals, intimidation and the illegal possession of high explosives', the country required 'vigorous treatment'. The immediate enforcement of conscription was impossible; and 'the lawlessness which prevents conscription is itself the strongest argument against the establishment of a Government dependent of the support of a population so utterly out of hand'.[70]

It is not surprising that historians have barely noticed the activities of the Cabinet committee on the Government of Ireland Amendment Bill, but it marked another step on the path to partition. The exclusion of 'Ulster' in some form was now definitely fixed: the effect of recent agitation had been 'to increase the hostility of Ulster and strengthen the Ulster case'. Up to this point, exclusion of Ulster had been envisaged in a number of forms – ranging from continued integration within the United Kingdom to some kind of special status within an Irish legislature. (The committee talked about both an 'Ulster committee' and a 'loaded parliament'.) But Long's 'interim report', by calling for a commission to 'investigate the Federal solution in its possible application to every part of the United Kingdom', signposted a different direction in the evolution of partition. A single Irish polity remained a technical possibility, but it was vanishingly improbable in political terms; the likely outcome now was that Ireland would have not one but two home rule parliaments.

5

The Cut

The war ended in November 1918 with conscription still hanging over the Irish. Ineffective yet provocative, it could serve as a symbol of the paralysis of British rule – the effect of governing a country according to the public opinion of another. For Unionists, of course, such a view was a nationalist distortion: there were not two countries but one, which could save itself if it displayed sufficient resolution. The general election which quickly followed the Armistice, however, showed how far the process of psychological separation had advanced since the outbreak of war. Sinn Féin proved to be less ephemeral than Lord French and Walter Long had imagined, and the 'constitutional' Irish Party was crushed – only six of its MPs survived, while the seventy-three elected Sinn Féiners refused to take their seats in parliament. At the same time the political separation of the north-east appeared in sharper relief. While Sinn Féin had swept the board in twenty-four counties, Unionists won 60 per cent of the poll in Ulster (more than the Protestant proportion of the population) with twenty-six MPs. Their social profile had changed; the once dominant landed gentry were reduced to a single representative; the majority of Ulster Unionists were now lawyers and merchants.[1]

The constitutional corollary of this was explicitly recognized in the election manifestos of both Coalition Liberals and Conservatives. While supporting Irish 'self-government', Lloyd George and Bonar Law spelt out that 'the forcible submission of the six counties of Ulster to a Home Rule parliament against their will' was a path which was closed (the other closed path being the one which led to 'a complete severance of Ireland from the British Empire').[2] When self-government would come, they did not say. The 1914 Act had always been expected to come into operation – with suitable 'safeguards' – on the cessation of hostilities. Many would now have liked to take that as meaning when all the post-war peace treaties had been ratified – but it became clear that, like the war itself, this process would take much longer than expected.

The balance within the Lloyd George coalition – the first in the party-political era to win a general election as a coalition – had shifted ominously, from an Irish nationalist viewpoint. Its 136 Liberals were now vastly outnumbered by 339 Unionists. Bonar Law, Long and Milner were all in Cabinet. The prime minister's personal dominance had if anything become even more marked than it had been in the war, but this had a malign effect on Irish policy: while he was virtually living in Paris settling the new world order, it was, as the Chief Secretary Edward Shortt noted, 'impossible to get [him] to appreciate the situation'. He 'means to take a bold line on the Irish question the moment he is able to give the matter his personal attention', Horace Plunkett observed, adding acutely 'the trouble is that while he is waiting for his opportunity England and Ireland are losing theirs'.[3] Irish policy was on hold: repeated parliamentary questions about the promised implementation of the 1914 Act were answered the same way – it was impossible to give any definite date. Austen Chamberlain displayed the government's fix with disarming clarity: 'You cannot safely repeal the Act of 1914. You cannot safely allow it to come into force.'

All you could do, evidently, was appoint another committee to draft yet another home rule bill. Even this process was left for several months, and by the time it began in late autumn, significant things had happened. Most striking was the unilateral declaration of independence issued on 21 January by the assembly of Sinn Féiners elected as MPs but now renamed 'deputies' (or in Irish, TDs), Dáil Eireann. Together with the fatal ambushing of a police escort by a group of Irish Volunteers at Soloheadbeg in Tipperary – coincidentally on the same day – it signalled the start of a completely new challenge to British rule.[4] The government had had fair warning of this in 1918, but it was simply not prepared to accept it, and at first watched the revolutionary assembly with bemusement. It was probably encouraged in this by the reaction of the Unionist press, mixing mockery of the Dáil with denunciation of Sinn Féin's motives. The 'German Plot' – the arrest of dozens of Sinn Féiners in May 1918 for alleged contact with Germany – denounced by nationalists as a fabrication, commanded implicit belief amongst Unionists.[5] They invoked it to buttress their view of Sinn Féin as less concerned with winning freedom than with wrecking the Empire. The Soloheadbeg attack seems to have passed unnoticed in the north, and it was not until the assassination of a former Belfast police inspector, now a Resident Magistrate, and a member of the Plymouth Brethren, at the end of March, that Unionists raised the alarm. They saw this attack in directly sectarian terms.[6]

As the marching season came on, Edward Carson dramatically abandoned his wartime moderation (what Wilfrid Spender called his 'bewildering appearance of tolerance') by delivering a speech on 12 July threatening to revive the UVF if any attempt was made to 'interfere with the rights and liberties of Ulster'. The government's new Chief Secretary (Shortt moved to the Home Office in the new year), Ian Macpherson – yet another Liberal – at first took the opposite line, favouring the release of gaoled Sinn Féiners, but as violence increased he veered inevitably towards 'a firm policy'. Early in May, Long (recently installed as First Lord of the Admiralty) cruised over to Dublin on the Admiralty yacht *Enchantress* to confer with French and Macpherson, and pressed 'the strong line'. After the dramatic rescue of a Tipperary Volunteer, Seán Hogan, at Knocklong railway station in mid-May, which happened even though Tipperary had been made a Special Military Area after the Soloheadbeg attack, Macpherson accepted French's argument that separatist organizations must be proclaimed illegal. There was resistance to this step in Cabinet – not only Liberals but also Bonar Law, who warned the absent prime minister, 'To proclaim Sinn Fein means in effect putting an end to the whole political life of Southern Ireland.' A ban would be politically dubious, but worse, it 'could not be effectively done'. Even Long put in a cautious note, instructing French on 21 May that 'in no country in the world is it so important' as in Ireland 'that strong measures should consist not merely of printed proclamations'.[7]

Lloyd George was thus well aware that a serious policy development was in the air and had no issue with it. When Tom Jones, the Cabinet Secretary closest to him, told him that Liberal ministers were very disturbed by the possibility that Sinn Féin might be 'proclaimed' an illegal organization (accepting that no 'constructive policy' could be put together in the prime minister's absence, 'they don't want the pitch queered in the meantime'), he got no response.[8] When French finally decided to ban all 'Sinn Féin' organizations – including the Irish Volunteers, Cumann na mBan, and the Gaelic League – in Tipperary after the assassination of a police inspector in Thurles on 23 June, there was no move to stop him. Long set aside his opposition to 'proclamation', and the Cabinet approved it 'on the condition that the Irish Government was unanimous in its favour'. So the first step in ending 'the political life of Southern Ireland' was taken. Dáil Eireann remained at large until September – Macpherson jibbed at banning an assembly of MPs – but eventually, when it then decided to require the Irish Volunteers to take an oath of allegiance to the Dáil, it too was declared illegal throughout Ireland.

A SENSE OF PROPORTION

During this extended period of drift, one significant step was taken: Irish electoral law was drastically altered. The introduction of proportional representation, which would form a significant element of the next home rule measure, and would continue, little changed, into the electoral system of the Irish republic, was a kind of quiet revolution. Alongside federalism, PR had its British advocates and occasionally entered public political debate – as indeed it had while the 1918 Representation of the People Act was under discussion. It had always been ruled out; but – as so often since the Union – Ireland was seen as suitable for political experimentation that had been rejected in Britain itself. In 1919 concern about minority protection – a big issue in the post-war settlement in Europe – helped this extraordinary constitutional innovation to gain traction.

Since 1914, Irish local elections, along with all voting in the United Kingdom, had been postponed for the duration. They were now due, but in 1919 the government found a reason to postpone them again. The accelerating political shift in Ireland in the wake of the conscription crisis had begun to cause alarm. From mid-1918 to the general election the Cabinet received a barrage of reports about the advance of Sinn Féin. Long, as usual citing his trustworthy sources, predicted that Sinn Féiners would win 90 per cent of seats outside Ulster if municipal elections were held in early 1919. Henry Robinson, analysing the election shortly before the count was declared, pointed out that Sinn Féin's showing would give it control over most local authorities, and French suggested that local councils would become 'absolutely Sinn Fein'.[9]

Robinson, who had assured Long in July 1916 that what 'everyone' in Ireland wanted was 'not to have anybody's experiments and panaceas forced on the country', now seemed quite content to try an experiment – which might 'give a chance to minorities and prevent the rebels sweeping the country'. The system emerged by a circuitous route, starting in 1906 when the Chief Secretary James Bryce had consulted with a leading PR proponent over the possibility that the system might reduce resistance to his contentious Irish Council bill. In early 1911 the president of the PR Society proposed a three- and five-seat single transferable vote scheme for Ireland to reduce minority fears over the Home Rule Bill, and after he spoke in Dublin in April a PR Society of Ireland was founded to press for its adoption. Amendments were successfully carried, though when the bill was put on ice the Irish PR society more or less disappeared. In 1918 a private member's bill (the Sligo Corporation Bill) introduced it for the Sligo borough election in January 1919. This was a highly unusual, if not unique, pathway to constitutional change, but the election proved a success.

One of the original members of the PR Society for Ireland was none other than Sinn Féin's founder, Arthur Griffith, who had begun to build PR into its political programme. He believed that by ensuring the minorities would retain a voice, it would help to reconcile Irish Unionists to the separatist policy.[10] The Sligo model figured prominently when the Local Government (Ireland) Bill was introduced in March 1919, with the Irish Attorney General warning of the risk that Sinn Féin would use local elections to break down British rule as had been done in Hungary – exactly Griffith's strategy, of course. He was armed with a letter from Robinson claiming that the scheme had cross-party support – 'men of all classes, politics and religions' were convinced of its 'urgent necessity'. This was indeed true outside Ulster; Sinn Féin, the intended victim of PR, stuck to its founder's commitment to the principle. Eamon de Valera, newly elected President of Dáil Eireann after his escape from Lincoln gaol, confirmed this at the Mansion House in Dublin on 29 April. When the bill was being debated in parliament in May, Ulster Unionists also stuck to their principle of not departing from British ways, maintaining that as it had been rejected in Britain, it should not be experimented with in Ireland. Carson labelled the use of such an experiment 'to deal with the menace of the Sinn Feiners' a 'political outrage'.[11]

Wilful ignorance played a part in this: denouncing its 'absurdity', Carson protested that he had 'listened to discussions of proportional representation for twenty years or more and I have never yet got the faintest idea of what it means'. (The clause in the bill carefully describing how the single transferable vote would work he professed to find 'mystical'.) Joe Devlin frankly admitted a similar failure, but – pointing to the high turnout and near-absence of spoiled papers in Sligo – sardonically observed that 'surely if the poor people of Sligo can understand proportional representation, it is not a very big compliment which the Right Honourable Gentleman and myself pay ourselves if we say we cannot'.[12] Devlin charged the Unionists with a less innocent motive: simply refusing to allow protection of the nationalist minority in Ulster. But Unionists also disputed whether this (or any) system could really protect minorities as small as the Protestants in, say, Clare. ('You might as well look for holy water in an Orange Lodge' as look for Unionists there.)

'A MEASURE OF FEDERAL DEVOLUTION'?

When the Act was passed in June 1919, with the first local elections to be held in December (1923 in Sligo), the home rule issue was still dormant. But federalism had its last hurrah at that moment – it was debated in the Lords in March, and a junior minister, Edward Wood (later to be Viceroy of India as Lord Irwin), tabled a motion in the Commons on 3 June calling for 'a measure of federal devolution' for

England, Scotland, and Ireland. Walter Long declared himself a supporter of the federal system, though he was clearly referring to
devolution within an essentially unitary state. He thus took issue
with Wood's proviso that a federal scheme need not 'prejudice' any
government proposals for Ireland: for Long, whatever the 'governing
reasons' for federalism, 'you should treat the United Kingdom as a
whole in the same way'. One of its charms for him, as before, was
that it would supersede all talk of Irish home rule, and above all the
hated 1914 Act. Federalism was not to be a question of 'different
nations', he insisted. (Robert Cecil had insisted even more forcibly the
previous year that 'colouring Federalism with Nationalism is like
painting a rat red – it kills the animal'.)[13] After this debate Lloyd
George, who was not an enthusiast, was persuaded to set up a parliamentary conference headed by the Speaker of the Commons. There
was no hurry: it was put together in September and eventually met on
23 October.

Long came back to the thorny issue of the 1914 Act after a visit to
Ireland in September. Like French he was still optimistic that Sinn
Féin was faltering, but he grasped that repression alone would not be
enough. While the government should of course be firm that it would
not tolerate lawlessness, and would not have any dealings with Sinn
Féin, it should not simply ignore the aspiration to self-government.
Since he agreed with Bonar Law that repealing the 1914 Act was not
an option, Long now suggested that a federal scheme with at least two,
possibly more Irish parliaments would 'give a definite prospect of
moderate self-government' ('in the future', naturally).[14] After taking
note of his proposals on 25 September, the Cabinet had a full discussion of the Irish situation on 7 October – its first since the end of the
war, and none too soon, it might be thought. Some ministers maintained that no policy should be adopted merely in response to popular
clamour, but the Cabinet decided to set up another committee to
assess the 'possible alternative Irish policies' in light of the probable
effect of each on Ireland, on Britain, 'and on opinion abroad'.[15] Its
chair was of course Walter Long.

American opinion bore heavily on the issue. When the 'massive'
Irish Race Convention tried to engage President Wilson during his
trip back to the United States in February 1919, alarm bells were

ringing in London. Wilson refused to consider presenting Irish claims to the Peace Conference, but a resolution of the House of Representatives (with the 'concurrence' of the Senate) on 4 March that 'it is the earnest hope' of Congress that the peace conference would 'favorably consider the claims of Ireland to the right of self-determination' was a real embarrassment. The Irish-American delegation which set off for Paris in April – the 'three accursed Americans' as Lloyd George called them – was equally alarming, and not much less so when after failure there two of its members went on to Ireland in May, and produced a report alleging widespread British atrocities and human rights violations there. Macpherson was impelled to apologize to the prime minister for the fact that his regime was getting such a bad press – now being compared with those of 'Buckshot' Forster and 'Bloody' Balfour in the nineteenth century. He produced a point-by-point public rebuttal of these charges in July.[16]

In June the Senate racked up the pressure with a resolution (which only one senator dared to oppose) that the American Peace Commission should try to get a hearing for the leading Sinn Féiners at the peace conference. Wilson's secretary, Joseph Tumulty, warned that 'you cannot overestimate the real intensity of feeling behind the Irish question' – it was 'growing every day and not at all confined to Irishmen'.[17] Britain's ambassador, Earl Grey – himself a notable federalist – reported in October that the absence of an announcement on Irish self-government was 'doing great harm'. Somewhat surprisingly, though, a survey of American press opinion suggested that partition itself was not a big issue – if included in a settlement it was seen as 'unlikely to last for long'.[18]

STATE RIGHTS FOR ULSTER

As late as September, the Cabinet Secretary – still in Paris – was asking his deputy Tom Jones to find out for him 'the exact terms of the Home Rule Act' and 'how soon after the ratification of Peace it comes into force if no action is taken'.[19] Things were at last beginning to move. Lloyd George met Lord French in London on 23 September and outlined the likely shape of the next home rule bill: 'three southern provinces should be together under one parliament'. Long, who had dined with French aboard the Admiralty yacht at Kingstown a week earlier, incorporated this template for partition in the memorandum he prepared for Cabinet on 25 September. The Cabinet went on to give its new Irish committee a complicated set of questions – first, what would happen if a home rule bill was passed and (i) the Irish people refused to touch it; (ii) a sufficient number of moderate nationalists were prepared to work it and form a parliament; (iii) Sinn Féin used the parliament to thwart the British government. Second, what should be the financial relationship between Britain and Ireland, particularly concerning customs, Land Act indebtedness, and the Irish contribution to the cost of the war. Third, what would be the effects of further postponing home rule, and finally, whether postponement would need a parliamentary resolution. The committee was empowered to consider a general federal scheme for the United Kingdom.[20]

Evidently the whole idea of devolution remained problematic, the pre-war policy of creating a single Irish parliament especially. When Long's committee met for the first time on 15 October, it discussed the possibility of an all-Ireland parliament, with exclusion of some areas on the basis of 'clean cut', county option, or plebiscite. It dismissed all these options. A plebiscite would produce an administratively unworkable area, it decided, as well as 'infallibly inflaming religious and political passion' which would 'do more to partition Ireland in spirit and temper and hinder eventual Irish unity than any separation imposed from outside' could. A clean cut six-county bloc would inevitably contain a large nationalist minority, and in any case it would preserve 'British rule' in part of Ireland. The committee dismissed the idea of a single parliament with 'safeguards' for Ulster. This it decided would be 'unworkable': it was simply no longer 'within the power of the Imperial Parliament to impose unity on Ireland' (except, of course, by maintaining the Union unaltered). Instead it concluded that there should be a northern and a southern parliament, together with 'a Common Council with certain powers for the whole of Ireland' designed to preserve a framework of unity and offer a route to closer integration. The set-up would be 'not inconsistent with' a United Kingdom federal scheme. The 'Council of Ireland' concept was a token of the government's reluctance to let go of an all-Ireland settlement of some kind. The idea that unity was the ultimate objective of UK policy was never to be officially abandoned.

In November, Long's committee delivered a second report, whose headline message was that Britain would 'follow the Peace Conference by respecting the principle both of responsible government and of self-determination'. The 'two parts of Ireland' would get 'state rights' (Long underlined this term) immediately, with 'a link between them' and 'the power to achieve Irish unity on any basis . . . which they can agree upon'. This would 'get rid of the tap root of the Irish difficulty by providing for the complete withdrawal of British rule from the whole of Ireland' – in terms of domestic government – so meeting the 'fundamental demand of the overwhelming majority of Irishmen since the days of O'Connell'. At the same time it would be 'entirely consistent with the Government pledges to Ulster'. Being asked to govern itself could not 'in any sense be called coercion'. If 'Ulster' saw it as a sacrifice, it was one which must clearly be made 'to heal the feud which has estranged Ireland and Great Britain for so many decades' and which was now jeopardizing Britain's relations with the rest of the Empire and the United States.

Home rule for Ulster was the key to the whole proposal; Long suggested it would 'enormously minimize the partition issue'. His argument for this arresting claim was that 'the division of Ireland becomes a far less serious matter if Home Rule is established for both parts of Ireland'. That way, 'no nationalists would be retained under British rule'. This was mainly for foreign consumption – Long must have been well aware that few northern nationalists were likely to find Ulster Unionist rule preferable. Given that some kind of partition was now inevitable, the committee wanted it to be implemented according to 'administrative convenience': this would mean that 'Ulster' was indeed Ulster. Retaining Ulster's 'historic' boundary would be 'far the most convenient' arrangement – which would (perhaps not incidentally) have the further advantage of 'minimising the division of Ireland on purely religious lines'. In the Parliament of Northern Ireland – the first appearance of this title – the two 'religions' would be 'not unevenly balanced'.[21]

What seemed a virtue to Long's committee, however, would strike others as the opposite. When the Cabinet met on the anniversary of the Armistice to discuss the proposal, the strongest objection was that, since Ulster Unionists as well as Sinn Féiners would dislike it – the latter opposed to any partition, the former now preferring to ditch the three 'Catholic' Ulster counties – the scheme would be dead in the water.[22] Lord Birkenhead (the ennobled F. E. Smith), the Lord Chancellor, and Sir Laming Worthington-Evans (Minister of Pensions, not then in the Cabinet) fired off a note insisting that unless the Cabinet was sure that 'responsible people' in Ireland were 'willing to undertake the duties of Government', they could not support taking the bill forward through parliament. Birkenhead added characteristically that he supported making the offer 'as an ingenious strengthening of our tactical position before the world' – but did so only because he was 'absolutely satisfied that the Sinn Feiners will refuse it'.[23]

Such cynicism may have been rare, but even amongst the majority who still hoped that the scheme could work there was an atmosphere of fatalism. As the Cabinet wrangled over the details of the proposal, the scope and timing of the powers to be transferred to the Irish parliaments occupied much of their time – the endlessly debated issue of customs powers was no easier to resolve than it had ever been, and legal powers remained a hugely complicated issue. But the question of the partition line also loomed large. It should not have surprised Long that the Ulster Unionist leader-in-waiting James Craig found the argument about the administrative convenience of a nine-county state unconvincing, and the argument about denominational balance wrongheaded. Balfour endorsed Craig's scepticism about 'historic' Ulster, though he took a fundamentally different line, sticking to the old Unionist demand that the excluded area should remain an integral part of the United Kingdom. The ultimate aim was not, for him, Irish unity, and as against the principle of parallel treatment for the two parts of Ireland, he now advocated giving the southern part Dominion status.[24]

The alacrity with which Craig grasped the offer of a devolved 'state' surprised many Unionists, though Long had already been amazed by the fervour of his conversion to home rule. Craig indeed called for a more rapid transfer of powers than the committee had envisaged. It duly adjusted the project to provide an immediate transfer of all the devolved powers, instead of the staged arrangement previously proposed. (Long now spoke dismissively of powers being 'bandied about between various different authorities and at different times' in his original plan.) When the Cabinet met to give the final go-ahead to the bill in December, its discussion of alternative arrangements was perfunctory. The prime minister reported a conversation with the Irish Chief Justice James O'Connor, who seemed to think that if the county option were adopted and the excluded counties remained part of the United Kingdom, they would be more likely to opt for eventual unification because the taxes in a home rule Ireland would be lower. But the Cabinet was against keeping the six counties an integral part of the UK, since it might well make eventual unity less likely, and indeed give the impression that partition was the aim of British policy. O'Connor took the view that, if the northern area were to have home rule, it should be limited to six rather than nine Ulster counties. But even though the Cabinet discussed it four times in December, the issue of the precise boundary of the northern unit remained unresolved. Various arguments against the nine-county area were considered, including the birth rate – the 'danger' that Protestants would eventually be 'swamped' in it – and the related notion of 'homogeneity' – one which would be increasingly invoked. The trend of discussion seemed to be definitely running in favour of six counties, yet the last meeting before the prime minister was due to move the resolution in the Commons on 22 December swung back to the 'historic' Ulster, which 'by its size was more suited to possessing a separate Parliament'.[25] At this point the nine-county area's larger Catholic population was actually presented – along with its wider economic diversity – as one of its positive features. Once again the key argument here was the presumed reception of the measure in the Dominions and the United States, which would depend on the prospect of eventual unification. The Cabinet reiterated more than once that the ultimate aim of British policy was 'a united Ireland with a separate Parliament of its own' (though this was also queried more than once by the handful of diehards still opposed to any home rule).

The mechanism it chose to provide a pathway to unification – or 'create a bond of union' – has received short shrift from nationalists and historians alike. The Curzon committee in 1917 had come up with the idea of a 'common council', and Long's committee suggested giving this body (which it named the Council of Ireland) 'certain powers for the

whole of Ireland'. The Irish parliaments should have 'far-reaching constituent power': if they passed identical legislation, they could secure the
transfer of any of the temporarily reserved services, and revise the constitution of the Council so it might become 'a Parliament elected by
electors for the whole of Ireland'. Long thought this did 'everything
which an outside authority can do to bring about Irish unity' – without
of course 'in any way infringing the freedom of Ulster to decide its own
relation to the rest of Ireland'. The Council would advise the Imperial
government on the administration of some services which were 'spe-
cially undesirable to divide' for one year, after which they would be
divided unless both Irish governments asked for them to be transferred
to the Council. (These included agriculture and technical education,
transport, old age pensions, and unemployment insurance.) This would
represent 'a powerful recognition of the objections to partition', with 'a
strong incentive to immediate action towards Irish unity'.

Long's belief that this plan would not infringe Ulster's freedom did
not survive contact with Ulster Unionist leaders.[26] James Craig asked
for the committee report to be shown to Dawson Bates, the UUC
Secretary, who 'knew the mind' of Ulster intimately and could advise
on how the plan would be received. The Cabinet immediately took
fright, thinking that Bates might 'engineer an agitation in order to
influence the government'. By December the committee had shifted
position, 'impressed by the objection that not enough powers had
been conferred from the outset' on the separate Irish governments.[27]
Long clung to the Council idea, though he could see that there was 'a
real weakness' in the proposal in the first draft of the bill, and suggested early in 1920 that – not least for practical reasons – it should
be given immediate responsibility for transport, fisheries, and animal
diseases.[28] (So that, as Professor Adams argued, this lone all-Ireland
institution should at least have a trial.)

'AS HOMOGENEOUS AS IT IS POSSIBLE TO ACHIEVE'

At this point a striking new concept was injected into the discussions.
Worthington-Evans, who was quietly arrogating some of Long's

claim to shape Irish policy, reported that Craig had suggested to him that a 'boundary commission' might examine the distribution of population along the six-county border, and take a vote in districts where there was doubt about the inhabitants' preferred allegiance.[29] This initiative never became public; indeed, a prominent historian of partition, Denis Gwynn, would firmly assert that 'there had been no question of any Boundary Commission' until it was proposed by Tom Jones to Arthur Griffith during the 1921 Treaty negotiations. (Its purpose at that point was to put pressure on the intransigent Ulster Unionists; Gwynn added that Craig found the idea 'odious'.) There was some support for it in the Cabinet, Lloyd George himself appearing notably enthusiastic, but it fell foul of an objection that would reappear in future – that the enquiries made by such a body might produce 'unrest'. It was shelved, but not forgotten: five years later, by which time Craig undoubtedly did find the idea odious, he would be awkwardly reminded of it.[30] It was still listed as one of the options the prime minister was to lay before parliament when he introduced the new home rule proposal. Shortly before he moved that resolution the Cabinet went back yet again to trying to gauge the likely reaction to it in the United States and the Dominions – worrying that if the powers transferred appeared to be less than those in the 1914 Act they would be found inadequate. By analogy with the powers of American states, it could be made clear that 'with a divided Ireland it would be quite impracticable to set up a customs barrier between North and South'.

In the Commons on the evening of 22 December, Lloyd George – his extended world-settlement mission finally over – staged an expansive performance, laying out the issue on a wide canvas. As Plunkett had with the Irish Convention, he took full advantage of its epic scale: he faced 'about as difficult a task as any Minister has ever been confronted with'. He did not fail to invoke the attempt to assassinate Lord French three days earlier as evidence of the malignity of history: the 'path of fatality which pursues the relations between the two countries'. Lloyd George highlighted two 'basic facts' – the inevitability of home rule and the parallel inevitability of partition. The union of 1801 was in effect finished because in Ireland – uniquely outside Russia – the 'classes', the mainstay of law and order everywhere else, no longer supported the law. Ireland had 'never been so alien-ated from British rule as she is today'. At the same time a significant part of Ireland was 'just as opposed to Irish rule as the majority are to British rule'. To 'force union' within Ireland would be 'to promote disunion'. It would be 'an outrage on the principle of self-government'. Still, the wider union had to be maintained in some way: an inde-pendent Irish republic 'might very well have been fatal' to the Allies in the war. 'Any attempt at secession' – here the American audience was clearly in mind – would be fought 'with the same resolve as the Northern States put into the fight against the Southern States'.[31]

When Lloyd George turned to the Ulster issue – 'a fairly solid population, a homogeneous population, alien in race, alien in sym-pathy, alien in tradition, alien in outlook from the rest of the population' – he used a long quotation from Father O'Flanagan's 'very remarkable' 1916 essay to support his argument for two-parliament home rule. (Remarkable not least of course because it was written by a prominent Catholic nationalist.) In speaking of race, sympathy, tradition, and outlook, Lloyd George had it seemed care-fully avoided mentioning religion, but when he moved on to the question of 'boundaries' it leapt forth. He dismissed rather brusquely the three options which had been publicly discussed over the last eight years for determining the size of the excluded area; 'historic Ulster', for instance, contained too large a 'Catholic and Celtic' pop-ulation; even a six-county 'clean cut' would incorporate too many people who were against it. Instead he held that 'we should ascertain what is the homogeneous North-Eastern section' – taking the six counties 'as a basis', and 'eliminating where practicable' Catholic and Protestant communities which would prefer to be on the other side of the line. The objective must be 'to produce an area which is as homo-geneous as it is possible to achieve'.[32] The prime minister's odd phraseology somewhat obscured the precise mechanics of his pro-posal, but he plainly envisaged some kind of 'enquiries', of the sort which the Cabinet had feared would produce unrest. These would, just as clearly, have to be carried out by some agency – whether or not it was called a 'boundary commission'.

Since Lloyd George had already greeted such an idea with enthusi-asm, and plebiscites to determine the same kind of ethnic frontiers were a key element of the peace settlements he had just negotiated, it does seem that is what he had in mind. (At that moment, for instance, the Inter-Allied Commission for Upper Silesia was embarking on such a project.)[33] Maybe his hearers were baffled by his presentation, but they did not make any response to the point. Apart from Labour leader Arthur Henderson's brief protest that there should be a 'county vote' to 'consult the Ulster people' – quickly silenced by demands that he declare whether his party was for or against partition – and Carson's routine denunciation of home rule, the only dispute was over whether there were any 'Irish members' in the house at that moment.

Carson, issuing dire warnings about how Sinn Féin could take over the southern Parliament, declare an all-Ireland republic, and use the parliament's powers to 'arm' and 'proceed to annex Ulster', made the point that you could not set up a parliament one day and take it down the next. 'You cannot knock parliaments up and down as you do a ball.' But he was reassured by the fact that the same would be true of Ulster's own parliament: 'once it is granted, it cannot be interfered with'. The debate petered out with the radical Josiah Wedgwood changing the subject entirely. After drily observing 'if only the Irish were nice, sad, sober, sensible and business-like Englishmen, what a perfect bill this would be', he proceeded to deliver a detailed denunciation of the Amritsar massacre eight months earlier, when Brigadier-General Dyer had ordered troops of the British Indian Army to fire on unarmed Indian civilians in Amritsar in the Punjab, killing at least 370 of them.

'AS MUCH OF ULSTER AS WE CAN HOLD'

Another two months would pass before the final draft of the Government of Ireland Bill received its first reading, on 25 February 1920. This was a discouraging period for British rule in Ireland. In January the first Irish Volunteer/IRA attacks on police barracks began – thirteen in that month, with the first actual capture of a barrack following in mid-February. On 21 January the Assistant Commissioner of the Dublin police was assassinated in daylight. Dozens of police posts were closed. Shortly after the attempted assassination of Lord French in December, the army was given a more prominent role in the attempt to subdue the republican military campaign, and a programme of mass arrests followed in early January. This would soon backfire, as the inadequacy of the existing police intelligence system became clear. To stiffen the police, 'Walter Long's idea to employ some discharged soldiers in the RIC' came to fruition in January, when English recruits were enrolled for the first time. These 'Black and Tans' would achieve a special reputation in the annals of counter-insurgency.[34]

Not until the day before the Government of Ireland Bill was introduced was the size of the northern area finalized. Long visited Ireland in January and was struck by the general lack of interest in his home rule measure. He interviewed a wide range of people in Ulster, finding them all less interested in the complex details of the bill than the likely line of partition. He seems to have been surprised to find that the 'inner circles' of Unionists wanted the 'new province' to consist of six counties only; presenting their argument that 'the inclusion of Donegal, Cavan and Monaghan would provide such an access of strength to the Roman Catholic Party [sic] that the supremacy of the Unionists would be seriously threatened' as if he had not encountered it before. The Catholics, on the other hand, seemed to be in favour of the nine-county area.[35] Long was also taken aback by the number of people – many of them his friends – who told him he ought to resign, accusing him of adopting home rule to stay in office. He naturally thought they were 'talking simple nonsense' (not least because his resignation would make no difference), but the atmosphere was fraught.[36]

Long's final revised draft of the bill went to the Cabinet on 5 February, but the Irish committee met again a fortnight later to reconsider the idea of offering to grant Customs powers – reserved to London under all previous home rule proposals – if the two Irish parliaments agreed to unite. But since Unionists did not want the powers in any case, and using them would set up 'a Customs barrier against this country', the idea was dropped. The question of the partition line still nagged away, and the committee hung on to the idea that a nine-county Ulster would make eventual unification more likely.[37] By this time, though, there could be no doubt that the Ulster Unionist decision-makers had plumped for a six-county unit with a 'clean cut' borderline. Intelligent arguments like that of the editor of the *Spectator*, St Loe Strachey, that homogeneity was more vital than geographical tidiness or even economic benefit – he urged Carson in February to 'cast out as many Catholic districts, unions and parishes as possible', even if that created a 'jigsaw' border – did not rival the convenience of a ready-made frontier. Still, the Cabinet clung to the possibility of separating the nine-county 'historic province', repeating yet again the abstract argument that its size would make it more suitable to have a parliament.

When the Cabinet met on 24 February, a day before the bill was to have its first reading, the nine-county arguments still seemed to hold sway. The issue was finally resolved not by the Ulster leadership's wishes but by a rather different argument. Balfour, vividly evoking 'all the troubles which we have had at Westminster during the forty years between the advent of Parnell . . . and the blessed refusal of the Sinn Feiners to take the oath of allegiance in 1918', stressed how 'irre-dentism' had haunted the Paris settlement negotiations: 'If you have a *Hibernia Irredenta* within the province of Ulster,' he said, you will merely reproduce the problem (albeit 'on a small scale') in Belfast. If that were to happen, 'there will be no Irish settlement'. This has been read as support for the six-county area, though Balfour did not quite say this: he spoke of 'carrying out logically the principle of self-determination'.[38] (Paris talk again.) This surely indicated a plebiscite of the kind the Cabinet had already rejected, or at least a survey of the kind Lloyd George had trailed on 22 December, rather than simply following the county border line.

When the bill was presented on 25 March 1920, the northern parliament's area had been hastily trimmed to six counties, and the bill did not contain the phrase 'self-determination' or any hint that the county borders might be adjusted. In the debate Charles Craig set out a brutally simple rationale for the six-county area – 'the defence of as much of Ulster as we can hold'. The final decision to abandon the three counties was 'heartbreaking', he declared, but recent events showed that 'the Sinn Feiners . . . would make government there absolutely impossible for us' as they had already made it impossible for 'the English government' in the rest of Ireland. 'To try to hold more than we could would seem an act of gross folly.'[39] Self-determination did haunt the fringes of the debate: Carson bitterly denounced it as part of the 'ridiculous phraseology' of the war which had done so much harm (like 'making the world safe for democracy').[40] Lloyd George offered an important refinement of the principle – 'self-determination does not mean that every part of a country shall have the right to say "we mean to set up an independent republic"'. That was 'the very thing that was fought for in the Civil war in America,' he claimed. 'There must be [some] limitation to that principle, otherwise you might carry it to every fragment and every area and every locality throughout the world.' The 'limitations' he suggested were 'those which common sense and tradition will permit'.

This was suggestive rather than definitive, but he was forthright on the inevitability of partition. Asquith might still maintain that the 1914 Act preserved Irish unity, but the exclusion of four counties, on whatever basis, 'is partition'. It might be four rather than six counties, 'but nevertheless it is partition'.[41] In a vivid psychological excursion, he advised nationalists to come to terms with it as the British had. It had 'hurt [British] national pride, it hurt the national vanity,' Lloyd George said, to 'recognize that Ireland wanted to go her own way'. Surely Ireland should likewise recognize that Ulster did not want to be governed from Dublin. 'Let them,' he urged, 'learn from the mistakes we have made with regard to Ireland as a whole'. As when he had introduced the bill, however, 'Ireland' (not just the abstentionist Sinn Féin MPs, but even the surviving handful of the Irish Party) was notably absent from his audience.

The Commons debate was desultory; the sense of resignation pervading the Cabinet's discussions seemed to be amplified in the chamber. Macpherson, on the point of quitting as Chief Secretary, admitted the 'diffidence' with which he would 'attempt to expound the principles of this Bill'. Several speakers asserted (without audible dissent) that there was not 'one iota' of support for the bill in Ireland. J. R. Clynes pugnaciously disputed the long-established mantra of not 'coercing Ulster' – 'why responsible statesmen who are answerable for the enforcement of the law . . . should go out of their way to announce beforehand that they are not going to enforce a law if it is carried is beyond my comprehension'.

The tone of debate sharpened momentarily when Devlin – who described the bill as 'conceived in Bedlam' and, perhaps more destructively, 'drafted by F. E. Smith' – charged that Lloyd George was 'violent in his hatred of people who differ from him', and had 'that rare quality, which powerful rhetoricians like himself generally use, of not only hating people, but knowing how to express his hatred'. When the prime minister retorted, 'So have you', Devlin said he was glad there was 'something in common between us'. When Carson cannily interjected 'you never really hate, you only pretend', Devlin acidly remarked 'that is probably why I have a lesser influence in public life than the right honourable Gentleman'.[42] Looking back after the second reading, in June, Earl Winterton archly remarked that 'when we consider the old Home Rule bills and the discussions and interest they attracted' – this was putting it mildly – 'one asks oneself whether this is a committee of the House of Commons passing an important Bill or a debating society in some provincial town'.

Large swathes of English members were probably prey to the same indecision as afflicted the Labour Party, though without being awkwardly put on the spot as the Labour leadership was when the bill appeared. Although Fabian public gurus like George Bernard Shaw might embrace federalism – Labour 'can never be a separatist party, it is a federalist party' – and suggest that partition 'may easily become an abusive name for quite beneficial measures of decentralization and local autonomy', party leaders trod more awkwardly. Clynes initially announced Labour's Irish policy as 'the fullest financial and economic liberty', subject to an annual contribution to 'expenditure which is common to us all', and with 'adequate protection for the Ulster people from any sense of danger to their life, their property or their faith'. All this he said would 'literally amount to self-determination' – but limited by the requirements of 'imperial unity and defence'. In other words, good old home rule. There was something of a flurry of objection to this across the Labour movement, with the *Daily Herald* proclaiming (26 February) that any reservation of powers was 'both illogical and impolitic', conflicting with the essence of self-determination.[43] The leadership still fought shy of this logic, but it found an escape route in the rejection of partition. It stressed the 'historic unity' of both Ireland and Ulster, declaring 'we oppose this scheme of self-government because it provides a form of partition founded on a religious basis.' On 18 May, Clynes announced that Labour would vote against the partition clause, and then withdraw from any further discussion of the bill.

The bill featured a Council of Ireland consisting of 'twenty representatives elected by each parliament and a President nominated by the Lord Lieutenant'. Its initial remit would be to 'initiate proposals for united action on the part of the two Parliaments', and bring them forward in them. Macpherson, reiterating the pious 'hope that division may be temporary', held that the bill had been framed 'in such a manner as may lead to a union between the two parts of Ireland'. The Council 'may become a real stepping stone on the way to the union'. But his lengthy exegesis of the arrangements for assembling the Council, and transferring to it a range of powers by agreement with both Irish parliaments was swiftly and brutally put into perspective by James Craig. 'I would not be fair to the House if I lent the slightest hope of the union arising within the lifetime of any man in this House.'[44] So (as Henry Robinson had warned) even the idea of giving the Council a trial by endowing it with fairly extensive powers was unlikely to persuade Ulster. Insisting on a trial would be seen as coercion.

The issue of the partition line would not quite lie down. In May, during the second reading, Philip Lloyd-Greame (the future Lord Swinton) put down an amendment proposing to substitute nine Ulster counties for six. He made several arguments for the Cabinet's preferred template, starting from the contention that since Irish unity was the 'fundamental purpose' of the bill, 'a complete Ulster' would work better both in this direction and in itself. He echoed a point previously made by Herbert Fisher, the danger of creating a new 'pale' in Ireland, then suggested it was undeniable that 'as an economic whole, it is a thousand times more desirable to have a complete province than the six counties only', invoking the question of railway administration. With rather less evidence, he argued that nationalists in the three border counties would no longer oppose being incorporated in the northern area as they had in 1913 and 1916; then they had to choose between home rule and no change, he said, but now their choice would be between home rule within either the Ulster parliament or the other – 'a perfectly different proposition'. The wider diversity of the province was crucial: a 'homogeneous area' might be easier to govern, but the real need was to demonstrate that wider Irish self-government could be a success.[45]

Such musings no doubt reflected much of the discussion within the Irish committee. Herbert Fisher himself candidly admitted that there was 'no question in connection with this Bill which has caused us greater anxiety than the limitation of this province of Northern Ireland', but simply said that to include three 'purely Catholic' counties would create 'very great difficulties for the new Parliament'. Carson acknowledged that naturally 'we should like to have the very largest area possible', which he called 'a system of land grabbing that prevails in all countries for widening the jurisdiction of the various governments'. But there was 'no use in our undertaking a Government which we know would be a failure if we were saddled with these three counties'.[46]

Urging MPs to accept that 'we have to refer in these matters to Protestant and Catholic' – to do otherwise would be 'the greatest camouflage of argument, because these are really the burning questions over there' – Carson nonetheless contended that the northern and southern parliaments would not diverge on religious questions. He predicted that the northern Parliament would be very largely 'labour', and the southern 'agricultural': 'they will diverge on this kind of question'. He remained silent on the ultimate unification of Ireland, leaving it to Ronald McNeill to point out that there were in fact many who did not see that as the 'cardinal point' of the bill. Long diverted the discussion back towards federalism: either six or nine counties could work for this. You could 'build the Irish wing first, as long as you could complete the rest of the building'. Lloyd-Greame's amendment showed that there was some interest in the issue, but not enough to carry it.

A 'RIDICULOUS BOUNDARY'

The lukewarm formality of the parliamentary debate was tellingly different from the intense dispute amongst Ulster Unionists over the bill just before its second reading. In calling the decision to abandon the three counties 'heartbreaking', Craig perhaps spoke more truly than his audience imagined. Although, in hindsight, it might seem to have been taken years earlier, in 1916, that was not clear to people in 1920. Long's commitment to the nine-county province reflected a still-potent belief rooted in the Covenant. Underlying it was the conviction, still widely held, that home rule would be a catastrophe for Britain and the Empire as well as for Ireland itself. This conviction had if anything been strengthened by the experience of the war. What had changed was that most Unionists now saw home rule as unavoidable, largely because English public support for 'Ulster's stand for union' had weakened. Carson's threatening speech of 12 July provoked widespread hostile reactions, from former supporters as well as opponents, and Unionists seem to have taken these to heart.[47] Craig told the Commons that the very fact that the government was introducing a home rule measure when the situation in Ireland was so bad proved that home rule was inevitable.

But the six-county area had not yet been conceded when the UUC considered what attitude it should take to the new bill in March 1920. In the 'prolonged and acrimonious debate' over the issue, the arguments for a nine-county Ulster came not only from the three marginal counties. They revolved round the effects of the 'ridiculous boundary' that would be created by six-county exclusion. Donegal would be cut off from its rivers and harbours, and would be accessible only via the six counties. Cavan and Monaghan formed a 'natural' southern boundary, while Monaghan projected into 'the very heart of the province'. The nine-county area was Belfast's economic hinterland, and would also spread the cost of maintaining the administrative apparatus of government and law courts. There was also, surprisingly, support for the view that the Unionist majority in a six-county parliament would actually be too great for healthy politics. (The fact that the southern parliament would have an overwhelming nationalist majority, they argued, was not a good reason to engineer a similarly 'deplorable' situation in the north.) The nine would produce a Unionist majority of twelve in a parliament of sixty-four (thirty-eight/twenty-six).

The three-county group claimed that the critical meeting of the

UUC on 10 March was stitched up by Thomas Moles, the MP for Belfast Ormeau, whose estimates of likely electoral statistics (presented without 'reasons') were wrongly preferred to theirs. The count was taken by show of hands only – they were 'thankful to see such a large number of the delegates from the Six counties respect the Covenant they had signed', and remained convinced that they represented 'a large majority of the Unionists of Ulster'. They forced a second meeting of the Council on 12 May, where Carson, in perhaps his last major political moment – 'evidently in pain and depressed by the neuritis he is suffering from' – spoke brilliantly against their cause. This time they were defeated indisputably, mustering just 80 out of 381 votes. The line of partition was now fixed, assuming the new home rule bill became law.

Invocation of the Ulster Covenant was a crucial point of rupture: its once totemic power no longer worked on the majority, who argued that it had applied to a different threat – one that had been headed off by the two-parliament scheme. The three-county group countered that since the 1914 Act was still on the statute book, the 'threatened calamity' of home rule remained a threat; and the Covenant had undeniably been an oath to defend the whole of Ulster. Abandoning the Covenant was certainly not easy. Sir James Stronge would only concede reluctantly that it was 'certainly well nigh out of date'. Fred Crawford was impelled to produce an extended analysis of five of the Covenant's key phrases to justify his 'voting for the six counties', managing to convince himself that 'if I had voted for the nine counties I would have been going against both the spirit and letter of the Covenant'. Stronge lamented that the decisive vote had been rushed, leaving the 'impression that the 3 Counties have been thrown to the wolves with very little compunction'. It would have been more honest to abrogate the Covenant openly than to quietly 'give it the "go by"'.[48]

In the middle of the Government of Ireland Bill's long parliamentary journey, the government had something of a wobble. Impressed (as well they might be) by the general lack of enthusiasm for it, and the certainty that Sinn Féin would never work it – points trenchantly made by the Head of the Civil Service, Sir Warren Fisher, when he inspected the Irish administration in May – some ministers returned to the idea of going beyond home rule to 'Dominion status'. While Long, chairing a new Irish Situation committee, piled on pressure for stronger repressive action, the top officials in Dublin were becoming increasingly vocal on the futility of coercion and the need for an imaginative political gesture if there was to be any hope of a settlement. This came to a head at a Cabinet Conference on 23 July, attended by all the senior Irish administrators. The only Liberal left on the Irish committee, Herbert Fisher, was particularly impressed by William Wylie, the Law Adviser at Dublin Castle, who argued with some passion that the alienation of Irish public opinion could not be reversed by military action. The armed Irish police would soon be little better than a mob. The rebels were more than just terrorists – the 'murder gang' as the government labelled them – and could be negotiated with. The head of the Dublin administration, Sir John Anderson, agreed with Wylie that the bill before parliament was a dead letter and something more was needed. Coercion was not an option.

James Craig's contribution to the discussion was short but to the point: the home rule bill 'ought to be pushed quickly through parliament'. Bonar Law and Long hastened to make clear that this could not be done – unless 'the Financial Clauses were abandoned'. The bill, and with it partition, was taking a battering: Lloyd George himself admitted that if the experts' view became public knowledge, 'it would be impossible to go on with' it. Even Fisher, almost alone in maintaining that it 'was a very good Bill and had been unfairly condemned', thought that an offer of Dominion status might be even better. Early in August the prime minister met a deputation of businessmen from Dublin and Cork, who were unanimous that the bill would not 'satisfy the country', and if carried would 'probably lead to Civil War'. (A worse conflict than so far existed, presumably.) Only a prompt, bold, and generous offer of Dominion status would restore peace. They reassured him that southern Protestants had 'no fears on the grounds of creed', and that if Dominion status brought financial independence, 'you will find that a two shilling income tax and no Excess Profit Duties will bring Ulster in like angels'. The Cork brewer Richard Beamish presented a radically different view of the insurgency from the Ulster Unionists': it was 'not a revolution' but 'the soul of the people aiming for a certain object' – maybe by the wrong methods, but 'they want to try honestly'.[49]

The late-July rethink might conceivably have changed the direction of policy: Fisher noted revealingly that it was the Cabinet's 'first real discussion' of the Irish issue in his time. Winston Churchill admitted that 'the unanimity of the experts' (the chief of police excepted) against the hope of crushing republicanism by force was a formidable point. But in the end Lloyd George ruled that, whatever else was done, the law 'and the machinery of the law must be strengthened'. Bonar Law quietly remarked that 'such a view upset the whole of Mr Wylie's case', and discussion petered out, leaving the bill to trundle on its course towards enactment.[50]

6

The Siege

In the summer of 1920 the IRA's house journal *An tOglac* (The Volunteer) published a 'War Map' showing the location of IRA operations in the second half of July. Just four took place in the six-county area, and three of those were mail raids – some of the easiest of all actions to mount.[1] This map spoke volumes about the nature and impact of the armed insurgency which had been intensifying through the year. The IRA's figures for a two-week period in May (6 operations in the six counties, 126 in the rest) and one in September (4 and 71) show that the pattern was consistent. 'The Anglo-Irish War was fought in the twenty-six counties', as one historian has put it.[2] Many revolutionary wars since the American revolution have been at the same time unavowed civil wars; in Ireland this was certainly so, though not often in a military sense. In most of the country, loyalists were a small minority who were not in a position to contest the republican campaign even if they wished to; in the north-east the situation was reversed. Even where, as in Londonderry, nationalists were in the majority, most Volunteer operations were ineffective or worse – their attempt to defend the Catholic diocesan college during the upsurge of street violence labelled the 'Derry pogrom' in June 1920 ended in an ignominious rout. In Belfast a cautious leadership kept activity minimal 'for fear of reprisals on the Catholic population'.[3]

In the Unionist view, the republican campaign directly threatened them as much as the British administration. Even attacks in the south could have a northern resonance, however unintentional. When the Cork Volunteers mounted their landmark first attack on British troops in Fermoy on a Sunday morning in September 1919, it is unlikely that they either knew or cared that the soldiers on church parade were Methodists. But in the north they definitely cared, and the shock of the assault outside a church door just before Sunday worship was intense. IRA actions were not yet automatically viewed as sectarian, but that would rapidly follow. After another attack in October, reported in the loyalist *News-Letter* as 'Farmer's House Burned Because He Was Friendly With a Protestant', the paper launched a blistering attack on the Catholic Church, whose 'bigotry and consistent efforts, open and secret, to increase its power' had brought much of Ireland into a state of lawlessness.[4] And whatever the framers of the new local government act may have hoped, the 1920 municipal elections dramatically sharpened this perspective. Although Sinn Féin was confined to 550 seats in Ulster, other groups taking 1,256, in conjunction with nationalists it took control of Derry city and nine other six-county urban councils. 'Londonderry' – 'less a territorial reality than a state of mind'[5] – had a Catholic lord mayor for the first time since the seventeenth century. His inaugural address, announcing that 'mighty changes are coming in Ireland' and that 'the Unionist position is no longer tenable', predictably raised widespread alarm.[6] This epochal takeover was symbolically read as the result of the Catholic hierarchy's ownership of the nationalist movement.

This latest 'invasion' of Ulster was ostentatiously signalled in Derry: the city council broke off its connection with the Local Government Board and struck Lord French's name off the list of freemen of the city. The republican tricolour flew over municipal buildings in place of the Union flag – an act of calculated illegality. When in mid-April a number of imprisoned republicans were moved to Bishop Street gaol in Derry, at a historic flashpoint for communal battles – just between the Catholic Bogside and the Protestant Fountain Street area – an hour-long street fight began. It was very often not the IRA which took the lead in escalating street violence, but rather the Hibernians, the Irish Party's enforcers, who were less concerned to avoid the appearance of sectarianism. The 'Hibs' were indeed frankly a sectarian, all-Catholic communal defence organization, directly mirroring the Orange order.[7] But the distinction between 'constitutional' nationalists and republicans, sharper in 1920 than perhaps ever before, was lost on Ulster loyalists: all nationalists now became in effect Sinn Féiners.

When, at Easter, the IRA burned a mass of income tax offices, including the Belfast Custom House, as well as some abandoned RIC barracks, groups using the name UVF set up roadblocks and rough-handled any Catholics they found at them. The tax office attacks were a turning point for northern Volunteers, who had no previous experience even of what Seamus Woods later called 'the proper use of petrol'.[8] A month later the IRA and RIC exchanged fire in Derry for four hours. In mid-June, Catholics were attacked in Prehen Wood and Catholic homes in the Waterside were burned; UVF men fired down 'for hours' from the old city walls on the 'exclusively Catholic' Long Tower district (the *Derry Journal* reported). In the six days of fighting (18–24 June) often labelled the 'Derry pogrom', fifteen Catholics and four Protestants died. Eoin MacNeill, the first to apply the 'pogrom' label, and one of the few Sinn Féin leaders to have been born in Ulster, insisted that the loyalist action was not spontaneous: the government had supplied the UVF with weapons. When the army was called in on 24 June, and liaised with the loyalist groups which it assumed to be on the side of law and order, it added to the death toll by itself firing into the Bogside. By the end of June, forty people had been killed in Derry.

The official response to this violence had its own malign effect on the polarization of attitudes. A group of senior Dublin officials – the Under Secretaries John Anderson and James MacMahon, the Law Adviser William Wylie, and the Police Chief Henry Tudor – who went to Derry on 25 June ('to show they really were concerned'), got a hostile reception.[9] The magistrates they met accused Dublin Castle of 'flouting the opinion of the city's representatives when they appealed for military aid to free the citizens from the reign of murderous terror': if troops had been sent immediately, many lives would have been saved, they alleged. 'The Irish government were allowing things to drift' and 'the people of Derry had no faith in what Dublin castle would do'. (So at least the *Belfast News-Letter* reported.) The paper's editorial flatly contradicted MacMahon's contention that 'a peace based on force would not be a lasting one', robustly declaring that 'all peace is based on force'.[10]

The intense gaze directed from north to south was not reciprocated. Sinn Féin was of course automatically against partition in principle, but this did not mean that it was concerned with the north in practice. It shared the view of Ulster adopted by earlier generations of nationalists, rooted in the assertion (repeated in the Irish Convention) 'We regard Ireland as a nation': not 'the Irish', but 'Ireland' – the people synonymous with the territory. Arthur Griffith was reported by the Irish Unionist Alliance in late 1917 to have declared that they 'must make up their minds either to throw in their lot with the Irish nation or to stand out as the English garrison'. If they stood out, 'the Irish nation must deal with them'. The IUA took, at that point, some comfort from Eamon de Valera's less belligerent remark that he 'would not like to see any man who was loyal as an Irishman, be he Unionist or Separatist, coerced'. But de Valera, depending on his audience, could sound different, and more often did. 'As far as the Unionists were concerned', he was reported as saying in Sligo in July 1917, 'as they were in the minority they must give way to the majority'. Their claim to self-determination he likened in 1918 to that of 'a robber coming into another man's house and claiming a room as his'.[11]

The protest of Louis J. Walsh, a leading Ballycastle Sinn Féiner, who told the 1919 Ard-fhéis (national convention) in Dublin that 'the organization had not sufficiently grappled with the situation' in Ulster, remained unanswered.[12] The handful of northerners amongst the members of the first Dáil did not manage (if indeed they tried) to persuade the republican government to develop a constructive, or even coherent, northern policy. The only direct effort to investigate the situation in the north on Sinn Féin's behalf was made by one of the rare Ulster Protestant Sinn Féiners, William Forbes Patterson, who reported in late 1919 that while the republican movement was dead in the water, labour was growing in strength and might threaten Unionist control. His advice that Sinn Féin should back labour may have been sensible, but hardly fitted with the party's idea of its mission. The Dáil's attitude to Ulster oddly resembled the baffled indifference to Ireland so long evident at Westminster. It remained, as the *Kilkenny People* declared after the Treaty, 'a truism amongst Irish Nationalists that the differences between North and South are largely, if not entirely, the creation of English interference'. As soon as that interference ended, differences 'would be amicably adjusted'.[13] The implications of this delusion would become disastrously apparent in 1920.

In late June republicans noticed 'an abrupt change' in the tone of the *Belfast Telegraph*, which had carried a reasonably fair account of the Derry events. Its editorial warned that the 'rebels in Londonderry' were aiming to 'hasten the day when an Irish Republic will give them control of the lives and property of the loyal citizens'.[14] The republican forces did not see a need to disprove such views. Ignorance or indifference was plain in the IRA's assassination of the RIC Divisional Commissioner for Munster, Colonel Gerald Smyth, at the Cork County Club on 17 July. Like Fermoy, this was a long way from Ulster; however, Smyth was not just a Protestant but an Ulsterman, from Banbridge in County Down. His death would have produced a strong loyalist reaction at any time, but five days after the central day of the loyalist calendar, 12 July, with tensions already screwed up to a high pitch, the resulting violence was catastrophic. The 12th itself had passed without significant violence, but Edward Carson had once again taken the opportunity to announce, at a Finaghy Field rally, that 'We in Ulster will tolerate no Sinn Fein' and deliver a warning that if the government failed 'to protect us from the machinations of Sinn Fein', 'we' would 'take matters into our own hands'. 'We will reorganise'.[15] And in a phrase which a number of historians have highlighted, he declared he was 'sick of words without action'.

The day of Smyth's funeral, 21 July, was the first full day back at work after the 12 July holiday. Smyth's body became a victim of the railwaymen's munitions embargo – refusing to carry troops or munitions – when no crew could be found to convey the coffin to Banbridge. 'The refusal of the railway people to carry his remains' acted, the RIC Commissioner thought, 'as a match to gunpowder'; and there were attacks on Catholics there and in neighbouring Dromore. In Belfast several (perhaps five) thousand shipyard workers responded to notices posted by the Belfast Protestant Association to 'Protestant and Unionist' workers to meet outside Workman Clark's south yard, where BPA speakers denounced the IRA campaign, Sinn Féin 'penetration' of Ulster, and 'disloyal' trades unionists who had allegedly become Sinn Féin's industrial wing.

The Workman Clark apprentices and 'rivet boys', armed with hammers and iron bars, sallied forth to Harland and Wolff's yard, where they searched for any they could identify as Catholics and socialists. The management's decision to lock the main gates at Queen's Island meant that many were trapped; some jumped into the Musgrave channel, where they were pelted with 'shipyard confetti' – nuts, bolts, rivets, and other steel scraps – and had to swim (according to one) two or three miles to escape. Next day a series of workplaces across the city were similarly invaded. Perhaps 10,000 were expelled over the next few days, including several hundred female textile operatives. Smaller-scale expulsions and physical intimidation went on into August and September. Some employers, possibly encouraged by the BPA, made clear that they could not guarantee the safety of expellees – including 'rotten Prods', Protestants who refused to sign an oath of 'loyalty' – if they returned to work.[16]

What was going on here? If this was a pogrom, it is hard to see that the state authorities, whether government or the security forces, had much to gain from this kind of communal violence. The commander-in-chief of the army, Sir Nevil Macready, a political liberal who would have become military governor in Belfast in 1914 if the threat of a UVF rebellion had escalated, was aghast at the prospect of the force re-emerging in the summer of 1920. The RIC, by now dismissed by loyalists as untrustworthy because of its overwhelmingly Catholic make-up, had even less interest in ramping up civil conflict. Local leaders may have taken a different view. The Ulster Unionist leadership had perhaps become less hostile to spontaneous loyalist street action than in the pre-war crisis. They were acutely anxious about the possibility that a growing labour movement might undermine the commitment of Protestant workers to the Unionist cause. The Belfast strike of January–February 1919, when both Protestant and Catholic workers took action to secure a forty-four-hour week in engineering and shipbuilding industries, had alerted leading Unionists to the danger. Dawson Bates, the UUC Secretary, warned James Craig at the end of January, 'the leaders are practically Sinn Feiners, who have taken advantage of some of the rank and file'.[17] In denouncing the republican campaign in his 12 July *grito*, Carson took care to stress the 'more insidious' process of 'tacking on the Sinn Fein question and the Irish republican question to the Labour question'. He hammered home the point that men who 'come forward posing as the friends of Labour care no more about Labour than does the man on the moon'.

The fusion of Sinn Féin and labour was not purely an Ulster Unionist nightmare. Fear of socialist revolution was acute during the wave of industrial action in the wake of the war: a Cabinet committee worried in early 1920 that 'the country would have to face in the near future an organized attempt to seize the reins of Government in some of the larger cities'.[18] Sir Henry Wilson, Chief of the Imperial General Staff, who attended this 'amazing meeting', noted that 'one after another said that we were going to have a triple Red revolution strike'; and 'one after another said there was nothing to be done'. Only Long and Churchill 'were prepared to put up a fight'.[19] It is not surprising that the potential of Irish republican socialism was exaggerated. Its modest future could hardly have been foreseen by people of any political stripe. The brief romance between Sinn Féin and the infant Soviet Republic – two outlaws desperate for any kind of international recognition – looked dangerous, and the even briefer upsurge of worker power in the 1919 Limerick Soviet confirmed for many the scale and imminence of the danger. The eagerness of Sinn Féin and Irish labour to speak up for Russia (echoing the trades unions' 'hands off Russia' movement in Britain) fed this perception.

Richard Dawson's *Red Terror and Green* of 1920 (which despite its sensational title presented a thoughtful analysis of what he called the 'new nationalism' in the works of James Fintan Lalor, James Connolly, and Aodh de Blacam) reflected and fed a potent suspicion. Dawson's cocktail was spiced with a few of the airier utterances of the Dáil Minister for Labour, Constance Markievicz. His contention that labour was already stronger than 'moderate' Sinn Féin far outran his evidence, but his prediction that it would surely not repeat its electoral self-abnegation of 1918 was reasonable enough. Nor was his suggestion that the notably ambitious Dáil government machinery indicated 'monetary assistance from Russia' entirely unreasonable. And his belief that the Irish revolutionaries now saw Britain as 'not only a country from whose rule they desire to escape, but a country which must be brought down in headlong ruin', was directly echoed by Ulster Unionists.[20] Craig would explain to the Cabinet in September that loyalists 'believe that the Rebel plans are definitely directed towards the establishment of a Republic hostile to the British Empire', and to that end they were 'working in conjunction with Bolshevik forces elsewhere'.[21]

Nationalists have stuck tenaciously to the allegation of a 'pogrom' (which fitted their political analysis of loyalism as the product of manipulation); even writers who have questioned the label have come down in its favour.[22] But if so, which higher power was instigating the violence? Some, like MacNeill himself, resolutely pinned responsibility onto the British government – with its traditional 'divide and rule' strategy of 'fostering religious and internecine strife' – while others like the *Irish News* blamed the Unionist party leaders. The most comprehensive statement of the pogrom charge, *Facts and Figures of the Belfast Pogrom* compiled in 1922 by the Rev John Hassan (using the name 'G. B. Kenna'), held that Belfast employers, rattled by the 1919 strikes, had created a fake union and set about provoking sectarian animosity. Not once in a 200-page manuscript, as Maurice Goldring has pointed out, did he mention 'that there was a war raging between Britain and nationalist Ireland, and the majority of Belfast's population felt itself to be on the front line'. Goldring saw Kenna's work as casting more light on the nature of conspiracy theory than on the actual processes at work, though that in itself says much about popular attitudes.[23] The most careful assessment of the 'pogrom' label in the Belfast context suggests that it 'seems a better guide to the depths of nationalist fears . . . than it is to understanding the overall dynamics of the conflict between communities'.[24]

The violence may have been indirectly encouraged from above, but its essential dynamism stemmed from below. Alongside the sectarian and political motives so consistently and plainly flagged, there was a social and economic impulse. Belfast's industrial boom peaked briefly in 1919, which the *Belfast News-Letter* called the *annus mirabilis* in the long history of the linen industry, and the shipbuilding workforce neared a historic high of 30,000. Thereafter they would be in competition for shrinking employment; within a few years of having a full order book in 1919, Harland and Wolff would be on the verge of bankruptcy. Insecurity would now have a material as well as moral dimension.

'THE ARMING OF THE PROTESTANT POPULATION'

The UVF had never entirely disappeared, though many in its ranks – maybe one-third – had gone off to war. It was indeed formally disbanded early in 1919, but the RIC went on sending in returns on the force's strength, and compiling lists of rifles it retained.[25] There was no move to seize or surrender these. Their existence probably encouraged a belief that the old force could be revived, and such a belief probably underlay a parliamentary question tabled in June, asking whether the government would accept the 'assistance of loyal volunteers to aid in the restoration of law and order', and suggesting that the Ulster Ex-Servicemen's Association (a group formed shortly after the war) had offered 3,000 trained officers and men.

In June 1920 the Fermanagh landowner Basil Brooke formed his Fermanagh Vigilance Force because 'the threat of raids was increasing'. He argued 'that [loyalist] hotheads might take the matter into their own hands if not organised', and even ordinary Ulstermen who wished for a quiet life . . . might turn to Sinn Fein' if they did not 'find support elsewhere'. He used UVF weapons he had stored on his Brookeborough estate since 1914. Similar groups appeared elsewhere, like the 'Protective Patrol' set up in Armagh city by a shopkeeper, which grew rapidly and secured 174 UVF rifles from the UUC in Belfast. According to Fred Crawford, Carson himself had seriously suggested the revival of the UVF in March, but only on 25 June did the UUC Standing Committee formally reconstitute it.[26] Wilfrid Spender was offered the command on 16 July, and was also given leave of absence from his post as 'Officers' Friend' at the Ministry of Pensions. As he later remembered it, Hamar Greenwood, the new Chief Secretary, told him that the revival had the tacit approval of the prime minister, though 'it would be politically unwise to announce this publicly'[27] (something of an understatement). Spender had gone on from the pre-war UVF staff to serve as GSO II in the 36th Division, but since leaving that in 1916 he had not been in Ulster, and he now presided over a force that never quite recovered its original impetus.

On 1 July the Viceroy, Lord French, told Long that the UVF would form 'a most useful and valuable contingent', but General Macready scouted the idea of using 'a body of undisciplined men over whom the Government would have no hold, and who would most assuredly paint the place red'. Spender charged Macready with being the main problem for loyalists; first 'his fatuous policy of transferring loyalist constabulary and other officials to the South, and replacing them in the North by extreme nationalists'; then his idea that 'if he could disarm everyone in Ireland he would secure peace'. Spender had confronted the Chief Secretary after the UVF acted to stop a republican attack on the Londonderry GPO and were then disarmed by the army, telling him 'I could not carry on unless the army and RIC authorities were told officially that the Government recognized the UVF and wished them to cooperate in keeping order'.[28]

Notices in the Unionist papers on 23 July announced the reorganization of the UVF and called on all members and former members to report for duty. Public figures like Lord Massereene and R. Spencer Chichester (the Deputy Lieutenants for counties Antrim and Londonderry) chaired recruiting meetings; Massereene himself became a county commander, along with General A. St Q. Ricardo in Tyrone, Colonel Perceval Maxwell in Down, and Basil Brooke in Fermanagh. Colonel George Moore Irvine, recently commander of the Army Ordnance depot at Carrickfergus, was sent to Derry city as full-time organizer. By early September, Spender was able to report to Craig that numbers were 'now fairly satisfactory', including a 'very large' proportion of ex-servicemen.[29]

Macready railed against the re-emergence of 'the same force who, for their own opinions, armed against the Government of the day' in 1914, warning Bonar Law (who of course had shared those opinions and approved that action) that 'the arming of the Protestant population of Ulster will mean the outbreak of civil war'.[30] On the day the UVF's relaunch was announced, Macready went to the Cabinet Conference in London where Wylie painted a vivid picture of the collapse of the civil administration and police in Ireland. Churchill responded by diagnosing the problem as caused by the 'prolonged strain' of the republican insurgency: his answer was to 'raise the temperature' of the conflict to 'a real issue and shock, and trial of strength'. He proposed raising '30,000 men in Ulster' to vindicate the authority of the Crown 'not only in Ulster but throughout Ireland'. Tom Jones, arguing for a Dominion settlement in the wake of the 23 July conference, told Lloyd George that even though the army was not adequate to implement 'a policy of "thorough"', Macready would resign if the UVF was officially recognized. In any case, the UVF would 'not fight outside Ulster', and even there would need many months to be brought into 'efficient condition'.[31]

The revived UVF was certainly a shadow of its former self. The twenty original Belfast battalions were all re-established, but they lacked numbers – most having no more than company strength. In more 'doubtful districts', Spender noted in September that people 'will watch to see how things pan out before committing themselves'.[32] Had war service put men off returning to paramilitary activity? Spender later recalled that though many of the men who had returned from war service 'were war weary', 'most' responded to the call to get the UVF 'on to a proper footing'. One disincentive was that the pre-war UVF's insurance scheme (which, as we have seen, had drawn some misplaced mockery from nationalists) was not revived. Spender found that few of the pre-war UVF commanders were prepared to resume their roles, and those few appeared unenthusiastic. The situation in 1920 was very different from that in 1914 – there were no central HQ or staff, no central Volunteer post office; everything was decentralized not only to counties but also districts. 'Because patrol duties etc were unpaid & putting a severe strain on our men, I put forward proposal that the UVF should be changed into three types of Special Constabulary and should be paid as such.'[33]

On 29 July the Cabinet's Irish Situation Committee discussed a paper on 'use of Ulster Volunteers' and agreed that advantage ought to be taken of 'the willingness of the North to protect themselves'. Steps should be taken 'to enlist Volunteers on a Special Constabulary basis'. The force should not, however, be used 'outside Ulster'. At a ministerial conference early in September, Craig spelled out in some detail his proposals for a special constabulary force, to ensure that adequate police posts were re-established throughout the six counties. It should be armed, organized as far as possible on military lines, and detailed for general duty within the six counties only. It should include a reserve force 'only to be called out in an emergency', commanded by its own local leaders. Craig suggested that the UVF organization should be used for this, 'as was done for the raising of the 36th Division'.[34]

'URGENT ACTION'

Another assassination of a police officer – this time in the Ulster heartland – triggered a further surge of street violence in August. District Inspector Oswald Swanzy had been serving in Cork in March when its Lord Mayor (and IRA brigade commander) Tomas MacCurtain was assassinated, and had been named amongst those responsible by the coroner's jury. On Sunday 22 August he was shot dead leaving Lisburn Cathedral after matins. According to the Belfast IRA commander Roger McCorley, the killing had been ordered earlier, before the July 'pogrom', but was delayed for fear of large-scale reprisals. Once communal violence began, 'the way was clear to carry out the operation'.[35] Fresh reprisals duly followed: the 'Sinn Fein murder of D. I. Swanzy', as the *Boilermakers' Monthly Report* labelled it, led to three days of attacks on Catholic pubs, homes, and businesses, wrecking more than three hundred, and turning almost the whole Belfast Catholic community into refugees. The RIC County Inspector unthinkingly, or perhaps revealingly, wrote of a 'crusade against all members of the Catholic faith'.[36] For Fred Crawford, visiting Lisburn shortly afterwards, it brought back memories of French towns 'bombarded by the Germans'. Michael Collins, who had ordered the killing and even sent MacCurtain's own revolver to do it with, saw it as a demonstration of republican power; for the northern IRA, the ferocious reaction demonstrated their fatal weakness. 'Inactive, small in number, and hopelessly isolated', they could do little more than watch 'the ebb and flow of sectarian violence'.[37] Similar attacks on a still larger scale soon followed in Belfast. Reaching once again for a now sadly familiar analogy, the *Daily News* suggested that it was 'probably unmatched outside the area of Russian or Polish pogroms'.

As the damage and casualties mounted – in one week of Belfast rioting, there had been 180 major fires – Craig spelled out its lessons for the Cabinet's benefit. Sinn Féin was 'already the predominant factor over a considerable proportion' of Ulster, and, with the natural advantage of attackers over defenders, 'rebel influences are spreading'. Now 'the Loyalist rank and file have determined to take action' to guarantee their own safety, and the Unionist leadership 'feel that the situation is becoming so desperate that unless the Government will take immediate action', they may have to 'see what steps can be taken towards a system of *organised* reprisals against the rebels'. There was a barely concealed threat here – alongside defeating the rebels, the system would be needed 'to restrain their own followers' from carrying out 'regrettable' acts. 'Unless urgent action is taken,' Craig warned, there would be 'civil war on a very large scale.'[38]

What kind of action should the government take? After its July wobble – and in face of the almost united opinion of its 'experts' – it had just rushed through a new coercion law, the Restoration of Order in Ireland Act, to replace the Defence of the Realm Act (the wartime emergency powers law due to expire at the same time the 1914 Home Rule Act sprang back to life). The only one of its experts in favour of coercion, the police commander General Tudor, was going ahead with Lloyd George's own evident preference for out-terrorizing the republicans. Along with the new law came new 'machinery' – the Auxiliary Division of the RIC, a special 'emergency gendarmerie' (another of Churchill's ideas). The 'Auxies', rather loosely connected to the RIC and prone to disciplinary problems, quickly became the most visible and energetic practitioners of the 'Black and Tan' strong-arm methods intended to break the grip of the IRA on the community.[39] Prominent amongst these methods were 'unofficial reprisals'.

In calling for 'organized reprisals', the Ulster Unionists were weighing in on one of the most vexed issues plaguing Britain's attempt to repress the republican movement. Retaliation by troops and police following IRA attacks became ever more frequent and destructive in the summer of 1920, and almost inevitably – given that the attackers themselves could not be identified, and dissolved back into their communities after attacks – it targeted those suspected of merely belonging to or supporting the republican movement. Retaliation of some sort was, as General Macready pointed out, certain to happen: forces with any *esprit de corps* would always respond, and 'the human endurance of the troops is rapidly reaching a point where restraint will be impossible'. For him, like many regular officers facing irregular fighting, the overriding issue was preserving military discipline. Retaliation had to be regularized and kept under control. 'Organised reprisals' were most forcefully advocated by Sir Henry Wilson, who had called in May for lists of known Sinn Féiners to be posted 'on the church doors all over the country'; 'whenever a policeman is murdered, pick five by lot and shoot them'. He repeated the call in September, not long after Craig's memorandum.[40]

Echoes of German 'frightfulness' no doubt ensured that the government would never agree to such a system. Churchill (who drily opined that the situation would not be improved 'by the kind of methods the Prussians adopted in Belgium') demanded to know in detail what measures Wilson advocated – 'It is no use ... saying "I should shoot", or "I should shoot without hesitation", or "I should shoot without mercy".' To Churchill's exasperation, Wilson affected not to understand the question.[41] But Lloyd George seems to have been satisfied that 'unauthorised' reprisals were proving effective; Wilson had been taken aback to hear from him that a 'counter-murder Association' set up by the head of police, General Tudor, was 'murdering 2 S.F.s to every loyalist the S.F.s murdered'. Wilson's concern was not that this would be more deadly than his own scheme, but that the prime minister would not take public responsibility for it. Lloyd George preferred 'gunning' to 'burning' but had no way of ensuring that the police followed his preference.[42]

Unauthorized reprisals hit the front pages on 20 September, when some sixty buildings in Balbriggan (near the RIC training depot in northern County Dublin) were burned by policemen after the killing of a Head Constable. Next day, in County Clare, police rampaged through three towns after an RIC patrol was ambushed, burning dozens of buildings and killing four people – including a boy who was trying to extinguish one of the fires they had started. From then on the army held the 'Black and Tans' – English recruits in the RIC – culpable for reprisals, and tried to get them removed from military areas. Macready – who had originally been offered joint command of the army and police, but refused – began calling for martial law, mainly to stop police indiscipline getting out of control. (He was supported by the respected *Observer* correspondent Stephen Gwynn, who said that martial law would be 'less barbarous and brutal and far less demoralizing than the present anarchic and futile campaign of revenge'.)[43]

'A DECLARATION OF WAR ON ONE PART OF THEIR OWN TERRITORY'

The political-psychological significance of the action taken by the republican government in response to the 1920 'pogrom' has not always been acknowledged. In August, Seán MacEntee presented the Dáil with a petition from the nationalist members of Belfast Corporation calling for action to stop the 'war of extermination being waged against us'. MacEntee (another of the select band of Ulstermen there), framing the violence as 'the first act of open rebellion against the Republic', acknowledged that a military response was impossible, but 'there was the more potent weapon of the blockade'. Everyone knew that, in the war, Britain had blockaded Germany with grim effect, and MacEntee argued that the Republic should do the same to the main 'distributing trades throughout Ireland' – or, as the petitioners more tersely put it, 'fight Belfast'. There was no doubt then or later of how far that fight might go – 'let grass grow in the streets of Belfast', as MacEntee would snort.

Ernest Blythe (also a northerner, but a Protestant) by contrast immediately saw that a 'blockade of Belfast' would destroy the possibility of a united Irish nation 'for ever'. Desmond Fitzgerald likewise protested that it would be 'a vote for partition'. Arthur Griffith recognized that the motion amounted to 'practically a declaration of war on one part of their own territory', but wanted to declare the imposition of denominational tests on employees illegal, and held that Belfast employers who refused to comply within seven days might indeed be boycotted. Since demands for a boycott grew ever louder, and several spontaneous boycotts had already started in the west (as early as February one district council in Mayo had called on traders to close their accounts with any Ulster firms which failed to 'declare themselves anti-partitionist'), it was perhaps inevitable that the Dáil government authorized a boycott of banks and insurance companies with headquarters in Belfast. Local activists quickly went further, adding other towns where there had been anti-Catholic violence, and extending the range of enterprises targeted. It seems to have been the IRA itself which decreed a blanket proscription of all goods 'manufactured or distributed from Belfast', and the IRA led the way in enforcing the ban by destroying such material. Exactly how they thought their actions would help their cause was never clear. Each of the eighty-odd local boycott committees had its own ideas, and the Dáil's Central Boycott Committee lost impetus when its director was arrested in October. No comprehensive blacklist of firms was compiled until 1921. Much of Ulster might have been only dimly aware of the economic war, but the IRA commander in Monaghan, Eoin O'Duffy, was a notable enthusiast for it and made it highly visible. His forces picketed Protestant stores, fined blacklisted firms, harassed any Catholic customers they had, and attacked trains and delivery vans.

The boycott has figured slightly if at all in standard nationalist accounts of the partition process such as Gwynn's. Yet it unquestionably 'heightened Unionist perceptions of . . . the whole Sinn Féin movement as the enemy of the unionist community'. And it (like the laughter with which Carson's name was greeted during the roll call of the first Dáil) 'demonstrated the extent to which the north-east was regarded as external to the true Ireland'.[44] The disenchanted Sinn Féiner P. S. O'Hegarty put it still more bitterly in his 1923 polemic *The Victory of Sinn Féin*: not only did it raise up in the south 'a hatred of the North', but it made the few remaining northern Protestant home rulers 'almost ashamed of their principles' – and, above all, 'turned apathetic Protestant unionists into bitter partisans'.

'STILL A GLADSTONIAN HOME RULER'

By the time the financial relations between Britain and the Irish governments under home rule were due to be debated for the last time in parliament, the surviving Cabinet Liberals had at last grasped that the Government of Ireland Bill did not go far enough to secure any substantial political support in Ireland. They thought it left 'too much British intervention in Irish affairs' – in particular 'the collection of customs, excise & income tax' (which would of course be done by 'English officials') would be an ongoing 'irritant'. Since it was obvious enough – to them as to others – that the bill was a staging post rather than a final settlement, they argued that it would be politically more honest to reduce its provisional elements. The government 'should have the courage of its convictions and say that this new solution was put forward in the belief that it would settle the question'. Giving complete financial autonomy to both parliaments would be a strong signal that 'no further concession could possibly be made'. Such a generous measure would be supported by, and would strengthen – as it clearly would need to – 'all moderate opinion in Ireland'.[45] That opinion was crucial not just to the eventual constitutional settlement, but more immediately to the 'breaking up of the murder gang' for which the government would need all the public support it could get. Defeating the republican insurgency was, indeed, a precondition of any settlement.

This attempt to bid for greater nationalist support was made on 13 October, at a time when the struggle between the security forces and the IRA was reaching a climax. Terence MacSwiney, lord mayor and IRA brigadier of Cork, had been on hunger strike for two months: he died in Brixton prison twelve days later. The Irish countryside, largely abandoned when police stations were evacuated in the winter, had never since been effectively controlled. Military and police patrols could only dominate small areas, and now in the autumn they were increasingly threatened with ambush by new full-time IRA units, the 'flying columns'. The reprisals which became so prominent in September were the target of growing criticism in Britain. But the situation in Ireland was increasingly detached from the legislative process, and in any case the issue of financial autonomy was a red line for the bill's framers. Walter Long had from the start opposed transferring customs and excise powers, arguing that Ulster did not want them and Sinn Féin would not be reconciled to the bill by them; moreover, handing them over would destroy 'the federal idea'.[46] Lloyd George vehemently rejected the Liberals' proposal.

His reaction casts light on his often opaque political strategy on Ireland. If the government adopted such a conciliatory attitude, he protested, 'nothing would be left with which to negotiate'. The prospects of getting anything in return were in any case small – about that he was surely right – and 'if this were done Ireland could not remain part of the United Kingdom'. The retention of customs was always regarded as a sign of unity, and other federal systems – he cited Germany and the United States – did not give such power to their federal states. The US government had had a major battle to gain central control of income tax – 'absolutely essential for defence' – and Lloyd George would not give it up. 'That was not the home rule on which he had been brought up'; he was 'still a Gladstonian home ruler'. Contradictorily, he asserted both that Sinn Féin 'would collect the taxes' and that they 'would not accept such a concession'. What he meant, evidently, was that 'if we retained these taxes the Sinn Feiners were at our mercy'. He might in the end give them up, but 'he would only consider it if it was impossible to get other terms'.[47]

With the final passage of the bill impending in December, official thoughts belatedly turned to what would happen if moderate nationalists failed to take up the home rule offer. Early in November a new clause, proposed by the minister without portfolio, Sir Laming Worthington-Evans (deputing for the absent Long), set out arrangements if either parliament was 'not properly constituted' – 'to prevent a farce being made of' them if members did not take their seats. But the only plan offered was for further elections to replace them.[48] The southern Unionist MP Colonel Guinness grimly told the government it was 'drifting into what I think will be a crowning blunder in Irish policy'. The speech introducing the new clause was 'a wonderful commentary on the absurdity of the position'. The minister 'would have made an admirable Peter Pan, but his fairyland happens in real life'. If Sinn Féiners were elected 'owing to your failure to meet the demands of reasonable Irishmen . . . you will be in a very great difficulty'. To take the bill forward in its present form would be 'taking an unjustifiable risk which must aggravate Irish opinion at best, and at the worst may land you into a terrible disaster'.[49]

After Lord Hugh Cecil also complained that the bill did not meet reasonable Irish – as well as international – demands, Bonar Law icily observed 'how difficult this problem is for anyone who does not think'. For him, the situation had gone beyond reasonable compromise. 'It is no good talking as my noble friend did about self-determination. What is the good of talking about that? What is the good of telling us that the Irishmen should get what they wish?' The reality was that there would be seventy members in the southern parliament pledged to an Irish Republic. 'What is the good of talking about this concession or that concession?' (A curious echo perhaps of W. B. Yeats's 'who can talk of give and take?' in his poem 'Sixteen Dead Men'.) Bonar Law preferred to spell out the equal importance of the other side of the real situation, what the British wanted. 'We are prepared to give Ireland the largest measure of self-government which commends itself to the people of Great Britain as well as to the people of Ireland.'[50]

'THE BIGGEST ADVANCE TOWARDS UNITY IN IRELAND'

The only positive proposal for coping with the oncoming disaster was made by Sir Ellis Hume-Williams, who asked whether the planned Council of Ireland might be utilized to provide an alternative to paralysis, by carrying on 'non-controversial government in Ireland'.[51] Although nobody else seemed interested in taking it up, this at least indicated that some scope for official initiative remained. From the inception of the 'partition act' to its passage into law, the official line was always that its essential principle was not division but union. The government's ultimate aim was to preserve some kind of all-Ireland political structure, and the key device proposed for this was the Council of Ireland. By the time the Government of Ireland Bill finally became law, this body had – erratically – evolved from a shadowy aspiration to an apparently substantial administrative mechanism. There can be no doubt how keenly the government – certainly its Liberal component – wanted to believe in the Council's feasibility; but it never cast off its air of forlorn hope.

The strength of the hope allowed it to withstand a series of more or less brutal doses of reality. The first was administered shortly after the Cabinet approved Long's idea that any viable Irish unity must emerge from the 'voluntary cooperation' of the two parliaments, not be imposed from outside. The original draft bill conferred no definite powers on the putative Council, seeing the very process of inter-parliamentary discussion about the services to be transferred as a joint project which might conjure up consensus. Sir Henry Robinson put in one of his heftiest papers, arguing that this very fact would ensure that it was a dead letter: unless it started out with a significant number of state functions, the northern parliament would probably not delegate powers or even send representatives to a council sitting in Dublin (whether the location would be part of the issue he did not say). Robinson identified twenty functions, which could be administered by the central authority 'without inconvenience or danger of political controversies' because 'sectarian considerations do not come in', and which affected northern interests directly enough that 'the Northerners cannot afford to keep outside the Council'. These included the Congested Districts Board, the Ministry of Transport, and the Dublin Metropolitan Police as well as the National Gallery and Museum, the Public Record Office, and the Registry of Deeds. By way of warning, Robinson reminded the Cabinet that the 'anti-English atmosphere' of the General Council of County Councils had impelled five Ulster councils to withdraw from it. If the same thing happened when the Government of Ireland Bill became law, 'it would be an end to all hopes of a Parliament of Ireland'.[52]

As a southern Unionist, Robinson was keen to assert that such a parliament was 'the underlying principle of the whole Bill' and the foundation of 'all hopes of a final settlement'. This may have gone beyond what the Cabinet would subscribe to, but that was not why it turned Robinson's plan down. Nor did it doubt his expert credentials; the fact that it received his memorandum directly showed that he was taken seriously. The problem lay in the fundamental ambiguity of its overall policy. Ten days after receiving it, a subcommittee of the Committee on Ireland reasserted the idea of voluntary cooperation, and suggested that pressuring the two parliaments to cooperate 'might be regarded as an infringement of the pledge to Ulster'.[53] The pledge of course related to the ban on 'coercing' the Ulster Unionists; what degree of indirect pressure might be interpreted as actual coercion was a delicate issue. Accordingly, the official line wavered. Awkward cases – whether, for instance, the National Gallery, Museum, Library, and Schools of Art and Science should be reserved to London control or transferred – drew conflicting opinions. On 24 February, just before the bill was to be introduced, the Cabinet changed tack on transport, deciding to transfer it to the Council. Carson objected that this would prevent the northern parliament from legislating for construction or improvement, which Long's committee accepted, but pointed out that unless the railways were under 'single control', effective administration would be impossible. A government amendment in October then diverged from this, enabling each parliament to authorize railway construction, extension, and improvement in its territory. But though the Council was thus deprived of this function, at the same time the principle of giving it specific executive powers had been re-established. A similarly complex issue of unitary control arose with Irish fisheries administration, which was eventually placed in the Council's remit.

At the very last moment before the bill became law, a third power – administration of the Diseases of Animals Acts – was added. Long's committee had never been in favour of this, and turned it down once again when the Irish Veterinary Medical Association called for the Council to be given the responsibility on 2 November. The government view stayed the same, since the bill set up two agriculture departments, and there would be no effective central machinery for agricultural administration. But when, in mid-December, a Lords amendment supported the vets' demand, the Cabinet decided to accept it (on the ground that it would be 'unadvisable' to stand out against an evidently strong feeling in favour). It has been suggested, fairly enough, that 'out of the vast range of public administration' in Ireland, these three matters 'would not appear to have represented much of a threat to Ulster'.[54] The government, with the apologetic line that the primary intention was not to increase the power of the Council but to provide the most 'business-like' mode of administration, was almost bending over backwards to avoid any hint of 'coercion'. Yet they failed to persuade Carson, who went on protesting that this transfer to the Council was too far-reaching, and even 'dangerous'.

At some point it must have occurred to someone that the bill contained no provision for the actual meeting of the Council – 'when the first meeting shall be called or by whom', as Worthington-Evans said. Even its title – Council of Ireland or Irish Council – remained uncertain: both forms were used right up to the final discussions on the bill. The timing of its actions carried more messages than might have been thought, as the dispute over whether it should consider plans for the unification of certain Irish services 'forthwith' or 'as soon as may be' demonstrated.[55]

The issue of minority protection came under the spotlight again in November, when it emerged that there was still no plan to establish 'Second Houses' or senates. Six months earlier, in committee on 18 May, when the absence of any provision for a Second Chamber in the bill was sharply criticized, Long had promised to present a 'definite scheme'.[56] Whether through his illness or lack of attention, nothing had been produced. Worthington-Evans implied that there had indeed been discussions, but they had turned up so many complications that the decision had been reached to make the Council of Ireland responsible for creating the Second Chamber. This received a dusty response from Samuel Hoare (a former head of the British intelligence mission to the Russian general staff, and a future Carlton Club plotter who would help to bring down Lloyd George in 1922). He was sorry that Long was ill, he said, but he protested 'against the attitude taken by the Minister without Portfolio today: he comes down virtually without excuse, and suggests that this is the only course to take because the difficulties are so great'. Hoare charged that the government had 'not consulted the minorities in the South and West'; 'they really – I will not put it higher than this – have made a very great mistake'.[57]

When the idea of a Second Chamber had been discussed in the spring, Hoare insisted, the aim was not to stop hasty legislation but 'with the sole object of attempting to find some practical safeguard for the scattered minorities'. Hoare had always thought that the Council should be given 'far greater responsibilities and powers', and asked why, if 'Irishmen' were to be entrusted with the constitution of their Second Chamber via the Council, should they not also be entrusted with the constitution of their First Chamber. But the main point was not for him about the functioning of the Irish Council – it was 'to provide immediately and without further delay a practical safeguard for minorities'.[58] In the situation that would exist when the Act came into operation, 'party feeling' would be 'most bitter' – this was putting it optimistically – so safeguards should not, he urged, be dependent on some such indefinite phrase as 'as soon as may be'. Colonel Guinness also charged that the government had 'most distinctly broken a parliamentary pledge' in failing to implement Long's undertaking. A more outright condemnation came from the rising Conservative star William Ormsby-Gore, who pointed to the sparse attendance in the Commons – 'the numbers attending this debate' and lack of interest in the new clause were 'a very fair measure of the reality behind the Clause. That is to say, there is practically no reality.' The clause was 'not meant to be operative and never will be'. Even if the Council did meet, it could not hope to get identical acts passed by the two parliaments. By refusing to 'give quite clear and definite constituent powers', the government was 'merely getting out of the proposal to set up Second Chambers altogether'.[59]

Bonar Law's answer was to invoke Britain's own constitutional problem – the long-delayed issue of the House of Lords. The fact that 'we have got to face the question of reform of our own Second Chamber next session' made it really 'impossible to discuss' the Irish case. It was impossible to advocate a nominated Chamber, he declared. But Carson as so often cut to the fundamental point – the north and the south presented radically different minority protection issues.[60] The Protestant minority would be 'without any representation whatsoever' in the southern parliament, whereas in the north the minority would be substantially represented, making a Second Chamber unnecessary. Clause 4, prohibiting the Irish parliaments from passing any discriminatory legislation, would provide enough protection. This effectively determined the eventual provisions, giving the southern and northern senates notably different aspects. The southern was to consist of representatives of the churches, the Irish peers, privy counsellors, and nominees representing commerce, labour, and the 'learned bodies' – a definite attempt to give some public voice to the minority. The northern senate would be made up of the Lord Mayor of Belfast, the Mayor of Derry, and twenty-four members elected by the House of Commons. At most the minority would have the same weight on the senate as it had in the lower house.[61]

Carson chose this point in the debate to issue a ringing endorsement of the Council idea. It was 'not going to be the impotent body that a number of people think it will be'. Indeed 'the biggest advance towards unity in Ireland was this conception of the Council'. His point was that whereas formal moves to unification would not work, this could well lead to 'measures and suggestions for the benefit of the whole of Ireland', and eventually something more. He was 'optimistic enough to hope' that the Council contained 'the germ of a united Ireland in [the] future'.[62] This might be kicking the issue into the long grass, in practical terms, but at the symbolic level it suggested that the concept had some moral traction.

The last serious discussion of unity came when the Ulster MPs put down an amendment to Clause 4 a couple of days later, requiring that any vote on unification could be carried only by an absolute majority of the northern parliament – not merely a majority of those present at the vote. Charles Craig insisted that 'a matter of such importance as the sweeping away of the Northern parliament . . . ought not to be left to a mere snap division'. Some further safeguard was needed. Interestingly, Craig suggested that a referendum would satisfy this, though evidently an absolute majority would be simpler to apply. Ronald McNeill added a further argument, that without this proviso 'the question whether the North is to unite with the South will come up again and again at every election' for the northern and probably the southern parliament as well. When Worthington-Evans suggested that the Ulster concern was exaggerated, Carson charged that he had 'not really grasped what those objections are': if you were going to bring about the union of the two parliaments 'you ought to take care that the majority which brings that about is really representative, on that question, of the particular jurisdictions which they purport to represent'. And 'if these Parliaments are to work at all . . . you ought not to have hanging over them at every election the question as to whether they would agree to the amalgamation of the North and South'. He did not believe there was any colonial constitution which would 'allow the abolition of a Parliament by a bare majority of those who happened to be present . . . You certainly could not do it in America . . . I do not know any Constitution under which you can do it.'[63]

The notion of an absolute majority was scoffed at by some MPs, who pointed out that no Westminster legislation secured such a majority, and that if people were deeply concerned about an issue, it would surely not pass on a 'snap vote'. 'I really do not think, when we are dealing with a matter so important to the aspirations of the Irish people, that we should go out of our way to rake up impossible things which cannot happen if adequate notice is given.' This, of course, not only confirmed for the Ulster MPs that the British saw the aspirations of the Irish people as paramount, but also that they regarded a vote for Irish union as a normal piece of legislation, not as a potentially catastrophic constitutional revolution. The debate petered out, with Worthington-Evans balancing the arguments. It may be said 'that we are putting up a barrier against union', that the bill 'is not trying to bring about union'. But 'a union which was not brought about by an absolute majority would not be a real union and would not work'. Still, he protested a little feebly, 'we do not want it to be said that there is anything in this Bill which puts up a barrier against union'.[64] In the end, the Ulster amendment was agreed.

The Council occupied a few more minutes of parliamentary time when the question of whether its powers would be 'delegated' or 'transferred' once again showed how far from fully baked the project was. The last issues that cropped up in the Home Rule Bill debate were the division of the police forces and the judiciary, and the tetchy old question of proportional representation. The government now proposed (in Clause 10) that the police should not be 'handed over' to Irish control until the parliaments had been working for three years. Then, if no other arrangements had been made, they would be split between the two administrations. Carson led the oppositional charge once again, protesting that 'in the present condition of Ireland, I cannot imagine anything more difficult to carry out than dividing up the police, and saying "You must have these police, whether you like them or not". This force,' he added, 'has always been an imperial force directed by this House, and never paid out of local funds.'[65] He certainly had a point, but this time he failed to carry it.

The Ulster MPs had never troubled to disguise their dislike of the proportional representation introduced in Clause 14. The question had become not whether but how long it would endure. Colonel Guinness had called for the bill to specify a minimum of ten years, but the Ulster Unionists wanted three. The government now proposed a period of six years, or two elections, before the system could be altered. It did not want 'to take away from any minority any security that proportional representation would give to it' (though it was clearly not prepared to make that security permanent). Minority protection was piously supported by some, though the issue as usual produced some derisory views – one MP calling PR 'a very harmless form of pleasure . . . a mild form of amusement which people with nothing better to do indulge in from time to time if they are not particularly strong in their minds'. He did make a more serious point as well: since the Act represented an attempt 'to entrust the two Irish peoples with their separate destinies', the sooner they could 'take full responsibility' the better.[66]

BETTER GOVERNMENT OF IRELAND?

The Ulster MPs, still flourishing their principled objection to home rule, abstained on the bill's final reading. The Government of Ireland Act received the royal assent on 23 December 1920, a full twelve months since Lloyd George had announced it. In that year the situation in Ireland had been transformed – disastrously, for the British government. When Long's committee put the bill together, IRA activity was largely confined to occasional raids for arms. Three days before Lloyd George spoke, it attempted to assassinate the Viceroy. The prime minister's sardonic reaction to the news – 'they are bad shots' – showed that he had some way to go before taking them seriously. By the time the bill was introduced, dozens of police posts had been attacked and one had been captured; over four hundred were abandoned as indefensible. Through much of the Irish countryside, security forces could only move in patrols ten or twenty strong. By the time the bill's committee stage was complete, the IRA had formed permanent 'flying columns' capable of ambushing such patrols. While parliament fretted over the timing of the transfer of functions to the Irish parliaments and council, the west Cork IRA annihilated one such patrol of the elite RIC Auxiliary Division, and in December, after another attack near the military HQ in Cork, the Auxiliaries duly took revenge by burning the centre of Cork city. By the time the bill was enacted, martial law had been declared in four south-western counties, Cork, Kerry, Limerick, and Tipperary. Four more were added at the end of the year.

7

The State

'A TABLE, A CHAIR AND AN ACT OF PARLIAMENT'

By the time the Government of Ireland Act finally became law, a key part of the Northern Ireland state apparatus had already been established. The process was accelerated by Unionist reaction to the republican military campaign – the demand that the government take 'urgent action' to head off civil war (and 'restrain' the loyalist rank and file from taking 'regrettable' action of their own). The Ulster leaders had called for 'a system of reprisals', but that, as we have seen, never materialized; the unsystematic reprisals which did erupt, effective though they may have been in increasing the flow of information from the public, were distinctly unsettling to the advocates of law and order. Instead Ulster Unionists were given a separate professional administrator, Sir Ernest Clark, tasked with establishing a governmental apparatus, equipped (as he later noted) with just 'a table, a chair and an Act of Parliament'.

Churchill's pugnacious query at the 23 July Cabinet conference, 'what would happen if the Protestants of the six counties were given weapons', and charged with maintaining law and order, had drawn a dusty response from the Castle officials. Lord Curzon had likewise seen 'the arming of Ulster' as 'a most fatal suggestion'. William Wylie was almost beside himself with alarm – 'in Belfast the Protestants would reduce the Catholics to a state of terror. In Tyrone there would be unceasing and unending civil war.' James Craig, unruffled as usual, asserted that if they were sworn in as special constables they would be effectively disciplined, and something like seven infantry battalions could then be redeployed to the rest of Ireland.[1] Churchill's idea of raising 30,000 men in Ulster was scouted by Henry Wilson, who sharply lectured him 'this would mean "taking sides", would mean civil war and savage reprisals'. (Wilson reminded himself that 'Winston does not realise these things in the least and is a perfect idiot as a statesman'.)[2]

The clarity of Wilson's awareness about the peril of 'taking sides' did not fully percolate to the situation on the ground, where the army was naturally inclined to see one of the two sides as posing less of an immediate threat. Fred Crawford crowed that Colonel Moore Irvine, the UVF organizer in Derry, had so impressed the army commander that 'the GOC now refers everything to him' – 'Irvine says he is virtually the governor of Derry'.[3] It was no doubt true that, as Crawford noted, 'the GOC recognizes that the UVF are for King and country', and were useful allies in a volatile situation. But it is worth noting that though it has become 'a common ploy in guerrilla wars to arm a native militia to do the dirty work', the British government 'never played the ethnic card'.[4] There was no repeat of the brutal Yeomanry and Militia campaigns of the 1790s. It has also to be said that nationalists naturally never appreciated this comparative perspective.

In retrospect the creation of the Ulster Special Constabulary (USC) has an air of inevitability. The regular police force, the Royal Irish Constabulary – concentrated in large stations where they 'were apt to shut and bolt the door at sunset and not emerge until the morning' – was dismissed as a broken reed. The resistance of Sir Nevil Macready, commander-in-chief of the army, to the gendarmerie idea had been outflanked, and the Lisburn inferno overcame his objection to arming the Protestants. (Though he thought it 'rather shakes one's faith in the "discipline" of the Ulster people' that 'no attempt was made to stop' the destruction.) In August, Belfast was festooned with placards announcing that the UVF was to be recognized, but on whose authority was unclear. Whether it would be a national or a provincial force and how it would be structured were also still uncertain. Under Secretary John Anderson and Macready both rejected the talk of Chief Secretary Hamar Greenwood 'enrolling loyal men in the North as Special Constables' as amounting to an acceptance of civil war, and Churchill had envisaged a force that would operate across the whole country. The military commander in Belfast warned at the end of the month that the re-formation of the UVF would 'only lead to more trouble and excitement, more nerves and consequently more attacks on the Catholic populations'.[5] In the end, the decision to raise an official force was taken primarily because a new Ulster administration refused to delay it any longer.

In September, while the Government of Ireland Bill was still drifting through the parliamentary circuit – three months before its eventual passage on to the statute book and nine months before the creation of the northern parliament – the government began preparations for the long-term administration of the six-county area. Clark, a senior Treasury official, was appointed Assistant Under Secretary in Belfast – a post created, as the Under Secretary told him, 'under pressure from the Members of Parliament of Northern Ireland'. This was Clark's later recollection: it seems unlikely that Anderson used the title 'Northern Ireland' at that point, though in briefing Clark on the remit of his post Anderson certainly wrote of an 'office for the six counties'.[6] The pressure was real, also. When Craig met the Cabinet on 2 September he pushed for two crucial initiatives: the appointment of an official who would report directly to the Chief Secretary, bypassing Anderson and the Dublin administration, whose nationalist sympathies were 'a matter of common knowledge'; and the raising of a full-time special constabulary 2,000 strong with a much larger local part-time reserve. He may have thought he had got the first, though the government soon rowed back, trying not to appear to be allowing Craig to set the pace. It made sure that Craig did not make the announcement first, and established that Clark would be Anderson's subordinate, not a parallel Under Secretary.

Some Ulster leaders had hoped to get not a civil servant but a Parliamentary Private Secretary for Ulster – Charles Craig's name was prominent. To dampen expectations of instant separation Clark went to Belfast via Dublin (to report to his chief), and issued a statement there specifically denying that his appointment was 'a preliminary step towards the partition of Ireland'.[7] His initial reception in Belfast was, as a result, guarded. Clark had set up the income tax system for Cape Colony, but seems to have known nothing about Ireland. He found Ulster strange, as well he might. When he first met the Ulster leaders in Greenwood's London office, before he was given the appointment, he found them 'full of grievances', painting 'a picture of the deathly peril which threatened all loyalists'. Their world view bore no resemblance to Clark's 'notions of an ordered government'. Then Craig came up, 'towering above' him, and said, 'Now you are coming to Ulster you must write this one word across your heart'; he 'tapped out with his finger on my chest, "U-L-S-T-E-R" '.[8] Unusual at an appointment interview, no doubt, but unsurprisingly it made a big impression on him. The Unionist leadership was determined that Clark should 'support the majority'; 'new government officials and all new appointments to constabulary etc should be those who are prepared to support this new form of government'. This view should be 'firmly impressed on the military and constabulary authorities, who hitherto have considered that their responsibility is to act as mediators between those holding "loyal" views and those desirous of establishing a republic'. The latter could not 'be regarded merely as a "political opponent" but must be repressed'.[9]

Clark ('virtually alone' in Belfast, as he recalled) was soon visited by a delegation urging him to request additional powers which would make him independent of Dublin Castle. He held firm, telling them he could not discuss the issue, and that he was 'an Assistant Under Secretary only'. Within a fortnight he and Hamar Greenwood, who was visiting Belfast, again had to face a Unionist deputation reiterating their total distrust of the Irish administration. 'We have not the smallest confidence in the officials in Dublin Castle.' Anderson's deputy James MacMahon in particular 'may or may not be in sympathy with Sinn Féin', but Sinn Féin certainly saw him as a friend – so he was not 'favourable to this province'.[10] Clark remained Anderson's subordinate, but the nature of his mission increasingly turned him into what the Unionists wanted him to be.

Carrying out Greenwood's instructions to 'do all in his power to ensure the restoration of normal employment' – getting the expelled workers back to work – he managed to negotiate a compromise by which expellees would not have to make a declaration of loyalty. Instead of formally renouncing any connection with Sinn Féin, they would be assumed 'on their honour' (in theory at least) to have none. But Clark tacked on a crucial rider: 'it would greatly add to the chance of a general return to work' if the Special Constabulary were enlisted 'without any further delay'.[11]

'WE WOULD NOT TOUCH YOUR SPECIAL CONSTABULARY WITH A 40-FOOT POLE'

The structure and conditions of service of the Ulster Special Constabulary were published on 22 October, with recruitment starting at the beginning of November. The three quite distinct classes of service, one full-time, one part-time, and one without fixed time commitments, seem to have been worked out by Clark himself (along with the enrolment forms, uniform designs, and the oath to be taken by new constables). The A Class were to be paid and equipped like the RIC, given a six-week training course, and placed under RIC discipline. The part-time B Class would receive clothing allowances and be equipped as each RIC County Inspector deemed appropriate; they would serve one evening a week as well as receiving training at other times. The C Class would only be called on to serve in emergency conditions. Clark drew up the regulations, but, as Wilfrid Spender's wife happily noted in her diary, the result was 'almost entirely' what her husband had suggested.

The remnant of the Irish Party greeted the news sardonically: 'the Chief Secretary is going to arm pogromists to murder the Catholics,' John Dillon told the Commons. 'Instead of paving stones and sticks they are to be given rifles.' The assumption that the USC would be a Protestant force was almost universal, and indeed Joe Devlin made sure it would be: 'we would not touch your special constabulary with a 40-foot pole'.[12] Recruitment notices, issued under the 1832 Special Constabulary (Ireland) Act (re-enacted in 1914) spoke neutrally of 'well-disposed citizens' between the ages of twenty-one and forty-five. Clark made a point of saying that if enough Catholics enrolled, Catholic units could be formed for Catholic areas; but though a handful of Catholics did apply, no coherent effort was made to encourage them directly.[13] They would have needed plenty of encouragement, since, as one liberal paper pointed out, 'all the eager spirits who have driven nationalist workmen from the docks or demonstrated their loyalty by looting Catholic shops' would be joining. And while most loyalist organizations urged their members to enrol, the nationalists actively discouraged theirs. Unexpectedly, though, the Grand Orange Lodge refused to commit the order to joining the Specials; Crawford protested, 'surely ... the more Orangemen we have in that force, the better it will be for Protestant interests'.[14]

Spender issued a circular to Battalion commanders of the Belfast UVF a week after this, 'to let you know the views of the UVF HQ in regard to this [SC] force'. Government plans were, he said, 'a great advance on all previous proposals' – they 'definitely recognize that there are two distinct elements among the population', the loyal and the rest. The government was asking for the 'help of all Loyalists of Ulster', 'to arm with Firearms, to confer certain privileges, to recognize them, and to indemnify them for injuries incurred in the performance of their duties'. He underlined the key role they would play in state building: 'the new Ulster Parliament will depend for its initial success in a large measure on the efficient way in which the Special Constables perform their duties'. 'I know that our Great Leader can feel certain that the good name of Ulster will depend upon their performing their duties conscientiously and impartially, under discipline, and with that restraint towards those who disagree with us which as always marked our Organization.'[15] The UVF commander in Londonderry, Moore Irvine, emphasized that recruits must be 'men of integrity and strength of character', because 'the establishment of a Special Constabulary force marks the beginning and foundation of our own rule in the province'.[16]

Everyone engaged in creating the USC was aware that its primary purpose was to provide the infant Northern Ireland state with the elementary capability to vindicate its authority. So were observers like the nationalist *Irish News* of Belfast, which on 1 November identified the enrolment of Special Constables 'with the proposed imposition of a bogus Parliament on six Ulster counties'. Moore Irvine – who moved seamlessly from his UVF command to the position of USC County Commandant for Londonderry – explained that the Specials might be the 'chief controlling agency during the forthcoming transition stages of government'.[17] Clark's enthusiastic embrace of the project (which went beyond mere bureaucratic facilitation) stemmed from his belief – as he explained to Anderson – that 'the feeling of insecurity' which existed in Belfast was a real social problem. Even if it were illusory, as he had originally assumed, it would have had significant effects, but he also concluded that 'the secret information in the possession of the Government . . . affords justification for the feeling'.[18] The danger was more of the spontaneous street-level action by loyalists which might rekindle and possibly worsen the violence of the summer.

General orders for the Ulster Special Constabulary issued on 17 November specified that administration was to be controlled in each county by an advisory board of three magistrates, the RIC County Inspector and the USC Commandant. Enrolment of the A Specials was brisk, with numerous ex-servicemen in the market for work, and the first two platoons completed their training at Newtownards early in December. In mid-December, Clark transferred control of the force to the new RIC Divisional Commissioner for Ulster, Lt Col Charles Wickham (previously on the staff of General Knox's anti-Bolshevik expedition in Russia).[19] By the end of the year 1,500 had been sworn in. By the spring of 1921, A Specials reinforcing the RIC made it possible to reopen thirty barracks which had been evacuated in 1919–20, a significant recovery of territorial control.

The A Specials were seen by some as more neutral than the part-timers. When General Ricardo (another UVF leader now a USC county commander) worried about the lack of B class recruits in County Tyrone, he suggested enrolling more A class, on the grounds that it could not be construed as the wholesale arming of Protestants. This may have been intended to counter financial objections, but in any case his advice was not taken.[20] The B class establishment was laid down in January as ten times the combined strength of RIC and A Specials in each county – a rate that would have produced 30,000 for the province. In fact it would not even reach two-thirds of that total, and recruiting would remain patchy. It was strongest in solid Protestant areas, where the Specials were not so necessary, though the recruitment records do not show how many were members of the UVF.[21] The wage bill has been described as 'astronomical'.[22]

The Divisional Commissioner's first orders for the B Specials were quite restrictive: they could only carry out raids or searches with their County Inspector's permission, and had to be accompanied by a member of the regular RIC. Patrols had to be ordered by the RIC;

Specials were 'under no circumstances' to act on their own initiative. 'In particular an order to fire must come from the senior member of the RIC present.' By February 1921 orders had been significantly modified: 'In the event of a Patrol not being accompanied by an RIC representative, the Special sergeant then must act on his own initiative.' Special Constabulary going on patrol were to 'inform the local DI and invite him or his representative to accompany the patrol'.[23] Independent patrolling was clearly recognized as an essential part of their duties in the first quarter of 1921. Some of the remaining restrictions indicated why the new force might attract criticism: 'The use of "Party Expressions" and words likely to give offence when passing the houses of the "other side" is strictly forbidden when on duty.'

By June the RIC County Inspector for Londonderry reported that a large number of B Specials had been enrolled and were now regularly patrolling all parts of the county at night. There had been no case of serious indiscipline, and relations with regular RIC had become 'most harmonious' (the RIC had initially been sceptical, he noted, but now realized the value of having a large organized armed force in the event of an IRA ambush campaign). The Unionist view was unequivocal: the Specials were 'more responsible for saving Northern Ireland from anarchy than either the army or the RIC'.[24]

'THE NORTH IS FREE'

Surprisingly, the belated appearance of the Government of Ireland Act was accompanied by a decline in sectarian violence, despite intense public interest in 'the political debate surrounding the impending legislation'.[25] People 'made a conscious effort to enjoy Christmas'. Generally, ordinary Unionists moved at this stage, as their parliamentary party had, from seeing devolution as an undesirable (and potentially dangerous) step, a 'sacrifice' on their part, to acceptance that it would provide them with as much security as they needed. This was a prelude to uncharacteristic enthusiasm.

In the wake of the bureaucracy, the political establishment of Northern Ireland took shape in early 1921. Carson, widely expected to become the first prime minister, demurred, pleading ill-heath and age – the task was, he suggested, one for the next generation. This could only mean Craig, who had mixed feelings about relocating his political career from Westminster to Belfast. Carson resigned the leadership of the Ulster Unionist Party on 4 February, and Craig resigned from the Admiralty (where he had just been appointed Financial Secretary) in March; his wife had 'never seen him so depressed' as when he came home after 'his last day at the House, giving up the keys of his locker, etc., and turning the card on the door of his room' – this despite 'a long chat with the Prime Minister'.[26] But as he announced in his election address, 'the cause is sacred and worthy of every personal sacrifice'. Carson departed with a statesmanlike admonition, 'From the outset let us see that the Catholic minority have nothing to fear from Protestant majority. Let us take care to win all that is best among those who have been opposed to us in the past.'[27] Craig's first task was to win the election of the northern parliament, set for 24 May – Empire Day – under a PR system which most Unionists feared would favour Sinn Féin. Gestures of amity across the sectarian divide recurred through the election campaign. The *Impartial Reporter* firmly insisted in February that 'the Roman Catholic must feel as safe and secure under the new condition of things as under the Imperial Parliament' (as long as they did not import 'the methods of the South'). The *Ballymena Observer* noted that moderate nationalists could help make a great success of the new parliament.[28] Less than three weeks before polling day, Craig went to meet de Valera in Dublin. This was, in light of the recent past (and the following half-century), truly extraordinary, but if it was intended to deliver on Carson's plea, it did not get beyond the level of gesture. More likely it was a dutiful response to pressure from Lloyd George, whose fixer Andy Cope set up the meeting. Hamar Greenwood, picking a figure apparently at random, described it as 'the most hopeful thing in 750 years'. And it has been said that Craig's 'willingness to put himself in the hands of the Dublin Castle liberal peace faction' was a 'really crucial development'; it showed that he did not object to their strategy as long as it did no harm to Ulster.[29]

Given the improbability of Craig's journey – escorted from Dublin, where he had met the Viceroy, to a 'suburban villa' (probably in Blackrock) by 'three of the worst looking toughs' he had ever seen – the substance of the encounter was sadly predictable. The Dáil President, by now often provocatively called the President of Ireland, was baffled to find that Craig 'spoke of the Union as if it were a mystical thing'. Craig, in turn, had to listen as decorously as he could to de Valera's long walk through Irish history: after half an hour he had reached Brian Boru, 'after another half an hour he had advanced to the period of some king a century or two later'.[30] Here the lack of a shared history was starkly plain, even if the President gave no sign of perceiving this. They parted politely after ninety minutes. Next time de Valera asked Craig to meet him, 'to learn the views of a certain section of our people of whom you are representative', Craig declined.

Since they had no intention of entering the southern parliament that the 1920 Act envisaged, Sinn Féin might simply have boycotted the elections, or decided to prevent them taking place. Indeed it was Macready's warning that the republicans had the power to do this – outside Ulster at least – that finally brought Lloyd George to accept that the Act would never operate in the 'South'. The republican leaders instead decided to use the electoral process to elect a 'Second Dáil', but the election impelled them belatedly to focus on the partition issue. Even now it took repeated requests from northern nationalists for policy guidance to start the process. Nationalists in western Ulster had rallied to Sinn Féin in the belief that the movement would be more effective in organizing resistance to partition than the parliamentary party, but when a conference in Omagh had asked Dublin for a definite steer in November 1920, it got no reply. Once the Government of Ireland Act had passed, they came calling again. As they saw it, the Tyrone nationalist leader George Murnaghan explained to Arthur Griffith on 4 January, they faced a choice between boycotting the election and contesting it on the basis of abstention. Murnaghan said he had always believed that 'it was never intended to set up the northern parliament', but had now changed his mind. When Griffith put the issue to the Dáil Cabinet, it was clear that several of them still thought, as Michael Collins put it, that 'this Partition Act will never come into force'. But Collins accepted that Sinn Féin should be ready in case it did: he advocated contesting the election with a pledge to 'ignore the Partition Act and carry on with their colleagues in the south of Ireland as a national body, in fact as the Dáil'.[31] He evidently still believed that the Belfast boycott would be of 'vital importance' in solidifying nationalist opinion behind Sinn Féin.

De Valera worried that unless Sinn Féin could win at least ten seats 'it would be boomed abroad that these counties were practically a homogeneous political unity which justified partition', so it might be better to boycott the elections; but on the other hand 'letting the elections go by default would seem to be the abandonment of the North as hopeless to us' – 'in a sense of partition'. It could 'kill the republican movement in the North'. So he followed Collins's line, adding that abstention could allow divisions to emerge between 'capital' and 'labour' among Unionist MPs.[32] Collins believed that Sinn Féin could expect to win thirteen or fourteen seats, and urged that they should maintain their previous policy of 'contesting every seat in Ireland'. The real importance of this course would be to prevent 'the idea and acceptance of Partition entering into the minds and actions of the Irish people'.[33] Collins held to the conviction that the north-east 'must be redeemed for Ireland'; it 'must not be allowed to settle down in the feeling that it is a thing apart from the Irish nation'. To this end, local authorities in Tyrone and Fermanagh, substantially republican/nationalist, should resist incorporation, 'secure these for Ireland & so reduce the partitioned counties to four'.[34]

Devising a joint electoral strategy proved difficult, and an arrangement was only reached because of common opposition to partition, assisted by the Catholic clergy's elastic definition of politics, and the nature of the proportional representation system. In February, Devlin's dismissal of the 'simulacrum of a Parliament' and exhortation to 'those who abhor partition' to organize and prepare was dramatically reinforced by Bishop MacRory in his Lenten Pastoral. MacRory's sense of the boundary between pastoral and political opinion had been made clear in his assertion (in August 1920) that bigotry in Belfast would continue 'until this city is taught that it depends on Ireland'. Now, after denouncing the Government of Ireland Act as 'a mockery of Ireland's claims' – a highly political assertion faintly disguised by his invocation of 'justice and fair play' – the bishop spelt out that the issues involved were not 'merely' political: 'the whole question of education is involved'. The bishops, indeed, were 'in a state of near-paranoia on the educational question'.[35] In it, 'eternal interests are at stake', MacRory said: 'the Catholic education of children is a vital matter'. So it would 'probably, very soon, be advisable for representative Catholics and Nationalists of the six counties to meet for counsel together'.

In the openly political world, De Valera and Devlin met in Dublin to try to reach 'some understanding by which joint and united action could be taken'. They fenced over the issue of boycotting the election (which Devlin initially favoured) and the number of candidates. Devlin held out against the 'fatal' idea of abstention, which de Valera insisted on as a basis for any arrangement between them. They set up a four-man working group which agreed over the next few weeks on the (hardly contentious) principle of self-determination and opposition to partition, and eventually to abstention. Both parties were to field twenty-two candidates, until de Valera belatedly analysed the mathematics of PR: equal division could be 'rather worse for us than for the Devlinites', since 'the preferences will be transferred to us rather too late'. He eventually prevailed, with Sinn Féin fielding twenty candidates and the nationalists twelve. The final agreement, drafted by Sean MacEntee, was brokered by Bishop MacRory. On 29 March the *Freeman's Journal* announced that a united front now existed in Ulster, approved by all the northern bishops. All but one of the candidates would be either proposed or seconded by clergy. Essentially, the continuance of constitutional nationalism had been 'purchased at the price of almost complete acquiescence in Sinn Féin policy'.[36] (Glumly noting that 'no one likes this arrangement except the bishops and priests', Dillon admitted that 'any alternative would be worse'.) Without a pact, Devlin said, it would have been impossible to get any nationalist to stand against Sinn Féin outside Belfast.[37]

Considering the magnitude of what was at stake, the northern election passed off fairly quietly. Not absolutely: Sinn Féin's chief election organizer, Eamon Donnelly, reported 'wholesale' intimidation'. 'Cars were set on fire and drivers taken off and beaten', and unsurprisingly some Catholics who returned to cast their votes in areas from which they had been driven out the previous year were attacked. In Belfast, shots were fired frequently enough to show the war was not over; seven people were killed in May, including a young Harbour Constable shot dead in a botched IRA attempt to seize his gun. The day after the poll, a Catholic ex-serviceman was killed, apparently by a sniper, in Butler Street. De Valera appealed to 'north-east Ulster' to use the 'quiet and privacy of the polling booth' (where presumably British bullying might not reach) to vote 'against war with your fellow countrymen' and for 'an end to boycott and retaliation, to partition, disunion and ruin'. Craig warned that 'the eyes of our friends throughout the Empire are upon us'. 'Rally round me,' he urged loyalists, 'that I may shatter our enemies and their hopes of a republic flag. The Union Jack must sweep the polls.' 'Loyalists, both Protestant and Roman Catholic, see that you vote early and give every assistance to the loyalist candidates . . . This is the last and only chance.'[38] Both sides showed some anxiety that the labour vote might split their ethnic bloc. In the event labour polled so weakly that it might as well have stood aside again, as it had in 1918.

Turnout, at 89 per cent, amply reflected the significance of the vote. Constituency boundaries in Belfast proved distinctly favourable to Unionists, with only a single nationalist – Devlin – being elected for four constituencies. The nationalist vote across the six counties was the biggest ever, but even so it was overwhelmed by the Unionist poll. Sinn Féin and the Irish Party ended up with six members each, as against forty Unionists. The 1921 election 'highlighted the existence of two Catholic norths'; the transfer agreement between the two nationalist parties proved very one-sided, with barely a fifth of Sinn Féin's transferable votes going to the parliamentary party.[39] After the count, a relieved *Impartial Reporter* exulted that 'the Union Jack has swept Ulster! . . . the North has put itself outside the bounds of all English party politics. The North is now independent, and nothing can rob her of her parliament . . . the Union is dead, the North is free.' The *Belfast News-Letter* more soberly announced that 'in the Six Counties we are masters of our own fate now, our political, social and economic future is in our own hands'.[40]

'OUR ULSTER'

James Craig became prime minister on 4 May, when the Government of Ireland Act came into effect – the day before his meeting with de

Valera. Besides the prime minister's department, six governmental ministries (Finance, Home Affairs, Labour, Education, Commerce and Agriculture) formed the 'executive committee of the Northern Ireland parliament', otherwise the Cabinet. (Wilfrid Spender became Cabinet Secretary.) The seven-ministry set-up was contentious. Clark had proposed five, and objected to Adam Duffin's call for eight because it would mean that more than a quarter of MPs would be ministers of some kind. Even seven he thought too many, though it is unlikely that a working government could have operated with fewer. The real problem with the administration would not be its size, but its limited outlook, and its low turnover: most ministers served for the rest of their lives, and Craig would never sack any of them. He himself would die in office in 1940. Aside from one member, Lord Londonderry – who left it in 1925 – the government would never diverge from its simple unionism to address the complex political challenge it faced.[41]

The Northern Ireland House of Commons met in Belfast on 7 June, in the council chamber of City Hall (loaned by the corporation for the event, as it had been for the signing of the Covenant, but perhaps more legitimately this time). The Cabinet was sworn in and a speaker elected. Four days later the Commons elected a Senate, supposedly on the same proportional principle as the Commons, though since no nationalists appeared and the only ex officio senator was the Mayor of Belfast, the Second Chamber emerged as entirely Unionist. The northern parliament would be a part-time legislature whose main function was to rubber-stamp government policy rather than hold it to account.

Ronald McNeill said that 'the new order of things was accepted with acquiescence rather than enthusiasm', until it became known that King George V had decided to open the 'Ulster Parliament' – in spite of the 'anarchical condition' of the country. When news arrived that the queen would accompany him, 'the enthusiasm of the loyal people of the North rose to fever heat'. The State Opening of parliament being 'one of the most ancient and splendid of ceremonial pageants illustrating the history of British institutions, the association of this time-honoured ceremonial with the baptism, so to speak, of the latest offspring of the Mother of Parliaments stamped the

Royal seal upon the achievement of Ulster'. For McNeill, it 'gave it a dignity, prestige and promise of permanence which might otherwise have been lacking'.[42]

Behind the scenes, though, it produced a test of Ulster's status in which it did not do so well. Craig assumed that as prime minister he would draft the king's speech, and Whitehall seems to have been happy with this until the king received Craig's text. He rebelled, complaining that he was 'being made the mouthpiece of Ulster rather than the Empire', and was reportedly 'greatly distressed'. At the same moment, General Smuts – by now the Empire's top elder statesman – was urging Lloyd George to use the king's speech to exploit what he believed was 'a real opportunity of touching Irish sentiment'. He thought it 'questionable whether the King should go at all'; but if he were to, his speech could be 'made use of to give a most important lead'. Since the opening of the parliament meant the removal of all possibility of coercing Ulster, Dominion status was now possible. 'The promise of Dominion status *by the King* would create a new situation which would crystallise opinion favourably' both in Ireland and elsewhere.[43]

Smuts pulled no punches in laying out the prime minister's fix: he had to get 'out of a situation which is well nigh desperate'. The situation in Ireland was 'an unmeasured calamity', a 'negation of all the principles of Government which we have professed as the basis of Empire', which would increasingly 'poison both our Empire relations and our foreign relations'. Almost as bad, 'the present methods are frightfully expensive' financially as well as morally – 'and what is worse, they have failed'. This was strong meat, and it is not surprising that Lloyd George's adviser Edward Grigg now opted for a rare defiance of Craig. The idea that he was 'ultimately responsible' for the king's speech turned George V into 'a provincial partisan'; Ulster could not 'dictate the King's utterances'. A new speech was hastily drafted and duly delivered by the thoughtful monarch. Its famous invitation 'to pause, to stretch out the hand of forbearance and conciliation, to forgive and forget', was suitably imprecise, and (tactfully in the circumstances) no direct offer of Dominion status was made, but the tables had been turned. Instead of Ulster using the king as a 'mouthpiece', the king used Ulster as a lever. And while that key phrase was a call to end armed conflict, it was also very clearly an appeal for 'all Irishmen' to unite – 'to join in making for the land the love a new era of peace'. It might indeed be read as a call to end partition.

Whatever its effect on 'Irish sentiment', the speech delivered on Smuts's objectives; the tempo of communications with the republican leadership quickened, and a military truce – a prelude to peace negotiations – was arranged early the next month. In the north, the state opening of the northern parliament – outwardly the perfect Ulster Unionist festival – was possibly the most successful royal visit ever made to Ireland. Its effects were not entirely straightforward, though. Opening the way to negotiations with Sinn Féin, meant, as a sympathetic historian of the northern state notes, that 'the ground appeared to be shifting under the very feet of the new government'.[44] The Truce which began on 11 July – greeted with a relief bordering on ecstasy across republican Ireland – carried a sinister undertone in the north-east. If there were to be negotiations, the issue of partition would inevitably be on the table; within weeks of Ulster's great triumph, the permanent settlement was once again in question. The Truce 'heralded a particularly vicious summer orgy of rioting in Belfast'.[45] The day it was agreed, a police patrol in west Belfast was attacked and one policeman killed. Rioting broke out, and went on through the 12 July festival; within a week over twenty people were killed.

The solidification of Ulster consciousness showed in extended agonizing in public over the boundary in 1920, with some newspapers, including the *Impartial Reporter*, suggesting like St Loe Strachey that homogeneity should be a primary objective, putting identity above territory, and arguing for a frontier line which would maximize not the northern state area but 'Our Ulster'. But when Craig, bearing out de Valera's pessimistic prognosis, claimed that Sinn Féin's participation in the election helped to legitimize the new state, his aim was to fix that state as it was, not embark on another shake-up.

BOUNDARY QUESTIONS

Before serious Anglo-Irish negotiations had even begun, the question of Ulster's status was raised again. Lloyd George invited Craig to meet and discuss the terms he would offer Sinn Féin, and got a dusty response: the northern Cabinet was 'disturbed', and grass-roots unionists openly outraged. Sinn Féin was for them not a political group but 'the incarnation of evil'; Craig was warned not to take part in any talks, or meet de Valera. One asked him, 'how can we forget the happenings at our very doors – when one word [from him] could have saved hundreds of lives – how can we forgive?'[46] In the third week of July, Craig and de Valera – separately – met Lloyd George in London. Craig advised him (in terms that spoke volumes) to send the British proposals to the Dáil 'in a document full of high-sounding phraseology, which would appeal to the imagination of the Southern Irish'. The prime minister sketched a number of ways in which Craig's government could meet de Valera's insistence that 'any measure of local autonomy' for 'the minority in North East Ulster' must be 'consistent with the unity and integrity of our island'.[47] Since this was in effect a demand that partition be reversed, Craig and his ministers rejected all Lloyd George's devices and returned to Belfast, after issuing a 'striking declaration' (in the opinion of the *Belfast Telegraph*) reaffirming the right of the Northern Ireland 'people' to self-determination.

Lloyd George encouraged Craig to meet de Valera again, if invited, to help him 'realise that Ulster is a fact which he must recognize, not a figment bolstered up by the British government'. Craig told his Cabinet he would not meet unless 'Mr de Valera gave a written statement' that he 'accepted the principle of Ulster's independent rights'.[48] But de Valera did not seek another meeting. Instead he reiterated that Ireland could not 'admit the right of the British Government to mutilate our country, either in its own interest, or at the call of any section of our population'. He did not say 'our people', but that was not intended as a concession.[49]

De Valera, now and later, repeatedly experimented with formulae which might square the circle. At a public session of Dáil Eireann in mid-August he was asked for 'a full and clear definition of his policy with regard to Ulster', and dismayed many by saying that 'if the Republic were recognised, he would be in favour of giving each county power to vote itself out of the Republic'. He had begun to move away from the unreflective hostility to Ulster unionism which

most of those present very clearly demonstrated, and adjust to a disagreeable reality. If they were to insist that Britain recognize an
all-Ireland republic, he told the Dáil, 'they were going to face war'.
Were they ready for that?[50] Throughout his career de Valera, though
popularly seen as the champion of a united Ireland – which was of
course his preferred outcome – would 'mull over some "second-
choice" policy': a federal solution short of a unitary state and vague
on whether it was an interim or a final settlement.[51] This set him
apart from republican fundamentalists, especially those across the
Atlantic: as his American confidant Joe McGarrity would put it at
the height of the civil war, the minimum demand must be a united
Ireland – 'and by that I mean all of Ulster in with the same rights and
privileges as any other part – nothing more, nothing less'.

If the Irish delegates had held to this position, the negotiations
would have broken down on the partition issue rather than, as the
British government would have wanted, the issue of Ireland's sover-
eign status. British public opinion was assumed to be solid against a
republic, but less reliably in favour of partition, at least in the form it
now took. In the event, by the time the crunch came, the Irish negotiating position had become more complicated. This was partly due
to another supposedly inflexible republican purist, Erskine Childers,
who was adopted by de Valera as his expert adviser on the Ulster
issue and sent to London as secretary to the Irish delegation. Childers
started drafting an extended memorandum on 'Ulster Powers' for de
Valera, but never fully completed it. De Valera also put together several drafts for a treaty, but since he had decided not to lead the Irish
delegation in person, the actual drafting of the Irish proposals on
Ulster was done by Arthur Griffith. When Griffith took the draft
treaty to London on 11 October, de Valera withheld the Ulster clause,
apparently intending to recast it, but then seems to have decided
against it. When Griffith asked for it shortly afterwards, he was
told 'I have scarcely changed it at all as you notice'.[52] The clause
allowed each constituency in the six counties – or 'a smaller number'
if they were 'contiguous and forming a territorially continuous group'
(a characteristic bracketing of synonymous adjectives) – to opt out
of the Irish parliament. They would 'be entitled to maintain a legislature' with the same powers as the existing Northern Ireland

parliament. They would send MPs to Dublin rather than Westminster, and it was clearly envisaged that, as Childers had put it, the Ulster parliament's powers 'could be amended and the province itself be abolished by a simple Act of the All-Ireland Parliament'.

This was enough to guarantee that Ulster Unionists would never entertain the proposal, so the issue became whether Britain would shift its own negotiating position to achieve an Irish settlement. If the talks threatened to break down on the point, there was at least a hope that this might happen; those ministers who had pressed for a nine-county Ulster still believed that, as Austen Chamberlain put it at the end of October, the six-county unit was 'illogical and indefensible' and would be the 'worst ground' on which to battle for British public support.[53] By that point, the British were offering Ireland Dominion status, with the exclusion of Ulster on the basis of a 'new delimitation' of the border. This new delimitation would, as Griffith explained to de Valera on 9 November, 'give us the districts in which we are in a majority'.

The 'boundary commission' which would do this first cropped up indirectly in mid-October, when Lloyd George told the Irish delegates that such a commission would produce 'a more overwhelming Protestant majority' than the present county border. (The clear implication was that a commission would remove a substantial Catholic element from Northern Ireland.) His point was that if 'Ulster' were ever to be persuaded to 'come in to an Irish unit', there would be 'an advantage in her having a Catholic population' – an argument which had of course been made many times in Cabinet and in parliament.[54] Michael Collins dissented on both points. 'There would have been an alternative to your Boundary Commission,' he said (his past tense here surprising) – 'local option'. He evidently thought this more likely than a commission to take all the 'solid blocks who are against partition' out of Northern Ireland, and he seems to have been unconcerned whether or not that made the remainder less disposed towards unity.

When the negotiations began, the partition issue had been expected to be both the most crucial and the most difficult of all – 'the crux of the problem' as Tom Jones put it to Bonar Law in July. Bonar Law agreed; while 'the longing for peace ... is a strong lever ... I am afraid of the partition difficulty'. He even suggested that success in resolving the 'real difficulty' – that while de Valera 'will find it impossible to treat Ulster as entirely outside his sphere . . . no settlement can be carried in England which imposes anything on the new Ulster Parliament' – would be 'almost as big as winning the war'. He tactfully expressed the hope that the 'very wise' prime minister 'will not make the mistake of trying to put pressure on Ulster to accept any arrangement which brought them in any way under the control' – 'however shadowy' – of a Dublin government.[55] Lloyd George, for his part, warned his colleagues that if the negotiations became 'entangled in the Ulster problem' and broke down over 'the question of Fermanagh and Tyrone, where we had a very weak case' – this would be the worst possible outcome.[56]

In light of all this, it is surprising that partition never derailed the negotiations. The reason for that lay in Lloyd George's renewed use of the idea he had briefly trailed earlier, the boundary commission. Early in November he made a serious effort to shift Craig's position, strongly implying that if he failed he would resign. (His resignation threats had a venerable history, of course, and this one has generally been discounted; the fact that he told private confidants like Lord Riddell and C. P. Scott he would do it may or may not make it more credible.) That he became emotionally invested in the Irish settlement seems beyond dispute. Since coming back from Paris, Lloyd George had spent a lot of time on Ireland. On 5 November his secretary-mistress, Frances Stevenson, noted that he had hardly taken his mind off the Irish talks 'for one minute' in the previous week.[57] A couple of days later he told Tom Jones, 'Craig will not budge one inch', so the negotiations would break down. 'I shall go out . . . I fear we are in for five or six years' reaction. I do not want to lead a reaction.' Then – ever the dramatist even alone with his secretary – he said, 'there is just one other possible way out'. If Sinn Féin would accept 'that the 26 counties should take their own Dominion Parliament and have a Boundary Commission', with 'Ulster' retaining its present powers ('plus the burden of taxation which we bear'), he 'might be able to put that through'. Jones sensibly double-checked his chief's precise meaning, asking, 'I take it that on no account would you give Dominion status to Ulster, and that it would be open to Sinn Féin to put up a customs barrier between the North and South?' Lloyd George 'agreed'.[58]

Once launched, the boundary commission ploy proved astonishingly successful, even though – or maybe because – its details remained hazy. Griffith told Jones they would 'prefer a plebiscite', but believed that 'in essentials' a boundary commission would be 'very much the same'. He reported it to de Valera as 'a tactical [move] to deprive "Ulster" of support in England by showing it was utterly unreasonable in insisting to [sic] coerce areas that wished to get out'. Although Jones had made clear to him that the commission's remit would cover all nine Ulster counties, he did not pass this on to the president. Griffith said he had declined Lloyd George's invitation to 'stand behind' such a proposal, but told him 'we realized its value as a tactical manoeuvre'; if he made it 'we would not queer his position'.[59] De Valera remained adamant that whilst he might perhaps understand Griffith giving up independence for unity, 'you have got neither this nor that'. He could not subscribe to an oath of allegiance or give 'N. E. Ulster power to vote itself out of the Irish state'. Evidently he, and probably Griffith himself, did not grasp how Griffith's carefully phrased undertaking might lead to the dramatic resolution engineered by Lloyd George on the night of 5 December. The 'most bitterly contested question' arising from the prime minister's proposal has always been 'whether he left the likely outcome . . . to the imagination of Griffith and Collins or told them directly, or implied, that the purpose of a commission would be a substantial rectification of an obvious anomaly in the 1920 partition'.[60]

Lloyd George's resignation threat was designed to hold both the Irish delegation and his own negotiating team, the 'British seven', to his line. With Craig he had less leverage. He believed that the threat to subject Northern Ireland to the United Kingdom's tax regime would sway the Ulster leaders – 'They have their hands on their hearts the whole time,' he told Stevenson, 'but if it comes to touching their pockets they quickly slap their hands back in.' This bit of cultural profiling he supported by telling him, 'I know – my wife is a Presbyterian!'[61] Even before it reached Craig, the threat produced a 'very acute discussion' among the British negotiators, with Worthington-Evans angrily protesting that since 'Ulster was to get all her powers under the 1920 Act . . . there could be no change in the matter of finance'. Lloyd George stuck to his guns, snorting that it was 'preposterous for Ulster if she [sic] stood out of the All-Ireland Parliament to send representatives to Westminster to put burdens on the Irish tax payer which they did not themselves share', but his insistence that they 'can't expect to get the benefits of both systems' turned the atmosphere 'electric'. It was only calmed by Churchill directing attention to some other drafting point. 'The little scene was over', but Chamberlain saw fit to instruct the prime minister that 'we were now not writing to Celts but to Anglo-Saxons'. The document was to be 'de-floridised'.[62]

Craig's riposte was to call for Dominion status for Northern Ireland, effectively ending the union. The loss of Westminster representation would be 'a less evil than inclusion in an all-Ireland parliament'. Curiously, Craig's intransigence seems to have encouraged Griffith, who read it as showing 'the cloven hoof of Ulster's sordidness' – selling out the supposedly sacred union 'for the sake of a lower income tax'. Griffith seemed happy to believe it when Jones told him that, if Sinn Féin stood by Lloyd George, 'we might have Ulster in before many months had passed'.[63]

Why did Griffith think Lloyd George might ever 'force Ulster in', abandoning the 'pledge', so often repeated, not to use coercion? Was it the 'scorn for political realities' which some would say marked Sinn Féin, a movement that 'despised politics as the art of the possible'?[64] Certainly Griffith had his own mix of idealism with realism: like all nationalists he believed that ultimately Ulster would not have to be 'forced'; it would be enough for Britain to stand back. But he also grasped the real threats to Lloyd George's position. The prime minister was undoubtedly on a knife-edge, depending on support from Chamberlain and Birkenhead, who backed him personally but found his Irish policy dangerous. Chamberlain at one point gave the Irish delegates a glimpse of the edge of the abyss, pleading 'do not press it too far I beg. You are not aware of the risks we are taking with our whole political future.'[65] Chamberlain was acutely aware of the threat to his position posed by Bonar Law, 'an Ulsterman by descent and spirit', and 'a very ambitious man . . . disposed to think the first place might & ought to be his'. Griffith was equally aware of the fear that Bonar Law would use the National Unionist conference in Liverpool – exactly at the moment he was presented with the border-revision prospect – to challenge Chamberlain's leadership. Even though this did not happen, the conference compelled the leading Unionist ministers to reiterate unambiguously the pledge not to coerce Ulster, and it seems likely that as the negotiations reached a climax in December, Griffith (like many others) believed that the Coalition government could fall by the end of the year. Bonar Law indeed had written violently that further pressure on Ulster would lead to 'the irretrievable smashing of the Coalition'.[66] If that happened, the Ulster clauses of the Treaty might – as Chamberlain noted on 5 December – 'be put into the waste paper basket with all other promises'.[67]

But just what Griffith believed he was getting in return for accepting partition as well as the oath of allegiance to the Crown – abandoning both unity and the republic, as republicans would see it – remains hard to pin down. In the evening of 13 November, Jones showed him a draft he and Chamberlain had drawn up, stating that if Ulster wanted to remain separate 'it would be necessary to revise the boundary of Northern Ireland'. This might be done by a commission, which would 'be directed to adjust the line both by inclusion and exclusion so as to make the boundary conform as closely as possible to the wishes of the population'. In the draft treaty presented to the Irish delegates three days later, a boundary commission would determine the border in accordance with 'the wishes of the inhabitants'.[68] The phrase 'inclusion and exclusion', implying that there might be transfers on both sides of the 1920 line, had disappeared. John Chartres, the delegation's secretary, later insisted that no limitation of its remit was mentioned in the first draft – there was 'not a word about economic or geographical considerations', and that Griffith had been given 'express' assurance that there would be no 'exclusion of large bodies' of nationalists from the Irish state. 'No one ever mentioned "minor rectifications" of the existing boundary.' When Lloyd George subsequently introduced the 'limiting phrase' it was specifically to deal with exceptional cases of 'small, non-contiguous districts' like the Glens of Antrim – which he apparently pointed out directly on the map ('in the presence of all the British none of whom made any demur').[69] The officials in attendance outside the negotiating room were not called in ('chiefly because of Childers', Jones would ruefully recall) to help draft what became article XII of the Treaty. Would they have made a difference? As Jones noted, 'there were half a dozen famous lawyers among the plenipotentiaries', but 'it is notorious that a lawyer cannot draft his own Will clearly'.[70] But one of them, the Lord Chancellor (Lord Birkenhead), would later intervene decisively – disastrously, for the Free State – in the interpretation of the boundary commission's remit.

'IMMEDIATE AND TERRIBLE WAR'

In light of subsequent republican charges of the duress applied to the Irish delegation, it is worth noting that the threat of force had been openly discussed, and deliberately discounted by both sides. At the fourth plenary session on 14 October, Lloyd George declared that 'force is not a weapon you can use. It would break in your hands.' He added, 'Mr Collins shakes his head', but 'you do not want to begin your new life with a civil war that would leave you with desolation in its train . . . force is impossible'. Collins, for his part, ruminated that 'By force we could beat them perhaps, but perhaps not. I do not think we could beat them morally. If you kill all of us, every man and every male child, the difficulty will still be there. So in Ulster.' Lloyd George went on to tell Tom Jones with almost comical solemnity on 8 November, 'I have made up my mind definitely . . . I do not make up my mind quickly . . . I will not be a party to firing another shot in the south of Ireland. I have told the King.'[71]

Still, it was Lloyd George's threat of 'immediate and terrible war' that probably – in all nationalist accounts certainly – overcame the resistance in the Irish delegation on 5 December. At that point in the long-drawn-out negotiations, the patience of the British negotiators was stretched thin. The key issues remained the status of both Ireland and Ulster. The 'oath of allegiance' to the Crown had been recast many times, and was now so mangled that it seemed to satisfy both sides (though it would prove to be the biggest sticking point for republicans). The symbolically crucial issue of naming the Irish state had been resolved, with the adoption of the title 'Irish Free State', a literal translation of the word *saorstát*, which had been used as a synonym for *poblacht* as the Republic's official title since 1919.[72] Still, the question of how, or whether Ireland would remain in the Empire was still unresolved, and almost caused a total breakdown in the talks on 4 December, when three of the delegates pressed once again for 'external association', and George Gavan Duffy said 'our difficulty is to come into the Empire'.

After that, the talks were only kept going by a private meeting between Lloyd George and Collins, who noted the prime minister's belief that 'the North would be forced economically to come in', and that 'we would save Tyrone and Fermanagh, parts of Derry, Armagh and Down by the Boundary Commission'. Collins dramatically predicted that if events like a recent police raid on Tyrone County Council were repeated, 'another such incident would inevitably lead to a conflict, and this conflict would inevitably spread through Ireland'. Only major border revision would prevent this.[73] He clearly thought Lloyd George agreed. (Oddly, though, when he briefed the northern IRA chiefs, Denis McCullough and Joe McKelvey, during the Treaty debate, he spoke only of areas 'near the borders of the Saorstát', while he went on to tell the Bishop of Dromore that 'no action and no desire of the Northern parliament' could take 'such places as south and east Down and a great part of Armagh' away from the Irish government.)[74] The final British formula, presented on 5 December, glossed allegiance to the Crown as representing 'the common citizenship of Ireland with Great Britain', and Ireland's 'adhesion to and membership of' – not the Empire but the British Commonwealth of Nations. The Irish delegates still resisted approving the 'Ulster clause', with border adjustment, until they knew Craig had accepted it, but Lloyd George was adamant that it be agreed before he sent it to Craig in time for a meeting of the northern parliament the next day. This was the hinge for his dramatic (if not melodramatic) performance, flourishing two letters, one saying that the Irish delegates had accepted the draft treaty, the other that the negotiations had broken down. If he sent the second, it would mean war 'within three days'.

It has always been easy to see, in retrospect, the implausibility of Lloyd George's precise and pressing schedule – the train 'waiting with steam up at Euston', the destroyer waiting at Holyhead, the messenger needing to have the answer by 10 p.m. if he was 'to reach Sir James Craig in time' – but much harder to recapture the suffocating atmosphere of that evening. The theatrics might not have worked, but for Griffith's previous acceptance of the boundary commission proposal, which Lloyd George now flourished to the dismay of Griffith's colleagues. Griffith, outwardly at least unruffled, agreed that 'if you stand by the Boundary Commission, I stand by you'. Maybe he realized he had been outmanoeuvred, but more likely he still believed that border revision would prove decisive in achieving ultimate unity. Force had been ruled out, as had 'coercion', and consent remained a distant prospect; but the pressure of realities – what Collins, in defending the decision to sign the Treaty, would call 'the duress of facts' – could impel voluntary realignment. There can be no doubt that although Collins still disliked the commission idea, it was central to the outcome of the intense, fractious meeting of the Irish delegates at which they decided to sign. Robert Barton's account, the most reliable, paints E. J. Duggan springing to life for the first time at this meeting, threatening that those who refused to sign would be 'hanged from lamp-posts' by irate Dubliners. Then Griffith 'stood in front of the fireplace, held up his hand' and said that if the Ulster Unionists 'don't agree to join us' the boundary commission would take away 'half their territory'. This he repeated several times: 'Griffith was highly optimistic about the results of a proposed plebiscite' [sic].[75]

That the British government got essentially what it wanted, while the Irish delegation (as de Valera said) did not get either of its core demands, has always been clear. Nationalist history, even the cogent Free Stater view of their inevitability, has always seen the Treaty terms as a disappointment at best – at worst a betrayal. A sophisticated recent version measures 'the magnitude of Lloyd George's achievement' by highlighting Tom Jones's jubilant report of the 'wonderful day' to Maurice Hankey, 'in essentials we have given nothing that was not in the July proposals'.[76] Jones's admiration for Lloyd George's 'extraordinary patience and alertness' was to be expected, as was his sheer relief at the outcome, but we may ask whether he was right. The answer depends primarily on how the boundary commission idea is interpreted. As Denis Gwynn rightly said, the Treaty was 'a repudiation of the Act' of 1920 – which he habitually referred to as the 'Partition Act' – not just in its concession of Dominion status. The boundary commission announced in Article XII of the Treaty 'seemed naturally to imply that the Ulster Unionists would not be allowed to retain the full Six-County area if they did refuse to enter the Free State'.[77]

The Treaty of course did not say this exactly. It provided that the powers of the Free State would 'not be exercisable as regards Northern Ireland' for a month after the Treaty was ratified, and no elections to the Free State parliament would be held there unless the northern parliament passed a resolution calling for them. If it also presented an address to the King 'to that effect', the Government of Ireland Act 1920 would 'continue to be of full force and effect' (including its Council of Ireland provisions). In that case, a commission should determine the 'boundaries' between the North and 'the rest', 'in accordance with the wishes of the inhabitants, so far as may be compatible with economic and geographic conditions'. That this was a new provision, with potentially dramatic implications for the North, can hardly be disputed. Alternatives to the county boundaries had been spoken of several times, but never formally discussed, let alone written into a statutory instrument. The implication that the county boundaries would be modified is very clear – otherwise it would hardly have been worth mentioning. And long before the article was framed, when one of the Irish delegates had objected to the 1920 Act, Lloyd George had told them that the alternative 'would have been a Boundary Commission', which would have created 'a more overwhelming Protestant majority' in the north.[78] The only way it could do that was by transferring extensive territories from the northern state.

The whole course of British policy over the years from 1910 has been seen by many, and by nearly all Irish nationalists, as being at root dedicated to satisfying Ulster Unionism and keeping 'Ulster' in the United Kingdom.[79] From the Unionist standpoint, though, it hardly looked that way. The sinister implications of the Treaty negotiations appeared, with Article XII, to have become a reality. The Government of Ireland Act had been modified, and, crucially, the scale of the modification remained unfixed. The fact that Irish republicans regarded the Treaty as a betrayal of their cause, and that the debate on it precipitated an increasingly violent split – culminating in civil war – provided little reassurance to Unionists; if anything the reverse.

In the Treaty debate in the Dáil, as in the negotiations, the partition issue was less salient than might have been expected. If we were to judge by the crude fact that only nine pages out of 338 in the record of the debate were taken up with partition, we might conclude that it was insignificant. That would certainly be wrong: it was rather that partition was detested by those who were for acceptance as much as those against the Treaty; but both sides expected the existence of Northern Ireland to be a short one. Michael Collins argued that it could not survive, in economic terms, in any case, and that the boundary commission would simply accelerate its collapse. Eamon de Valera, in drawing up his alternative treaty draft – 'Document No. 2' – in mid-December, simply incorporated the Ulster clauses of the Treaty, doing no more than add a declaratory clause asserting Ireland's essential unity. The document came to have a significance he would regret: at the time he called it 'the sort of document we would have tried to get', and 'only a bad best'. He did not intend it to be published, in either its original form or the revision he made in January 1922 which omitted the Ulster clauses entirely (just 'a slight change of form', he claimed). It was Arthur Griffith, infuriated by this, who leaked both versions to the press.[80]

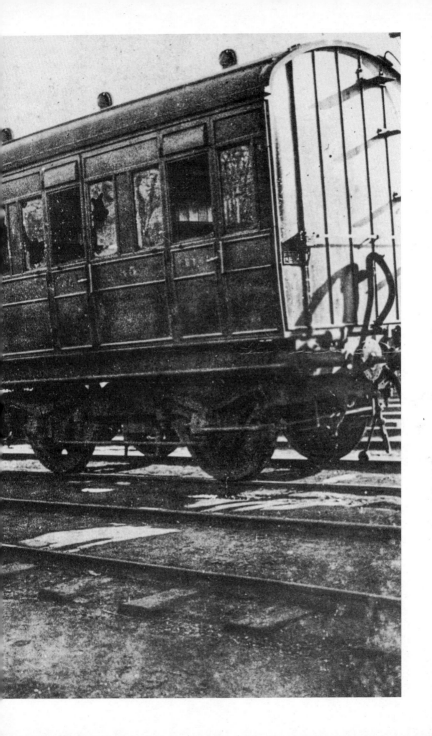

8

The Frontier

It is hardly surprising that Unionists saw the new-minted Northern Ireland as 'a state under siege', or that this perception set the tone for the administration built up over the following months. It has percolated into historical writing too.[1] 'Siege mentality' has become a common characterization of Ulster politics; the *New History of Ireland* suggests that 'a siege mentality prevailed even after the siege had lifted'.[2] There was of course never a 'siege' as such – certainly not of the state – but rather a potent metaphor evoking the visceral fear of being surrounded by natives, the fear that animated the annual celebration of Londonderry's resistance to an actual siege in 1689. The sense of insecurity was sharpened by any sign that British support was faltering.

In 1921 British responses to northern government requests became gradually less obliging, and a note of actual hostility appeared at the end of the year. James Craig's early request for officials from the Treasury to provide an administrative cadre was only hampered by the reluctance of some officials to move to Ireland – they worried about both physical and financial security, reasonably enough as their pension rights were not clear. Under the Government of Ireland Act, existing Irish officials were to be allocated to the two administrations by a Civil Service Committee, and shortly after he withdrew from the negotiations in London in July, Craig asked for that committee and the Joint Exchequer Board to be set up immediately, to accelerate the establishment of a northern administrative service. He was told that the boards would not operate until both parliaments were functioning under the Act; and it became clear that the British government was unwilling to invoke the Act's provision that if either Irish parliament failed to emerge its area would revert to Crown

Colony government. Hamar Greenwood advised the Cabinet in early October that this would prejudice the negotiations with Sinn Féin. When Craig tried another tack, asking that the Lord Lieutenant appoint the southern members of the boards by Order in Council (as per section 69 of the Act), he got the same response.

At the crux of the negotiations a month later when, as we have seen, Lloyd George intended to 'touch Ulster's pockets', Craig plainly felt ambushed. He and his wife were in London, to visit their children at their English school, when he was summoned to meet Lloyd George – to be told that the negotiations now hinged on Northern Ireland accepting an all-Ireland parliament. Craig was furious, and shocked to find 'so many "backsliders" among his old friends and colleagues'. His Cabinet assembled in London on 9 November, to consider Lloyd George's warning that if they did not accept, they would face economic dislocation and a damaging customs barrier on the border. They rejected the proposal 'with scarcely concealed indignation'.[3] The tone of the British press had changed noticeably by this point: Craig later complained of a press campaign against the people of Ulster 'without parallel in British history'. A chorus of minatory advice ranged from the *Birmingham Post*'s warning that if Ulster proved unhelpful in reaching an Irish settlement, 'she will do the greatest disservice it is possible to imagine to the Empire she professes to love', to *The Times*'s stark assertion that Ulster now had to 'make answer to the Empire, and to Great Britain, whether she stands for peace or against it'. The *Daily Express* reversed the famous Unionist slogan with the headline 'Ulster will be wrong', and pulled out all the stops by charging that if it did not abandon its uncompromising attitude 'the Ulster Cabinet' would be 'guilty of the greatest political crime in history'.[4]

'OUR PECULIAR CONDITIONS'

The northern government was acutely conscious of its lack of full autonomy, above all in the sphere of public security itself. Accounts of the 1920–22 period often focus on the assertion of Protestant dominance over the northern Catholic community – the nationalist view in effect. Those (rather few) more sympathetic to the Unionist position present a very different view, where the northern government's dependence on unhelpful British authorities – to the point indeed of 'impotence' – fuelled a deep sense of insecurity.[5] As Belfast was convulsed by riots after the Truce, Craig's government called for the reimposition of the curfew, citing 'the situation which has arisen in Belfast through attacks on Constabulary'. Curfew, along with most of the security measures imposed in Ireland under emergency laws (the 1920 Restoration of Order in Ireland Act and the 1887 Crimes Act) over the previous two or three years, was suspended. The 'choking off' that Churchill spoke of during the Truce talks extended to the USC, which was effectively stood down in July, without consulting the northern government. Wilfrid Spender, now Secretary to the Cabinet, seems merely to have been informed that deploying the Specials with guns would be a breach of the Truce, and deploying them unarmed would be a breach of the undertaking given to them on enlistment.

Predictably, Unionists strongly resented this decision and saw it as the result of nationalist pressure to disband the force.[6] The day after the Truce, Belfast's police commissioner was in 'despair' over the situation in the city, telling Spender that his force could not cope without military support. On 15 July the northern government asked the GOC Belfast for the Restoration of Order in Ireland Act (ROIA) to be 'again re-established', only to be told that indeed the act was still in force, but military measures would be 'guided by the spirit' of the Truce.[7] Since, as one judicious legal historian notes, the British government was proving 'largely unresponsive to demands from Belfast', the northern Cabinet made its own security plans for a breakdown of the Truce, deciding on 22 July to introduce identity cards and prepare for the internment of 'five or six hundred people'.[8]

A distinctive Northern Ireland security policy, which was to culminate in the emblematic Special Powers Act of 1922, was now launched. The Treaty negotiations, and the uncertainty they generated, were the backdrop to a series of outbreaks, with loyalist groups such as the Ulster Protestant Association – originally formed the previous autumn as a vigilante force in east Belfast – becoming more active. In August, the police commander Charles Wickham warned

Spender that unless the Specials were mobilized the population could not be 'restrained from taking the law into their own hands'. Spender fired off to London a blood-curdling report, warning of a 'general massacre – which you people who do not know the North, slow to anger but terrible in just wrath, cannot believe possible in the 20th century', if the negotiations went badly.[9] Dawson Bates informed the Cabinet that 'the aggression of Sinn Féin and the lack of defensive measures by the authorities' had led to 'the formation of Provisional Committees and the organization of armed loyalists to supply protection'.[10] Rioting at the end of August, when according to police reports gunmen 'gained control of a large part of the York street area', mills and shops were forced to close, and shipyard workers attacked, caused six deaths. The northern government, subjected to sharp loyalist criticism for failing to suppress IRA drilling and enforcement of the Belfast boycott, pressed 'with anger and a growing sense of frustration' for strong measures. A series of crisis meetings registered the point that 'nothing can be more disastrous to any community than to allow the rank and file' (as Spender put it) 'to imagine that Civil Authority has broken down', and demanded the reactivation of the USC as well as of the ROIA. Only internment would suffice to deal with 'the gunmen and other suspected individuals'.[11]

General Macready dashed up to Belfast with Andy Cope to smother the incipient security crisis. The commander-in-chief disliked his Belfast commander's proposal of troop reinforcements coupled with the use of internment under the ROIA; having reluctantly swallowed the establishment of the Specials, he now thought they should take the leading role. Cope – detested by many Ulster Unionists for his contacts with Sinn Féin leaders – followed the Dublin Castle line, arguing that this would provoke further disorder, and expose the government to 'lying propaganda' – painting it as 'having taken a party side'. Security forces had to intern both Protestants and Catholics if they were to have general support. These discussions, the most open of any yet on northern security, led to better communication between military and police chiefs, but the underlying issues – notably the use of the ROIA – were left unresolved.[12] When the year's third round of rioting began in Belfast a month later, the northern government unilaterally remobilized the USC.

The army took control of the police, including the USC, at the end of September, but though disturbances dropped away for a few weeks, more rioting followed in November, along with large-scale parades: the extravagantly named Ulster Imperial Guards (formed out of the Ex-Servicemen's Association in November, and surviving barely six months) mustering no fewer than 13,000 in Belfast. Loyalists found the attitude of the military authorities trying. The Specials were not brought up to full strength, or fully armed. Military communiqués mostly described the disturbances as sectarian clashes, instead of recognizing that – as loyalists saw things – they represented a political struggle against republicanism. Worse, when the ROIA was reapplied, the army used it to arrest Protestants as well as Catholics. Samuel Watt, the Permanent Secretary at Home Affairs, argued that the law had been designed to deal with Sinn Féin, and suggested it had never been 'contemplated that these extraordinary powers should be used against those who are loyal to the Crown'.[13] His minister cautiously dissented, but did go on to ask the army whether it intended to bring three 'respectable' Unionists it had arrested to trial.

The USC's survival seemed to be in the balance. Even if the British government ignored the fact that its existence contravened the GIA, it looked unlikely that Imperial funds would be available again. There was a danger that the USC itself would resist disbandment, and begin to operate outside the northern government's control: it had a potential leader in Fred Crawford. (On 21 March, the head of the Belfast detective department apparently offered him 200 revolvers if he could find men to use them; Crawford assembled an oath-bound group he called the Ulster Brotherhood, or 'Crawford's Tigers'.) Craig was concerned to 'wrest the USC from the grasp of the Imperial parliament before it was too late'.[14] Convinced that the Truce would break down, Craig stepped up his bid to get control of security. Late in October he had a long talk with the GOC Belfast, Major-General Cameron, who mentioned that his orders were to return to GHQ in Dublin if martial law was declared. Craig wrote to Henry Wilson to point out that Cameron had 'learned a great deal' in a short time of 'our peculiar conditions', and was 'going down very well with the people' (who had taken him to heart, as 'a Scot with staunch

Protestant views'). If he was to be moved, the change should be made '*at once* in order that whoever has to go through with the operations should pick up all the local circumstances *before* the truce ends'. (A thinly disguised code for falling in line with Craig?)

Cameron also told Craig that Wilson was in favour of 're-raising the Ulster Division' rather than re-utilizing the USC. Craig strongly opposed this idea, telling Wilson that he would be lucky to get more than a few hundred volunteers. Men would not risk enrolling in a military force even with a guarantee that they would not have to serve outside the province, because the volunteers for the Ulster division had been 'given an equally definite promise' that they would not be sent to other formations, and that promise had been broken. 'Another reason', Craig offered – surely the real one – was that men were now accustomed to the Special Constabulary, 'which they look upon as being raised to protect their homes', and would not 'leave their homes' and join another force 'where this purpose was not equally plain to their minds'.[15] In case the army worried that Specials might refuse to serve outside the six counties, Craig assured Wilson that they were 'anxious' to serve in Donegal, Cavan, and Monaghan – 'any number' of the A Specials would volunteer to serve 'just outside the six counties for the better protection of our [sic] province'. He believed that Macready 'has I think thoroughly realized the importance of getting arms over in Ulster before the truce breaks down, and he writes that he hopes to get 13,000 quietly into Carrickfergus during the next few days'. There must be 'no question about this', he insisted, since previous promises had (yet again) not been fulfilled: 'if we lose a number of casualties simply because arms are not available to let the people defend themselves' there would be 'very serious trouble'.

Finally, with the government facing a vote of no confidence, Whitehall gave way on the transfer of services, and from 22 November the Northern Ireland government became responsible for 'services in connection with the maintenance of law and order and the administration of justice'. In mid-December it put through a rather unusual law: the Local Government (Emergency Powers) Act (Northern Ireland) gave the Minister of Home Affairs power to dissolve local authorities and replace them by 'such person as the Ministry thinks fit'.

DEBATING THE BORDER

The Treaty, and especially Article XII, sent a shiver of dismay through the north. Having been established separate and free to stay that way unless it decided to join an Irish parliament, Northern Ireland would now be part of the Free State until it voted itself out. If it did – as it certainly would – it now faced the hazard of a boundary commission. The possible implications were alarming. A fear that Tyrone and Fermanagh 'may be taken from us' was widely voiced, and Craig protested to Bonar Law that there was nothing in the Treaty terms 'to show that the Boundary Commission must necessarily limit its functioning [to] little readjustments'. His brother Charles was more sanguine, reassuring him a fortnight after the Treaty that with the 'right' chairman (either Lord Dunedin or Clyde, he thought) 'and with our friend as our Commissioner, nothing very serious could happen to us'. (A calmer assessment than he was apt to provide in the chamber at Westminster.)

Craig first thought that as long as any Unionists who were transferred to the Free State got 'full compensation', he would appoint a Commissioner, and he approached 'our [unnamed] friend'. But when Lloyd George spoke in the parliamentary debate on the Treaty on 14 December his language rattled loyalists: there was 'no doubt', he confidently asserted, that 'the majority of the people of two counties prefer being with their Southern neighbours to being in the Northern Parliament'. This majority was there whether you took it 'by constituency or by Poor Law unions, or if you like by counting heads'. The prime minister added a somewhat convoluted gloss: there should be a 're-adjustment of boundaries ... not for the six counties but the North of Ireland, which would take into account where there are homogeneous populations of the same kind as that which is in Ulster, and where there are homogeneous populations of the same kind as you have in the South'. Explaining the need to 'take into account geographical and economic considerations', he instanced 'a little area of Catholics right up in the North-east of Antrim, cut off completely from the South'. Nobody proposed taking that away from the north, he said.[16]

Was it alarmist to read this prime ministerial homily as a steer to the boundary commission? When Asquith asked whether the commission was to 'operate' by counties, or any specific areas, or 'merely an enumeration of population', Lloyd George protested that 'we avoid giving directions of that kind to the Arbitrator' (who would, he said, be 'a man of distinction and a man whose impartiality will commend itself to all parties'). This seems to have defused the issue, and even Charles Craig, replying to the prime minister, elected not to probe it, simply saying that while admittedly 'the boundaries are not in every way satisfactory, they are fixed, and there is an end of them'. But he warned him, 'there is nothing that he could have done more calculated to rouse the ire and suspicion of the Ulster people than the appointment of this Boundary Commission'. Later, Ronald McNeill was able to draw from the prime minister a specific denial that he had 'told the Sinn Feiners that, inasmuch as they had a majority in Tyrone and Fermanagh, they would get the whole of those counties'. But he repeated the point he had made two days before: the boundary adjustment might add to Ulster or diminish it; the first time, though, he had talked of area – this time of population.[17] Austen Chamberlain tried to head off Ulster objections by suggesting that if only 'they had been present here in London' (when the Treaty was finalized), 'I have no doubt we and they would have come to an amicable arrangement'. From a statesman often credited with honesty, perhaps too much of it for his own political good, this was worryingly disingenuous. Challenged by McNeill to explain why, since 'the area was finally fixed by the Act of 1920, did you alter it?', Chamberlain sounded apologetic. If, he asked, 'in exchange for those who were unwilling to submit to their rule you can give them those who long to be under their rule, what injury have we done?'[18]

The government's contribution to the parliamentary debate on the Treaty plainly did nothing to assuage Ulster Unionist anxiety, and it would have been perhaps too much to expect them to be reassured by the Dáil debate on the Treaty, which ignored its Ulster provisions, while dragging on so long that it disrupted the timetables planned by the leading signatories on both sides. (Lloyd George had undertaken to put the Treaty to parliament 'as soon as possible', and Arthur Griffith wanted the Dáil to debate it within a week of signature.) Speed was critical, with the diehard republicans who had walked out of the Dáil after the Treaty vote regrouping to attack the Treaty and the ministers who signed it. When the Irish Free State bill – ratifying the Treaty – came before parliament in mid-February, the boundary commission loomed uncomfortably large for the government.

Indeed Churchill, who introduced its second reading, was quickly on the defensive, when he came 'to the difficult part of what I have to say'. He knew that Charles Craig was about to put down an amendment calling for the elimination of the commission, or at least making its award dependent on the consent of the northern parliament. At this dangerous moment he dug deep into his rhetorical armoury, vividly evoking the toils of the pre-war exclusion negotiations: 'the differences had been narrowed down not merely to the counties of Fermanagh and Tyrone, but to parishes and groups of parishes inside the areas of Fermanagh and Tyrone'. And yet, 'even when the differences had been so narrowed down, the problem appeared to be as impenetrable as ever'. Then, he said, came the great war. 'Every institution, almost, in the world was strained. Great empires have been overturned. The whole map of Europe has changed. The position of countries has been violently altered. The modes of thought of men, the whole outlook on affairs . . . all have encountered violent and tremendous changes in the deluge.' But, 'as the deluge subsides and the waters fall short we see the dreary steeples of Fermanagh and Tyrone emerging once again. The integrity of their quarrel is one of the few institutions that has been unaltered in the cataclysm which has swept the world.'[19]

This sonorous (and justly famous) passage heralded a more awkward (and less often quoted) observation. Even Churchill's style suddenly became awkward: stressing 'the great strength of the Ulster position', he admitted that there was 'one weak point: certain of these districts in Fermanagh and Tyrone, even in [sic] the county boundary, may be districts in which – I am not prejudging – the majority of the inhabitants will prefer to join the Irish Free State'. The commission could 'conceivably' affect the existing frontiers of Ulster 'prejudicially'. He went on wrestling almost apologetically with the difficulty for some time – the best part of an hour: 'if our supporters in the House feel convinced that we have done wrong in the Boundaries Clause, into which we have entered, and from which, having pledged ourselves to it, it is altogether out of our power to recede . . . they should do their duty as we have endeavoured to do ours'.[20] The argument he produced to mitigate the wrong was already a familiar one. Stressing that nobody could predict what the commission would decide, he proposed 'an extreme and absurd supposition'. If the commission, 'going far beyond what any reasonable man would expect, and far beyond what those who signed the Treaty meant, were to reduce Ulster to its preponderatingly Orange areas . . . would that not be a fatal and permanent obstacle to the unity and co-operation of Ireland?'

'TO SETTLE BOUNDARIES, NOT TO SETTLE TERRITORIES'

What Churchill meant exactly by 'far beyond' the intentions of the signatories remained obscure, despite repeated demands from MPs during the debate for clarification. The Attorney General blankly refused to offer any guidance, merely echoing the terms of Article XII – 'the commission having ascertained, I presume by suitable methods and with the help of appropriate machinery, what the wishes of the inhabitants are', would then have to 'take into account' the economic and geographic conditions. But as Ronald McNeill instantly pointed out, he had 'skilfully avoided' the real question: 'the inhabitants of what?' – a province, a county, a city or a parish?[21] Sir William Davison, the Armagh-born Kensington MP, claimed that most of his fellow MPs believed that the border question 'was merely a question of a pocket here or a pocket there, with practically even concessions on either side'. If they had thought that 'the arbitrators would have power to bring in Fermanagh and Tyrone, Londonderry city and parts of Armagh and Down', they would not 'for one moment' have ratified Article XII.[22]

Neville Chamberlain (Austen's younger brother), asking whether fears that it 'might be interpreted in such a way as to allow big chunks of territory to be cut away from Ulster', insisted that parliament had understood it to mean that the boundary commission would 'adjust boundaries' rather than 'transfer large territories'. He invoked Bonar

Law's statement that if the commission worked in the spirit of the Agreement – 'which means not the possibility of throwing out counties but of a real adjustment of boundaries' – Ulster would be wrong to refuse to have anything to do with it.[23] He lamented the failure of the government or its law officers to provide guidance as to 'how this Clause should naturally be interpreted'. Another speaker suggested that if the government really believed that the commission would merely 'trim the fringes of Ulster' they should surely accept Craig's amendment. Asked yet again how wide would be the areas consulted, Worthington-Evans sharply dismissed the interrogation: it was, he said, 'absolutely impossible to say whether it is one yard or a hundred yards, one mile or more'. He brusquely maintained that everyone knew 'perfectly well what those general phrases are intended to cover' – though they had repeatedly shown they did not.[24]

James Craig upped the stakes a notch, warning Austen Chamberlain that many of his followers now believed that 'violence is the only language understood by Mr Lloyd George and his Ministers'. Chamberlain hastily pointed out that although Bonar Law had objected to Article XII, he had just offered a correct interpretation of the commission's 'spirit and method'. Revision of the boundary would not be 'carried out by counties as a whole'. There would be no threat to the Unionist position.[25] Lord Carson himself, bitterly attacking the Treaty in the Lords, concentrated on the financial provisions and did not mention the boundary commission. But it haunted the parliamentary debate as it went on into March. Worthington-Evans and even Chamberlain compounded the proposal's opacity, one saying that the commission's purpose was 'to settle boundaries, not to settle territories' (without saying what 'territories' meant), while the other argued that unless the boundary was redrawn they would face fighting a war 'to preserve within the boundary of the Northern government populations the majority of which desire to leave their sway'.[26]

When the Free State Bill went into committee the next month, there was even a dispute over whether calling the Anglo-Irish agreement a 'treaty' was 'a gross abuse of language'. Lord Hugh Cecil suggested that 'the Government think the more difficult the situation the more remote your declarations ought to be from the truth'. He put down an amendment declaring – 'for the removal of doubts' – that in consenting to Article XII the government and parliament 'did not intend to agree to the transfer of the main area of any of the six counties of Northern Ireland . . . but only to such minor adjustments (if any) . . . as might without economic injury . . . satisfy the desires of bodies of persons of homogeneous opinions in respect to their territorial situation'.[27] This cumbersome formulation showed that even the government's critics had difficulty in laying out their views precisely. But it was clear enough that they wanted minimal change to the border – as one put it, nothing should be altered 'except straightening the boundaries'; the border should be 'like Euclid's line, length without breadth'; while another found it obvious that had 'partition' (of Northern Ireland) rather than 'readjustment' been intended, 'the words would have been very different, and a different machinery would have been set up'.[28]

Davison – justifiably surprised that neither the prime minister nor the leader of the house 'thought fit to be present when a matter of such vital importance' was under discussion – again insisted that if there was to be arbitration 'the arbitrator should know what is the matter on which he has to decide'. He challenged any MP to say definitely 'what it is that the Boundary Commission will have to determine'. Hugh Cecil put down yet another amendment requiring that the chairman of the boundary commission must be approved by both houses of parliament. The government resisted all these proposals, holding that they would alter the Treaty, and that could not be done. Charles Craig's response was blunt enough – to set up a commission which might 'possibly deal with territories which belong to us' was 'beyond the moral powers of the government'. It had 'no right in the world to interfere with' them.[29] The government inevitably carried the ratification of the Treaty without amendments, but the Ulster border question had not passed quietly through.

A 'BARBAROUS BORDER'

Early in 1922 the security situation verged on the critical. The Irish Free State Provisional Government, formed on 7 January, the day the

Dáil finally ratified the Treaty, developed a two-sided northern strategy. The meeting between Craig and Collins in London on 21 January, which produced the 'Craig-Collins Pact', indicated a policy of peaceful coexistence. The Belfast boycott was to be wound down while the northern government ended anti-Catholic discrimination. But neither party was enthusiastic, and the meeting only took place under pressure from Churchill. The leaders agreed that the boundary commission should be replaced by a bilateral arrangement, which Collins evidently believed would work better because the British would be sidelined. (He seems to have thought there was more to be feared from their appointed chairman than from the Ulster Unionists – once again showing the rooted nationalist belief that British manipulation was at the root of the problem.) Craig went as far as to suggest an all-Ireland conference to discuss the north–south relationship. But this promising idea was quickly dropped, and so was the border negotiation. Within a week Craig was reiterating, for the benefit of the UUC, that there would be no boundary change that left 'our Ulster area any less than it is'. Facing the Unionists, Collins's instincts were confrontational. For one thing, hostility to the northern state provided a rare instance of common ground between pro- and anti-Treaty groups. And, realist though he was, he shared the nationalist conviction that the northern government 'could stop all the outrages in the North if they set their hands to do so'. He was prepared to abandon the boycott (which was coming in for increasingly vocal criticism on the nationalist side) but not to stop putting pressure on what nationalists now uneasily mocked as 'Carsonia' to prevent it from becoming 'normalized' in the minds of both sides.

In February, when the Provisional Government decided to lay out the 'maximum Irish demand' to Britain, Churchill made a point of dismantling the long-held nationalist hope that if Northern Ireland's territory was significantly cropped it would become economically unviable and be forced into unity. He accepted that the boundary commission award might affect Northern Ireland's frontier 'prejudicially' but argued that the idea that it might be reduced to its 'preponderatingly Orange areas' was 'absurd'. This would create a 'fatal and permanent obstacle' to unity, permanent because, if Ulster was 'maltreated and mutilated', Britain would be bound to support

Northern Ireland as an 'economic entity'. At the same time Collins was gloomily contemplating the possibility that a dramatic territorial reduction would force an angry 'North East' into a united Ireland, which would find it 'impossible to govern'.[30]

Early in 1922 the fractured IRA began to set a northern campaign on foot, with Eoin O'Duffy in Monaghan, Seán MacEoin in Longford, and Frank Aiken in Armagh linking up to form the Ulster Council, headquartered in the Monaghan border town of Clones – also the HQ of another IRA division (5th Northern). A few miles from the Tyrone and Fermanagh borders, Clones became the strategic hinge of the so-called 'Joint IRA offensive', combining pro- and anti-Treaty forces, planned for May 1922. North–south relations deteriorated dramatically after the arrest by Tyrone police on 14 January of several members of the Monaghan Gaelic Football team, on their way to the final of the Ulster championship in Derry. Some were of course IRA men, one of them the commander of the 5th Northern Division, Dan Hogan, and documents relating to a plan to rescue three prisoners under death sentence in Derry gaol were found on them.

O'Duffy insisted to Collins that the boycott be maintained until Hogan was released and told him he had 'arranged for the kidnapping of one hundred prominent Orangemen' in Fermanagh and Tyrone.[31] Early in February the IRA crossed the border and took forty-two Specials, Orangemen, and Unionist officials hostage. This 'deliberate and organized attack on Ulster', as Craig described it to Lloyd George, brought the 'constant state of tension' on the border 'almost to fever pitch'.[32] Tension climaxed when, on 11 February, the IRA killed four A Specials on a train from Newtownards to Enniskillen (and arrested/kidnapped several others) in a gunfight at Clones station. The nineteen-strong police squad – all uniformed, six of them armed – had been sent by a route that was quicker, but it involved crossing Free State territory to change trains at Clones. The choice of route has been described as 'provocative', but the police seemed unaware of this as they got refreshments at Clones station. The local IRA commandant, the up-and-coming Matt Fitzpatrick (wounded a year earlier and held under guard at Monaghan County Infirmary, the Monaghan brigadier had taken the flying column to

rescue him) arrived, revolver in hand, and called on the Specials –
who had boarded their connecting train – to surrender. He was
instantly shot dead. His men deluged the train with gunfire, killing
four policemen and wounding many other passengers. The chaos and
damage were spectacular, and the incident seemed like the prelude to
major events. When the blood-bespattered train reached Lisbellaw
the local Protestants drove Catholics out of the town. The British
army – which had evacuated Clones shortly before – halted its withdrawal from Irish garrisons. This 'merciless episode', as Churchill
called it, 'reduced the border to barbaric conditions'.[33]

Craig sharply enquired if there was 'any legal obstacle to our
sending a flying column of 5,000 constabulary to recover the kidnapped Loyalists'. He also suggested that the army should occupy
a piece of southern territory for every individual kidnapped until
they were released.[34] This vividly illustrated the nature of his
thinking about the security issue. When he called for a big consignment of arms and vehicles (including 100 Lancias, 100 Crossley
tenders, and 100 Lewis guns), Churchill referred the request to the
Belfast GOC to decide what Northern Ireland needed for 'defensive purposes', while he warned the Provisional Government that
if kidnapping continued 'we will have a fortified frontier', which
would necessarily be garrisoned by Imperial troops ('because they
would be more impartial than Northern Ireland troops'). Collins
was unimpressed, pushing ahead with the creation of a new active
service force in Belfast, the Belfast City Guard, conceived as an
elite unit made up of fifteen picked men from each of the city's four
battalions. The IRA Ulster Council now planned a series of attacks
on police barracks, three of which near the border were raided in
March, with no fewer than seventy-five rifles being seized at
Pomeroy in County Tyrone.

Simultaneously, the shooting of policemen in Belfast produced a
ferocious reaction. The grisly slaughter of the McMahon family near
the Crumlin Road gaol on 24 March was symptomatic of a widespread sense of dislocation, albeit especially acute in this sector of the
city. A sharp analysis of this deliberately transgressive act points out
that however strong the fundamental position of the Protestant community was, its self-perception was of vulnerability: 'They had no

faith in the old hierarchy of the decaying RIC. They felt betrayed by the British army. They were surrounded on three sides by hostile areas.' They needed to demonstrate that they 'had the stomach for the fight'.[35] It may be putting it too strongly to say that in late March 'north and south were to all intents and purposes openly at war', but it felt perilously close to that.[36]

It hardly needed a sophisticated intelligence service to enable Craig to identify the IRA campaign as being inspired and possibly controlled from the Free State. He pointed out to Churchill on 21 March that Seán McEoin, one of the Free State's most prominent generals, had made a speech in Cork offering to lead the flying column that was being organized for duty in Ulster. 'While some local members of the IRA may have taken part it is certain the whole matter has been organized and men imported from the Free State to take part in these raids.'[37] IRA attacks in border areas were indeed increasing dramatically, and the Free State deputy Chief of Staff, Eoin O'Duffy, consistently determined to make life hot for the Unionists, was directly involved.[38] IRA orders showed a will to pursue the campaign ruthlessly: reprisals were ordered to be 'taken at once', and 'must be six to one to prevent the enemy from continuing same'. Spies and informers were to be shot 'at sight', 'no mercy to be given'.[39] Although much of this venom had little practical application, there could be no doubt of the hostile intent.

Even so, support for the USC became an awkward issue in 1922. Craig was struggling to balance his tight budget, negotiating with an unsympathetic Treasury after the transfer of services in November. Whitehall asked Ernest Clark and R. G. Hawtrey to devise an arrangement to eliminate the deficit while staying 'within the four corners' of the Government of Ireland Act. The climate was chilly; few senior ministers and 'none of the senior Imperial officials involved with Irish affairs' either understood or tried to understand the problems facing Northern Ireland in 1922.[40] Eventually the circle was squared, it seemed magically, by Lloyd George's idea of reclassifying Specials as a 'military force' – so paid by London. But in mid-December, Otto Niemeyer, a top Treasury official, and increasingly sharp critic of Belfast's financial demands, held that this was not within the terms of either the 1920 Act or the Treaty, and was maybe even illegal. The Treasury recommended terminating British support as soon as it was 'legal or possible'.

The chancellor reassured Niemeyer that there was no intention of letting Northern Ireland 'have Specials ad libitum', but in fact another grant of £850,000 was made by the Cabinet in early March, to underwrite the Specials for the first half of the next fiscal year.[41] On 17 March, Tom Jones, who now seemed to see himself as partly responsible for the Treaty (perhaps not without some reason), and 'very disquieted at the position we are moving into in relation to Ulster', addressed an unusually vehement protest to the prime minister. To go forward 'paying for the SCs, making other grants to Ulster, cloaking a military force under the guise of a police force', and 'allowing Henry Wilson to proceed unchallenged to prepare his "scheme" . . . bringing us back to the position we were in 1914' (but with the preparations made 'legally and with the money of the British Government'), he urged, would certainly be a breach of faith if not of the letter of the Treaty.[42]

A second Craig–Collins 'pact' on 30 March was launched with the resonant phrase 'peace is today declared' – it was fostered by Churchill – which would have been more reassuring if the word 'peace' had carried the same meaning for the two sides. There was agreement on enrolling a proportion of Catholics in the police, who were not to operate except in uniform; arms and ammunition were to be more carefully controlled; a special court was to try certain offences without jury; and a joint Catholic–Protestant committee would investigate complaints about outrages and intimidation. Political prisoners were to be released, and expellees allowed to return, while Britain would provide a half-million-pound relief fund, a third of it to go to Catholics. As the pact was signed, though, the new Special Powers Act was imminent: it became law on 5 April. And the police were getting a new, politically loaded title – unknown to Collins. A committee of fifteen (two of them Catholics) appointed by Dawson Bates recommended on 28 March that the new force should be called the Ulster Constabulary, and a month later King George V added the prefix 'Royal'.[43] The old RIC had received its royal title to mark its firmness in face of the Fenian insurrection of 1867; the reason for likewise honouring its Ulster successor was left unexplained.

SPECIAL POWERS

In March 1922, Northern Ireland took a big step towards complete separation, launching a new police force and its own special powers law. Craig asked Henry Wilson, who was elected as MP for North Down three days after retiring as Chief of the Imperial General Staff, to advise the northern government on security matters, even though the two did not quite see eye to eye. Wilson was dismissive of Craig himself – 'a very second-rate man . . . well pleased with himself', and still more so of the Home Affairs minister Dawson Bates – 'a small man in every way & thought'. Indeed he pushed to have Bates sacked. Wilson's dim view of the northern government bolstered his preference for formal military rather than police forces (the police commander Wickham was merely 'a Major of average ability'). Worried that 'no Catholics could be found for the SC',[44] he recommended that Catholics should be encouraged to join the police 'equally with the other religions'; he also discouraged the idea already circulating of introducing flogging as a punishment for carrying arms, as it might 'alienate English public opinion'.[45] Republicans of course knew none of this; for them his appointment symbolized the north's increasingly draconian administration; Collins thought him 'a violent Orange partisan'.[46] Wilson – who had ostentatiously refused to shake hands with Collins when introduced to him at 10 Downing Street – would suffer the ultimate penalty for this perception when he was shot dead outside his London home in June. (Whether at the direct instigation of Collins has never been clear.)[47]

Wilson picked Major-General Arthur Solly-Flood to be head of security forces – his lack of any police experience was not surprising, and not a barrier. On the same day he was appointed, the Civil Authorities (Special Powers) Act passed into law. This Act, perhaps the most famous – certainly the most notorious – statute passed by the northern parliament, would become for nationalists (and civil libertarians) a key emblem of the northern state. By the time a headline report by the National Council for Civil Liberties in 1936 condemned it as establishing 'a permanent machine of dictatorship', it seemed to have outlived its justification; and by the time it was finally repealed after the reversion to British direct rule in 1973 it was an ugly antique. But in 1922 its immediate descent from the wartime Defence of the Realm Acts via the 1920 Restoration of Order in Ireland Act made it look less anomalous. The kind of statutory martial law embodied in the previous acts undoubtedly reassured many people who had no idea of how or whether it really worked; it represented a declaration of intent. Of its thirty-five initial regulations, thirty-two were taken from the 1914 Defence of the Realm Act (DORA), and two others from the ROIA. But though the powers were largely similar, there were significant divergences: in place of the 'Competent Military Authority' in whom DORA and ROIA powers were vested, the new act set the 'Civil Authorities' – in essence, just a single one, the Home Affairs minister, who could delegate 'any or all his [sic] powers' to any police officer. In June a raft of new regulations added powers to stop and search, to close buildings and roads, and restrict residence, as well as banning the IRA and some other nationalist organizations, and imposing restrictions on the wearing of uniforms.

Solly-Flood quickly came up with a large-scale quasi-military scheme, which seemed emblematic of a steady militarization.[48] James Craig told Wickham and the Ministry of Home Affairs that Solly-Flood was 'in supreme control of all the constabulary forces of Northern Ireland for all purposes' and could deal directly with the Ministry of Finance in matters of 'essential, urgent expenditure of a military character'. But there were limits to militarization. When the supreme controller tried in mid-June to argue that, by analogy with the position of the Competent Military Authorities under DORA and ROIA, 'full powers under [the Special Powers Act] should be delegated to him', Craig did not support him. And though a number of cross-border roads were blocked, Solly-Flood's very military proposal to close the frontier entirely to interdict IRA movements was turned down.[49] Still, when the anti-Treaty IRA occupied the Four Courts in Dublin, he put forward an even more elaborate scheme: on top of the 3,000 regular RUC (half as big again as the old RIC strength), there would be 8,290 A Specials, 25,000 B Specials (2,000 of them mobilized full-time), and a new C1 class 15,000–17,000 strong. The latter would be in effect a Northern Ireland territorial army.

In May, Craig was able to exploit the reaction in London to the Collins–de Valera electoral pact, designed to minimize violence by ensuring that the two sides kept the share of votes they already held, but evidently a travesty of the 'normal' electoral process. It was furiously denounced by Churchill as an 'outrage on democratic principles'. He was now convinced a republic would be declared if British troops were withdrawn from Dublin, and talked of 'having to retain what he called the "English capital" '.[50] A Cabinet committee examined coercive measures including possible blockade as well as military action, and in early June the Committee of Imperial Defence discussed plans to occupy the waterline of lakes and rivers from Donegal to Dundalk to defend the north against invasion.[51] Craig took the opportunity to deliver his most outright public rejection of border revision, insisting to his parliament on 23 May that 'we will hear no more about a Commission coming to decide whether our boundaries shall be so and so'. His peroration was resonant: 'What we have now we hold . . . against all combinations'.

Churchill, angry at being given no warning of this ('I cannot understand why it was not possible to communicate with me before making a declaration'), now rounded on Craig in turn, fuming that it would put British public opinion off involvement in Irish affairs, weaken Britain's capacity to deal with the Provisional Government, and make it more difficult to comply with Craig's request for 'enormous financial aid and heavy issues of arms'. It was 'not within your rights to state that you will not submit to the Treaty . . . and at the same time ask the British Government to bear the overwhelming burden of your defensive expenses'.[52] Unruffled by this finger-wagging, Craig insisted that the boundary commission idea had been 'at the root of all evil', and the Collins–de Valera pact had been the perfect moment to jettison the 'preposterous proposal'. Things were unlikely to go 'from bad to better' rather than bad to worse, but even if they did the 'imposition of the Border Commission would only once more start the vicious circle of trouble and recrimination' with 'sad loss of life and devastation'. He cheekily predicted that Churchill would later 'thank God that we got it out of the way so cleverly', and generously credited him with being 'shrewd enough to take full advantage of this escape from an impossible position'. Now the air was cleared for what Craig labelled 'the defence of Ulster against the Republic'.[53]

The Joint-IRA campaign moved up a gear with the offensive planned for May, opening with an advance which showed just how readily border entanglements could develop. At this stage the border had become very ill-defined 'with border posts largely abandoned and small parties of IRA and Specials roaming the frontier areas exchanging fire and insults in acts of threatening bravado'.[54] Potentially far more serious than the Clones affray in February – though it has gone down in history as a semi-comical fiasco – the Belleek–Pettigo fighting at the end of May was the closest the IRA came to engaging in pitched battle with British troops. The IRA occupied Pettigo, a Protestant village in the 'triangle', an area cut off from the rest of Fermanagh by Lough Erne and the river Erne, and an old fort near Belleek. Basil Brooke, the Fermanagh USC commandant (and future prime minister), took a strong force – sixty-four A and B Specials, with a Lancia armoured car – across the lake by boat, only to be driven back with the humiliating loss of the armoured car and three Crossley tenders. When British troops were sent into the triangle on 3 June, the IRA fended off their assault, and held out until artillery was brought up. The troops occupied Pettigo on 4 June and finally seized the fort at Belleek – in Free State territory – four days later: they remained there until August 1924.[55]

If the IRA's aim was to destabilize the north, it seemed a promising start. The panic created among loyalists by this 'incursion' was deep and long-lasting.[56] A British official later reported that 'the events of last May have reduced the local Unionists to a state of nerves' comparable only in his experience 'to the panic among the better class of inhabitants of villages which the Bolsheviks have once held and threaten to revisit'. Many believed, he felt sure, that 'the Republicans and their local allies are only waiting for the withdrawal of the British troops to enter the village and massacre them'.[57] Since the incursion coincided with Collins's demand for an inquiry into the McMahon murders, Craig naturally talked up the threat – 'De Valera and Collins desire to accomplish the fall of Ulster'. De Valera might indeed have desired it, and Collins was certainly taking action. Although most historians have implied that the Pettigo incursion was made by anti-Treaty Republicans, there seems no doubt that Free State forces also took part. This gave some colour to Craig's objection, after the civil war broke out at the end of the month, that British arms supplies to the Provisional Government might be used against Northern Ireland. When the Unionist MP William Twaddell, a founder of the Imperial Guards, was assassinated on 22 May, the killing created an even bigger public shock than the Pettigo battle.

Patrick Shea, a Catholic teenager (son of the RIC Head Constable in Clones), got the sense that at this time 'the N Ireland administration seemed in danger of collapsing in anarchy', and he was not alone in invoking that thrillingly alarming notion.[58] Between 6 December and the end May 1922, 236 people were killed – 16 members of the Crown forces, 147 Catholic and 73 Protestant civilians. Injuries were almost equally shared, with 166 Catholics and 143 Protestants recorded as casualties of disorder. This was a civil war of sorts, seeming to pose a life-and-death issue for the northern state – which 'was scarcely master in its own house' as one historian puts it. The cooperation of the Imperial authorities 'could never be relied upon and had to be constantly fought for'.[59] The old RIC (which in any case many loyalists distrusted) was being wound down, to be finally disbanded on 31 May 1922. Its replacement was reassuringly named the Royal Ulster Constabulary, but took some time to be brought up to its planned strength of 3,000. The Specials, excluding the old class C – an unarmed local reserve – reached 32,000, including 5,500 in class A and 7,500 in the new class C1 – 'in effect a Northern Ireland territorial army'. This was a substantial total (as big as the former military garrison for the whole island) but it was not cheap, and the cost was always beyond the northern state's means.

The northern government's feeling of abandonment by Britain was of course paralleled amongst the Provisional Government: Collins complained to Tom Jones at the end of May that the British 'would do nothing to put Belfast right', and that 'even the PM was incredibly callous about the murder of Ulster Catholics'. The PG's demand for either a judicial inquiry or the use of martial law to control the police only produced another half-measure, an investigation into the reasons for the breakdown of the March pact carried out by a single civil servant, Stephen Tallents. Lloyd George's idea seems to have been that if Tallents found 'there was ground for a public inquiry', the northern Cabinet would have to agree.[60] The former private secretary to the Viceroy, now given the title Imperial Secretary for Northern Ireland, produced another unflattering picture of some Ulster ministers – Dawson Bates was 'a weak man and a political hack', whose 'two chief assistants are also violent political partisans', and though he found Hugh Pollock 'more intellectual than his colleagues', he noted that 'his word was to be taken absolutely' on 'any question but politics'. Solly-Flood was 'a soldier without police experience, whose name carries no weight in the country which seems destined to finance his plans'. Craig, though, emerged in one piece – 'not a clever man but one of sound judgment and can realise a big issue'; he had 'a great desire to do the right and important thing'. And Tallents blamed the breakdown of the pact primarily on the failure to deliver 'the cessation of IRA activities in the Six Counties' promised by Collins. His key conclusion, ultimately, was that there was no need for a judicial inquiry, which might 'inadvertently encourage northern Catholics in their refusal to recognize the Northern government'.[61]

From now on, things looked up for Northern Ireland. Not only had its take on the border crisis been officially endorsed, but the Joint-IRA offensive had collapsed. The security clampdown after the May events – notably the use of internment – had tightened the pressure on republicans. After an anti-Treaty IRA group defied the Provisional Government by occupying the Four Courts in Dublin on 13 April, the Free State came under increasing pressure from Britain to demonstrate its rejection of republicanism. The delivery of the draft Free State constitution in London produced yet another Anglo-Irish crisis – Lloyd George exasperatedly called it 'a complete evasion of the Treaty & setting up of a republic with a thin veneer'. At the same time Northern Ireland also flexed its political muscles at the highest level as it moved to dismantle a detested element of the 1920 Act, proportional representation. A bill to remove PR in local elections was brought in on 31 May – at the height of the Belleek–Pettigo crisis. Collins immediately protested against the destruction of 'Catholic and Nationalist' representation, claiming that while safeguards for Unionists in the Free State had been 'frequently demanded and readily granted', the Craig regime did not protect minority interests 'in the slightest degree'. This invocation of minority protection, a key issue in the debates on the Government of Ireland Act, was indeed awkward for the British government, whether or not it accepted Collins's contention that abolishing PR would help Craig 'wipe out the Boundary Commission'.[62] (By making it impossible, for instance, for authorities such as Derry city council to refuse to recognize the northern state.) When Churchill told Craig that London had the right, and indeed duty, to insist that PR be maintained, Craig simply replied that, if it did, he and his Cabinet would resign. This was enough to ensure that the 'Imperial government', with only the alternative of resorting to Crown Colony rule, would limit its resistance to briefly delaying the royal assent. Republicans played their part in getting Craig off the hook: the assassination of Henry Wilson by two London IRA men on 22 June – whether it had any strategic intent beyond simple revenge – was effectively the last act in Collins's aggressive northern strategy, and produced yet more outrage in the British establishment. Finally, a week later, the Free State army moved to evict the anti-Treaty IRA from the Four Courts; pro- and anti-Treaty forces began a life-and-death struggle for control of 'southern' Ireland.

9

The Fix

In the autumn of 1922, as the Irish civil war intensified, a series of events shifted the dynamic of the border question. Both the leading Irish signatories of the Treaty, and the two with the most direct investment in Clause XII, died in August – Arthur Griffith from a brain tumour and Michael Collins in an ambush. One British insider went as far as to say that only the early death of Collins saved the Treaty.[1] In October, after four years in office, the Coalition government, which had framed the 'Partition Act' and negotiated the Anglo-Irish Treaty, fell. The threat of a diehard backlash against Lloyd George had pressured the Irish delegation to sign, and in the Tory rebellion which overthrew him not only the prime minister but also the leading signatories, Chamberlain, Birkenhead, Churchill, and Worthington-Evans, were ejected from power. All, in the diehard Tory view, had betrayed the union.

The new prime minister, Bonar Law, though not a signatory, nonetheless endorsed the Treaty (to the surprise of some of his party), and on 7 December 1922 Northern Ireland duly exercised its right to opt out of the Free State. The boundary commission should have been set up immediately, but in fact it would not be convoked for almost two years. Why? Much of the answer lies in the events of the autumn. Bonar Law accepted the Treaty as a fait accompli but did not like it, least of all the commitment to boundary revision. His government was assertively Conservative, with Treaty-sceptics like Leo Amery, Sam Hoare, and William Joynson-Hicks on board. More surprisingly – even though Collins had traded it in the Craig–Collins pact – but no less definitely, the Provisional Government in Dublin also soft-pedalled on the Commission.

The Free State's incoherent northern policy began to be clarified even before Collins's death. Ernest Blythe, a leading member of a new policy committee, put in a weighty memorandum arguing that to adopt a 'pacific and friendly disposition immediately' would be 'no more than bare sanity'. This would mean recognizing the northern government and ending the attempts of northern nationalists 'to prevent its working'. It is not entirely clear that this direct reversal of Collins's approach 'logically implied' (as has been suggested) 'the abandonment of any territorial claims on the North' – these could be pursued by non-confrontational means.[2] But it certainly set an altered frame for the activities of the North-Eastern Boundary Bureau (NEBB), which was set up at the beginning of October to study the issues that would arise around the boundary commission. When Blythe, its first director, was moved to Local Government (for reasons still unclear), he was followed by Kevin O'Shiel, Assistant Legal Adviser to the Executive Council, who presided over various enterprises such as detailed studies of the plebiscitary procedures used in Silesia, Schleswig-Holstein, Klagenfurt, and Hungary.

Early in 1923 the Bureau produced two blueprints, 'our claim for two lots of territory' as O'Shiel put it. The 'maximum demand' they could 'argue well from the wishes of the inhabitants point of view' but 'not so well from the economic and geographic point of view'. The 'minimum', on the other hand, was 'supported with unanswerable statistical, economic and geographic arguments'.[3] Even this would deliver them 'all Fermanagh and the greater part of Tyrone, west and south Derry, south Armagh and south and east Down'. The difficulty with arguing the maximum demand related to the notion – which had of course been freely advocated by Griffith – that it might make Northern Ireland unviable. In fact, O'Shiel's technical advisers, who included the Trinity College economist Joseph Johnston, made clear that viability had little or nothing to do with territorial extent: they instanced states in the USA, Australia, and Canada which had powers 'at least as great as those of Northern Ireland' with much smaller populations than would remain in the north.[4]

Naturally, given his task, O'Shiel did not take the view that border revision was logically inconsistent with government policy; but he was very cautious, insisting that because 'we must be in a position to maintain public order and guarantee the protection of the lives and property of possible future citizens' – those to be transferred to the Free State by it – the boundary commission should not begin to act until the end of the civil war.[5] He defined his Bureau's objective not as 'wresting as much territory as possible from Craig', but achieving 'a much more lasting thing than any temporary arrangement of purely arbitrary and utterly absurd boundaries'; the object was '*National Union*' – underlined and capitalized to make clear its sacral status. Although this echoed Blythe's line, O'Shiel was careful to invoke Collins in support. He claimed that 'the late general [Collins] never made any secret of his distrust in the Boundary Commission as a means of settlement per se'. He had often said it would 'settle nothing', since however the border was drawn, 'there would still be an "Hibernia Irredenta" to disturb the peace of future generations'.[6]

The Bureau's magnum opus, its *Handbook of the Ulster Question*, turned out to be a rather slim volume, mustering O'Shiel's pick of arguments – primarily against partition in principle, but also in favour of plebiscites as the way of determining the border if partition should occur. A surprisingly spacious historical introduction, stretching back to 350 BC and taking ten pages to reach the Ulster Plantation, set the tone of the Free State's approach. The partition issue was not addressed until page 25. O'Shiel's philosophical approach was also ambitious, resting on an analysis of 'the idea of the nation'. Admitting the severe difficulty of defining nations, the *Handbook* suggested that they rest on 'common possession of a rich heritage of memories' as well as 'actual consent, the desire to live together'.[7] The obvious response, that both qualities – notably the second – were missing in Ireland, was sidestepped. Instead, the *Handbook* went on to insist that religious differences were not significant in an 'organic' nation – rather they 'strengthen the national unit by bringing to its service the widest possible variety of character'. Nature was also, naturally, invoked: the existing frontier was (the *Handbook* oddly remarked) 'historic' – but not 'natural' – while the island of Ireland was a 'natural design'.[8]

Surveying ways of building composite national unions, O'Shiel took an international perspective: the USA, Germany, Italy, Canada, and above all South Africa provided examples of the process. (Czechoslovakia was missing from the list.) He, like Lloyd George, clearly believed that the 1909 South Africa Convention – presided over, interestingly, by the anti-partitionist Lord Selborne – offered a relevant blueprint. But if the 'fixing of boundaries' had to be done, the *Handbook* made clear that all the partitions recently carried out in Europe under the auspices of the League of Nations had been based on a clear demarcation of areas, and had put the wishes of the inhabitants of 'each district (as the instructions for S[ch]leswig put it) taking into account the particular geographic and economic conditions of the locality'. It instanced Balfour's statement (in a letter to *The Times* shortly before the Anglo-Irish Treaty) that 'the Treaty of Peace' – i.e. the Paris Treaty – 'put the population first and industry second' in territorial adjustments. But though the *Handbook* gave the impression that plebiscites were the usual way of ascertaining the wishes of the inhabitants, it said that the Irish boundary commission must do it 'by the various means at its disposal'.[9]

O'Shiel went on advising delay even after the civil war ended. A month after the anti-Treaty IRA dumped arms in May 1922 he suggested that they should wait until the Free State could join the League of Nations (which it would in September 1923). But Irish public opinion – not a factor he had weighed – began to bear heavily on the government that summer with the approach of the first general election to be held under the Free State constitution. W. T. Cosgrave's administration, focused thus far on winning the war, needed to reinvent itself as a political party based on implementing the Treaty – and showing that it could work against partition.

In July, the Executive Council, believing that 'certain progress must be made in the matter of the Boundary Commission' before the election, at last sent the British government its official request to activate Article XII of the Treaty. Deciding that O'Shiel's 'minimum line' was the claim 'beyond which they could not recede',[10] on 20 July the Free State put Britain firmly on the spot by announcing its appointment as boundary commissioner. This was Eoin MacNeill – author of the famous tract 'The North Began', which had led to the foundation of the Irish Volunteers in 1913 – and another of the select band of Ulstermen who had played leading parts in the Irish revolution. Even so, Lionel Curtis (who respected and even 'loved' Cosgrave, but worried that Ireland's accession to the League of Nations opened up the possibility of international interference) went on working to head off the commission idea. He could see that the six-county border was 'neither natural nor convenient' and bore 'no relation to the line separating the predominantly Nationalist and predominantly Unionist areas', but thought that any alteration should be made by intergovernmental agreement rather than a commission. Better still, it should be rendered unnecessary by 'some wider solution' in which the Free State would enter a federal structure with the north.[11] It is worth noting that, as late as December 1923, O'Shiel himself was still telling the Executive Council that a commission was 'not an ideal solution' since it could as easily lead away from national union as towards it.[12]

'GUESSWORK SELF-DETERMINATION'

Curtis went as far as to ask Francis Bourdillon, an Oxford expert on frontier definition and self-determination (who had advised the Foreign Office on the Upper Silesian Commission), to advise the government on the possible use of plebiscites for border revision. In mid-December, Bourdillon sent him two substantial draft articles, which did nothing to remove his worries about a commission. Assessing the use of plebiscites in five places in Europe, Bourdillon laid out several key points. The first was that satisfactory results 'were not obtainable unless the two parties are agreed that the general conditions are just'. It was crucial that the areas involved were placed under neutral control. (He instanced the vote in western Hungary in December 1921, taken with Hungarian police and irregular forces present throughout, and Hungarian troops nearby, as showing how not to do it.) The lists of inhabitants needed to be accurate, and the areas carefully defined to avoid creating 'irredentas' (the key concept Balfour had deployed to argue against a nine-county Northern Ireland). Using what he called plebiscites by 'zones', rather than village by village, had 'led to irredentas in every case when it was applied'. Fair conditions required 'the association of representatives of both parties with every step', controversial questions being settled by outside authority, and the executive government of the plebiscite area being taken out of the hands of either of the parties.[13]

Bourdillon was not against plebiscites – far from it. He stressed that despite the problems inevitably involved in taking a vote, the alternative – using 'existing evidence' such as language, religion, or electoral records – was 'so unreliable as to be an exceedingly dangerous guide' to the wishes of the inhabitants. Such 'guesswork self-determination', he told Curtis privately, was exactly what the Free State Boundary Bureau's *Handbook* was presenting. The Bureau was clearly taking 'existing evidence' as if it 'proved the wishes of the inhabitants on a question they have never had put to them'. In an even heftier memorandum focusing on the Irish case ('The Scope of the Boundary Commission'), he made clear that everything would depend on the interpretation of Article XII. Was the intention merely to correct local incongruities, or adjust a 'limited border area' – perhaps 5 to 15 miles wide – or even the 'whole area in which there is any doubt'? Bourdillon offered a detailed analysis of the provisions necessary in each scenario, suggesting for instance that the border should be divided into three plebiscitary zones, placed 'under separate administrations'. The biggest issue was the balance between the wishes of the inhabitants and the geographic/economic conditions. In Europe, 'much controversy arose over cases where the Treaty specified that [these] should be taken into account but did not indicate how far they should override the voting'. He thought that an Irish commission 'must have wider powers than an ordinary Boundary Commission' because it would have to resolve this issue. For him, 'the most important point is that the interpretation given to the Treaty should be given by a body whose verdict is accepted beforehand by the two states'.[14] This key point was, obviously, potentially fatal.

Bourdillon's repeated insistence that there was no substitute for a plebiscitary vote certainly did not appeal to Curtis's senior Colonial Office colleague Geoffrey Whiskard. He had been part of John Anderson's Dublin Castle team and believed he knew Ireland: 'the holding of a plebiscite in a neutral area' would never be possible, and even discussing plebiscitary methods 'merely confuses the issue'. The prospect of having to establish independent administrations was predictably unappealing. Curtis held to the idea that the way forward was an inter-governmental boundary conference which would make a commission unnecessary.

The revival of the Commission proposal, which Unionists believed

Craig had killed off, triggered a new spate of public consternation in the north, where it 'dominated the public utterances of Unionist politicians and newspaper editorials and indeed news columns', right through to the final settlement in December 1925.[15] This time, though, the issue did not spill over into communal action. Unionist nerves were not eased by the disappearance from politics of the perennially sick Bonar Law, who retired for a second time in May 1923. His successor, Stanley Baldwin, who traded on his image as an archetypal English Tory squire, had never taken a strong position on the Ulster question. The Commission loomed large in the Free State general election in August, and again (in Ulster at least) in the UK general election of November, which was labelled a border referendum in the two border counties contested (the two-seat Fermanagh and Tyrone constituency). The nationalist majorities in both racked up the Unionist press alarm triggered when Baldwin's government – then commanding the biggest parliamentary majority since 1910 – summoned both Irish governments to a boundary conference.

The original invitation, issued before the elections, was first put on hold because Craig was again ill, and then delayed over the election campaign. By the time of the first actual meeting, when Cosgrave, Kevin O'Higgins, and Hugh Kennedy went to London early in February 1924, Ramsay MacDonald was in Downing Street. Baldwin had lost his overall majority, and the improbable (and to many unbelievable) advent of a Labour government – albeit a minority government – further stoked Unionist anxiety. Labour was indeed formally opposed to partition, but the question was whether it was ready to incur political costs (potentially high for an administration without a parliamentary majority) to pursue unity. There was little evidence of this, or that it was readier than the Conservatives to put pressure on the Ulster Unionists. But the new Chancellor of the Exchequer, Philip Snowden, falling in with the Treasury officials' view, began promisingly by refusing to confirm the million-pound grant promised by his predecessor for the Special Constabulary. (Oddly perhaps for a Labour minister, Snowden denounced the Special Constabulary grant as a concealed unemployment subsidy.)

At the February meeting, MacDonald came up with the suggestion that Westminster might transfer the proposed Council of Ireland powers in Northern Ireland to a joint Dublin–Belfast body, which would be given statutory authority by both Irish parliaments meeting together (alternately in both capitals). Craig himself seemed prepared to accept this idea, but his cabinet dismissed the joint sessions as 'unthinkable'. The Free State cabinet rejected the whole project as utterly inadequate and renewed its call for the Commission. The 1924 'army mutiny' – a protest by aggrieved ex-IRA officers – was no more an actual mutiny than the Curragh incident had been, but was an equally murky business, and perhaps an equally disturbing sign of political volatility. It alarmed the northern government and put pressure on W. T. Cosgrave's government in Dublin; Tom Jones noted on 19 March that 'having been weak in handling the mutiny, [they] are determined to show themselves strong on the Boundary issue, and have sent a stiff letter to us asking that the Commission be set up forthwith'. Later that month, Curtis enrolled a hesitant Jones, reluctant to 'put my foot in the Irish bog again'; he had 'lost touch with what had been happening over there'. Nonetheless he went to Dublin and met all the Free State leaders, to try to persuade them to make 'one more desperate effort at a solution which would further postpone boundary issue'. A month later he thought he had got to the brink of agreement 'on the lines of a voluntary commission to be set up by Craig and Cosgrave, to consist of local experts'. But Craig scuppered that by requiring that, if that happened, the Free State should surrender its right to a commission under Article XII.[16]

Unsurprisingly, when in May Britain eventually delivered a formal request that Northern Ireland appoint its boundary commissioner, it was rejected.[17] MacDonald kept talking, and when he met the two Irish premiers on 31 May, he managed to rattle Craig by invoking the Silesian partition, suggesting that the process should start by determining the area to be considered. Craig's alarm at 'the prospect of large areas such as whole counties' being even brought into the frame was plain. But what was inescapable was the absolute opposition between Craig's and Cosgrave's conception of how any transfers should be decided. When the issue of how to count heads – by unanimity or majority – arose, MacDonald concluded that if the former were used, Craig would probably be willing to appoint a commissioner, but in that case Cosgrave would probably withdraw his.[18]

Harried by the repeated demands of the Free State Governor General, Tim Healy, that the government fulfil its Treaty obligation, MacDonald announced on 5 June that the Commission would be chaired by Richard Feetham, a member of the South African Supreme Court. He 'reminded' MPs that Feetham had advised on Indian constitutional questions, and chaired an inquiry into the division of functions between India's central and provincial governments ('the complexity and importance of which would be difficult to overstate').[19]

But the problem of the missing northern Commissioner remained. The Judicial Committee of the Privy Council, which was then asked whether Britain could act in Northern Ireland's place, reported at the end of July that the royal prerogative could not be used for this. Faced with the 'beastly awkward' decision, the government knew how hard it would be to get the Tories to agree to legislation. Sent to 'beg' Stanley Baldwin to cooperate, Tom Jones was taken aback by the 'diehard reaction' he got, more so than he could 'ever remember having before from him': Baldwin fumed about 'assassination' and Irish 'behaviour in the war', all unforgivable. (Jones was driven to point out that MacDonald's own war record – as a leading pacifist – had not been 'conspicuously helpful'.)[20] More fruitless inter-governmental conferences followed through August and September, before MacDonald's government accepted the inevitability of legislation empowering it to appoint a third commissioner. The bill was a disagreeable one for Labour to have to push through parliament, and it showed how explosive the underlying issues still were. In an ill-tempered debate, diehards on all benches pressed a series of contentions designed to restrict or undermine the boundary commission. They argued that once the British government had appointed a chairman, it had no further legal obligation; if Northern Ireland did not wish to appoint a commissioner, that would be the end of it.[21] Some, notably the former Foreign Secretary Lord Grey, a very lukewarm home ruler, held that any conflict between Britain's 'honourable understanding with Ulster' in 1920 and its 'definite engagement with the Free State' should be resolved in favour of Ulster. If the Free State wanted to become a republic as a result, what did it matter? The bill went through, but plenty of notice had been served that the very existence of the boundary commission, as well as its terms of reference, were divisive. Indeed the idea of prioritizing the 'wishes of the inhabitants' was directly challenged, on the grounds that it might lead the commission to 'include the whole of Tyrone, Fermanagh, and a large portion of county Down' in the Free State.[22] So when the Boundary Commission finally met for the first time on 6 November – with Francis Bourdillon as its secretary – it was not in an entirely peaceful atmosphere.

That week Craig's position was bolstered when the political scenery shifted again, and such pressure as might have been put on him eased. In October MacDonald resigned, and on 3 November another general election brought back Stanley Baldwin. With him reappeared not only the leading Tory figures of the Coalition, Birkenhead and Austen Chamberlain, but also the double renegade Winston Churchill. Returning to the Conservative fold required all of them, but especially Churchill (now Chancellor of the Exchequer), to play down their commitment as signatories of the Treaty – still widely seen in the party as the great betrayal. This was easy enough for Birkenhead, who had always taken a cynically instrumental view of it, but Churchill's investment had been more positive, and his vocal hostility to Ulster Unionism as a Liberal minister still echoed. He immediately reversed Snowden's stand on the one-off grant for the Special Constabulary, to the exasperation of the top Treasury officials, who argued that giving Craig what he wanted would be a breach of the Treaty. The Controller of Finance, Sir Otto Niemeyer, pointed to the political embarrassment that would follow if the Northern Ireland government were to reject the Boundary Commission's ruling and then use the constabulary to resist border changes. Churchill, already demonstrating greater sympathy for the difficulties facing the northern government 'through no fault of their own', maintained that the fact that the Commission was sitting 'makes it all the more necessary that the Northern Govt. should be solidly supported'.[23]

'A CHAIRMAN OF EXACTLY THE KIND YOU CONTEMPLATED'

The Boundary Commissioners have not been kindly treated by history. The least contentious of the three – perhaps surprisingly – was the last one to be named, the veteran barrister-journalist J. R. Fisher, long-standing editor of the *Northern Whig*. Although he was appointed by the British, not Northern Ireland, government, the solidity of his Ulsterism was beyond question; he was an early enthusiast for exclusion – on its own merits, not just as a device to stop home rule. In 1914 he had advised Carson that 'if the principle of exclusion by plebiscite is conceded, you have won a very great point'. He had striking ideas about the need to maximize Ulster's homogeneity. In 1922 he had told Craig 'with north Monaghan *in* Ulster and South Armagh *out*, we should have a solid ethnographic and strategic frontier to the south', and if east Donegal was included 'a hostile "Afghanistan" on our north-west frontier would be placed in safe keeping'.[24] Unfortunately his ideas on this were unusual. As Commissioner he did exactly what might have been expected, including keeping his government informed of all the Commission's deliberations (and, less reasonably, breaching the Commissioners' mutual agreement that their proceeding should be kept strictly secret).

It was otherwise with MacNeill, the Free State nominee. The 'scholar-revolutionary' had a big national reputation, as a pioneer of Gaelic studies who had founded the Irish Volunteers and led the breakaway from Redmond in 1914, and – less auspiciously maybe – issued the 'countermanding order' trying to pull the Volunteers back from the brink of rebellion in 1916. On appointing him, Cosgrave chose, rather oddly, to emphasize MacNeill's qualifications as a Catholic, a northerner, and a minister. None of them was obviously relevant; O'Shiel had suggested that what was needed was 'a man of great weight and sagacity' who might be from any part of the country, or 'even from outside our shores'. His key attribute would be readiness 'to act on the government's slightest suggestion'. MacNeill, however, seems to have taken the Commission's commitment to secrecy as a kind of purdah; he barely communicated with the government or the community. A northern priest grumbled to Blythe nearly a year after the Commission started up, 'Fisher keeps them [his people] well informed. We can get no news.'

The choice has never been satisfactorily explained. Kevin O'Shiel would have been a more obvious candidate, already fully briefed on the whole issue; Hugh Kennedy, chief legal adviser to the Irish government since the Treaty, had experience of complex constitutional negotiations. And what MacNeill expected from the Commission is not clear: academic though he was, his political career had been marked by realism as much as idealism. F. S. L. Lyons attributed to him the same optimism about the border settlement as Griffith, but his biographer has suggested that he deliberately placed himself in a situation that would have threatened the career of a younger minister. In other words, he assumed that the outcome was likely to be a setback, and Cosgrave himself may have thought the same. Invoking Shakespeare, rather than any Gaelic source, MacNeill mused on King Richard II's dismissal of John of Gaunt – 'the ripest fruit first falls'. This was scarcely optimistic, though he cannot have imagined quite how catastrophic the outcome would prove for his reputation.[25] MacNeill's very distinction coupled with the immense public expectation would make the charge that he had buttressed, not diminished, partition all the more destructive.[26]

The key member of the Commission, obviously, was its chairman, who took the lead in interpreting 'the maddeningly few words he was left by the Treaty-makers' to specify the Commission's procedures.[27] Sir Richard Feetham appears as a rather neutral and even stateless character in modern histories, which in one sense is an improvement on his virulently hostile depiction ('Feetham-Cheat'em') in early nationalist accounts. He is often described simply as a 'South African Judge', and 'coming from an overseas Dominion';[28] but any implication of national kinship with Smuts is misleading. Feetham was a classic representative of the imperial administrative class, born in Monmouthshire, educated at Oxford, a member together with his friend Lionel Curtis of Milner's 'kindergarten' in South Africa, where he rose to the Supreme Court in 1923. Feetham was not the first choice to head the Commission. Curtis (who had wanted him to prepare the final draft of the Treaty) recommended him, but only after Sir Robert Borden, former prime minister of Canada, had turned the job down. With one eye on the Orange vote in Toronto, Borden insisted that he would take it on only if both governments appointed Commissioners, and he was 'assured that my acting is desired by both'; intentionally or not, this guaranteed his escape.[29]

Feetham might have been well advised to do the same, but here his national identity probably did figure. Curtis urged him to take up the task with a laconic telegram, sent in the name of the Milnerite group 'The Moot', which read 'England expects'. Just what Curtis thought was expected was indicated in his assurance to Churchill that Feetham – 'a chairman exactly of the kind you contemplated' – would resist the Free State's 'preposterous and extravagant claims'.[30] Maybe this amounted to little more than saying that he was a senior judge (to point out his 'conservative temperament' was surely supererogatory) whose 'legalism and remoteness from political realities', as one historian of the Commission sagely noted, formed 'perhaps the other side of his conscientious precision'.[31] How far the Labour government, in turning from Borden to Feetham, was deliberately avoiding a big political issue (the sort of thing it so often did, as Leonard Woolf thought) is not clear. The Colonial Secretary, J. H. Thomas, was aware that Borden thought the Commission should be used as a lever towards Irish unity on the Canadian federal model.[32] Feetham's known conservatism was probably not unwelcome.

Because Article XII was put together to meet the needs of a high-wire negotiation process, it did no more than the minimum necessary to sidestep further dispute. If Feetham himself had indeed been asked to compose the final draft, it would surely have read differently. It was not, as Tom Jones ruefully admitted, 'drafted like an act of Parliament'. As it was, the article – as Lord Buckmaster told the Lords in March 1922 – was 'full of grave and dangerous ambiguity'. (In this, as in its superficially appealing brevity, it perhaps resembled the similarly drafted Balfour Declaration on Palestine.) Feetham would stress in the Commission report how different it was from the boundary settlement provisions of the Versailles Treaty, which contained 'precise directions as to the limits of the areas to be dealt with, as to who are to be regarded as inhabitants, as to the expression of the wishes of the inhabitants by votes taken for the purpose, and as to the units of area in which wishes are to be ascertained'.

Article XII apparently left all this to the discretion of the Commission, but was that discretion limited or unlimited? In the absence of definite directions, Feetham produced his own elaboration of the clause by legal interpretation. He addressed a set of key questions.

Could the Commission shift the boundary in either direction? Could it transfer large areas and populations, or merely make minor adjustments to the existing boundary? What was the relationship between the 'three factors', wishes of inhabitants and economic and geographic conditions? Who qualified as an inhabitant and how were their wishes to be ascertained – was unanimity required, or would a bare majority be sufficient? And on what principle should units of area be chosen for this purpose?

Simply listing these questions starkly displays the makeshift nature of Article XII. None of these key issues had been identified by the Treaty makers, though the first had been hinted at in the draft approved by Griffith on 13 November 1921, with its phrase 'by inclusion and exclusion'. This dropped out, perhaps being seen as redundant; Griffith did not insist on it. More surprisingly, the questions would not be formally laid out until September 1925, after the Commission had already spent ten months gathering evidence. This in spite of Lord Curzon's insistence in the House of Lords, in October 1924, that 'the first condition of the success of such Commissions was to define in precise language the duty they were called upon to discharge'. It was vital, he said, to say 'what machinery are you to set up' to determine the wishes of the inhabitants? How are 'geographic and economic conditions' to be 'appraised and ascertained'? Curzon suggested that, given fellow Commissioners who were partisans of the opposing sides, 'you are placing upon the shoulders of [the Chairman] a responsibility that any human being might shrink from bearing'.[33] Curiously, though, when Curzon returned to the Cabinet in November, he does not seem to have persisted in his call for precise definition of the Commission's remit. Most surprising of all, surely, was that when Eoin MacNeill finally saw Feetham's list of questions in September 1925, he made no fuss about it. It has been suggested that Feetham's memorandum passed 'without formal dissent on MacNeill's part but without his support', and this seems true. Although he did record on 19 September that he did not accept that the Commission could transfer territory from the Free State to Northern Ireland, he did not press this point.

It may be, as has been suggested, that 'the most vital of all the questions' was the one about the 'three factors' – how would the conditions qualify the wishes? It would certainly take up a lot of the Commission's time. But surely the fundamental question was how to establish those wishes in the first place. What were the 'units of area' whose inhabitants' wishes would count, and how would their wishes be counted? Feetham's invocation of the Versailles plebiscites, and the question of what kind of majority would be needed, seemed to assume a public vote. How else could a majority be counted? Eoin MacNeill had insisted months before that 'a hard and fast stand must be made on the plebiscite system'.[34] The Free State government declared, in September 1924, that the Commission's 'first step' must be to hold plebiscites for each poor law union in the border counties. Yet, of course, no voting was ever to take place, in any unit of area. A plebiscite was ruled out, despite being 'the only means by which precise figures as to the wishes of the inhabitants could be ascertained', on the ground that it was not specified in Article XII. 'It is clearly impossible' – the voice of the supreme court judge can be heard here – 'to conduct a plebiscite except under the authority of special legal provisions of a comprehensive and stringent character'. Instead the Commission would hold consultations with 'persons claiming to speak on behalf of inhabitants of different areas' and took written evidence – notably census returns and election results. The latter seldom if ever related exactly to areas the Commission was assessing, leaving the possibility that 'the evidence available does not show the existence of a decisive majority in favour of transfer'.[35]

In fact Feetham knew that the absence of 'special legal provisions' was only a secondary reason for rejecting the idea of a plebiscite. He had been told on 31 July by the Crown law officers that special legislation would be necessary, and when he returned to the issue in September, while the Commission bill was being debated, he was told by the Colonial Office that such legislation would be politically hazardous. It is not clear what Feetham's starting point was – he certainly appeared to expect a plebiscite – but it is clear that Geoffrey Whiskard once again delivered a decisive steer. He told Curtis that if a bill was introduced to enable the Commission to take a plebiscite, 'amendments would be moved defining within a very limited area the districts within which the plebiscite could be taken'; clearly it was impossible for such amendments to specify 'limits of deviation to which plebiscites are to be confined. To do that it would be practically necessary to attach a map as a schedule ... the description of these limits would occupy pages'. Curtis took note of this, but was more impressed by Whiskard's argument that 'the real objection to plebiscites is ... the practical difficulty of holding them', the same kind of difficulty which would be encountered 'when the time comes to give effect to the award by handing over areas to the Free State'.[36]

Whiskard warned that 'some definite conflict of authority which could not or need not be construed as repudiation or rebellion might arise during the period of bringing a case before the Court', and 'such a conflict might in the last resort require the occupation of the disputed territory by British troops pending the final decision'. This would be a 'highly undesirable' way (to put it mildly) 'to meet a contingency which it is reasonable to hope can be met by some less drastic medicine'. Curtis argued that 'HMG will only stultify themselves ... unless they are prepared to ensure if necessary by military occupation the execution of the award'. He had already pointed out that, since the Commission's award would have immediate statutory effect, if the northern government refused to cooperate Britain would have to use force to implement it. Force would also be required to restore Cosgrave's government if it fell and the republicans repudiated the Treaty. (Curtis hoped this could be done by blockade, 'the most merciful course', rather than direct military action – Curtis optimistically suggesting that 'control would then gravitate into the hands of the more reasonable and propertied classes'.)[37] After receiving this unappealing appreciation, the War Office concluded that the commitment of the army would be 'unlimited, indefinite, and fraught with serious danger'.

Curtis worried away at the presentational as well as substantive problems involved. Feetham, he said, had only raised the issue 'to enable the Government to think out in advance certain likely contingencies if they arise' – if the Commission reported they could not discharge their task without taking plebiscites and could not take plebiscites without statutory authority, such powers might 'be nugatory unless HMG are prepared to maintain and enforce order'. What, he wondered, 'would be said of the Powers who signed the Treaty of Versailles if the Silesian Commission had reported that they could

not delimit the frontier without powers, machinery and military support, and the Powers had told the Poles that they did not propose to
meet the request of their own Commission?' It would be a mistake,
he believed, to think that the Free State would acquiesce if the Commission was refused such powers. The Free State had been forced into
the position of saying they could not settle the boundary by agreement 'because their supporters in Northern Ireland have definite
rights under the Treaty – to declare their wishes by a Plebiscite', and
these rights could only be abrogated by their consent. 'Cosgrave has
said this again and again. That he has drifted into this position is one
of the penalties we are paying for protracted delay.' If powers were
asked for and refused, the Free State would say the Treaty had been
broken. In Curtis's view, Feetham was 'not the kind of man to ask for
any legislative powers which are not in his deliberate judgment necessary for his task'. Yet since there seemed to be no way to square the
circle, Curtis advised that 'he be told that it is, for obvious reasons,
extremely inadvisable to bring the proceedings of the commission
into the arena of parliamentary discussion'.[38] He must have known
that this *verbum sapienti* would suffice.

'NORTHERN IRELAND
MUST STILL BE
RECOGNIZABLE'

It is not easy to explain why the Free State failed to take the stand
MacNeill had called for. Feetham and the Commissioners held two
hearings with its representatives, the first on 4–5 December 1924.
This was a long meeting, and Feetham seemed genuinely anxious to
get the Irish government's advice on how to proceed. (The Executive
Council had simply issued a bare statement that 'it was not contemplated by the Treaty that any area within "Northern Ireland" should
have the right to withdraw permanently' from the Free State 'unless
the majority of the inhabitants of such area were in favour of this
course'.)[39] He wanted to know what kind of areas might be used to
establish the wishes of the people, and there was extended discussion
of the Commission's powers to hold plebiscites. Feetham was

concerned that the Treaty had not specified this in the way that the Versailles treaties had; the Free State's Attorney General, John O'Byrne, who had been the Irish delegation's legal adviser, explained that it was 'a very short document, prepared in a certain amount of hurry'. He held that while census information might give 'a certain loose indication' of the people's wishes, it could not be exact. (Since this was precisely the point that the Commission's secretary Bourdillon had made to Curtis, he may have been quietly cheering O'Byrne on.) Here Fisher intervened, saying 'we come back to a plebiscite', for which an Act of Parliament would be needed: otherwise 'I do not see anyone in a disturbed district opening a polling post; the police might simply move them on.'[40] Various areas – from counties to townlands – were surveyed to find an equivalent to the 'commune' specified in the Upper Silesian case. Because poor law unions were the smallest administrative area (townlands having no official status), O'Byrne urged that they were the nearest analogue. As to which precise areas should be polled, Feetham suggested that existing evidence – census material, election statistics, and so on – should be the basis for deciding. When he asked if the Free State government wished to offer any evidence immediately, O'Byrne said that since it had expected the Commission to 'take a vote', it had not prepared any.[41]

Thus it was left: it seemed to be understood that the Commission would assemble written evidence, and hold consultative hearings (Feetham duly noted that they would have no power to compel witnesses to attend, any more than to set up polling stations), as a preliminary process. But Feetham's scepticism was unmistakable. It was obvious enough to Cahir Healy, writing to the NEBB's solicitor early in December, that unless they could get the Commission to specify its terms of reference, 'we are going to be diddled'. They should insist on a plebiscite, 'and if that is denied us, leave the Commission'.[42]

The Commission's ruling on the extent of territory that might be transferred dealt a double blow to nationalist expectations. First, it ruled that it had power 'to shift the existing boundary line in either direction'. This was a shock to some nationalists but it hardly dented their hopes. Much more serious was the issue of whether, as Griffith and Collins had believed, and so many still believed, entire counties, or certainly large segments of them, could be transferred. In Newry, where 'the Boundary Commission was an unending topic of conversation', the certainty that the town would become part of the Free State survived even past the Commissioners' visit in March 1925 ('stories were told of the cool reception they had given to Unionists who had appeared before them to argue their case').[43] Such optimism could not survive Feetham's ruling that – while its scope was 'not limited to mere correction of irregularities' – there was to be 'no wholesale reconstruction of the map'. The fundamental 'proviso' (unstated in Article XII) was that 'the Commission is not to reconstitute the two territories, but to settle the boundaries between them'. The reason for rejecting 'reconstitution' went well beyond the terms of Article XII: when the 'boundaries' had been determined, Feetham said, 'Northern Ireland must still be recognizable as the same provincial entitity'. How was it to be recognized? The changes made 'must not be so drastic as to destroy its identity', or to 'make it impossible for it to continue as a separate province . . . with its own parliament and government under the Government of Ireland Act'.[44] This invocation of statute was of course consonant with the Treaty; but the invocation of 'identity' went a long way beyond 'economic and geographical conditions' into the realm of political culture. Economic and geographical factors, however complicated, were in principle measurable. Identity was not.

How did Feetham come up with this game-changing 'proviso'? Part of the answer may lie in one of the shadiest British documents of the whole Treaty process – a letter from Lord Birkenhead to Balfour originally written in 1922 – and the still more dubious action of Winston Churchill in arranging its publication in September 1924. Birkenhead had written to 'reassure' Balfour 'as to the meaning of' Article XII. The 'main purpose' of that Article, he held, was 'to preserve to Northern Ireland' the provisions of the 1920 Act – in essence, 'the maintenance of Northern Ireland' not as a 'new State to be brought into existence' when the Treaty was ratified, but as 'an entity already existing', 'a creature already constituted'. It was 'inconceivable that any competent and honest arbitrator could take the opposite view'. Birkenhead dismissed Craig's fear that the Commission might make drastic changes by insisting that if the Article had meant that, it would have 'been drafted in very different words'. Such changes would not, he suggested, have been 'committed to a Commission': 'the natural course would have been that the Governments concerned should retain everything but details in their own hands' – in accordance with the precedents set by 'innumerable' treaties in the nineteenth century. (He instanced in particular the establishment of Bulgaria by the 1878 Treaty of Berlin, providing his own translation 'for clearness sake'.)[45]

Churchill's intentions in nudging his former colleagues into publishing the letter are plain enough. Although he generously told Balfour it 'will do you good' with the Diehards, the real good would be done for himself. Not just in opposition, but in political limbo, he was trying to return to the Conservative Party; lingering diehard Tory anger over the Treaty – in particular the unfinished business of border adjustment – was a big obstacle. For Churchill the letter, as he told a correspondent in Fermanagh shortly before it was published, 'shows most clearly that the British signatories of the treaty intended that Article 12 should only deal with a readjustment of boundaries and not with a redistribution of territory'. (He went on to say that 'we then received the highest legal advice . . . that no impartial commissioner could take any other view'.)[46] So once the letter was made public, Feetham faced the possibility of being labelled either incompetent or dishonest by the former Lord Chancellor if he took a different line. A more deliberate and public attempt to nobble him would be hard to imagine. And if, as he would later imply, Eoin MacNeill was unaware of this, it is hard to understand why.

Indeed, Feetham first aired the idea three months after the Balfour letter, at the hearing with the Free State representatives, when he suggested that the 'new territory' of Northern Ireland 'should be capable of maintaining a Parliament and Government'. He seems to have deduced this from the Government of Ireland Act. The Free State's Attorney General was clearly taken aback – 'I do not know,' he protested, 'that the consideration which you suggested a moment ago is a proper suggestion for this Commission.' As he pointed out, the territory of Northern Ireland should consist simply of that 'homogeneous population in favour of' separation from the Free State. It would have a local parliament, but to consider it as being a more or less independent state 'would be an absolutely false analogy'. Did Feetham take this point? He did not respond; Eoin MacNeill, who did, seems to have missed it; he turned the discussion towards the self-governing status of the Free State.[47]

WISHES AND CONDITIONS

In rejecting the possibility of a plebiscite (or plebiscites), Feetham decided that there could be 'no precise rule as to the requirements which must be fulfilled' in any particular areas so that 'the wishes of their inhabitants' could prevail. Its method had the virtue of avoiding the thorny question of balancing the transient will of the people against their long-term, structural interests. Public will was assumed to follow religious affiliation. How justified was this assumption? O'Byrne had warned that it could be no more than a 'loose indication' – saying perhaps surprisingly that, for instance, 'plenty of Catholics' would vote to be in Northern Ireland.[48] In Upper Silesia – where the Commission's Chief Technical Assistant, Major Boger, had been present during the plebiscite – the vote revealed some unexpected deviations from expected preferences (on the basis of language). Identities there were perhaps more fluid than in Ulster, but the force of Bourdillon's point that the Commission's method basically assumed the answer to a question that had never been asked remains.

The lapse of time since the Treaty was a problem for the nationalists; the original intention of the signatories was that the Commission would start work immediately after ratification. This had not happened, for reasons the Free State preferred not to dwell on. Nonetheless, nationalists demanded that border adjustment be based on the situation at the time of the Treaty, since when an unknown number of people had moved in or out of the border area. But this was obviously inconsistent with any call for a plebiscite, and indeed could only be done by something like Feetham's method. They may have hoped that the two methods could somehow be combined, but in practice went along with the Commission's gathering of indirect testimony.

Shortly after the hearing with the Free State representatives, the Commissioners crossed to Armagh and spent a week touring the border area. In Derry city on 21 December, Feetham told a nationalist deputation that the Commission did not have the power to hold a plebiscite, but would take account of all available written evidence.[49] Early in 1925 the Commission invited written statements to be submitted before its formal sittings opened at the beginning of March, when it embarked on a four-month sequence of hearings – fifty-five altogether – with representations from well over five hundred people, in bodies ranging from the Belfast and County Down Railway Company via the Armagh County Council to the County Donegal Protestant Registration Association (who were heard twice, the second time over a period of four days), and individuals and groups, including 'certain inhabitants of the Poor Law Union of Londonderry'. It amassed some 150 written submissions.[50] Assessing the wishes of the inhabitants by this method was a demanding process, and Feetham threw himself into it with persistence and pertinacity. Weighing evidence and examining witnesses was, after all, his profession, and most likely more congenial than presiding over a public vote, however much more rapid and unambiguous that might have been. In fact a public vote did take place: just a month after the hearings began, Craig held elections to the Northern Ireland parliament. His clear intention was to impress Feetham by re-emphasizing the solidity of the Unionist community. The outcome of this plebiscite at one remove was less unequivocal than Craig hoped. Nationalists improved their representation across the province as a whole, though in the border counties the Unionist vote increased slightly.

The definitional issues that underlay the whole project broke through repeatedly. When the Commissioners sat at Enniskillen in late April 1925, for instance, the town council turned down Feetham's invitation to meet them, saying they thought that the Commission was only to consider the immediate vicinity of the border – Enniskillen was ten miles from it. (Instead, the Fermanagh nationalist MP Cahir Healy turned up, to insist that his re-election – with Thomas Harbison – in the last two elections demonstrated the 'right that the people of the county had acquired under the Treaty of remaining in the Free State'.)[51] Sometimes Feetham got into fascinating and revealing analytical and syntactical debates, as with Archdeacon Tierney of Enniskillen, one of those who maintained that the wishes of the inhabitants must predominate, and economics and geography be secondary. Feetham disputed this apparently straightforward reading of Article XII, insisting that 'the terms used show that sometimes economic and geographic conditions are to prevail against the wishes'. When Tierney made the (indisputable) point that the wishes of the inhabitants were the sentence's principal clause, with the second clause on economic and geographic conditions subordinate, Feetham said – equally accurately – 'it is also qualifying'. If it could never prevail, there would have been no point putting it in.

It would probably have been impossible to measure the population changes that had taken place since the Treaty, especially the displacements triggered by the border conflict between 1920 and 1924, and the Commission did not try to.[52] But the impact of changing 'facts on the ground' since 1921 on Feetham's assessment was nowhere more striking than in the case of the Silent Valley reservoir, work on which had only begun late in 1923. The site in the Mourne mountains, some forty miles from Belfast, had been chosen because of its high rainfall and the quality of its water; but it also served as a counterweight to the universal nationalist expectation – and unionist fear – that south Down would be awarded to the Free State. Although the project was incomplete – the dam would not be finished until 1933 – and alternative sites could in principle have been used, the Belfast City and District Water Commissioners' argument, that to guarantee the safety of the city's water supply it must stay in Northern Ireland, was accepted. The indisputable wishes of the Catholic majority in south Down must be subordinated to the vital interests of the Belfast region's half a million people.

All along the line, Feetham set himself to build a hypothetical projection: would being one side or the other of the border help or hinder the economic development of each area examined? In the case of three-quarters Catholic Newry, for instance, where nationalists were so sure that it must be in the Free State – 'that the area was predominantly "nationally-minded" had been demonstrated in election after election' – he asked could it preserve its prosperity as a coal-trade port, and a centre of the flax-spinning and linen-weaving industry, if it left Northern Ireland? The analysis of Newry was undoubtedly substantial – a full four pages of the Commission's report. The answer was negative: the changes that would 'be involved in the separation of Newry and its surrounding area from Northern Ireland cannot be regarded as ... "compatible with social and economic conditions" '. This was yet another syntactical shift, slight but significant.

The Commission's hearings induced an outpouring of communal beliefs and attitudes. Nationalists preferred to couch their arguments in the language of civil rights and minority protection – it would be outrageous to force them to live in a state ruled by bigots determined to deprive them of equal voting rights. Unionists tended to ground their arguments in the habitually greater rateable capacity of Protestants, which gave them a greater stake in the country even where they were in the minority. Many also argued that many Catholics would prefer to stay outside the Free State, challenging the automatic identification of Catholic with nationalist. Some even challenged the right of Catholics to the land, claiming, like the Afrikaners, that it had been empty when their ancestors arrived. The Irish had arrived later, as 'parasites' on Protestant industriousness.[53] But Unionists could also be more unguarded in displaying their cultural attitudes (which of course they regarded as the only attitudes a normal, moral person could hold). The Rector of Castle Caldwell in Belleek fully bore out his plaintive confession, 'I can't get over my upbringing', by rolling forth the full gamut of timeless stereotypes of the native Irish. Southern Ireland would always be 'a second Mexico'; the Catholics of Fermanagh were 'a restless and discontented people', not because of oppressive government but because – whether in Fermanagh or in the packing yards of Chicago (or indeed, presumably, the governmental buildings in Dublin – the native Irish were feckless, violent, and cowardly. He himself had no 'Celtic blood'.[54]

All this was an interesting symptom of the problem at issue, but as evidence it was far from what had been expected from the phrase 'compatible with conditions', which Lloyd George had introduced, as he said, only to deal with obvious absurdities. Just as Feetham set himself to preserve the viability of Northern Ireland as a unit, so he did the same with each small border unit he examined. This was what he meant when he told the Free State representatives in late August 1925, in a revealing phrase, that the Commission's award would use economic conditions with the aim of 'protecting the inhabitants of a given area from themselves'.[55] People would not be allowed to sacrifice their prosperity on the altar of freedom. The identity of Northern Ireland might be protected, but that of border communities would not.

'A STRONGER AND MORE COMPACT TERRITORY'

Weighing the wishes of the inhabitants against economic and geographic conditions was admittedly a process which could never be simple or straightforward. The question of what would represent a 'decisive majority' of wishes, on the other hand, could in principle have been decided with absolute certainty. Feetham (with at least the tacit consent of his fellow Commissioners) refused so to decide, concluding merely that a case for transfer could not be 'made out unless the majority in favour of the change appears to be a substantial majority'. This remarkably vague formulation was followed by another purporting to clarify the term 'substantial' – 'i.e. a majority representing a high proportion of the total number of persons entitled to rank as inhabitants of the district directly concerned' – which did no such thing. Substance and height alike were left unmeasured. This otiose formula seems to have been Feetham's own, and though it did him little credit as a draftsman, it confirmed his determination to avoid precision.

At what point did this confession of statistical bankruptcy become fixed? The general outline of the award was clear well before the final report was written, which itself was sooner than many expected. Fisher, reporting to a friend in May 1925 that 'our staff is steadily growing, and we shall want a pantechnicon to convey our maps and other documents alone', added, 'Our Engineer, Major Boger . . . mentioned cheerfully that that after all their regular commission work on the Polish frontier, it was *eighteen months* before the final surveys were completed and the reports presented'.[56] Two months later, when the Commission was still gathering evidence at Omagh, he sent the wife of an Ulster Unionist MP a fairly definite report of the pending outcome. The 'more extravagant claims' had been 'practically wiped out', he told her. 'It will now be a matter of border townlands for the most part . . . and although we may have to go pretty deep in some places, the result will be a stronger and more compact territory, with not inconsiderable bits added'.[57]

Possibly at that stage MacNeill still thought there would be large transfers to the Free State. He finally saw the draft report on 11 September, a fortnight after the Commission's second hearing of the Free State representatives on 25 August. (The Free State government had left this late: the best part of a year had passed since the first hearing, the gathering of evidence was complete, and there had been no plebiscites.) Discussion there focused on the phrasing of Article XII – the intended balance between 'the wishes of the inhabitants' (however defined) and 'economic and geographic considerations'. The Free State argued repeatedly that this proviso was put in only 'to prevent absurdities and anomalies', and that the wishes of the inhabitants must be paramount. Feetham dismissed this: 'they are not paramount where the result they indicate is not compatible with economic and geographic conditions . . . Though the wishes of the inhabitants are put first [in Article XII], I am not sure they can rightly be described as the governing factor.' He suggested that the reference to economic conditions was there because the inhabitants could not be 'trusted to take a sufficiently enlightened view of their own interests'.[58]

The Free State's Attorney General was baffled by this, and in mid-September the Chief Justice, Hugh Kennedy, fired off an angry note condemning Feetham's 'over-narrow' interpretative method. Mac-Neill's response was half-hearted; he said (on 10 October) that 'nothing is to be gained by antagonizing' the chairman, though 'a great deal may be gained by sturdy impersonal argument'.[59] Coming at this late stage, the Free State government might surely have realized that the game was up. MacNeill never explained how much he had gained by 'sturdy argument'. What proved to be Feetham's final draft was initially treated as 'not . . . a document formally before the Commission' and was only discussed informally. There is no evidence that MacNeill secured any alterations, however. His eventual explanation in the Dáil of his inaction was lame: 'the details came before us in a very gradual and piecemeal manner', and 'there was at no time any debate . . . as to the principles of interpretation'.[60] No definite decision which could produce 'consistent application' of any princ-iples was ever taken. It surely must be asked, why on earth not?

In the public memory, the Boundary Commission joined other footnotes to history like the Irish Convention and the Council of Ire-land. But if its award had been signed by all the Commissioners, it would have been legally binding on governments and would have been implemented. The adjustments it proposed – however short they might fall from nationalist hopes – were not as trivial as is often sug-gested. Most of the transfers were to be on the Fermanagh border, but they would also include a four-mile-wide strip of east Donegal around Derry city, and a substantial chunk of south Armagh. Cross-maglen would have become part of the Free State. Altogether 183,290 acres were to be transferred to the Free State, 49,242 acres to North-ern Ireland. Just over 31,000 people – nearly 28,000 of them Catholics – would be brought into the Free State. The frontier would be shortened from 280 to 229 miles, albeit still far longer than Fish-er's idea of a militarily defensible line. But it was not merely the scale of adjustments, rather the idea of losing Free State territory – with 2,764 Catholic inhabitants – to Northern Ireland, which impelled Eoin MacNeill to resign. The three Commissioners approved the draft award on 5 November (exactly a year after their first meeting), but the appearance of a supposed copy of the Commission's map in the *Morning Post* two days later unleashed a storm of nationalist denunciation. MacNeill resigned on 20 November without signing the report. Only after that did he publicly condemn Feetham's crucial 'importation' of 'a new governing and dominant condition' into Art-icle XII, the insistence that the border adjustment must not significantly disadvantage Northern Ireland. MacNeill identified this as 'a political consideration which was made a dominant consider-ation'; he was absolutely right, but fatally late.

The possibility of transfers lingered briefly after this, though Tom Jones believed that the premature publication had 'broken con-fidence' in the Commission. Feetham and Fisher, apparently taken aback by MacNeill's sudden resignation, signed the report and expected it to take effect. Indeed they told the British government that they 'regarded his resignation as ineffective and void – he had no power to resign and the Free State Government had no power to

accept his resignation'. It could not 'touch their right to reach a decision'.[61] Craig, though he had trademarked the 'not an inch' demand,
and never showed any sign of embracing Fisher's ideas of a drastically
shortened frontier, could see that this was not a bad deal. The Donegal and Armagh transfers, in particular, were uncannily close to
what Fisher had earlier urged him to go for. Fisher himself wrote to
Carson that the award 'would not shift a stone or a tile of your enduring work for Ulster . . . If anybody had suggested twelve months ago
that we could have kept so much I would have laughed at him.'[62]
Soon, though, it became clear that the report would not be published –
in fact it would be locked away until 1968. In Newry the leak at first
provoked derision, then (when there was no official denial) dismay;
but 'the outcry died quickly, the Boundary Commission was quietly
forgotten'.[63] Still, its ferocity, however brief, seemed to leave the Free
State with no option but to reject the award.

So there was to be one more partition crisis – this time the last. Craig
indicated that, given the right financial settlement, he might accept
the Feetham award. His terms infuriated Churchill, but Baldwin persuaded him that the way forward was to reach an agreement with
Cosgrave. Cosgrave duly dashed to London, hoping to secure the
release of republican prisoners in the north (regarded by nationalists
as 'political prisoners', by Unionists as criminal terrorists) in return
for leaving the border unchanged – the only feasible option left to his
government, but now much less attractive to Craig than it would have
been earlier. Craig offered the Cabinet's Irish Committee his usual
blunt line – they 'should rule out of their minds any idea that Ulster
would be prepared to sacrifice territory to save Mr Cosgrave's face'.
(Chamberlain put forward the idea that 'it might be better to maintain the existing boundary if there were to be an exchange of
population', but this went no further.)[64] Craig offered a mere thirty
prisoners; Cosgrave dashed back to Dublin to present the offer to his
colleagues, who duly denounced it as political suicide. Next day the
Free State's sharpest negotiator, Kevin O'Higgins, went to see Baldwin. He, together with the Attorney General and the Minister for
Commerce, arrived at Chequers on 28 November. Baldwin's line –
announced to Craig before he met the Free State group – was that if
the latter 'cannot take the old boundary . . . they must take the new'.

The leaked map was 'full of inaccurate suggestions' and 'the proposed line is much more favourable to the Free State' than it suggested.[65] O'Higgins was unimpressed by this. 'Newry was the acid test', for them – 'an award which left Newry and its hinterland within the jurisdiction of the North' could not be squared with either their interpretation of the Treaty or the evidence.

O'Higgins underlined how crucial the issue was to the survival of the Free State government. 'We cannot stand on the *status quo* plus prisoners' – they would be seen as having been 'tricked and cheated'. It was not just a case of 'six or seven men facing extinction' – there was 'no coherent party ready to take over from us and carry on on the basis of the Treaty'. The only thing that could save them was a 'substantial improvement in the condition of the Catholics of Ulster' who were now living 'in conditions of Catholics prior to Catholic Emancipation'. How could this be done? Craig protested that he had already got the 'ban against Roman Catholics in shipyards removed'; more than that, a Protestant doctor had recently opened a Catholic bazaar 'and Lady Craig had been asked to a Catholic whist drive'! (O'Higgins's reaction to this news is not recorded.) Craig proposed regular governmental meetings to 'get to the bottom of' charges of discrimination. O'Higgins preferred something more positive – the restoration of proportional representation – drawing from Craig the inevitable response, 'I can't stick PR. Does not seem British. Too Continental.' It turned out, of course, that Cosgrave agreed with him.

The talks circulated interminably around the issue of joint meetings, but after three days (and, as Jones wearily recorded, thirty-six meetings of the Committee on Irish Affairs since 23 November) it proved to be financial adjustments that would secure consent to the boundary. On 2 December, with Churchill warning again of the dire consequences if there was no settlement, the British agreed to abandon the Treaty provision (in Article V) for the Free State to contribute a share of the UK's war debt, moving Cosgrave to say that the proposal 'showed a spirit of neighbourly comradeship which had never before been revealed'. In return he agreed to take over liability for malicious damage compensation claims. The decision about which of Northern Ireland's prisoners should be released would be made by Britain. The Colonial Secretary, Leo Amery, who wanted to use 'the present opportunity . . . to eliminate the obligation that would exist after 1927 of bringing into existence' the 'unworkable' Council of Ireland, succeeded in getting the powers reserved to the Council under the 1920 Act transferred to Northern Ireland: the wraithlike life of the Council was ended.[66] The Boundary Commission would, in Baldwin's word, be 'buried'.

Feetham went on protesting that the report had real value – 'the present order was an accident', and 'the grievances found at particular places were serious'. At the very least it ought to be published 'so that the public should not be left permanently under a delusion'. Most importantly perhaps for him, 'the good faith of the tribunal was at stake' – here he adopted a judicial concept which reflected his view of his task throughout. Churchill poured the inevitable balm – the fact that this 'admirable report' should not be published was 'a great sacrifice'. It had achieved something of importance: the problem of Tyrone and Fermanagh had wrecked the home rule negotiations, nearly wrecked the Government of Ireland Bill and the Treaty, but had now been 'settled out of court'. The Commission's work had 'led to this settlement'.[67] Churchill was surely right. But as it was, even well-informed Irish nationalists could believe, twenty years later, that the 'fatuous' Commission 'never once ran the risk of taking . . . a square inch' from the territory of Northern Ireland.[68]

'A DRASTIC REALLOCATION OF TERRITORY'?

There was an instructive coda to the negotiations. Shortly after the *Morning Post* leak, Craig proposed that 'persons transferred against their will to the Free State' should receive financial compensation. This drew a remarkable response from the Home Secretary, William Joynson-Hicks. He scouted the idea as 'inadmissible', but was struck by the fact that Craig appeared to contemplate payments only to Protestants. The implication disturbed him: 'if it were really the case that no Roman Catholic would willingly remain under the jurisdiction of the northern government, the argument for a drastic reallocation of territory would be almost unanswerable'.[69] Coming from any minister, this would have been a striking admission, but from the arch-diehard 'Jix', a prime mover (with Ronald McNeill) in the overthrow of Lloyd George, and 'the most puritanical and protestant Home Secretary of the twentieth century', it confirmed how disastrously the Free State had failed to present northern nationalist opinion. Small wonder that Cahir Healy, even before he testified to the Boundary Commission, charged that 'none of the Irish leaders understood the northern situation or the northern mind'.[70]

Epilogue
The Long Division

In Spike Milligan's comic novella of the Irish border, *Puckoon*, the eponymous village is the last piece of the border to be determined by the Boundary Commission. The Commissioners, eager to be done with it and get to the pub, jointly grasp the pencil and pull it across a giant map of Ireland. Their tussle, had it happened, might have provided a better explanation of the mazy borderline than the real one. Milligan had a pardonably hazy idea of the Commission's make-up, but more importantly he – like many others – assumed that it had determined the line. Feetham would have been duly mortified. In reality, lines that were never intended even as internal administrative borders became an international frontier.

In Puckoon, the frontier bisects O'Toole's pub, placing 'two square feet in the corner of the public bar' in Northern Ireland, 'where the price of drinks is thirty per cent cheaper'. There 'a crowd of skinflints' somehow manage to huddle, while the rest of the pub stands empty. The reality of partition was not much less absurd. Some of its results were trivial – when Colm Tóibín walked the border in the 1980s he met a man whose house straddled the border; 'the only bother he had was people like me asking did he sleep in the north or the south?' But some of the human dislocation was serious. The largely unavowed refugee crisis that followed the Treaty was over by 1925, and could probably not have been reversed by any border adjustment.[1] Even so, the evident inappropriateness of the county line as a political frontier might well have led to efforts to adjust it. But political investment in it was too strong on both sides. Unionists held to Craig's 'not an inch', nationalists demanded 'reunification'. The border must not be redrawn, but abolished. The timetable for this was variable. Republicans persisted with direct confrontation, while

Eamon de Valera's Fianna Fáil in its first general election campaign loudly denied that it stood for 'attacking "Ulster"' – 'it will accept EXISTING REALITIES'. But as de Valera made clear, 'acceptance' was ambiguous. ('We must of course recognise existing facts, but it does not follow that we must acquiesce in them.')[2]

In power after 1932, de Valera resisted demands to use the Free State's increasingly prominent position in the League of Nations to internationalize the partition issue, but when he rewrote the Free State constitution in 1937 he recast its status. The new constitution insisted that the national territory was the whole island and gave the state a name in the Irish language, Eire (in the English language, 'Ireland'). In also recognizing the 'special position' of the Catholic Church, in Article 44, it stepped away from the secularism of both the Free State and Northern Ireland constitutions. Thus, as an acerbic critic said, 'the Protestants of Northern Ireland were declared incorporated *de jure* into a state which recognised the special position of the Roman Catholic church'. It would, he added, 'be hard to think of a combination of propositions more likely to sustain and stiffen the siege-mentality of Protestant Ulster'. If de Valera was interested on wooing the north, the constitution 'was an odd bouquet to choose'.[3]

De Valera stoutly maintained in 1937 that the prospect of voluntary unification was growing – Ulster unionist 'hallucinations' of the danger of persecution were receding. But he was still ready to envisage unification by a simple majority. At Monaghan in June that year he pointed out that the nationalist vote in the six counties was already one-third; 'if you can get another one-sixth of the population' to support unity, 'the problem will be solved'. For him, the restoration of the Irish language was a more urgent issue than partition; even if the language was a barrier to unity, there was 'no use in being an imitation country'.[4] The Irish-Ireland bar would not be lowered to accommodate dissenters. As Seán MacEntee put it in 1936, 'if these people want to come in with us they will have to accept the Republic as well as every other thing'.

By 'the Republic', MacEntee evidently meant not so much a political form as the whole Irish–Ireland cultural package. The formal declaration of a republic did not come until over ten years later, and it was not made by de Valera, who was temporarily out of power. He had steered a slightly awkward course through the Second World War, maintaining Ireland's neutrality – vital as an assertion of Irish sovereignty, but inevitably pointing up yet again the distinction of 'loyal Ulster'. A significant casualty of the policy, as well, was American goodwill towards the ending of partition.[5] The frontier itself, which divided belligerent and neutral territories during the war, remained open – recognition of its essential indefensibility in military terms. By that time it had generated a distinct border culture, in which smuggling (accelerated by the Anglo-Irish 'economic war' of the 1930s) was notoriously prominent, together with a high level of bicycle ownership, and even a certain amount of cross-dressing.[6]

'A LOGIC INHERENT IN THE IRISH SITUATION'

The declaration of the Republic by the Inter-Party government brought an unlooked-for restatement of British policy in the form of the Ireland Act, guaranteeing that 'in no event' would Northern Ireland cease to be part of the United Kingdom 'without the consent of the parliament of Northern Ireland'. Although this had been perfectly well understood from the start, the somewhat gratuitous reiteration projected it into a new generation. But the Act also restated the common citizenship of the two countries, and hence the unique status of the Irish border: Ireland was not a 'foreign country'. De Valera was none the less incensed, speaking out repeatedly against the 'calamitous', 'almost incredible', fantastic, outrageous, 'stupid' and 'mad' guarantee. 'If this thing is done to our country,' he fumed, 'then feelings will go back to what they were in 1919 to 1921.' He read it as making unification 'an impossible task'.[7]

Many thought he had made it so. One of his most persistent parliamentary critics, Frank MacDermot, dismissed his unity policy as a compound of 'stale claptrap and weary fallacies', and called on the Dáil to reject the 1937 constitution: 'while purporting to establish a Constitution for the whole of Ireland, it offers no basis for union with the North and contains various provisions tending to prolong partition'. One of these was Article 44, which 'really means nothing' but would not be seen that way in the north. MacDermot went further, saying he had heard prominent politicians from both major parties suggest that 'the North would be an embarrassment to us' – 'we were better off without them'.[8]

This picked up a line of thought about partition first suggested by Arthur Clery, and more definitely advanced in 1916 by Michael O'Flanagan – that partition became more likely, and indeed desirable, as a more authentic Irish cultural identity developed. It was a line which had never held any attraction for most Irish nationalists. Partition continued to be presented, as it was in Denis Gwynn's well-known *History of Partition*, not as 'a logic inherent in the Irish situation' but as merely 'the outcome of many extemporized compromises which were always devised in haste and imposed against the considered judgment of all parties'.

Michael Sheehy's tersely argued *Divided We Stand*, published in 1955, was a rare exposition of that inherent logic. Sheehy held that 'Southern demands on the North' became increasingly unreasonable in the revolutionary period, and that the 'national effort' to achieve separation from Britain 'was in large part unnecessary'. The 'spiritual division it caused' was 'a gratuitous tragedy'.[9] This argument had two corollaries: first, that Redmond's strategy had represented the best chance of achieving both freedom and unity, and second, that Britain was powerless to materially alter the outcome. As the veteran nationalist writer John J. Horgan noted in a foreword to Sheehy's book, the unanimous nationalist denunciation of partition as an English device ignored the reality that 'all the English parties without exception have sought at one time or another to find a solution, even to the extent of betraying their Northern adherents'.[10] Reminding his readers that the 'much-abused Government of Ireland Act of 1920' provided for a Council of Ireland 'given sole power to legislate for the whole country in respect of railways, fisheries' and so on, Horgan suggested that the 1920 Act 'did not divide Ireland but provided a straight road to Irish unity'. It was really the Treaty, negotiated by the Sinn Féin leaders themselves, 'which divided Ireland into two absolutely separate and irreconcilable units'.[11]

Arguments like this barely ruffled mainstream nationalist attitudes. An immediate riposte appeared in *The Indivisible Island*, a highly readable traditional account of partition by Frank Gallagher, a former Irish government propaganda director. Although for one critic its very title displayed the weakness that had always bedevilled nationalist thinking about partition, 'a complete refusal to face facts', and Ernest Blythe called it 'an elaborate rehash of the widely accepted but misconceived and lopsided propaganda which has prevented us from facing up to the many difficulties that must be overcome if we are to end partition', there could be no doubt that Gallagher's take was 'widely accepted'.[12] Republicans, even if weakened by two decades of repression initiated by de Valera, never gave up on the idea of ending partition by force. Shortly after Sheehy's book appeared, the IRA launched a border campaign intended to restart the struggle abandoned in 1922. The plans for 'Operation Harvest' drawn up by the Chief of Staff, Seán Cronin, even envisaged flying columns crossing from the Republic, the stuff of Unionist nightmares. A series of attacks began in December 1956, including assaults on two Fermanagh police stations. It looked to threaten a return to the chaos of the 1920s. But though over five hundred incidents followed before the campaign was abandoned early in 1962, it never generated enough momentum or public support to destabilize Northern Ireland as Cronin had expected.[13] The 'patriot game' seemed to be up.

ULSTER NATIONALISM

While the IRA was still in action, a geographer from the Free University of Amsterdam, Marcus Heslinga, arrived in Belfast to start research for a cultural study of the border. He produced a remarkable example of 'human geography', a kind of geographically informed social history, evaluating the border as a 'cultural divide'. Easily the most comprehensive and theoretically aware study, it formed a kind of belated Unionist parallel to the Boundary Bureau's *Handbook of the Ulster Question*. Heslinga himself noted the parallel, pointing out the dearth of significant historical studies of Ulster, certainly in comparison with the plethora of nationalist histories of Ireland. One of the earliest, D. A. Chart's *History of Northern Ireland* in 1928, which helped to furnish the new state with a genealogy much more extended than its few years of actual existence, was also an isolated one.[14] It was not until after the Second World War that a sustained movement to study Ulster folk history, inspired by Estyn Evans, a Welsh geographer at Queen's University, began to give real depth to the idea of an Ulster identity. Its focus, though not its manner, was political. When the Committee on Ulster Folklife and Customs was set up in 1955, the first number of its journal stressed the 'great importance' of the 'collection of the oral traditions of the people of the six counties of Northern Ireland'.

Heslinga became an enthusiast for Evans's project. His thesis deployed geographical analysis to refute the *Handbook*'s central contention that Ireland formed a single entity with no natural internal barriers. Heslinga argued, for instance, that while the Central Irish Lowlands might appear to be an ideal 'historical kernel area', in fact they had served for most of Irish history as 'a "natural dividing zone" between the north and south of the island rather than as a unifying force'.[15] His study elaborated an Ulster identity – he called it 'Ulsterism' – which was to all intents a national one. It was 'a form of nationalism' because it had 'too many political implications to be considered mere regionalism'.[16] The border was not an arbitrary compromise between transient political forces but a reflection of deep physical and cultural realities. The careful structure of Heslinga's analysis, with plentiful citation of an extensive range of secondary material, gave it an air of scientific assurance, allowing him to add numerous unsupported or unquantifiable asides, such as the remark that 'quite a number of' southern Protestants 'share with their Roman Catholic fellow-countrymen the traditional allergy to – if not dislike of – the Ulstermen'.[17] Since his analysis was 'the most effective declaration of the two nations theory', not everyone found it equally convincing. Indeed it took its place in the ongoing dialogue of the deaf. 'Irish unionists have embraced his thesis, and Irish nationalists have ignored it.'[18]

Even though Heslinga supplied it with some weight, the two-nations concept remained politically marginal. Its implications were flirted with by the Ulster Vanguard movement, launched by William Craig (a former Home Affairs minister who had banned the October 1968 Civil Rights march) in 1972. Vanguard's manifesto was challengingly entitled 'Ulster – A Nation', but the short-lived movement was never committed to the principle of independence. The two-nations idea was also pushed by a maverick nationalist writer, Desmond Fennell, and enjoyed a curious half-life when it was adopted by the Irish (later British and Irish) Communist Organisation. It also figured in an influential analysis by Peter Gibbon, who argued that the territorial basis of the identity fostered by Ulster Unionism made it 'a form of nationalism'.[19]

This idea was given a searching appraisal in the most persuasive historical study of loyalism yet to appear, David W. Miller's *Queen's Rebels*. Miller argued for a Protestant 'community' which never quite became a nation. Gibbon suggested that 'a new being, the "Ulsterman"', was born in 1892 and supplied with unique characteristics by 'an array of publicists'. Miller carefully examined this (relatively modest by nationalist standards) celebratory literature, looking for the 'rhapsodies on national heritage and character' characteristic of national movements. He found the Ulster literature oddly reticent on the point of nationality – indeed only one author (Herbert Moore Pim, a renegade Sinn Féiner) directly argued that Ulster was a nation. Even the apparent racism of Ernest Hamilton's frenetic *Soul of Ulster* is, as Miller notes, quirky: though Hamilton insisted that the settlers 'had not a drop of Irish blood in their veins', he clearly believed that the two 'races' could actually 'merge' were it not for the Catholic Church – in other words, they were not biologically distinct. In effect they were cultures, not races.[20]

Miller concluded that the rejection of home rule was not grounded in a sense of 'Ulster' nationhood – or even British nationhood: as he astutely saw, the Britain to which loyalists were attached was 'less the real Britain than a vague concept of a Greater Britain which the Empire might come to embody'. So he took Ulstermen's invocation of empire – so often dismissed as a ploy to gain British sympathy – more seriously than most. Their ambivalence on the issue of nationality was 'really a symptom of the irrelevance of nationality to their claim, as they understood it'.[21] But if they were not nationalists, what were they? Miller noted the vital place of loyalty – a moral choice, not an accident of birth – in Edward Saunderson's early picture of the 'two Irish nations'. Loyalism, as he argued, was conditional (hence the often mocked situation of 'loyalists' resisting the king's government); it was none the less coherent for that. Irish Catholics, whose fundamental allegiance was to a foreign ruler, were sadly, perhaps irretrievably disloyal.

BORDERLINE CRAZY

In the mid-1970s an official interest in the idea of border adjustment briefly appeared. The suspension of the northern parliament and the return of direct British rule in 1972 under the impact of the revived IRA assault brought the border back into contention. The British authorities at first took the view that 'any permanent physical barrier' would be counterproductive, and any attempt to 'close the border' would suck too much military force away from the real points of conflict, Belfast and Derry.[22] But soon dozens of 'unapproved' crossings (there were some 150 of them) were being cratered by the army, leading to clashes as local people assembled to fill the craters in.[23] The frontier became once again a conflict zone. For some years, between the publication of a 1972 Bow Group pamphlet, *Ireland: A New Partition*, and the more substantial 1986 *Two Ulsters* by Liam Kennedy of Queen's University Belfast, the idea of re-partition was in the air.

Merlyn Rees, the Northern Ireland Secretary who in 1975 famously labelled south Armagh 'bandit country', began to think of 'giving it to the Republic'. He discovered that if the Feetham Commission award had been implemented, Crossmaglen would indeed have been within the Republic, but found that 'neither the British nor the Irish government was very interested'.[24] Margaret Thatcher's government did briefly consider the issue; her question why the border could not be redrawn, straighter and more defensible, was squashed by the Cabinet Secretary's assertion that the 'nationalist communities were not all in one place'.[25] The Northern Ireland Office saw re-partition as both difficult and risky, while the Irish government under Garret FitzGerald was strongly opposed to it.

So cratering and bridge-breaking were followed by the building of huge concrete barriers; forts and watchtowers were exected, helicopters ferried garrisons to and fro. When Conor Cruise O'Brien (then the Irish Labour Party spokesman on northern issues) toured the 'border land of low wooded hills, lakes and small farms' of south Fermanagh in 1980, he thought you could 'smell in the air' the 'sectarian civil war already smouldering'. The small farms were sites of a battle which the British army was losing; as one staff officer put it, 'what amounts to ethnic cleansing over a long period does not only constitute a failure but can go largely unnoticed'.[26] By the military command, perhaps, but not by the farmers. A few years later, walking along the border just after the 1984 Anglo-Irish agreement, Colm Tóibín found attitudes which precisely echoed reactions to home rule a hundred years earlier – 'they want us off the land, out of business, they want us gone'. Amongst a raft of telling vignettes, none is more so than the moment when a policeman reassures an anxious landowner 'Ye bought your land'. He meant that they had not 'come during a Plantation or Confiscation'; they had bought their land – in 1732. As Tóibín notes, 'people remembered'.[27] When his book was reissued, he changed its title. ('It was never a walking book.') He called it *Bad Blood*.

Denis Gwynn's point that partition was 'against the considered judgment of all parties' is hard to dispute. Almost nobody wanted it; but any implication that a better arrangement was possible, and somehow squandered through haste and carelessness, would be misleading. The intensity of Unionist hostility to home rule presented a political challenge of exceptional difficulty. Once Joseph Chamberlain had talked of a separate parliament for Ulster, it would have needed a major reconstruction of nationalist ideas to make a unitary home rule arrangement viable. That adaptation was not made, or even attempted, mainly because nationalists were doomed to believe that any resistance within Ireland to home rule was illusory. Even amongst others, partition was never embraced with enthusiasm. It was a negative concept, connoting at best failure, at worst abuse of statesmanship. Schoolchildren were taught the partition of Poland as a parable of the evils of absolutism. When the first proposals that northern counties have the option to stand out from home rule were made, the term used was temporary exclusion; nobody in official circles at that stage would have accepted Lloyd George's later remark that 'exclusion was partition'.

'Hindsight', it has been suggested, 'may conclude that partition was the worst possible solution for Ireland but, in 1920, it was almost certainly the only feasible expedient.'[28] Was there a feasible alternative to the partition? It has recently been said, fairly enough, that 'when partition threatens, the appropriate slogan should be . . . "Give power-sharing a chance"'.[29] That would now be axiomatic, but it was not then on the menu of political options. The most sophisticated alternative theory available was federalism, and in theory it might have worked. It never quite did, even though the last home rule bill was conceived and designed as the first step in a UK-wide scheme. But such a scheme never looked like taking off; it would have called for a creative effort which was well beyond English political capacity. When federalism's moment seemed to arrive, at the end of the war, was it in any case too late for Ireland? Even in the 1930s, Eamon de Valera was exploring a federal 'Irish Commonwealth', but it assumed two dominions in his personally designed relationship with Britain, 'external association'. That could not work in 1936, and certainly could not have done in 1919. Here was the 'lacuna in English political thought', the 'caution and enduring pessimism' identified by Nicholas Mansergh.

IN AND OUT OF THE EU

The Northern Ireland peace process was premised on the gradual erosion of national frontiers as the European Union, which the United Kingdom and the Republic both joined (as the Common Market) in 1973, evolved. The European framework encouraged expectations that 'the meaning of state sovereignty and therefore of borders would diminish'.[30] And over the best part of two decades after the 1998 Belfast Agreement, the border effectively disappeared from contention. Crossings, notably the bridge between Fermanagh and Cavan at Aghalane (destroyed in 1972) in 1999, were ceremonially restored. That year, a Centre for Cross-Border Studies (CCBS) was set up, launching an energetic programme mixing research with the promotion of cooperative projects. Numerous cross-border schemes were funded by Europe. In 2006 the last watchtower was taken down. Even 12 July was turning into the kind of general carnival prematurely greeted by Thomas Larcom in the 1840s. It is not hard to see why, ten years later in 2016, when Britain – really England this time – voted to leave the EU, the Irish government insisted that any settlement must guarantee an open border, although this made a 'no deal' exit practically unavoidable. The Leave campaign dismissed the border as a tiresome diversion rather than a big issue, and 'a succession of clownish Tories revealed the depth of their ignorance and contempt when it came to Ireland'.[31] In 2020 the border returned to the status of an international frontier, but with little prospect of going back to the quirky coexistence of its first fifty years.

Nearly half a century's experience with power-sharing (taking the Sunningdale project as a beginning and reading the Belfast Agreement as 'Sunningdale for slow learners') may possibly have given the 'slow learners' some reason to accept that it might be adapted for the whole island of Ireland. Nationalist pressure for a 'border poll' (as provided by the Belfast Agreement) simply reasserted de Valera's view of the northern problem as mathematical; and most have not grasped how deeply the Belfast Agreement entrenched partition, in legal terms.[32] Other awkward realities remain; the 'peace walls' in Belfast are still doing their work, and have if anything grown, in number and size.[33] Most analysts find that polarization has not receded during the peace process. Some indeed suggest it is sharper than ever, and more visible. Segregation carries a significant financial cost, beyond its malign social and political implications.[34] Identity may always be fluid to a degree, but some 47 per cent of Northern Ireland citizens still identify as 'British', rather close to the 48 per cent who live in Protestant households. Many have resisted the charm of power-sharing, and still see the issue – symbolized by the Irish language, which precipitated the breakdown of the power-sharing government in 2017 – simply in terms of domination and subjection. A 2018 Sky News poll found that while an overwhelming majority of Catholics would be 'upset' by the return of border controls, 56 per cent of Protestants would not.[35] When the CCBS held its twenth-anniversary conference in 2019 (in the shadow of the killing of Lyra Mckee) it was clear that the border had once again become an issue to be problematized. Power-sharing had not got beyond 'power-snaring', and the 'border in the mind' was as much an issue as the physical frontier.[36] The fundamental attitudes which produced partition are still in play a century later.

Acknowledgements

This book has its origin in a conference at the Centre for the Study of Terrorism and Political Violence at St Andrews, aimed at assessing the security issues involved in the centenary of the 1916 Irish rebellion, and other events in the 'decade of centenaries' in Ireland. I am most grateful to Richard English, then Director of the Centre, for inviting me. (At that time, it appeared that the centenary of partition was likely to present a definite security risk, but also that there was some uncertainty about the exact date of that anniversary. This book will I hope at least demonstrate that there is no simple answer on that point, but of course the whole problem has since been transformed by the UK's withdrawal from the EU.) My other debts must be expressed in more general form: principally, as should go without saying, to the true specialists in all the issues involved in the process of partition, on whose work I have depended, and further to the staff of libraries and archives I have worked in over many years, notably the British and Bodleian libraries, the National Archives of the UK and Ireland, the Public Record Office of Northern Ireland, and the Parliamentary Archive at Westminster.

The staff at Penguin Random House have coped admirably with bringing the book to publication amidst the disruption of the worst global pandemic for a century. The handover of the annotated typescript on a Wandsworth park bench, and of the corrected page proofs in a Holiday Inn car park, will live in my memory. Simon Winder initially took up the idea of the book with encouraging enthusiasm, and has read it with impressive care. Eva Hodgkin's unfailingly cheerful assistance, notably with the selection of illustrations, has been sincerely appreciated.

Wandsworth and Keele, January 2021

Bibliography

Adams, R. J. Q., *Bonar Law* (London: John Murray, 1999)

Aiken, S. et al. (eds), *The Men Will Talk to Me: Ernie O'Malley's Interviews with the Northern Divisions* (Dublin: Merrion Press, 2018)

Akenson, D., *Education and Enmity: The Control of Schooling in Northern Ireland, 1920–1950* (Newton Abbot: David & Charles, 1973)

—*Between Two Revolutions: Islandmagee, County Antrim 1798–1920* (Dublin: Academy Press, 1979)

—*Small Differences: Irish Catholics and Irish Protestants, 1815–1922* (Montreal and Kingston: McGill–Queen's University Press, 1991)

Anderson, J., 'Ideological Variations in Ulster during Ireland's First Home Rule Crisis: An Analysis of Local Newspapers', in Williams and Kofman (eds), *Community Conflict*

Anderson, J. and L. O'Dowd, 'Imperialism and Nationalism: The Home Rule Struggle and Border Creation in Ireland 1885–1925', *Political Geography* 26 (2007)

Anderson, M. and Eberhard Bort (eds), *The Irish Border: History, Politics, Culture* (Liverpool University Press, 1999)

Baker, S. E., 'Orange and Green: Belfast 1832–1912', in H. J. Dyos and M. Wolff (eds), *The Victorian City: Images and Realities*, vol. II (London: Routledge & Kegan Paul, 1973)

Bardon, J., *A History of Ulster* (Belfast: Blackstaff Press, 1992)

Bell, G., *Troublesome Business: The Labour Party and the Irish Question* (London: Pluto Press, 1982)

Bew, P., *Ideology and the Irish Question: Ulster Unionism and Irish Nationalism 1912–1916* (Oxford University Press, 1994)

—*Ireland: The Politics of Enmity 1789–2006* (Oxford University Press, 2007)

—*Churchill and Ireland* (Oxford University Press, 2016)

—, P. Gibbon, and H. Patterson, *The State in Northern Ireland 1921–72* (Manchester University Press, 1979)

Bowman, J., *De Valera and the Ulster Question 1917–1973* (Oxford University Press, 1982)

Bowman, T., *Carson's Army: The Ulster Volunteer Force, 1910–22* (Manchester University Press, 2007)

Boyce, D. G., *Englishmen and Irish Troubles: British Public Opinion and the Making of Irish Policy 1918–22* (London: Jonathan Cape, 1972)

—'British Opinion, Ireland and the War, 1916–1918', *Historical Journal* 17 (1974)

—'Federalism and the Irish Question', in A. Bosco (ed.), *The Federal Idea*, vol. 3 (London: Lothian Foundation Press, 1991)

—and Alan O'Day (eds), *The Ulster Crisis 1885–1921* (Basingstoke: Macmillan, 2006)

Brooks, Sydney, 'The Problem of Ulster', *North American Review* 198, no. 696 (November 1913)

Buckland, P., 'The Southern Irish Unionists, the Irish Question, and British Politics, 1906–1914', *Irish Historical Studies* xv, no. 59 (1967)

—*Irish Unionism,* vol. 2: *Ulster Unionism and the Origins of Northern Ireland 1886–1922* (Dublin: Gill & Macmillan, 1973)

—*The Factory of Grievances: Devolved Government in Northern Ireland 1921–39* (Dublin: Gill & Macmillan, 1979)

—*James Craig* (Dublin: Gill & Macmillan, 1980)

—'Carson, Craig and the Partition of Ireland, 1912–21', in Collins (ed.), *Nationalism and Unionism*

—(ed.), *Irish Unionism 1885–1923: A Documentary History* (Belfast: HMSO, 1973)

Budge, I. and C. O'Leary, *Belfast: Approach to Crisis* (London: Macmillan, 1973)

Burgess, M., 'Mapping the Narrow Ground: Geography, History and Partition', *Field Day Review* I (2005)

Campbell, C., *Emergency Law in Ireland 1918–1925* (Oxford: Clarendon Press, 1994)

Canning, P., *British Policy towards Ireland 1921–1941* (Oxford: Clarendon Press, 1985)

Clayton, P., *Enemies and Passing Friends: Settler Ideologies in Twentieth-Century Ulster* (London: Pluto Press, 1996)

Collins, P. (ed.), *Nationalism and Unionism: Conflict in Ireland 1885–1921* (Belfast: Institute of Irish Studies, Queen's University, 1994)

Coogan, T. P., *Michael Collins* (London: Hutchinson, 1990)

Dangerfield, G., *The Strange Death of Liberal England* (New York: Harrison Smith and Robert Haas, 1935; London: Serif, 1997)

De Brun, F., ' "Ulsteria": The Fortunes of the Irish Language under Stormont, 1921–72', in Parkinson and Phoenix (eds), *Conflicts in the North of Ireland, 1900–2000*

Dicey, A. V., *England's Case against Home Rule* (London: John Murray, 1886)

—*A Leap in the Dark* (London: John Murray, 1892)

Doherty, G. (ed.), *The Home Rule Crisis, 1912–14* (Cork: Mercier, 2014)

Dooley, T., 'Monaghan Protestants in a Time of Crisis, 1919–1922', in R. V. Comerford (ed.), *Religion, Conflict and Coexistence in Ireland* (Dublin: Gill & Macmillan, 1990)

—*The Plight of Monaghan Protestants, 1912–26*, Maynooth Studies in Irish Local History (Dublin: Irish Academic Press, 2000)

Ellison, G. and J. Smyth, *The Crowned Harp: Policing Northern Ireland* (London: Pluto Press, 2000)

English, R., *Armed Struggle: The History of the IRA* (London: Macmillan, 2003)

—and G. Walker (eds), *Unionism in Modern Ireland: New Perspectives on Politics and Culture* (London: Macmillan, 1996)

Ervine, St John, *Craigavon: Ulsterman* (London: Allen and Unwin, 1949)

Fanning, R., 'Anglo-Irish Relations: Partition and the British Dimension in Historical Perspective', *Irish Studies in International Affairs* 2, no. 1 (1985)

—*Fatal Path: British Government and Irish Revolution 1910–1922* (London: Faber and Faber, 2013)

Farrell, S., *Rituals and Riots: Sectarian Violence and Political Culture in Ulster, 1784–1886* (Lexington: Kentucky University Press, 2000)

Ferriter, D., *The Border: The Legacy of a Century of Anglo-Irish Politics* (London: Profile, 1919)

Fisher, J. R., 'Historical Retrospect', in Rosenbaum (ed.), *Against Home Rule*

Fitzpatrick, D., *The Two Irelands 1912–1939* (Oxford University Press, 1998)

—'The Orange Order and the Border', *Irish Historical Studies* xxx, no. 129 (2002)

—*Descendancy: Irish Protestant Histories since 1795* (Cambridge University Press, 2014)

Fletcher, I., ' "This Zeal for Lawlessness": A. V. Dicey, *The Law of the Constitution*, and the Challenge of Popular Politics, 1885–1915', *Parliamentary History* 16, no. 1 (1997)

Follis, B. A., *A State Under Siege: The Establishment of Northern Ireland 1920–1925* (Oxford: Clarendon Press, 1995)

Foster, J. Wilson (ed.), *The Idea of the Union* (Vancouver: Belcouver Press, 1995)

Foster, R. F., 'Remembering 1798', in McBride (ed.), *History and Memory in Modern Ireland*

Fox, C., *The Making of a Minority: Political Developments in Derry and the North 1912–25* (Londonderry: Guildhall Press, 1997)

Fraser, T., *Partition in Ireland, India and Palestine: Theory and Practice* (London: Macmillan, 1984)

Gallagher, F., *The Indivisible Island: The History of the Partition of Ireland* (London: Gollancz, 1957)

Gibbon, P., *The Origins of Ulster Unionism: The Formation of Popular Protestant Politics and Ideology in Nineteenth-Century Ireland* (Manchester University Press, 1975)

Gibbons, I., 'The First British Labour Government and the Irish Boundary Commission 1924', *Studies* 98, no. 391 (Autumn 2009)

—'The Anglo-Irish Treaty 1921: The Response of the British Parliamentary Labour Party and Labour Press', *Labour History Review* 76, no. 1 (April 2011)

—*The British Labour Party and the Establishment of the Irish Free State, 1918–1924* (Houndmills: Palgrave Macmillan, 2015)

—*Drawing the Line: The Irish Border in British Politics* (London: Haus, 2018)

Glassie, H., *Passing the Time: Folklore and History of an Ulster Community* (Dublin: O'Brien, 1982)

Goldring, M., *Belfast: From Loyalty to Rebellion* (London: Lawrence & Wishart, 1991)

Good, J. Winder, *Ulster and Ireland* (Dublin: Maunsel, 1919)

Gribbon, Sybil, 'The Social Origins of Ulster Unionism', *Irish Economic and Social History* 4 (1977)

Gwynn, D., *The History of Partition (1912–1925)* (Dublin: Browne & Nolan, 1950)

Hamilton, Lord E., *The Soul of Ulster* (London: Hurst & Blackett, 1917)

Hammond, J. L., *Gladstone and the Irish Nation* (London: Longmans Green, 1938; Frank Cass, 1964)

Hand, G. J., *Report of the Irish Boundary Commission 1925* (Shannon: Irish University Press, 1969)

—'MacNeill and the Boundary Commission', in F. X. Martin and F. J. Byrne (eds), *The Scholar Revolutionary: Eoin MacNeill 1867–1945 and the Making of the New Ireland* (Shannon: Irish University Press, 1973)

Harbinson, J. F., *The Ulster Unionist Party 1882–1973: Its Development and Organisation* (Belfast: Blackstaff, 1973)

Harris, M., *The Catholic Church and the Foundation of the Northern Irish State* (Cork University Press, 1993)

Harris, R., *Prejudice and Tolerance in Ulster: A Study of Neighbours and 'Strangers' in a Border Community* (Manchester University Press, 1972)

Harrison, H., *Ulster and the British Empire 1939* (London: Robert Hale, 1939)

—*The Partition of Ireland: How Britain Is Responsible* (London: Robert Hale, 1939)

Hempton, D., *Religion and Political Culture in Britain and Ireland: From the Glorious Revolution to the Decline of Empire* (Cambridge University Press, 1996)

Hennessey, T., *Dividing Ireland: World War I and Partition* (London: Routledge, 1998)

Hepburn, A. C., *Catholic Belfast and Nationalist Ireland in the Era of Joe Devlin 1871–1934* (Oxford University Press, 2008)

Heslinga, M. W., *The Irish Border as a Cultural Divide* (Assen: Van Gorcum, 1971)

Hezlet, A., *The 'B' Specials: A History of the Ulster Special Constabulary* (London: Tom Stacey, 1972)

Hirst, C., *Religion, Politics and Violence in Nineteenth-Century Belfast: The Pound and Sandy Row* (Dublin: Four Courts Press, 2002)

Holmes, A., *The Shaping of Ulster Presbyterian Belief and Practice, 1770–1840* (Oxford University Press, 2006)

Hoppen, K. T., *Elections, Politics and Society in Ireland 1832–1885* (Oxford: Clarendon Press, 1984)

—'An Incorporating Union? British Politicians and Ireland 1800–1830', *English Historical Review* CXXIII, no. 501 (April 2008)

—*Governing Hibernia: British Politicians and Ireland 1800–1921* (Oxford University Press, 2016)

Irish Boundary: Extracts from Parliamentary Debates, Command Papers, etc, relevant to questions arising out of Article XII. Cmd. 2264 (1924)

Jackson, A., *The Ulster Party: Irish Unionists in the House of Commons 1884–1911* (Oxford: Clarendon Press, 1989)

—*Colonel Edward Saunderson: Land and Loyalty in Victorian Ireland* (Oxford University Press, 1995)

—'Irish Unionism, 1905–21', in Collins (ed.), *Nationalism and Unionism*

—*Home Rule: An Irish History, 1800–2000* (London: Weidenfeld & Nicolson, 2003)

Jackson, D., *Popular Opposition to Irish Home Rule in Edwardian Britain* (Liverpool University Press, 2009)

—and D. MacRaild, 'The Conserving Crowd: Mass Unionist Demonstrations in Liverpool and Tyneside, 1912–13', in Boyce and O'Day (eds), *The Ulster Crisis 1885–1921*

Jalland, P., *The Liberals and Ireland: The Ulster Question in British Politics to 1914* (Brighton: Harvester Press, 1980)

Jay, R., 'Nationalism, Federalism and Ireland', in M. Forsyth (ed.), *Federalism and Nationalism* (Leicester University Press, 1989)

Jeffery, K., *Field Marshal Sir Henry Wilson: A Political Soldier* (Oxford University Press, 2006)

—(ed.), *The Military Correspondence of Field Marshal Sir Henry Wilson 1918–1922* (London: Army Records Society/Bodley Head, 1985)

Jones, T. (ed. K. Middlemas), *Whitehall Diary*, vol. III: *Ireland 1018–1925* (London: Oxford University Press, 1971)

Kendle, J., *Ireland and the Federal Solution: The Debate over the United Kingdom Constitution, 1870–1921* (Kingston and Montreal: McGill–Queen's University Press, 1989)

—*Walter Long, Ireland, and the Union, 1905–1920* (Kingston and Montreal: McGill-Queen's University Press, 1992)

Kennedy, D., *The Widening Gulf: Northern Attitudes to the Independent Irish State 1919–1949* (Belfast: Blackstaff, 1988)

—' "Border Trouble": Unionist Perceptions of and Responses to the Independent Irish State, 1921–39', in Parkinson and Phoenix (eds), *Conflicts in the North of Ireland, 1900–2000*

Kettle, T. (ed. S. Paseta), 'The Hallucination of "Ulster" ', in *The Open Secret of Ireland* (University College Dublin Press, 2007)

Kiely, B., *Counties of Contention: A Study of the Origins and Implications of the Partition of Ireland* (Cork: Mercier, 1945)

Kockel, U., 'Braveheart and the Irish Border: Ulster-Scottish Connections', in Anderson and Bort (eds), *The Irish Border*

Laffan, M., *The Partition of Ireland 1911–1925* (Dundalk: Dublin Historical Association, 1983)

Lavin, D., *From Empire to International Commonwealth: A Biography of Lionel Curtis* (Oxford: Clarendon Press, 1995)

Leary, P., *Unapproved Routes: Histories of the Irish Border 1922–1972* (Oxford University Press, 2016)

Lee, J., *Ireland 1912–1985* (Cambridge University Press, 1989)

Lewis, G., *Carson: The Man Who Divided Ireland* (London: Hambledon Press, 2005)

Loftus, B., *Mirrors: Orange and Green* (Dundrum: Picture Press, 1994)

Loughlin, J., *Gladstone, Home Rule and the Ulster Question* (Dublin: Gill & Macmillan, 1986)

—'Parades and Politics: Liberal Governments and the Orange Order, 1880–1886', in T. G. Fraser (ed.), *The Irish Parading Tradition* (Basingstoke: Macmillan, 2000)

—'Creating "A Social and Geographical Fact": Regional Identity and the Ulster Question 1880s–1920s', *Past & Present* 195 (May 2007)

Lustick, I., *State-Building Failure in British Ireland and French Algeria* (University of California, Berkeley: Institute of International Studies, 1985)

Lynch, R., *The Northern IRA and the Early Years of Partition* (PhD thesis, University of Stirling, 2003)

—*The Partition of Ireland 1918–1925* (Cambridge University Press, 2019)

Lyons, F. S. L., *John Dillon* (London: Routledge & Kegan Paul, 1968)

—*Culture and Anarchy in Ireland 1890–1939* (Oxford: Clarendon Press, 1979)

—and R. Hawkins (eds), *Ireland under the Union: Varieties of Tension* (Oxford: Clarendon Press, 1980)

McBride, I. R., 'Ulster and the British Problem', in English and Walker (eds), *Unionism in Modern Ireland*

—*The Siege of Derry in Ulster Protestant Mythology* (Dublin: Four Courts Press, 1997)

—*Scripture Politics: Ulster Presbyterians and Irish Radicalism in the Late Eighteenth Century* (Oxford: Clarendon Press, 1998)

—(ed.), *History and Memory in Modern Ireland* (Cambridge University Press, 2001)

McColgan, J., *British Policy and the Irish Administration, 1920–22* (London: Allen and Unwin, 1983)

McDermott, J., *Northern Divisions: The Old IRA and the Belfast Pogroms 1920–22* (Belfast: BTP, 2001)

McDowell, R. B., *The Irish Convention 1917–18* (London: Routledge & Kegan Paul, 1970)

McGimpsey, C., *'To Raise the Banner in the Remote North': Politics in County Monaghan, 1868–1883* (PhD thesis, University of Edinburgh, 1982)

McKay, S., *Northern Protestants: An Unsettled People* (Belfast: Blackstaff, 2000)

McNeill, R., *Ulster's Stand for Union* (London: John Murray, 1922)

—*The Irish Boundary Question* (National Unionist Association, 1924)

Macknight, T., *Ulster As It Is*, 2 vols (London: Macmillan, 1896)

MacRaild, D., *Culture, Conflict and Migration: The Irish in Victorian Cumbria* (Liverpool University Press, 1998)

—*Irish Migrants in Modern Britain 1750–1922* (Basingstoke: Macmillan, 1999)

Magee, J., 'The Monaghan Election of 1883 and the "Invasion of Ulster"', *Clogher Record* 8, no. 2 (1974)

Mansergh, N., *The Government of Northern Ireland: A Study in Devolution* (London: Allen and Unwin, 1936)

—*The Unresolved Question: The Anglo-Irish Settlement and Its Undoing 1912–72* (New Haven: Yale University Press, 1991)

—*The Prelude to Partition: Concepts and Aims in India and Ireland*, Commonwealth Lecture 1976, in D. Mansergh (ed.), *Nationalism and Independence: Selected Irish Papers* (Cork University Press, 1997)

Matthews, K., *Fatal Influence: The Impact of Ireland on British Politics, 1920–1925* (University College Dublin Press, 2004).

Maume, P., 'Nationalism and Partition: The Political Thought of Arthur Clery', *Irish Historical Studies* XXXI, no. 122 (November 1998)

—*The Long Gestation: Irish Nationalist Life 1891–1918* (Dublin: Gill & Macmillan, 1999)

—'The *Irish Independent* and the Ulster Crisis, 1912–21', in Boyce and O'Day (eds), *The Ulster Crisis 1885–1921*

Meredith, J. C., *Proportional Representation in Ireland* (Dublin: Edward Ponsonby, 1918)

Middlemas, K. (ed.), *Thomas Jones Whitehall Diary*, vol. III: *Ireland 1918–1925* (Oxford University Press, 1971)

Miller, D. W., 'Presbyterianism and "Modernization" in Ulster', *Past & Present* 80 (1978)

—'The Roman Catholic Church in Ireland 1898–1918', in O'Day (ed.), *Reactions to Irish Nationalism*

—*Queen's Rebels: Ulster Loyalism in Historical Perspective* (Dublin: Gill & Macmillan, 1978; University of Dublin Press, 2007)

Milligan, Spike, *Puckoon* (London: Anthony Blond, 1963)

Monypenny, W. F., *The Two Irish Nations: An Essay on Home Rule* (London, 1913)

Morgan, A., *Labour and Partition: The Belfast Working Class, 1905–23* (London, 1991)

Moulton, M., *Ireland and the Irish in Interwar England* (Cambridge University Press, 2014)

Munck, R., 'Class and Religion in Belfast – A Historical Perspective', *Journal of Contemporary History* 20 (1985)

Murphy, R., 'Walter Long and the Making of the Government of Ireland Act, 1919–20', *Irish Historical Studies* xxv, no. 97 (May 1986)

Murray, Paul, *The Irish Boundary Commission and its Origins 1886–1925* (University College Dublin Press, 2011)

Murray, Peter, *Citizenship, Colonialism, and Self-Determination: Dublin in the United Kingdom 1885–1918* (PhD thesis, Trinity College Dublin, 1987)

Murray, R. H., 'The Evolution of the Ulsterman', *Quarterly Review* 220 (January 1914)

Nash, C. and B. Reid, 'Border Crossings: New Approaches to the Irish Border', *Irish Studies Review* 18, no. 3 (2010)

—B. Reid, and B. Graham, *Partitioned Lives: The Irish Borderlands* (London: Routledge, 2016)

O'Brien, C. C., *States of Ireland* (London: Hutchinson, 1972)

O'Callaghan, M., 'Old Parchment and Water: The Boundary Commission of 1925 and the Copper-Fastening of the Irish Border', *Bullán: An Irish Studies Journal* 4, no. 1 (1999/2000)

O'Day, A., *Irish Home Rule 1867–1921* (Manchester University Press, 1998)

—(ed.), *Reactions to Irish Nationalism* (London and Ronceverte: Hambledon, 1987)

O'Donoghue, B., *Activities Wise and Otherwise: The Career of Sir Henry Augustus Robinson 1898–1922* (Sallins: Irish Academic Press, 2015)

O'Halloran, C., *Partition and the Limits of Irish Nationalism: An Ideology under Stress* (Dublin: Gill & Macmillan, 1987)

O'Leary, B., *Debating Partition: Justifications and Critiques* (Queen's University, Belfast: MFPP Working Paper no. 28, 2006)

—*A Treatise on Northern Ireland*, Vol. I: *Colonialism: The Shackles of the State and Hereditary Animosities* (Oxford University Press, 2019)

O'Leary, C., *Irish Elections* (Dublin: Gill & Macmillan, 1979)

Oliver, F. S., *The Alternatives to Civil War* (London: John Murray, 1913)

Paarnila, O., *Race, Religion and History in the One-Ireland and Partition Arguments* (University of Jyväskylä, 1998)

Parkinson, A., *Belfast's Unholy War: The Troubles of the 1920s* (Dublin: Four Courts Press, 2004)

—and E. Phoenix (eds), *Conflicts in the North of Ireland, 1900–2000: Flashpoints and Fracture Zones* (Dublin: Four Courts Press, 2010)

Patterson, H., *Class Conflict and Sectarianism: The Protestant Working Class and the Belfast Labour Movement 1868–1920* (Belfast: Blackstaff, 1980)

—*Ireland's Violent Frontier: The Border and Anglo-Irish Relations during the Troubles* (London: Palgrave Macmillan, 2013)

Pearce, E., *Lines of Most Resistance: The Lords, the Tories and Ireland, 1886–1914* (London: Little, Brown, 1999)

Peatling, G. K., *British Opinion and Irish Self-Government, 1865–1925: From Unionism to Liberal Commonwealth* (Dublin: Irish Academic Press, 2001)

Phoenix, E., 'Northern Nationalists, Ulster Unionists and the Development of Partition, 1900–21', in Collins (ed.), *Nationalism and Unionism*

—*Northern Nationalism: Nationalist Politics and the Catholic Minority in Northern Ireland 1890–1940* (Belfast: Ulster Historical Foundation, 1994)

Rankin, K. J., 'The Role of the Irish Boundary Commission in the Entrenchment of the Irish Border: From Tactical Panacea to Political Liability', *Journal of Historical Geography* 34 (2008)

Ridden, J., *'Making Good Citizens': National Identity, Religion, and Liberalism among the Irish Elite, c.1800–1850* (PhD thesis, King's College London, 1998)

—'The Forgotten History of the Protestant Crusade: Religious Liberalism in Ireland', *Journal of Religious History* 31, no. 1 (2007)

Rosenbaum, S. (ed.), *Against Home Rule: The Case for Union* (London: Frederick Warne, 1912)

Ruane, J. and J. Todd, 'The Social Origins of Nationalism in a Contested Region: The Case of Northern Ireland', in J. Coakley (ed.), *The Social Origins of Nationalist Movements* (London: Sage, 1992)

Saunderson, E., *Two Irelands; or, Loyalty versus Treason* (London: P. S. King & Son, 1884)

Shea, P., *Voices and the Sound of Drums: An Irish Autobiography* (Belfast: Blackstaff, 1981)

Sheehy, M., *Divided We Stand* (London: Faber & Faber, 1955)

Sibbett, R. M., *Orangeism in Ireland and throughout the Empire* (Belfast: Henderson & Co., 1914)

Smith, J., 'Bluff, Bluster and Brinkmanship: Andrew Bonar Law and the Third Home Rule Bill', *Historical Journal* 36, no. 1 (March 1993)

—*The Tories and Ireland, 1910–1914: Conservative Party Politics and the Home Rule Crisis* (Dublin: Irish Academic Press, 2000)

Staunton, E., *The Nationalists of Northern Ireland, 1918–1973* (Dublin: Columba Press, 2001)

Stewart, A. T. Q., *The Ulster Crisis* (London: Faber & Faber, 1967)

—*The Narrow Ground: Aspects of Ulster 1609–1969* (London: Faber & Faber, 1977)

—*Edward Carson* (Dublin: Gill & Macmillan, 1981)

Tannam, E., 'Continuity and Change in the Cross-Border Relationship', in Anderson and Bort (eds), *The Irish Border*

Thackeray, D., 'Rethinking the Edwardian Crisis of Conservatism', *Historical Journal* 54, no. 1 (March 2011)

Theodorson, M., *Policing and Internal Security in Northern Ireland 1920–1939* (PhD thesis, Keele University, 2006)

Todd, J., 'Two Traditions in Unionist Political Culture', *Irish Political Studies* 2 (1987)

Tóibín, C., *Walking along the Border* (London: McDonald Queen Anne Press, 1987); reissued as *Bad Blood: A Walk along the Irish Border* (London: Picador, 1994)

Townshend, C., *Political Violence in Ireland: Government and Resistance since 1848* (Oxford: Clarendon Press, 1983)

—*Making the Peace: Public Order and Public Security in Modern Britain* (New York: Oxford University Press, 1993)

—*Easter 1916: The Irish Rebellion* (London: Allen Lane, 2005)

—*The Republic: The Fight for Irish Independence, 1918–1923* (London: Allen Lane, 2013)

—(ed.), *Consensus in Ireland: Approaches and Recessions* (Oxford: Clarendon Press, 1988)

'Ultach', 'Orange Terror', *Capuchin Annual* (1943)

Walker, B., *Ulster Politics: The Formative Years, 1868–86* (Belfast: Ulster Historical Foundation and Institute of Irish Studies, 1989)

—*Dancing to History's Tune: History, Myth and Politics in Ireland* (Belfast: Institute of Irish Studies, Queen's University 1996)

Wall, M., 'Partition: The Ulster Question (1916–1926)', in Desmond Williams (ed.), *The Irish Struggle 1916–1926* (London: Routledge & Kegan Paul, 1966)

Wheatley, M., 'John Redmond and Federalism in 1910', *Irish Historical Studies* 32, no. 127 (2001)

Whelan, I., *The Bible War in Ireland: The 'Second Reformation' and the Polarization of Protestant–Catholic Relations 1800–1840* (Madison: Wisconsin University Press, 2005)

Whyte, J., *Interpreting Northern Ireland* (Oxford: Clarendon Press, 1990)

Williams, C. H. and E. Kofman (eds), *Community Conflict: Partition and Nationalism* (London: Routledge, 1989)

Wilson, T., *Frontiers of Violence: Conflict and Identity in Ulster and Upper Silesia, 1918–1922* (Oxford Historical Monographs, Oxford University Press, 2010)

—' "The most terrible assassination that has yet stained the name of Belfast": The McMahon Murders in Context', *Irish Historical Studies* xxxvii, no. 145 (May 2010)

—'The Strange Death of Loyalist Monaghan, 1919–1921', in S. Paseta (ed.), *Uncertain Futures* (Oxford University Press, 2016)

Winder Good, J., *Ulster and Ireland* (Dublin: Maunsel, 1919)

Wingfield-Stratford, E., *Home Rule and Civil War: An Appeal to the British People* (London: Bell and Sons, 1914)

Wood, I., *God, Guns and Ulster: A History of Loyalist Paramilitaries* (London: Caxton, 2003)

Wright, F., 'Protestant Ideology and Politics in Ulster', *European Journal of Sociology* 14 (1973)

—*Two Lands on One Soil: Ulster Politics before Home Rule* (Dublin: Gill & Macmillan, 1996)

Notes

PROLOGUE

1 P. Livingstone, *The Monaghan Story* (Enniskillen: Clogher, 1980), 239, q. D. Hempton, *Religion and Political Culture in Britain and Ireland* (Cambridge University Press, 1996), 77.

2 Eugenio Biagini, 'The Third Home Rule Bill in British History', in G. Doherty (ed.), *The Home Rule Crisis, 1912–14* (Cork: Mercier, 2014).

3 K. T. Hoppen, *Governing Hibernia: British Politicians and Ireland 1800–1921* (Oxford University Press, 2016), ch. 10.

CHAPTER I: THE UNION

1 J. Byrne, *An Impartial Account of the Late Disturbances in the County of Armagh* (Dublin, 1792), q. D. W. Miller, *Peep O'Day Boys and Defenders* (Belfast: Public Record Office, 1990), 44.

2 Col. W. Blacker's account, PRONI T.2595, q. Miller, *Peep O'Day Boys*, 117ff.

3 J. Bardon, *A History of Ulster* (Belfast: Blackstaff Press, 1992), 243.

4 H. Glassie, *Passing the Time: Folklore and History of an Ulster Community* (Dublin: O'Brien, 1982), 268.

5 T. Garvin, *The Evolution of Irish Nationalist Politics* (Dublin: Gill and Macmillan, 1981), 10–11; B. O'Leary, *A Treatise on Northern Ireland. Vol. I: Colonialism: The Shackles of the State and Hereditary Animosities* (Oxford University Press, 2019), 207.

6 Bardon, *History of Ulster*, 245–6.

7 S. Farrell, *Rituals and Riots: Sectarian Violence and Political Culture in Ulster, 1784–1886* (Lexington: Kentucky University Press, 2000), 92.

8 T. Bartlett, 'Emergence of the Irish Catholic Nation', *The Oxford Handbook of Modern Irish History* (Oxford University Press, 2014), 529–32.

9 K. T. Hoppen, 'An Incorporating Union? British Politicians and Ireland 1800–1830', *English Historical Review* CXXIII, no. 501 (April 2008), 341.

10 Ibid, 343.

11 HC Deb 5s vol. 125, c. 611, 16 February 1920.

12 Hoppen, 'An Incorporating Union?', 349–50.

13 I. Lustick, *State-Building Failure in British Ireland and French Algeria* (University of California, Berkeley: Institute of International Studies, 1985), 36–8.

14 N. Mansergh, *The Government of Northern Ireland: A Study in Devolution* (London: Allen and Unwin, 1936), 82.

15 Cf. Lustick, *State-Building Failure in British Ireland and French Algeria*, 37–8.

16 I. Whelan, *The Bible War in Ireland: The 'Second Reformation' and the Polarization of Protestant-Catholic Relations 1800–1840* (Madison: Wisconsin University Press, 2005), passim.

17 S. J. Connolly, *Priests and People in Pre-Famine Ireland* (Dublin: Gill & Macmillan, 1982), 86.

18 F. Wright, *Two Lands on One Soil: Ulster Politics before Home Rule* (Dublin: Gill & Macmillan, 1996), 304.

19 D. Akenson, *Small Differences: Irish Catholics and Irish Protestants, 1815–1922* (Montreal and Kingston: McGill-Queen's University Press, 1991), 124.

20 The outlook of this community is carefully analysed in A. Holmes, *The Shaping of Ulster Presbyterian Belief and Practice, 1770–1840* (Oxford University Press, 2006).

21 M. Elliott, *When God Took Sides: Religion and Identity in Ireland – Unfinished History* (Oxford University Press, 2009), 132.

22 P. Maume, 'Ulstermen of Letters', in R. English and G. Walker (eds), *Unionism in Modern Ireland*, (London: Macmillan, 1996), 75.

23 St J. Ervine, *Craigavon: Ulsterman* (London: Allen and Unwin, 1949), vii.

24 I. McBride, *Scripture Politics: Ulster Presbyterians and Irish Radicalism in the Late Eighteenth Century* (Oxford: Clarendon Press, 1998), 230.

25 Ibid, 186, 194–5.

26 R. F. Foster, 'Remembering 1798', in I. R. McBride (ed.), *History and Memory in Ireland* (Cambridge University Press, 2001), 90.

27 R. H. Murray, 'The Evolution of the Ulsterman', *Quarterly Review* 220 (January 1914).

28 P. Gibbon, *The Origins of Ulster Unionism: The Formation of Popular Protestant Politics and Ideology in Nineteenth-Century Ireland* (Manchester University Press, 1975), 136.

29 Bardon, *History of Ulster*, 400.

30 Elliott, *When God Took Sides*, 119.

31 M. W. Heslinga, *The Irish Border as a Cultural Divide* (Assen: Van Gorcum, 1971), 70, 74.

32 J. Winder Good, *Ulster and Ireland* (Dublin: Maunsel, 1919), 4.

33 J. White, 'Partition', *The Month* XVII (1957).

34 Elliott, *When God Took Sides*, 121, citing D. H. Akenson, *God's Peoples: Covenant and Land in South Africa, Israel and Ulster* (Ithaca: Cornell University Press, 1992), 26–32.

35 F. S. L. Lyons, *Culture and Anarchy in Ireland 1890–1939* (Oxford: Clarendon Press, 1979), 129.

36 Wright, *Two Lands on One Soil*, 182.

37 Heslinga, *The Irish Border as a Cultural Divide*, 62.

38 Lyons, *Culture and Anarchy*, 138.

39 Bardon, *History of Ulster*, 255, 257.

40 Wright, *Two Lands on One Soil*, 50.

41 *Belfast News-Letter*, 13 July 1849, q. Bardon, *History of Ulster*, 301–2.

42 Bardon, *History of Ulster*, 291, 287.

43 J. M. Roberts, *The Mythology of the Secret Societies* (London: Paladin, 1974), 160–67.

44 Winder Good, *Ulster and Ireland*, 158, 162.

45 Ibid, 153.

46 Ibid, 159.

47 *Belfast Mercury*, 14 May 1784, q. D. W. Miller, *Queen's Rebels: Ulster Loyalism in Historical Perspective* (Dublin: Gill & Macmillan, 1978; University of Dublin Press, 2007), 54.

48 H. Senior, *Orangeism in Ireland and Britain, 1795–1836* (London: Routledge & Kegan Paul, 1966), 284.

49 D. MacRaild, *Irish Migrants in Modern Britain 1750–1922* (Basingstoke: Macmillan, 1999), 113ff.

50 *Barrow Herald*, July 1884, July 1880, q. D. MacRaild, *Culture, Conflict and Migration: The Irish in Victorian Cumbria* (Liverpool University Press, 1998), 137.

51 C. Hirst, *Religion, Politics and Violence in Nineteenth-Century Belfast: The Pound and Sandy Row* (Dublin: Four Courts Press, 2002), 84.

52 Winder Good, *Ulster and Ireland*, 150.

53 I. R. McBride, *The Siege of Derry in Ulster Protestant Mythology* (Dublin: Four Courts Press, 1997), 60.

54 A. T. Q. Stewart, *The Narrow Ground: Aspects of Ulster 1609–1969* (London: Faber & Faber, 1977), 72.

55 Ibid, 62.

56 Hirst, *Religion, Politics and Violence*, 84, 35.

57 M. Elliott, *The Catholics of Ulster: A History* (London: Allen Lane, 2000), 348.

58 Wright, *Two Lands on One Soil*, 4, 56.

59 *Belfast News-Letter*, 17 July 1846, q. Hirst, *Religion, Politics and Violence*, 71.

60 *Belfast News-Letter*, 20 July 1849, q. Bardon, *History of Ulster*, 303.

61 Quoted in Elliott, *Catholics of Ulster*, 351.

62 M. Goldring, *Belfast: From Loyalty to Rebellion* (London: Lawrence & Wishart, 1991), 100–104.

63 *Belfast Mercury*, 25 September 1857.

64 Lord Chancellor to Lord Lieutenant, Co. Down, 3 October 1857. NLI Ms7624.

65 *Banner of Ulster*, 4 June 1859, q. Hirst, *Religion, Politics and Violence*, 125.

66 Hirst, *Religion, Politics and Violence*, 127, 130.

67 Wright, *Two Lands on One Soil*, 232.

68 *Downshire Protestant*, 10 June 1859; Wright, *Two Lands on One Soil*, 234–6.

69 *Report of the Commissioners of Inquiry, Belfast Riots 1857*.

70 Hirst, *Religion, Politics and Violence*, 159.

71 Belfast riots commission 1864 report, q. Hirst, *Religion, Politics and Violence*, 169.

72 Larcom note, 26 August 1864, NA HO 45/7649; Peel to Larcom, 17 August 1864, NLI Larcom MSS 7626; C. Townshend, *Political Violence in Ireland: Government and Resistance since 1848* (Oxford: Clarendon Press, 1983), 44.

73 Hirst, *Religion, Politics and Violence*, 131–7.

74 Farrell, *Rituals and Riots*, 173.

75 *Dublin Evening Mail*, 4 August 1864, q. Farrell, *Rituals and Riots*, 159.

76 Report of Sub-Inspector of Constabulary, August 1872, q. Hirst, *Religion, Politics and Violence*, 171.

77 Hirst, *Religion, Politics and Violence*, 172.

78 Lyons, *Culture and Anarchy*, 143.

79 HC Deb 3s vol. 15 c. 259, q. Stewart, *The Narrow Ground*, 165.

80 A. Jackson, *Home Rule: An Irish History, 1800–2000* (London: Weidenfeld & Nicolson, 2003), 33.

81 Mansergh, *Government of Northern Ireland*, 83.

CHAPTER 2: THE REMOTE NORTH

1 Lord Rossmore, *Things I Can Tell* (London: Eveleigh Nash, 1912), 241–4.

2 T. Wilson, 'The Strange Death of Loyalist Monaghan, 1919–1921', in S. Paseta (ed.), *Uncertain Futures* (Oxford University Press, 2016), 179–80.

3 *Dublin Weekly Mail*, 20 October 1883.

4 T. Macknight, *Ulster As It Is*, 2 vols (London: Macmillan, 1896), 11.

5 C. McGimpsey, *'To Raise the Banner in the Remote North': Politics in County Monaghan, 1868–1883* (PhD thesis, University of Edinburgh, 1982).

6 *Northern Standard*, 30 June 1883, q. McGimpsey, *'To Raise the Banner in the Remote North'*, 490.

7 J. Loughlin, *Gladstone, Home Rule and the Ulster Question* (Dublin: Gill & Macmillan, 1986), 125.

8 J. Loughlin, 'Parades and Politics: Liberal Governments and the Orange Order, 1880–1886', in T. G. Fraser (ed.), *The Irish Parading Tradition* (Basingstoke: Macmillan, 2000), 39.

9 Macknight, *Ulster As It Is*, vol. ii, 95–6.

10 Ibid, 130.

11 Miller, *Queen's Rebels*, 89. Irish Boundary Commission, 6 June 1925 (D. McCrossan). NA CAB 61/148.

12 F. Moore, *The Truth About Ulster* (London: Eveleigh Nash, 1914), 54.

13 H. C. G. Matthew, *Gladstone, 1875–1898* (Oxford: Clarendon Press, 1995), 217.

14 A. V. Dicey, *England's Case against Home Rule* (London: John Murray, 1886), 156, 17.

15 Ibid, 280, 72, 74, 281.

16 J. Bryce, 'Irish Opinions on the Irish Problem' (11 December 1885); C. Russell, 'Memorandum on the Ulster Problem', 12 March 1886; Loughlin, *Gladstone, Home Rule and the Ulster Question*, 39–40, 134–5.

17 Russell, 'Memorandum on the Ulster Problem', 17 March 1886. Loughlin, *Gladstone, Home Rule and the Ulster Question*, 135–6.

18 Matthew, *Gladstone*, 236.

19 Speech in Cork, *Cork Daily Herald*, 17 June 1886, q. Loughlin, *Gladstone, Home Rule and the Ulster Question*, 129.

20 Mansergh, *Government of Northern Ireland*, 87.

21 B. Walker, *Ulster Politics: The Formative Years, 1868–86* (Belfast: Ulster Historical Foundation and Institute of Irish Studies, Queen University 1989), 42–3, 262.

22 B. Walker, 'The 1885 and 1886 General Elections – a Milestone in Irish History', *Dancing to History's Tune: History, Myth and Politics in Ireland* (Belfast: Institute of Irish Studies, 1996), 19.

23 Dicey, *England's Case Against Home Rule*, 290.

24 J. Morley, *The Life of William Ewart Gladstone* (3 vols, London: Macmillan, 1903), vol. iii, 327. Bright to Sinclair, 6 June 1887, q. G. Walker, 'Thomas Sinclair', in English and Walker (eds), *Unionism in Modern Ireland*, 26.

25 C. H. D. Howard, 'Joseph Chamberlain, Parnell and the Irish "central board" Scheme, 1884–5', *Irish Historical Studies* VIII no. 32 (1953), 324–61.

26 Paul Murray, *The Irish Boundary Commission and its Origins 1886–1925* (University College Dublin Press, 2011), 24.

27 Chamberlain to Labouchere, 2 May 1886; J. L. Hammond, *Gladstone and the Irish Nation* (London: Longmans Green, 1938; Frank Cass, 1964), 491.

28 'Chamberlain's Memoranda of the Round Table Conference (1887)', Garvin, *Chamberlain*, II, 286–7.

29 *Londonderry Sentinel*, 27 April and 8 May 1886, q. J. Anderson, 'Ideological Variations in Ulster during Ireland's First Home Rule Crisis: An Analysis of Local Newspapers', in C. H. Williams and E. Kofman (eds), *Community Conflict: Partition and Nationalism* (London: Routledge, 1989), 155.

30 Macknight, *Ulster As It Is*, vol. ii, 382–3.

31 Miller, *Queen's Rebels*, 92.

32 Walker, 'Thomas Sinclair', 27.

33 P. Buckland, 'The Southern Irish Unionists, the Irish Question, and British Politics, 1906–1914', *Irish Historical Studies* xv, no. 59 (1967), 370.

34 Loughlin, *Gladstone, Home Rule and the Ulster Question*, 142–3.

35 ILPU, *Union or Separation*, 1886; P. Buckland, *Irish Unionism*, vol. 2: *Ulster Unionism and the Origins of Northern Ireland 1886–1922* (Dublin: Gill & Macmillan, 1973), 20–21.

36 Miller, *Queen's Rebels*, 88.

37 L. Doyle, *An Ulster Childhood* (London: Maunsel & Roberts, 1921).

38 K. T. Hoppen, *Elections, Politics and Society in Ireland 1822–1885* (Oxford: Clarendon Press, 1984), 479.

39 Miller, *Queen's Rebels*, 90.

40 P. Bew, *Ideology and the Irish Question: Ulster Unionism and Irish Nationalism 1912–1916* (Oxford University Press, 1994), 3.

41 R. McNeill, *Ulster's Stand for Union* (London: John Murray, 1922), 57–8; A. T. Q. Stewart, *The Ulster Crisis* (London: Faber & Faber, 1967), 69.

42 McGimpsey, 'To Raise the Banner in the Remote North', 431.

43 Irish Office memo, '1886–1913 Arms Importation and Distribution'. NA CO 904/28, q. T. Bowman, Carson's Army: The Ulster Volunteer Force, 1910–22 (Manchester University Press, 2007), 17.

44 Ulster Gazette, 19 June 1886; Townshend, Political Violence, 190.

45 Morning News, 18 June 1886; RIC Report, Armagh, 21 June 1886. NA CO 904/28/1.

46 RIC Crime Special Branch report, 20 March 1893. NA CO 904/28/1.

47 Miller, Queen's Rebels, 93.

48 Macknight, Ulster As It Is, vol. ii, 329–30.

49 The Times, 5 April 1893.

50 Macknight, Ulster As It Is, vol. ii, 349.

51 The Times, 25 May 1893.

52 'An Irishman', Is Ulster Right? (London: John Murray, 1913).

53 Loughlin, Gladstone, Home Rule and the Ulster Question, 167.

54 Report of the Belfast Riots Commission, 1887, 17.

55 Crawford to Earl of Ranfurly, 14 December 1906; Buckland, Irish Unionism, vol. 2, 202.

56 F. McLaughlin to R. H. Wallace, 8 April 1899; Buckland, Irish Unionism, vol. 2, 185.

57 Dillon to Edward Blake, 31 October 1900. Blake MSS, q. A. O'Day, Irish Home Rule 1867–1921 (Manchester University Press, 1998), 93.

58 D. Ferriter, The Transformation of Ireland 1900–2000 (London: Profile, 2004), 66.

59 P. Buckland, 'Carson, Craig and the Partition of Ireland, 1912–21', in P. Collins (ed.), Nationalism and Unionism: Conflict in Ireland 1885–1921 (Belfast: Institute of Irish Studies, Queen's University, 1994), 83.

60 T. Crowley, Wars of Words: The Politics of Language in Ireland 1537–2004 (Oxford University Press, 2005), 102.

61 Akenson, Small Differences, 134.

62 P. Bew, Conflict and Conciliation in Ireland 1890–1910: Parnellites and Radical Agrarians (Oxford: Clarendon Press, 1997), 7.

63. In P. Bull, Land, Politics and Nationalism: A Study of the Irish Land Question (Dublin: Gill & Macmillan, 1996).

64 Jackson, Home Rule, 96–7.

65 The Leader, 27 July 1901, q. D. W. Miller, 'The Roman Catholic Church in Ireland 1898–1918', in A. O'Day (ed.), Reactions to Irish Nationalism (London and Ronceverte: Hambledon, 1987), 196.

66 Crowley, Wars of Words, 139.

67 Akenson, Small Differences, 138.

68 Rev. P. Forde, *The Irish Language Movement: Its Philosophy* (1901), q. Crowley, *Wars of Words*, 156.

69 Crowley, *Wars of Words*, 153.

70 *Sinn Féin*, 26 April 1913, q. Bew, *Conflict and Conciliation*, 6.

71 *Sinn Féin*, 21 February 1914.

72 Lyons, *Culture and Anarchy*, 132.

73 A. Clery, 'The Partition of Ulster', *The Leader*, 17 February 1906, q. P. Maume, 'Nationalism and Partition: The Political Thought of Arthur Clery', *Irish Historical Studies* XXXI, no. 122 (November 1998), 230.

74 Macknight, *Ulster As It Is*, vol. ii, 380.

75 *The Times*, 5 April 1893.

76 Garvin to Balfour, 25 October 1910, q. G. K. Peatling, *British Opinion and Irish Self-Government, 1865–1925: From Unionism to Liberal Commonwealth* (Dublin: Irish Academic Press, 2001), 129.

77 Strachey to Honey, 2 May 1912; Strachey Mss PA STR 21/1/8.

78 Strachey to Moore, 29 December 1910; Strachey Mss PA STR/21/1/6.

79 Strachey to Lynn, 10 November 1913, PA STR 21/1/15.

80 Jackson, *Home Rule*, 122.

81 Carson memo, 18 November 1911, PA BL 24/3/57.

CHAPTER 3: THE CRISIS

1 L. T. Hobhouse, 'Irish Nationality and Liberal Principle', in J. H. Morgan (ed.), *The New Irish Constitution* (London: Hodder and Stoughton, 1912), 367; Peatling, *British Opinion*, 77.

2 G. Dangerfield, *The Strange Death of Liberal England* (New York: Harrison Smith and Robert Haas, 1935; London: Serif, 1997), 42.

3 P. Jalland, *The Liberals and Ireland: The Ulster Question in British Politics to 1914* (Brighton: Harvester Press, 1980), 29.

4 W. G. S. Adams to Tom Jones, 31 January 1948, q. R. Fanning, *Fatal Path: British Government and Irish Revolution 1910–1922* (London: Faber and Faber, 2013), 35.

5 William Martin, *Statesmen of the War in Retrospect 1918–1928* (London: Jarrolds, 1928), 311.

6 R. Churchill, q. Fanning, *Fatal Path*, 37.

7 J. Kendle, *Walter Long, Ireland, and the Union, 1905–1920* (Kingston and Montreal: McGill–Queen's University Press, 1992), 41.

8 A. Jackson, *The Ulster Party: Irish Unionists in the House of Commons 1884–1911* (Oxford: Clarendon Press, 1989), 299; A. T. Q. Stewart, *Edward Carson* (Dublin: Gill & Macmillan, 1981), 74.

9 Jackson, *Ulster Party*, 310.

10 Ibid, 312.

11 F. H. Crawford, *Guns for Ulster* (Belfast: Graham & Heslip, 1947).

12 J. Loughlin, 'Creating "A Social and Geographical Fact": Regional Identity and the Ulster Question 1880s–1920s', *Past & Present* 195 (2007), 181.

13 It was recently reissued, appropriately, under the Forgotten Books imprint.

14 M. McCarthy, *Rome in Ireland* (London: Hodder & Stoughton, 1904), 97, 99, 104.

15 M. Laffan, *The Partition of Ireland 1911–1925* (Dundalk: Dublin Historical Association, 1983), 6.

16 'The Church View', in S. Rosenbaum (ed.), *Against Home Rule: The Case for Union* (London: Frederick Warne, 1912), 207.

17 'The Nonconformist View', in ibid, 220.

18 HC Deb 5s vol, 21 c. 169, 7 February 1911.

19 T. Sinclair, 'The Position of Ulster', in Rosenbaum (ed.), *Against Home Rule*, 175–6.

20 M. Harris, *The Catholic Church and the Foundation of the Northern Irish State* (Cork University Press, 1993), 15–16.

21 P. Murray, *Citizenship, Colonialism, and Self-Determination: Dublin in the United Kingdom 1885–1918* (PhD thesis, Trinity College Dublin, 1987), 80, 78.

22 Ronan Fanning's *Fatal Path*, for instance, never quite labels the Ulster mobilization as a product of British influence, but manages not to mention either the Ulster Clubs or the Orange Order.

23 G. A. Birmingham, *The Red Hand of Ulster* (London: Hodder & Stoughton, 1914), 15.

24 Ibid, 315.

25 Craig to Crawford, 20 April 1911. PRONI D 1700/5/6/1, q. Jackson, *Ulster Party*, 316–17.

26 H. Montgomery Hyde, *Carson: The Life of Sir Edward Carson, Lord Carson of Duncalm* (London: William Heinemann, 1953), 286–7.

27 McNeill, *Ulster's Stand for Union*, 49, 51.

28 Jackson, *Ulster Party*, 320.

29 J. Kendle, *Ireland and the Federal Solution: The Debate over the United Kingdom Constitution, 1870–1921* (Kingston and Montreal: McGill-Queen's University Press, 1989), 112, 133.

30 A. V. Dicey, *A Leap in the Dark*, 2nd edn (London: John Murray, 1892), xxiv–xxv.

31 Dicey to Bonar Law, 21 January 1912. PA BL 25/1/44.

32 Kendle, *Ireland and the Federal Solution*, 137–40.

33 Strachey to Bonar Law, 17 November 1911. PA BL/24/3/50.

34 Buckland, 'Southern Irish Unionists', 374–5.

35 Biagini, 'Third Home Rule Bill', 415.

36 A. J. Ward, *The Irish Constitutional Tradition: Responsible Government and Modern Ireland 1782–1992* (Dublin: Irish Academic Press, 1994), 65–6.

37 Jackson, *Home Rule*, 112–13.

38 Jalland, *Liberals and Ireland*, 88–9.

39 HC Deb 5s vol. 39, cc. 771–4, 11 June 1912.

40 HC Deb 5s vol. 36, cc. 1086–7, 1088, 12 April 1912.

41 HC Deb 5s vol. 39, cc. 1079–89, 13 June 1912.

42 *The Times*, 12 June 1912; D. Meleady, *John Redmond: The National Leader* (Dublin: Merrion, 2014), 217.

43 HC Deb 5s vol. 39, cc. 1065–79, 13 June 1912.

44 Ibid, c. 734, 11 June 1912.

45 Fanning, *Fatal Path*, 65.

46 Birrell to Churchill, 26 August 1911. Verney MSS, q. Jalland, *Liberals and Ireland*, 59.

47 P. Bew, *Churchill and Ireland*, (Oxford University Press, 2016), 48.

48 McNeill, *Ulster's Stand for Union*, 63; *The Times*, 9 February 1912.

49 E. Childers, *The Framework of Home Rule* (London: Edward Arnold, 1911).

50 Diary of Richard Holt, 5 February 1912. Holt MSS, q. Jalland, *Liberals and Ireland*, 61.

51 Asquith to the king, 7 February 1912. Asquith MSS, q. Jalland, *Liberals and Ireland*, 63–4.

52 Jalland, *Liberals and Ireland*, 64.

53 McNeill, *Ulster's Stand for Union*, 97.

54 Jackson, *Home Rule*, 123.

55 Harris, *Catholic Church*, 18–19.

56 Stewart, *Ulster Crisis*, 54.

57 B. Kiely, *Counties of Contention: A Study of the Origins and Implications of the Partition of Ireland* (Cork: Mercier, 1945), 110.

58 Sydney Brooks, 'The Problem of Ulster', *North American Review* 198, no. 696 (November 1913), 620.

59 Ibid, 627.

60 Bonar Law, 'Preface', in Rosenbaum (ed.), *Against Home Rule*, 13.

61 J. Loughlin, 'Creating "A Social and Geographical Fact"', 172.

62 McNeill, *Ulster's Stand for Union*, 126.

63 Bowman, *Carson's Army*, 20.

64 D. Fitzpatrick, 'Militarism in Ireland 1900–1922,' in T. Bartlett and K. Jeffery (eds), *A Military History of Ireland* (Cambridge University Press, 1996), 183.

65 Bowman, *Carson's Army*, 24–31.

66 Ibid, 45.

67 Ibid, 48–53.

68 UVF Confidential Circular, PRONI D.1327/4/21, q. Townshend, *Political Violence*, 252.

69 W. B. Spender, Foreword to Crawford, *Guns for Ulster*.

70 R. Holmes, *The Little Field-Marshal: Sir John French* (London: Jonathan Cape, 1981), 166, 169.

71 Report of meeting in London, 17 December 1913. PRONI D.1327/4/21. Buckland, *Irish Unionism*, 240–2.

72 Dunleath to Carson, 9 March 1915. PRONI D/1507/1/1915/7; Buckland, *Irish Unionism*, 261–2.

73 Churchill to Lloyd George, 21 August 1912. R. Churchill (ed.), *Winston S. Churchill*, vol. 2, Companion, part III, 1,396.

74 Carson to Lady Londonderry, 27 March 1912. Londonderry MSS, q. J. Smith, 'Bluff, Bluster and Brinkmanship: Andrew Bonar Law and the Third Home Rule Bill', *Historical Journal* 36, no. 1 (March 1993), 168.

75 Smith, 'Bluff, Bluster and Brinkmanship', 165.

76 HC Deb 5s vol. 54, cc. 371–2, 18 June 1913.

77 Bonar Law MSS, q. D. G. Boyce, *Englishmen and Irish Troubles: British Public Opinion and the Making of Irish Policy 1918–22* (London: Jonathan Cape, 1972), 104.

78 Jackson, *Ulster Party*, 156.

79 Dicey to Bishop of Ossory, 24 September 1913; I. Fletcher, ' "This Zeal for Lawlessness": A. V. Dicey, *The Law of the Constitution*, and the Challenge of Popular Politics, 1885–1915', *Parliamentary History* 16, no. 1 (1997), 325.

80 F. S. Oliver, *The Alternatives to Civil War* (London: John Murray, 1913), 35.

81 'What Civil War Means for the Army', *Spectator*, 22 November 1913.

82 *Further Notes on the Movement in Ulster* (November), *Further Notes from Ulster* (4 December 1913). NA CAB 37/11.

83 Note on 'Points discussed at dinner at 11 Downing Street', 12 November 1913; PA LG C/14/1/10.

84 B. Wasserstein, *Herbert Samuel: A Political Life* (Oxford: Clarendon Press, 1992), 149–51.

85 Dillon to T. P. O'Connor, 2 October 1913. Dillon MSS, q. Laffan, *Partition of Ireland*, 35.

86 Strachey to Lynn, 29 December 1913. PA STR 21/1/15.

87 I. Colvin, *The Life of Lord Carson*, vol. II (London: Victor Gollancz, 1934), 259–71.

88 Redmond's memo of interview with Asquith, 2 February 1914. NLI Ms 15165.

89 Asquith to Redmond, 7 March 1914, q. Meleady, *Redmond*, 263.

90 Devlin to Redmond, 5, 6, 7 March 1914, q. Meleady, *Redmond*, 263.

91 Dangerfield, *Strange Death of Liberal England*, 275.

92 French MSS, q. Holmes, *Little Field-Marshal*, 181.

93 RIC Crime Special Branch, 13 July 1912. NA CO 904/28/2.

94 'Alleged Storage of Arms', 1 August 1913. NA CO 904 28/2.

95 'Alleged Importation of Rifles into Ulster', 12 August 1912. NA CO 904/28/2.

96 'Illegalities in Ulster', 29 November 1913. NA CAB 37/117.

97 CIGS, *Position of the Army with regard to the situation in Ulster*, December 1913. Mottistone MSS, q. Holmes, *Little Field-Marshal*, 169.

98 J. Augusteijn (ed.), *The Memoirs of John M. Regan: A Catholic Officer in the RIC and RUC, 1909–48* (Dublin: Four Courts Press, 2007), 82.

99 T. Wilson (ed.), *The Political Diaries of C. P. Scott 1911–1928* (London: Collins, 1970), 84 (26 March 1914).

100 Milner memorandum. Milner MSS, q. J. Smith, *The Tories and Ireland, 1910–1914: Conservative Party Politics and the Home Rule Crisis* (Dublin: Irish Academic Press, 2000), 173.

101 Amery memorandum, 18 January 1914. Amery MSS, q. D. Thackeray, 'Rethinking the Edwardian Crisis of Conservatism', *Historical Journal* 54, no. 1 (March 2011), 204.

102 Hobhouse to Scott, 2 May 1914; Wilson (ed.), *Political Diaries of C. P. Scott*, 84.

103 C. F. N. Macready, *Annals of an Active Life*, vol. I (London: Hutchinson, 1924), 191.

104 *Covenanter*, 24 June 1914, q. D. Jackson, *Popular Opposition to Irish Home Rule in Edwardian Britain* (Liverpool University Press, 2009), 250.

105 Biagini, 'Third Home Rule Bill', 422.

106 Jackson, *Popular Opposition to Irish Home Rule in Edwardian Britain*, 184.

107 Long MSS, q. Smith, 'Bluff, Bluster and Brinkmanship', 161.

108 Dougherty to Birrell, 11 May 1914. Birrell MSS, Bodleian MS Eng.c.7034, ff. 78–80. See C. Mulvagh, 'Ulster Exclusion and Irish Nationalism: Consenting to the Principle of Partition, 1912–1916', *Revue Française de Civilisation Britannique (French Journal of British Studies)*, XXIV, no. 2 (2019).

109 Robinson to Birrell, 6 May 1914. B. O Donoghue, *Activities Wise and Otherwise: The Career of Sir Henry Augustus Robinson 1898–1922* (Sallins: Irish Academic Press, 2015), 176–83.

110 Bonar Law memorandum, 17 July 1914. PA BL MSS 39/4/43, q. R. J. Q. Adams, *Bonar Law* (London: John Murray, 1999), 163.

111 Dangerfield, *Strange Death of Liberal England*, 336.

112 Asquith to the king, 25 July 1914. Bod. MS Asq 7, f. 147.

113 Jalland, *Liberals and Ireland*, 259.

CHAPTER 4: THE WAR

1 N. Mansergh, *The Unresolved Question: The Anglo-Irish Settlement and Its Undoing 1912–72* (New Haven: Yale University Press, 1991), 87.

2 C. Petrie, *The Life and Letters of the Right Hon. Sir Austen Chamberlain*, vol. II (London: Cassell, 1940), 5–14.

3 C. Townshend, *Easter 1916: The Irish Rebellion* (London: Allen Lane, 2005), 62–4.

4 Meleady, *Redmond*, 394–5.

5 T. Bowman, 'The Ulster Volunteer Force and the Formation of the 36th (Ulster) Division', *Irish Historical Studies* XXI, no. 128 (2001), 498–518.

6 Inspector General RIC, Monthly Report, April 1915. NA CO 904/94.

7 McNeill, *Ulster's Stand for Union*, 244.

8 Memoranda by PM, 19, 21 May 1916. NA CAB 37/148/18; Mansergh, *Unresolved Question*, 90–92.

9 Lord Mayor to PM, 8 May 1916. PRONI D 1507/1/1916/17.

10 Memoranda by PM, 19, 21 May 1916. NA CAB 37/148/18.

11 PA LG/D/14/1/7.

12 F. S. L. Lyons, *John Dillon* (London: Routledge & Kegan Paul, 1968), 395.

13 D. G. Boyce, 'British Opinion, Ireland and the War, 1916–1918', *Historical Journal* 17 (1974), 580.

14 Buckland, *Irish Unionism,* vol. 2, 106.

15 Montgomery to C. H. Montgomery, 22 June 1916. PRONI D 627/429.

16 F. H. Crawford, 'Why I Voted for the Six Counties, April 1920'. PRONI D 1700/5/16. P. Buckland (ed.), *Irish Unionism 1885–1923: A Documentary History* (Belfast HMSO, 1973), 409–11.

17 Robinson to Long, 18 July 1916, q. O'Donoghue, *Activities Wise and Otherwise*, 248.

Midleton to Lloyd George, 26 May 1916. PA LG/D/14/1/26.
   ›randum of Interview, 29 May 1916. Midleton MSS, NA PRO
   ⸻/.31.
20 Lloyd George to Dillon, 10 June 1916; Lyons, *John Dillon*, 390–91.
21 Headings of a Settlement as to the Government of Ireland, 17 July 1916. NA CAB 37/151/39. Minute by Thring, 30 May 1916. PA LG/D/15/1/7.
22 Meleady, *Redmond*, 381.
23 Ibid, 382.
24 C. C. O'Brien, *States of Ireland* (London: Hutchinson, 1972), 90–98.
25 'Questions to be Considered', *Freeman's Journal*, 20 June 1916, q. O. Paarnila, *Race, Religion and History in the One-Ireland and Partition Arguments* (University of Jyväskylä, 1998), 160–61.
26 T. Hennessey, *Dividing Ireland: World War I and Partition* (London: Routledge, 1998), 147.
27 W. H. Long, 'The Irish Difficulty', 23 June 1916. NA CAB 37/150/15.
28 Long to LG, 11 June, and reply, 12 June 1916. PA LG/D/14/2/22, 39.
29 WHL, 'The Irish Scheme', 13 June; 'Irish Negotiations', 15 June; 'The Irish Situation', 15 June 1916. Cited in Kendle, *Walter Long*, 111–12.
30 Kendle, *Walter Long*, 121.
31 Ibid, 122.
32 Ruby Carson's diary, q. G. Lewis, *Carson: The Man Who Divided Ireland* (London: Hambledon Press, 2005), 190.
33 Memorandum, 'Ulster and the Irish Crisis', 24 June 1916; C. Shannon, *Arthur J. Balfour and Ireland, 1874–1922* (Washington DC: Catholic University of America Press, 1988), 219–21.
34 A. J. Ward, *Ireland and Anglo-American Relations 1899–1921* (London: LSE and Weidenfeld and Nicolson, 1969), 112.
35 Lord Robert Cecil, 'Ireland 1916', memorandum to Cabinet, 26 June 1916. NA CAB 37/150.
36 Ward, *Ireland and Anglo-American Relations*, 146–7.
37 Dillon to Redmond, 29 June 1916, q. Meleady, *Redmond*, 383.
38 Long to Selborne, 29 June 1916. Selborne MSS 80:224–5, q. Kendle, *Walter Long*, 121.
39 HC Deb 5s vol. 84, cc. 61–2, 10 July 1916.
40 Meleady, *Redmond*, 385.
41 Carson to Samuel, 21 July 1916; Wasserstein, *Herbert Samuel*, 180.
42 Meleady, *Redmond*, 385–6.
43 S. Gwynn, *John Redmond's Last Years* (London: Edward Arnold, 1919), 234.
44 Frances Stevenson's diary, 26 July 1916; J. Grigg, *Lloyd George: From Peace to War 1912–1916*, vol. II (London: HarperCollins, 1997), 353–4.

45 D. Officer, '"For God and for Ulster": The Ulsterman on the Somme', in McBride (ed.), *History and Memory in Modern Ireland*.

46 P. Orr, *The Road to the Somme: Men of the Ulster Division Tell Their Story* (Belfast: Blackstaff Press, 1987), 194.

47 Lyons, *John Dillon*, 391.

48 Hoppen, *Governing Hibernia*.

49 Kendle, *Walter Long*, 127.

50 Ibid, 137.

51 H. A. L. Fisher diary, 29 April 1918, q. E. O'Halpin, 'H. E. Duke and the Irish Administration, 1916–18', *Irish Historical Studies*, no. 88 (1981), 375.

52 Kendle, *Walter Long*, 138.

53 Adams to Lloyd George, 1 March 1917. PA LG F/63/1/1.

54 Alvin Jackson, *Ireland 1798–1998: Politics and War* (Oxford: Blackwell, 1999), 241.

55 S. Hartley, *The Irish Question as a Problem in British Foreign Policy, 1914–18* (London: Macmillan, 1987, 161.

56 Letter of Transmission from the Chairman, 8 April 1918, in *Report of the Proceedings of the Irish Convention*, 7.

57 Lloyd George to Bonar Law, 12 January 1918. PA BL 82/8/4.

58 Montgomery to Londonderry, 26 February 1918. PRONI D 627/433; Buckland, *Irish Unionism*, vol. 2, 112.

59 J. R. Fisher, 'Ulster and the Irish Angle', *Nineteenth Century* lxxxii (January–June 1918), 1,088.

60 Duffin to his wife, 28 November 1917, q. Buckland, *Irish Unionism*, vol. 2, 109.

61 Lloyd George to Plunkett, 25 February 1918, in *Proceedings of the Irish Convention*, 21–2.

62 Draft Government of Ireland Bill 1917. NA CAB 27/46.

63 Lewis, *Carson*, 216.

64 War Cabinet, 23 October 1917. NA CAB 23/13.

65 Hankey to Lloyd George, 20 April; Sykes to Hankey, 27 April 1918. GT4269. NA CAB/24/49.

66 C. Townshend, *The Republic: The Fight for Irish Independence, 1918–1923* (London: Allen Lane, 2013), 11.

67 Kendle, *Walter Long*, 164.

68 Ibid, 156.

69 Long to Lloyd George, 18 April 1918. PA LG/F/32/5/23.

70 War Cabinet Committee on Government of Ireland Bill, Interim Report by WHL, 14 June 1918. GT 4839. NA CAB/24/46.

CHAPTER 5: THE CUT

1 D. Fitzpatrick, *The Two Irelands 1912–1939* (Oxford University Press, 1998), 76.

2 NA CAB 27/68, q. Mansergh, *Unresolved Question*, 120.

3 Fanning, *Fatal Path*, 193.

4 See e.g. Townshend, *The Republic*; M. Hopkinson, *The Irish War of Independence* (Montreal and Kingston: McGill–Queens University Press, 2002).

5 Townshend, *The Republic*, 15–17.

6 D. Kennedy, *The Widening Gulf: Northern Attitudes to the Independent Irish State 1919–1949* (Belfast: Blackstaff, 1988), 37–8.

7 Strathcarron MSS, q. C. Townshend, *The British Campaign in Ireland* (Oxford: Clarendon Press, 1975), 25.

8 Jones to Davies, 23 May 1919; Jones, *Whitehall Diary*, vol. I, 87.

9 Lord Lieutenant to the king, 18 December 1918. French MSS, q. O'Donoghue, *Activities Wise and Otherwise*, 318.

10 B. Maye, *Arthur Griffith* (Dublin: Griffith College, 1997), 166–7.

11 HC Deb 5s vol. 114, c.133, 24 March 1919.

12 Ibid, c. 161, 24 March 1919.

13 T. Jones, (ed. K. Middlemas), *Whitehall Diary*, vol. III: *Ireland 1918–1925* (London: Oxford University Press, 1971), 11 and 23 October 1918.

14 'The Situation in Ireland', Cabinet memo, 24 September 1919. G.T. 8215, NA CAB 24/89.

15 War Cabinet, 7 October 1919. W.C. 628, NA CAB 23/12.

16 Ward, *Ireland and Anglo-American Relations*, 174–81.

17 Tumulty MSS, q. ibid, 183.

18 Telegram from Grey, 4 October 1919; 'American Opinion on the Irish Question', PA LG/F/180/1/3.

19 Jones MSS, q. Fanning, *Fatal Path*, 202.

20 W.C. 628, 7 October 1919. NA CAB 23/12.

21 First Report of Cabinet Committee on the Irish Question, 4 November 1919; C.P. 56, CAB/24/92.

22 Cabinet, 11 November 1919; CAB 23/18.

23 Joint Note by the Lord Chancellor and the Minister of Pensions (Circulated with reference to C.P. 56); C.P. 103, NA CAB 27/68.

24 A. J. Balfour, 'The Irish Question', 25 November 1919. C.P. 193, NA CAB 24/93.

25 Cabinet, 19 December 1919. C.16 (19), NA CAB 23/18.

26 J. McColgan, *British Policy and the Irish Administration, 1920–22* (London: Allen and Unwin, 1983), 37.

27 Committee on Ireland, 4th report, 2 December 1919. C.P. 247, NA CAB 24/94.

28 Memo by W. H. Long, 1 January 1920; CI 46, NA CAB 27/69.

29 Cabinet, 19 December 1919; NA CAB 23/18; Mansergh, *Unresolved Question*, 130–31.

30 L. S. Amery to Craig, 4 October 1924; Jackson, *Home Rule*, 208–9.

31 HC Deb 5s vol. 123, c. 1170.

32 Ibid, c. 1176.

33 T. Wilson, *Frontiers of Violence: Conflict and Identity in Ulster and Upper Silesia, 1918–1922* (Oxford Historical Monographs, Oxford University Press, 2010), 29.

34 Townshend, *British Campaign in Ireland*, 25, 44; D. Leeson, *The Black and Tans: The British Police and Auxiliaries in the Irish War of Independence* (Oxford University Press, 2011), 24.

35 NA CAB 27/69. C.I. 58, 4 February 1920.

36 Long to Ross of Bladensburg, 10 February 1920, q. Kendle, *Walter Long*, 187.

37 Cabinet Committee on Ireland: Report by Bonar Law, 17 February 1920. CAB/27/68 C.P. 664.

38 CAB 24/98, q. Fanning, *Fatal Path*, 218. Fanning suggests that this 'lays bare the reasoning behind the preference for six counties' but does not consider its attitude to the partition line.

39 HC Deb 5s vol. 127, c. 990–92, 29 March 1920.

40 Ibid, c. 1288, 31 March 1920.

41 Ibid, c. 1323, 31 March 1920.

42 Ibid, c. 1134, 30 March 1920.

43 G. Bell, *Troublesome Business: The Labour Party and the Irish Question* (London: Pluto Press, 1982), 49.

44 HC Deb 5s vol. 127, c. 984–5, 29 March 1920.

45 HC Deb 5s vol. 129, c. 1305–7, 18 May 1920.

46 Ibid, c. 1316, 18 May 1920.

47 Buckland, *Irish Unionism*, vol. 2, 116.

48 Stronge to Montgomery, 12 March 1920, and F. H. Crawford, *Why I Voted for the Six Counties*, April 1920, in Buckland (ed.), *Irish Unionism*, 409–11, 417.

49 Jones, *Whitehall Diary*, vol. III, 34–5 (4 August 1920).

50 Ibid, 25–31.

CHAPTER 6: THE SIEGE

1 *An tOglac* ii, no. 17, 15 August 1920.
2 Laffan, *Partition of Ireland*, 75.
3 Townshend, *The Republic*, 173–5.
4 Kennedy, *Widening Gulf*, 39–40.
5 McBride, *Siege of Derry*, 71.
6 D. Murphy, *Derry, Donegal and Modern Ulster: 1790–1921* (Londonderry: Aileach Press 1981), 253–4.
7 Wilson, *Frontiers of Violence*, 128.
8 O'Malley MSS, UCDA P176/107. S. Aiken et al. (eds), *The Men Will Talk to Me: Ernie O'Malley's Interviews with the Northern Divisions* (Dublin: Merrion Press, 2018), 87.
9 McColgan, *British Policy*, 24.
10 *Belfast News-Letter*, 25 June 1920, q. McColgan, *British Policy*, 24.
11 J. Bowman, *De Valera and the Ulster Question 1917–1973* (Oxford University Press, 1982), 34.
12 E. Phoenix, *Northern Nationalism: Nationalist Politics and the Catholic Minority in Northern Ireland 1890–1940* (Belfast: Ulster Historical Foundation, Queen University 1994), 65.
13 28 January 1922, q. Hopkinson, *Irish War of Independence*, 154.
14 J. McDermott, *Northern Divisions: The Old IRA and the Belfast Pogroms 1920–22* (Belfast: BTP, 2001), 30.
15 *Northern Whig*, 13 July 1920.
16 A. Parkinson, *Belfast's Unholy War: The Troubles of the 1920s* (Dublin: Four Courts Press, 2004), 35–6.
17 Buckland, *Irish Unionism*, vol. 2, 431.
18 Supply and Transport Committee, 15 January 1920; C. Townshend, *Making the Peace: Public Order and Public Security in Modern Britain* (New York: Oxford University Press, 1993), 85.
19 Wilson's diary, 15 January 1920, q. K. Jeffery, *Field Marshal Sir Henry Wilson: A Political Soldier* (Oxford University Press, 2006), 245.
20 R. Dawson, *Red Terror and Green: The Sinn Fein-Bolshevik Movement* (London: John Murray, 1920), 259.
21 Jones, *Whitehall Diary*, vol. III, 38.
22 McDermott's chapter entitled 'Troubles or Pogrom?' reaches no definite judgement, taking refuge in the undoubted but irrelevant fact that 'it would have mattered little to members of the minority if the attacks were technically pogroms or not'. *Northern Divisions*, 35.
23 Goldring, *Belfast*, 63.

24 T. Wilson, 'The Most Terrible Assassination That Has Yet Stained the Name of Belfast', *Irish Historical Studies* 145 (2010), 89; Elliott, *Catholics of Ulster*, 174–5.

25 Bowman, *Carson's Army*, 190.

26 With Major Horace Haslett as its provisional commanding officer. Bowman, *Carson's Army*, 192.

27 M. Farrell, *Arming the Protestants: The Formation of the Ulster Special Constabulary 1920–27* (London: Pluto Press, 1983), 21.

28 Spender memoir, c.1959. PRONI D 1295/2, Buckland, *Irish Unionism*, vol. 2, 445–6.

29 Farrell, *Arming the Protestants*, 24.

30 Macready to Bonar Law, q. Fanning, *Fatal Path*, 235.

31 Jones, *Whitehall Diary*, vol. III, 31.

32 Spender to Craig, 9 September 1920, q. Bowman, *Carson's Army*, 192–3.

33 W. Spender memoir, C.1959. PRONI D/1295/2. Buckland, *Irish Unionism*, vol. 2, 445–7.

34 Minutes of Cabinet Conference, 2 September 1920. NA CAB/23/22.

35 INA BMH WS 389.

36 CI Antrim monthly report, August 1920. NA CO/904/112.

37 R. Lynch, *The Northern IRA and the Early Years of Partition* (PhD thesis, University of Stirling, 2003), 37.

38 Memorandum to Cabinet, 1 September 1920. Jones, *Whitehall Diary*, vol. III, 38.

39 Leeson, *The Black and Tans*, 31ff.

40 Jeffery, *Field Marshal Sir Henry Wilson*, 266.

41 Churchill to Wilson, 26 June 1920. K. Jeffery (ed.), *The Military Correspondence of Field Marshal Sir Henry Wilson 1918–1922* (London: Army Records Society/Bodley Head, 1985), 181–2.

42 Wilson's diary, 1, 7, 10 July 1920. Jeffery, *Field Marshal Sir Henry Wilson*, 265.

43 *Observer*, 26 September 1920. Townshend, *British Campaign in Ireland*, 115–16.

44 Kennedy, *Widening Gulf*, 88–9; G. Martin, 'The Origins of Partition', in Anderson and Bort (eds), *The Irish Border*, 81–2.

45 Minutes of Conference of Ministers, 13 October 1920. NA CAB/23/23. McColgan, *British Policy and the Irish Administration*, 44.

46 Committee on Ireland, 13th meeting, 17 February 1920. NA CAB 27/68, q. Kendle, *Walter Long*, 188

47 McColgan, *British Policy and the Irish Administration, 1920–22*, 45–6.

48 HC Deb 5s vol. 134, c. 945, 8 November 1920.

49 Ibid, cc. 948–9.

50 Ibid, c. 953–44.

51 Ibid, c. 962.

52 Robinson, 'Powers of the Council of Ireland', 17 January 1920. C.I.48, CAB/27/69.

53 Committee on Ireland, report of the sub-committee, 30 January 1920. C.I.55, NA CAB/27/69.

54 McColgan, *British Policy and the Irish Administration, 1920–22*, 49.

55 HC Deb 5s vol. 134, cc. 894–5, 8 November 1920.

56 Ibid, c. 906.

57 Ibid, c. 911.

58 Ibid, c. 912.

59 Ibid, cc. 912, 914, 919.

60 Ibid, cc. 922, 925.

61 Buckland, *Irish Unionism*, vol. 2, 124–5.

62 HC Deb 5s vol. 134, cc. 925–7, 8 November 1920.

63 Ibid, cc. 1219, 1220, 1224, 1225–6, 10 November 1920.

64 Ibid, cc. 1228, 1231.

65 Ibid, c. 1235.

66 Ibid, cc. 1241, 1243.

CHAPTER 7: THE STATE

1 Jones, *Whitehall Diary*, vol. III, 28–9 (23 July 1920).

2 Wilson's diary, 26 July 1920, q. Bew, *Churchill and Ireland*, 95–6.

3 Farrell, *Arming the Protestants*, 23.

4 P. Hart, 'Ethnic Conflict and Minority Responses', *The IRA at War* (Oxford University Press, 2003), 145.

5 Bainbridge to Spender, 30 August 1920, q. Bowman, *Carson's Army*, 194.

6 Anderson to Clark, 12 October 1920. PRONI FIN 18/1/87.

7 *Irish News*, 17 September 1920, q. B. A. Follis, *A State under Siege: The Establishment of Northern Ireland 1920–1925* (Oxford: Clarendon Press, 1995), 10.

8 Clark, Autobiographical notes, q. Follis, *A State under Siege*, 8.

9 Memorandum about New Administration, PRONI CAB 5/1, q. Farrell, *Arming the Protestants*.

10 Clark to Anderson, 1 October; Minutes of meeting 13 October 1920, q. Follis, *A State under Siege*, 22, 20.

11 Clark to Anderson, 23 September 1920. PRONI FIN 18/1/176.

12 HC Deb 5s vol. 133, c. 1505, 25 October 1920.

13 A. Hezlet, *The 'B' Specials: A History of the Ulster Special Constabulary* (London: Tom Stacey, 1972), 45.

14 Crawford to Col. R. H. Wallace, Grand Master, 18 December 1920. Buckland, *Irish Unionism*, vol. 2, 450.

15 Buckland, *Irish Unionism*, vol. 2, 447–8.

16 Lt. Col. Moore-Irvine to Londonderry City UVF, 26 November 1920. PRONI FIN 18/1/131, q. Follis, *A State under Siege*, 17.

17 Ibid.

18 Clark to Anderson, 3 December 1920; Follis, *A State under Siege*, 14.

19 Follis, *A State under Siege*, 15.

20 Hezlet, *'B' Specials*, 29.

21 Bowman, *Carson's Army*, 195.

22 Parkinson, *Belfast's Unholy War*, 333.

23 Tyrone Special Constables' Handbook, 18 February 1921, q. Hezlet, *'B' Specials*, 31–2.

24 Hezlet, *'B' Specials*, 47.

25 Parkinson, *Belfast's Unholy War*, 100.

26 Lady Craig's diary, 21 March 1921. PRONI D 1415/38, q. Buckland, *Irish Unionism*, vol. 2, 129.

27 Hyde, *Carson*, 449.

28 *Impartial Reporter*, 10 February 1921; *Ballymena Observer*, 11 February 1921. P. Clayton, *Enemies and Passing Friends: Settler Ideologies in Twentieth-Century Ulster* (London: Pluto Press, 1996), 106–7.

29 He even seems to have thought that his Cabinet would prefer Cope to Ernest Clark as Under Secretary. P. Bew, *Ireland: The Politics of Enmity 1789–2006* (Oxford University Press, 2007), 413.

30 Bowman, *De Valera and the Ulster Question*, 47–8.

31 Collins to Griffith, 11 January 1921. INA DE 2/266.

32 De Valera to Collins, 13 January 1921. UCDA P150/1381.

33 'Partition Act', memo by Collins, 15 January 1921. INA DE 2/266. Phoenix, *Northern Nationalism*, 109.

34 Phoenix, *Northern Nationalism*, 109–10.

35 E. Staunton, *The Nationalists of Northern Ireland, 1918–1973* (Dublin: Columba Press, 2001), 287.

36 Phoenix, *Northern Nationalism*, 119.

37 A. C. Hepburn, *Catholic Belfast and Nationalist Ireland in the Era of Joe Devlin 1871–1934* (Oxford University Press, 2008), 223–5; Phoenix, *Northern Nationalism*, 113–19.

38 *Impartial Reporter*, 19 May 2021.

39 7,016 out of 34,654. Staunton, *The Nationalists of Northern Ireland*, 285.

40 *Belfast News-Letter*, 27 May 1921.

41 P. Buckland, *The Factory of Grievances: Devolved Government in Northern Ireland 1921–39* (Dublin: Gill & Macmillan, 1979), 10.

42 McNeill, *Ulster's Stand for Union*, 282–3.

43 Smuts to Lloyd George, 14 June 1921. Jones, *Whitehall Diary*, vol. III, 75.

44 Follis, *A State under Siege*, 52.

45 Parkinson, *Belfast's Unholy War*, 143.

46 Unionist supporter to Craig, 27 June 1921, q. Follis, *A State under Siege*, 54.

47 De Valera to Lloyd George, 19 July 1921. PA LG/F/14/6/11.

48 'Proposals of the British Government for an Irish Settlement', 20 July 1921. PRONI CAB/10/4; Follis, *A State under Siege*, 56.

49 Bowman, *De Valera*, 52.

50 Ibid, 55.

51 Ibid, 59–60.

52 De Valera to Griffith, 14 October 1920. INA DE 2/304/1. Bowman, *De Valera*, 61.

53 Ibid, 63.

54 Jones, *Whitehall Diary*, vol. III, 131 (14 October 1921).

55 Bonar Law to Jones, 30 July 1921. *Whitehall Diary*, vol. III, 91–2.

56 Inverness Cabinet, 7 September 1921. Jones, *Whitehall Diary*, vol. III, 108–11.

57 A. J. P. Taylor (ed.), *Lloyd George: A Diary by Frances Stevenson* (London: Hutchinson, 1971), 234–5.

58 Jones, *Whitehall Diary*, vol. III, 154–5 (2 November 1921).

59 Griffith to de Valera, 9 November 1921. DE 2/304/1, Bowman, *De Valera*, 63.

60 Murray, *Irish Boundary Commission*, 99.

61 Stevenson's diary, 11 November 1921. Taylor (ed.), *Lloyd George*, 236.

62 Jones, *Whitehall Diary*, vol. III, 159–60 (10 November 1921).

63 Ibid, vol. III, 163 (12 November 1921).

64 Fanning, *Fatal Path*, 286.

65 Jones, *Whitehall Diary*, vol. III, 132 (14 October 1921).

66 Bonar Law to Lord Rothermere, 16 November 1921. PA BL/107/4/6; Boyce, *Englishmen and Irish Troubles*, 166.

67 Chamberlain notes, NA CAB 21/253/1, q. K. Matthews, *Fatal Influence: The Impact of Ireland on British Politics, 1920–1925* (University College Dublin Press, 2004), 55.

68 F. Pakenham, *Peace by Ordeal: An Account from First-Hand Sources of the Negotiation and Signature of the Anglo-Irish Treaty 1921* (London: Jonathan Cape, 1935), 294, 369.

69 Chartres to Mulcahy, 5 February 1924. INA D/T S 1801/E, q. Matthews, *Fatal Influence*, 53.

70 Jones, *Whitehall Diary*, vol. III, 234 (31 July 1924).

71 Ibid, 130–31, 156 (14 October, 8 November 1921).

72 Ibid, 177 (18 November 1921).

73 Collins note, q. T. P. Coogan, *Michael Collins* (London: Hutchinson, 1990), 270.

74 Murray, *Boundary Commission*, 101, 106.

75 Robert Barton, BMH WS 979.

76 Jones to Hankey, 6 December 1921, q. Fanning, *Fatal Path*, 311.

77 D. Gwynn, *The History of Partition (1912–1925)* (Dublin: Browne & Nolan, 1950), 203.

78 Jones, *Whitehall Diary*, vol. III, 131 (14 October 1921).

79 For a pioneering indictment, cf H. Harrison, *The Partition of Ireland: How Britain is Responsible* (London: Robert Hale), 1939.

80 Bowman, *De Valera*, 66.

CHAPTER 8: THE FRONTIER

1 See Follis, *A State under Siege*; the final chapter of the more neutral P. Buckland's *Irish Unionism*, vol. 2, is entitled 'Northern Ireland Besieged'.

2 M. Hopkinson, in J. R. Hill (ed.), *New History of Ireland*, vol. VII: *Ireland 1921–84* (Oxford University Press, 2003), 59.

3 D. Harkness. *Ireland in the Twentieth Century: Divided Island* (Basingstoke: Macmillan, 1996), 11.

4 Boyce, *Englishmen and Irish Troubles*, 162–3.

5 Buckland, *Factory of Grievances*, ch. 8.

6 Ibid, 183–4.

7 PRONI H/20/A/1/2; C. Campbell, *Emergency Law in Ireland 1918–1925* (Oxford: Clarendon Press, 1994), 272.

8 PRONI CAB 4/10, q. Campbell, *Emergency Law in* Ireland, 272.

9 Spender to Jones, August 1921. Jones, *Whitehall Diary*, vol. III, 104.

10 Cabinet memo, 10 September 1921. PRONI HA20/A/12, q. Follis, *A State under Siege*, 82.

11 'History of Attempts to Get Peace Keeping Forces on Satisfactory Footing', PRONI CAB 4/17, q. Buckland, *Factory of Grievances*, 187.

12 Ibid, 188–90.

13 Memorandum by Watt, 5 October 1921. Buckland, *Factory of Grievances*, 192–3.

14 M. Theodorson, *Policing and Internal Security in Northern Ireland 1920–1939* (PhD thesis, Keele University, 2006), 58.

15 Craig to Wilson, 28 October 1921. Jeffery (ed.), *Field Marshal Sir Henry Wilson*, 302–5.

16 HC Deb 5s vol. 149, cc. 40–41, 14 December 1921.

17 Ibid, cc. 314–5, 16 December 1921.

18 Ibid, cc. 357–8, 16 December 1921.

19 HC Deb 5s vol. 150, cc. 1269–70, 16 February 1922.

20 Ibid, c. 1273.

21 Ibid, c. 1327.

22 Ibid, cc. 1320–21, 16 February 1922.

23 Ibid, c. 1310.

24 Ibid, c. 1393, 17 February 1922.

25 Craig to Chamberlain, 15 December, and reply, 16 December 1921, q. Matthews, *Fatal Influence*, 59–60.

26 HC Deb 5s vol. 150, c. 1326, 16 February 1922, vol. 151, c. 553, 2 March 1922.

27 HC Deb 5s vol. 151, c. 707, 2 March 1922.

28 Ibid, cc. 748–9, 3 March 1922.

29 Ibid, cc. 761, 781, 3 March 1922.

30 Murray, *Irish Boundary Commission*, 108.

31 F. McGarry, *Eoin O'Duffy: A Self-Made Hero* (Oxford University Press, 2005), 99.

32 Buckland, *Factory of Grievances*, 195.

33 W. S. Churchill, *The World Crisis: The Aftermath* (London: Thornton Butterworth, 1929), 321.

34 M. Hopkinson, *Green Against Green: The Irish Civil War* (Dublin: Gill & Macmillan, 1988), 79–80.

35 Wilson, 'McMahon Murders in Context', 106.

36 Buckland, *Irish Unionism*, vol. 2, 154.

37 PRONI HA/5/189, q. Lynch, *The Northern IRA*, 119.

38 McGarry, *Eoin O'Duffy*, 98–102.

39 2nd Northern Division IRA orders, 26 March 1922, q. Lynch, *The Northern IRA*, 120.

40 Buckland, *Factory of Grievances*, 198.

41 Matthews, *Fatal Influence*, 71–2.

42 Jones, *Whitehall Diary*, vol. III, 194–5 (17 March 1922).

43 G. Ellison and J. Smyth, *The Crowned Harp: Policing Northern Ireland* (London: Pluto Press, 2000), 19.

44 Hezlet, *The 'B' Specials*, 78.

45 Ministry of Home Affairs conference, 17 March 1922. PRONI HA20/A/18, q. Follis, *A State under Siege*, 92.

46 Jeffery, *Field Marshal Sir Henry Wilson*, 280.

47 Ibid, 284–5; Hart, 'Michael Collins and Sir Henry Wilson', *The IRA at War*, 194–220.

48 Theodorson, *Policing and Internal Security*, 66.

49 N.I. Cabinet Conference, 2 June 1922. PRONI CAB 4/47.

50 Jones, *Whitehall Diary*, vol. III, 201 (16 May 1922).

51 CID Subcommittee on Ireland, 1–8 June 1922. NA CAB 16/42, q. J. M. Curran, *The Birth of the Irish Free State 1921–1923* (Alabama University Press, 1980), App. IV.

52 Churchill to Craig, 24 March 1922. Churchill, *The Aftermath*, 332–3.

53 PRONI CAB 4/45/6, Fanning, *Fatal Path*, 328.

54 Lynch, *The Northern IRA*, 154.

55 'Invasion of Northern Ireland by Republican Forces', C.P. 4017, NA CAB 43/7.

56 Buckland, *Factory of Grievances*, 195.

57 Tallents to Masterton Smith, 13 November 1922. NA CO 739/1.

58 P. Shea, *Voices and the Sound of Drums: An Irish Autobiography* (Belfast: Blackstaff, 1981), 76.

59 Buckland, *Factory of Grievances*, 197.

60 Minutes of meeting, NA CO 906/26. Bew et al., *The State in Northern Ireland*, 55.

61 Report by Imperial Secretary, 6 July 1922. NA CO 906/30.

62 Collins to Churchill, 28 June 1922. NA CAB 27/160.

CHAPTER 9: THE FIX

1 Lionel Curtis, q. Murray, *The Irish Boundary Commission*, 127.

2 J. Lee, *Ireland 1912–1985* (Cambridge University Press, 1989), 141–2.

3 Memo by K. O'Shiel, 17 May 1923. Mulcahy MSS, UCDA P7/B/288.

4 'Report on Possible Boundary Lines', 9 January; Memo by K. O'Shiel, 21 April 1923. Blythe MSS, UCDA P24/171, q. Lee, *Ireland 1912–1985*, 149.

5 Memo by K. O'Shiel, 10 February 1923. Mulcahy MSS, UCDA P7/B/288, q. Murray, *The Irish Boundary Commission*, 145–6.

6 Memo by K. O'Shiel, 29 May 1923. Mulcahy MSS, UCDA P7/B/288, q. Lee, *Ireland*, 142–3.

7 North Eastern Boundary Bureau, *Handbook of the Ulster Question* (1923), 39.

8 Ibid, 89–90.

9 Ibid, 151–2.

10 Executive Council minutes, 5 June 1923. NAI G 2/2.

11 Curtis, 'The Irish Boundary Question', draft memo, q. D. Lavin, *From Empire to International Commonwealth: A Biography of Lionel Curtis* (Oxford: Clarendon Press, 1995), 208.

12 O'Shiel to Executive Council, December 1923. MacNeill MSS, UCDA LA/1/96/1, q. Murray, *The Irish Boundary Commission*, 147.

13 F. J. P. Bourdillon, 'The Recent Experiments in Self-Determination', draft in Bourdillon to Curtis, 14 December 1923. NA CO 739/25.

14 F. J. P. Bourdillon, 'The Scope of the Boundary Commission', in Bourdillon to Curtis, 7 December 1923. NA CO 739/25.

15 Kennedy, *Widening Gulf*, 135–6.

16 Jones, *Whitehall Diary*, vol. III, 227–9.

17 Introduction, G. J. Hand, *Report of the Irish Boundary Commission* (Shannon: Irish University Press, 1969), ix.

18 Ivan Gibbons, 'The First British Labour Government and the Irish Boundary Commission 1924', *Studies* 98 (Autumn 2009), 327.

19 HC Deb 5s vol. 174, c. 1400, 5 June 1924.

20 Jones, *Whitehall Diary*, vol. III, 233 (29 July 1924).

21 Matthews, *Fatal Influence*, 186.

22 HC Deb 5s vol. 174, cc. 551–2, 7 October 1924.

23 Niemeyer to Churchill and reply, 15 November 1924, q. Matthews, *Fatal Influence*, 203–4.

24 Quoted in Ervine, *Craigavon*, 481–2.

25 Tierney, *Eoin MacNeill*, 341–2.

26 Lyons, *Culture and Anarchy in Ireland*, 492.

27 Hand, *Report of the Irish Boundary Commission 1925*, xiii.

28 As he is in the recent *Cambridge History of Ireland*, vol. 4 (Cambridge University Press, 2018), 311. Cf also *Oxford Companion to Irish History* (Oxford University Press, 2019), 53; K. J. Rankin, 'The Role of the Irish Boundary CCommission in the Entrenchment of the Irish Border: From Tactical Panacea to Political Liability', *Journal of Historical Geography* 34 (2008), 436.

29 Matthews, *Fatal Influence*, 154–5; Lavin, *Lionel Curtis*, 222.

30 Curtis to Churchill, 19 August 1924. Curtis MSS, q. Matthews, *Fatal Influence*, 155.

31 Hand, *Report of the Irish Boundary Commission 1925*, x.

32 Borden to Thomas, 2 June 1924. Beaverbrook MSS, q. P. Canning, *British Policy towards Ireland 1921–1941* (Oxford: Clarendon Press, 1985), 93–4.

33 HL Deb 5s vol. 174, cc. 653–4, 662–3, 8 October 1924.

34 G. J. Hand, 'MacNeill and the Boundary Commission', in F. X. Martin and F. J. Byrne (eds), *The Scholar Revolutionary: Eoin MacNeill 1867–1945 and the Making of the New Ireland* (Shannon: Irish University Press, 1973), 226.

35 *Irish Boundary Commission, Report* (9 December 1925), 30, NA CAB 61/161.

36 Memorandum by G. C. Whiskard, 18 September 1924. Feetham MSS, Bodleian S.1793/7/2.

37 L. Curtis, 'Appreciation of the Present Position in Ireland', May 1924. NA CAB 21/281.

38 Note by Mr Curtis, 'Plebiscites', 18 September 1924. Feetham MSS, Bodleian S.1793/7/2.

39 Preparatory Statement, 20 November 1924. *Irish Boundary Commission, Report* (9 December 1925), App II, NA CAB 61/161.

40 Hearing of Counsel Representing the Government of the Irish Free State, 4 and 5 December 1924. *Irish Boundary Commission, Report* (9 December 1925), App. I, 26, NA CAB 61/161.

41 *Irish Boundary Commission, Report* (9 December 1925), App. I, 40, NA CAB 61/161.

42 C. Healy to G. Murnaghan, 5 December 1924. NEBB Corr., q. Phoenix, *Northern Nationalism*, 310.

43 Shea, *Voices and the Sound of Drums*, 95–6.

44 *Irish Boundary Commission, Report* (9 December 1925), 29, NA CAB 61/161.

45 Birkenhead to Balfour, 3 March 1922. *The Times*, 8 September 1924.

46 Churchill to William Coole, 5 September 1924, q. Bew, *Churchill and Ireland*, 133,

47 *Irish Boundary Commission, Report* (9 December 1925), App. I, 9, NA CAB 61/161.

48 *Irish Boundary Commission, Report* (9 December 1925), App. I, 26, NA CAB 61/161.

49 Phoenix, *Northern Nationalism*, 311.

50 Irish Boundary Commission: Records 1924–5. NA CAB/61.

51 Eamon Phoenix, 'Cahir Healy (1877–1970), Northern Nationalist Leader', in Parkinson and Phoenix (eds), *Conflict in the North of Ireland*, 145.

52 There is a good account of the refugee issue in Lynch, *Partition of Ireland*, ch. 7.

53 Boundary Commission, 28 April 1925 (Colonel Barton). NA CAB/61/66.

54 Ibid (Rev. W. Naylor).

55 Hearing of Counsel, 25 August 1925. *Irish Boundary Commission, Report* (9 December 1925), App. III, 59, NA CAB 61/161.

56 Quoted in Ervine, *Craigavon*, 409.

57 Ibid, 499–500.

58 Hearing of Counsel, 25 August 1925. *Irish Boundary Commission, Report* (9 December 1925), App. IV, 58, 61, NA CAB 61/161.

59 Tierney, *Eoin MacNeill*, 345.

60 Dáil Eireann Debates, 24 November 1925, vol. XII, c. 802. Tierney, *Eoin MacNeill*, 345.

61 Cabinet Committee on Irish Affairs (25), 1st minutes, 24 November 1925. NA CAB 27/295.

62 Fisher to Carson, 18 October 1925, q. Matthews, *Fatal Influence*, 221.

63 Shea, *Voices and the Sound of Drums*, 96.

64 Cabinet Committee on Irish Affairs (25), 3rd minutes, 26 November 1925. NA CAB 27/295.

65 Jones, *Whitehall Diary*, vol. III (29 November 1925), 239.

66 Cabinet Conference, 3 December 1925. NA CAB 27/295.

67 Ibid.

68 Kiely, *Counties of Contention*, 151.

69 Cabinet memorandum by Home Secretary, 16 November 1925. NA CAB 27/295.

70 Phoenix, 'Cahir Healy', 146.

EPILOGUE: THE LONG DIVISION

1 R. Lynch, *The Partition of Ireland 1918–1925* (Cambridge University Press, 2019), 167–96.

2 Bowman, *De Valera*, 99, 102.

3 O'Brien, *States of Ireland*, 120–21.

4 Bowman, *De Valera*, 155.

5 Ibid, 250.

6 P. Leary, *Unapproved Routes: Histories of the Irish Border 1922–1972* (Oxford University Press, 2016), ch. 4.

7 *Irish Press*, 2 May 1949.

8 Bowman, *De Valera*, 129, 151–2.

9 M. Sheehy, *Divided We Stand* (London: Faber & Faber, 1955), 24, 35.

10 Ibid, Foreword by J. J. Horgan, 10.

11 Even in August 1921, Horgan had insisted that the partition door had been 'slammed, banged and bolted long ago'. Bowman, *De Valera*, 337.

12 E. de Blaghd, *The Leader*, 3 August 1957.

13 H. Patterson, *Ireland's Violent Frontier: The Border and Anglo-Irish Relations during the Troubles* (London: Palgrave Macmillan, 2013), 7–14; R. English, *Armed Struggle: The History of the IRA* (London: Macmillan, 2003), 73–6.

14 M. Burgess, 'Mapping the Narrow Ground: Geography, History and Partition', *Field Day Review* I (2005), 122–3.

15 Heslinga, *The Irish Border as a Cultural Divide*, 44.

16 Ibid, 62.

17 Ibid, 59.

18 Burgess, 'Mapping the Narrow Ground', 127.

19 Gibbon, *Origins of Ulster Unionism*, 136

20 Miller, *Queen's Rebels*, 110–14.

21 Ibid, 121, 119.

22 Patterson, *Ireland's Violent Frontier*, 27–30.

23 For an account of one such clash, at Aghafin near Rosslea in January 1972, see Leary, *Unapproved Routes*, 164–6.

24 Q. in T. Harnden, *'Bandit Country': The IRA and South Armagh* (London: Hodder & Stoughton, 1999), 148.

25 D. Ferriter, *The Border: The Legacy of a Century of Anglo-Irish Politics* (London: Profile, 1919), 106.

26 Q. in Patterson, *Ireland's Violent Frontier*, 193.

27 C. Tóibín, *Bad Blood: A Walk along the Irish Border* (London: Picador, 1994), 114.

28 G. Martin, 'Origins of Partition' in Anderson and Bort (eds), *Irish Border*, 100.

29 O'Leary, *Treatise on Northern Ireland*, vol. I, 391.

30 E. Tannam, 'Continuity and Change in the Cross-Border Relationship', in M. Anderson and Eberhard Bort (eds), *The Irish Border: History, Politics, Culture* (Liverpool University Press, 1999), 139.

31 Ferriter, *The Border*, 138.

32 See R. Humphries, *Beyond the Border: The Good Friday Agreement and Irish Unity after Brexit* (Dublin: Merrion 2018).

33 G. Patterson, *Backstop Land* (London: Head of Zeus, 2019), 131–6.

34 Economic Policy Centre, Ulster University, 'Cost of Division: A Benchmark of Performance and Expenditure', January 2016. S. Fenton, *The Good Friday Agreement* (London: Biteback 2018), 89.

35 *Belfast Telegraph*, 9 April 2018.

36 Cf C. Gormley-Heenan and A. Aughey, 'Northern Ireland and Brexit: Three Effects on the "border in the mind"', *British Journal of Politics and International Relations*, June 2017.

Index

Craig, Charles 112, 143–4, 177, 184, 218, 219, 222, 223
Craig, James (Prime Minister of Northern Ireland 1921–40) 9, 45, 58, 62, 99, 101, 107, 109, 136, 138, 139, 146, 150, 159, 160, 163, 164, 166, 182, 184, 185, 190, 194, 201, 202, 207, 212, 216, 217, 218, 222, 224, 226, 227, 229, 232, 234, 235, 240, 245, 247, 248, 256, 259, 265, 266, 267, 269
Craig, William 276
Craigavon, Co. Down 40, 62–3, 74
Craig–Collins pacts (1922) 228, 238
Crawford, Frederick H. 44, 58, 62, 86, 101, 149, 162, 165, 183, 216
Crawford, Robert Lindsay 59
Crewe, Earl (Marquess) of (Lord Privy Seal 1908–15) 81, 105
Criminal Law and Procedure (Ireland) Act (1887) 214
Cromwell, Oliver xxii
Cronin, Sean 275
Crossmaglen, Co. Armagh 264, 276
Cumann na mBan 129
Curragh incident (1914) 84, 88–9, 245
Curtis, Lionel 241–2, 245, 249, 252–4, 255
Curzon, Earl (Marquess) (Lord President 1916–19, Foreign Secretary 1919–22) 106, 116, 118, 119, 122, 137, 182, 251

Dáil Eireann 127, 129, 168–9, 191, 198, 199, 209, 219–20, 263, 273
Daily Chronicle 60–61
Daily Express 213
Daily Herald 145
Daily News 165

Dangerfield, George 84, 91
Davis, Thomas 46
Davison, Sir William 221, 223
Dawson, Richard 160
De-Anglicization 47–8
De Broke, Lord Willoughby 79, 86–7
Defence of the Realm Act (1914) 110, 230
Defenders 2, 3, 4, 17
Derry city 83, 154–6, 163, 183, 225, 259, 264, 278
Derry Journal 156
Derry 'pogrom' 154, 156, 168
De Valera, Eamon 131, 157, 190–91, 193–4, 198, 199, 201, 202, 209, 232, 272, 273, 275, 280, 281
Devlin, Joseph (MP for Belfast West) 60, 70, 83, 102, 103, 109, 121, 131, 145, 186, 193, 194
Devolution Crisis (1904) 44, 57, 58
Diamond, battle of the 2
Dicey, A. V. 31–2, 35, 63–4, 78, 79, 88
Dillon, John 33, 45, 46, 82, 97, 99, 102, 112, 193
Diseases of Animals Acts 174
Dolly's Brae 19
Dominion status 69, 150, 165, 200, 201, 203
Donegal, county 49, 90, 100, 142, 217, 231, 248, 264, 265
Donnelly, Eamon 193
Dougherty, Sir James (Under Secretary, Irish Office) 90
Down, county 66, 68, 77, 90, 102, 163, 206, 221, 239, 247
Drew, Dr Thomas 14
Dromore, Co. Tyrone 29
Drummond, Thomas 18

ALLEN LANE
an imprint of
PENGUIN BOOKS

Also Published